GOODNIGHT SAIGON

GOODNIGHT SAIGON

Charles Henderson

BERKLEY CALIBER, NEW YORK

THE BERKLEY PUBLISHING GROUP
Published by the Penguin Group
Penguin Group (USA) Inc.
375 Hudson Street, New York, New York 10014, USA
Penguin Group (Canada), 90 Eglinton Avenue East Suite 700, Toronto, Ontario M4P 2Y3, Canada
(a division of Pearson Penguin Canada Inc.)
Penguin Books Ltd., 80 Strand, London WC2R 0RL, England
Penguin Group Ireland, 25 St. Stephen's Green, Dublin 2, Ireland (a division of Penguin Books Ltd.)
Penguin Group (Australia), 250 Camberwell Road, Camberwell, Victoria 3124, Australia
(a division of Pearson Australia Group Pty. Ltd.)
Penguin Books India Pvt. Ltd., 11 Community Centre, Panchsheel Park, New Delhi—110 017, India
Penguin Group (NZ), 67 Apollo Drive, Rosedale, North Shore 0632, New Zealand
(a division of Pearson New Zealand Ltd.)
Penguin Books (South Africa) (Pty.) Ltd., 24 Sturdee Avenue Avenue, Rosebank, Johannesburg 2196,
South Africa

Penguin Books Ltd., Registered Offices: 80 Strand, London WC2R 0RL, England

Copyright © 2005 by Charles W. Henderson
Cover design by Steven Ferlauto
Cover photo courtesy of Bettman/Corbis
Book design by Kristin del Rosario

PRINTING HISTORY
Berkley Caliber hardcover edition / January 2005
Berkley Caliber trade paperback edition / September 2008

Berkley Caliber trade paperback ISBN: 978-0-425-22402-1

The Library of Congress has catalogued the Berkley Caliber hardcover edition as follows:

Henderson, Charles, 1948–
    Goodnight Saigon / Charles Henderson.—1st ed.
        p. cm.
    ISBN 0-425-18846-9
        1. Vietnamese Conflict, 1961–1975—Vietnam—Ho Chi Minh City. 2. Ho Chi Minh City
(Vietnam)—History. 3. Vietnamese Conflict, 1961–1975. I. Title.

    DS559.9.S24.H46 2005
    959.704'342—dc22   2004057466

PRINTED IN THE UNITED STATES OF AMERICA

10 9 8 7 6 5 4 3 2 1

In Memoriam
for my beloved nephew,
Jody Glenn Henderson.
He lost his life trying to save others.

 **ACKNOWLEDGMENTS**

WORDS FALL SHORT to express the depth of my gratitude to the many men and women who appear in this book, who took the time with me to relive some very stirring and often painful memories. Their trust in my reverence for them as human beings and my respect for the roles that they played in the historic events that led to the climax of the Vietnam War leave me humbled and sincerely thankful to each of them.

Significantly, I thank President Gerald R. Ford for spending the hours with me talking privately about the events of the war's end and sharing with me his feelings about those days, the situations, and the people who surrounded him at that time. His personal reflections and his candor gave me valuable insight and greatly helped me to paint a realistic picture of those events with words.

I normally hold a great deal of cynicism toward most politicians. For me, politics and integrity seem mutually exclusive. However, after having the chance to get to know President Ford and to spend the time that I did with him, realizing the great sincerity, integrity, and stalwart honesty that lives in this man's heart, I came away feeling only the utmost respect for this good man. I am very deeply honored to know him and to have sat in his presence.

Another man who holds a high place on my short list of people I hold most honorable is General Al Gray, former Commandant of the Marine Corps and a man whom I have revered since I first met him more than thirty years ago. I thank him most profoundly for his time, his part of this story, and his warmth of Marine Corps brotherhood that he has always shown to me.

Sincere appreciation and thanks go to the eight Marines who were among the eleven Marine security guards left stranded on the roof of the United States Embassy in Saigon on April 30, 1975. They accompanied me back to Vietnam and told me their stories in the city where it all happened.

Thanks also to Lieutenant General Richard Carey for his insights and guidance and suggestions for further information. Also, my sincere thanks to former South Vietnamese Premier and Air Vice Marshal Nguyen Cao Ky, for his insightful conversations and his guidance in pursuing this story.

I also thank the men and women of the diplomatic missions of Vietnam for allowing me entrance into their country before the United States had established formal relations with them. They went out of their way to make me feel welcome and allowed me wide latitude to roam the hinterlands from one end of their nation to the other, and from borders with Cambodia and Laos to the coast. Although at times life got quite adventurous, I never felt at any great risk.

General Tran Van Tra and Colonel Vo Dong Giang could have only given me lip service, shaken my hand, fed me a few canned tidbits, and sent me on my way. However, these gentlemen, my former enemies, graciously welcomed me and spent many hours struggling with me through chapter and verse of their perspectives of the war's final days and the people who surrounded them. Their generosity with their time with me, patiently detailing the facts and their perspectives greatly helped me to understand their side of the story. My humble words of thanks seem so little in comparison to what they gave me in insight and knowledge.

I also thank the host of others who sat patiently with me in Vietnam, helping me to comprehend the stories of their experiences. People like Nguyen Duc Cui, who tearfully shared their intimate memories with me, a stranger and a former enemy, leave me humbled and grateful to each of them.

People like Huynh Thit, a former cost accountant for the First Marine Aircraft Wing in Da Nang, a woman who remained in the fallen city and then struggled under persecution year after year, yet never lost her love for America and her Marines, and who shared her memories with me and then went all the way to the airport to hug my neck good-bye and to tell me she has never lost hope in America, stir my heart to this day. How can mere words thank her? Or thank people like Nguyen Manh Tuan, a former artillery commander, trained and educated in America, who endured years of imprisonment and poverty and still wonders about his friends in America?

I hope that my honest portrayal of them in this book demonstrates my thanks better than my few words here.

A profound thank you goes to Hoang Huy Chung, my escort and my translator. During the weeks that I spent zigzagging my way from Saigon to Hanoi, Hoang remained by my side. At Xuan Loc, when we were arrested by the local warlord's police and held in their local stockade for a day, Hoang took the brunt of the not-so-friendly constabulary's aggression toward us. His pleas, promises, and homage paid to the Xuan Loc chieftain finally got us freed. During those weeks, Hoang endured the dirt, rough rides, bad food, and long days and nights, and never stopped smiling.

Then comes my friend, colleague, and fellow adventurer, Dirck Halstead. One of the world's great photojournalists, he and I traced every battle site of the Vietnam War's last campaign, venturing far from civilization into Vietnam's most remote reaches. Dirck never complained nor ever winced at any adversity, but simply kept his video cameras rolling with enthusiasm.

During those many weeks that we ventured together around the world, Dirck gave me his insights and shared his memories of Vietnam's last days. Dirck also introduced me to people like Peter Arnett, his old friend who also accompanied us with his CNN crew to Saigon and during the trek told me his stories of the war. I thank Peter for sharing with me. Then in Bangkok, Dirck helped me cut through the ice with more of his old friends, Alan Dawson, Hubert Van Es, and Derek Williams, so that they told their tales of those days to me with clear and colorful detail.

While I had known David Hume Kennerly from my time in Beirut in 1983, Dirck called on his long and close friendship with Kennerly to open that door wide and provide fly-on-the-wall insights of the White House and Vietnam. I am deeply grateful to David Kennerly for sharing that with us.

However, in the end I am most profoundly thankful to Dirck Halstead not only for the doors that he opened for me, such as that with President Ford, but for his long-lasting friendship over these many years and his willingness to join me on other great adventures.

There are few friends in this world like Dirck Halstead, and I am very blessed to count him among mine.

Lastly, my deepest appreciation goes to my editor, who has become my friend over the years, Tom Colgan. While I languished well past the date we all thought this book would find completion, he stuck with me. He absorbed the flack and kept urging me onward. I had once compared him to Maxwell Perkins, the great editor of Ernest Hemingway and F. Scott Fitzgerald. Tom continues to live up to that image, taking good care of his authors and cultivating their best work. I hope that Penguin USA knows what a rare gem that they have in Tom. He, along with my agent and old friend, Bob Markel, keep me going and keep me believing. My eternal thanks to them both.

GLOSSARY OF CHARACTERS

NORTH VIETNAMESE AND VIET CONG LEADERS

Dang, Tra Bach, Communist Party boss for Saigon.

Duan, Le, Communist Party First Secretary, principal mastermind of the North Vietnamese final campaign and politburo mainstay supporting the campaign to ultimate victory.

Dung, General Van Tien, Chief of Staff, North Vietnamese Army, Supreme Commander of all Communist Forces.

Giang, Colonel Vo Dong, Deputy Foreign Minister, North Vietnam, also known to many as Colonel Ba, a member of the Joint Military Commission in Saigon.

Hung, Pham, politburo member and Chief Political Officer and First Secretary for the South Vietnam regions.

Ky, Nguyen Xuan, Commander of Viet Cong forces for the Saigon region.

Tan, General Le Truong, Vice Commander of the North Vietnamese Army, commander of Communist forces in victories over Da Nang and Xuan Loc.

Tho, Le Duc, born Phan Dinh Khai on October 14, 1911, helped found Vietnam's Communist Party, the Vietnam Workers' Party, and in 1945 established the Vietnam Revolutionary League (Viet Minh) with Party Chairman Ho Chi Minh and General Vo Nguyen Giap, leading the Viet Minh rebellion against France in South Vietnam. He was the figurehead of the Viet Cong, a highly revered politburo member, and Communist South Vietnam's chief negotiator opposite Henry Kissinger at the Paris Peace Talks. He was the corecipient with Kissinger of the 1973 Nobel Peace Prize for leadership in the peace negotiations in Paris. However, Le Duc Tho refused to accept the award because he said that his country was not yet at peace. A key politburo member and leader of the Communists' final offensive in South Vietnam in 1975, Tho died on October 13, 1990, in Hanoi.

Thoa, Lieutenant General Hoang Minh, Deputy Chief of Staff, North Vietnamese Army.

Tra, General Tran Van, Commander in Chief of the Viet Cong and among the senior leadership of the North Vietnamese Army, deputy commander to General Dung.

NORTH VIETNAMESE AND VIET CONG SOLDIERS

Can, Ha Thuc, CBS News cameraman, and was secretly a Viet Cong who used the Western press access provided by being an international journalist to gain intelligence information for the Communists.

Cui, Nguyen Duc, Communications Officer, 320th NVA Division, carried the shoes of a dead friend in his pack for many years so that he could wear them in the victory parade in Saigon at the war's end.

Luong, Nguyen Thien, Viet Cong commander of forces attached to NVA 320th Division, annihilating the ARVN II Army Corps at Cheo Reo.

Phung, Dang Quang, architect at Tan Son Nhut Air Base and Viet Cong spy.

Reung, Le Van, Viet Cong guerrilla who fought for many years in the Central Highlands and in the southern reaches of I Corps up to Da Nang and Chu Lai and led insurgent platoon in the attack of Ban Me Thuot.

Than, Le Cong, Vice Commander of the Forty-fourth Line Front, Viet Cong, led his units in the assaults outside Hue and Da Nang simultaneously as the assault on Ban Me Thout took place and converged his units on Da Nang as it fell.

The, Colonel Hoang Duc, North Vietnamese Army regimental commander in the Second NVA Division attacking Hue and Da Nang.

Thi, Truong Quang, NVA battalion commander with 320th Division, participating in the Cheo Reo massacre.

Trung, First Lieutenant Nguyen Thanh, AFRVN, South Vietnamese Air Force pilot who defected to the Viet Cong on April 8, 1975, flying his F-5 jet fighter to Song Be Airfield at Phuoc Long after dropping the plane's bombs on the South Vietnam Presidential Palace.

Tuan, Nguyen Sinh, NVA soldier and documentary photographer.

Wahn, Ky, photographer with the Saigon Associated Press, worked closely with AP Correspondent Peter Arnett; also a Viet Cong spy.

SOUTH VIETNAMESE LEADERS AND MILITARY

Dao, Brigadier General Le Minh, commander of the ARVN Eighteenth Division, held the NVA at Xuan Loc for thirteen days.

Ky, Air Vice Marshal Nguyen Cao, former Premier of the Republic of Vietnam and Commander of the South Vietnamese Air Force.

Lan, Brigadier General Bui The, Commandant of the South Vietnamese Marine Corps.

Phu, Major General Pham Van, ARVN, Commanding General of Military Region 2 and the II Army Corps.

Thieu, Nguyen Van, President of South Vietnam.

Toan, Nguyen Van, ARVN III Army Corps Commanding General and Commander of Military Region 3.

Toan, Lieutenant Colonel Tran Ngoc, Vietnamese Marine Corps, commander of the Fourth Battalion of the ill-fated 147th Brigade, lost on the beach at Tan My attempting to redeploy from Hue as it fell.

Truong, Lieutenant General Ngo Quang, ARVN, Commanding General, Military Region 1.

Tuan, Lieutenant Colonel Nguyen Manh, an artillery battalion commander in the ARVN II Army Corps, lost at Cheo Reo.

SOUTH VIETNAMESE CIVILIANS

Ca, Nha, one of the most widely read novelists in South Vietnam, received acclaim for her criticism of the Vietnamese Communists, also the wife of Tran Da Tu.

Chinh, Kieu, South Vietnamese actress, that country's most popular motion picture star of that time.

Nguyen, Bich-Van, second oldest daughter of Nguyen Giap Ty and Ninh Thi Tran.

Nguyen, Vanny Low, youngest daughter of Nguyen Giap Ty and Ninh Thi Tran.

Nguyen, Son D., younger son of Nguyen Giap Ty and Ninh Thi Tran.

Nguyen, Tuong-Van, oldest daughter of Nguyen Giap Ty and Ninh Thi Tran, disabled with Down's syndrome.

Nguyen, Nam K., older son of Nguyen Giap Ty and Ninh Thi Tran.

Thao, Mai, South Vietnam's most renowned novelist and newspaper publisher, author of more than fifty books.

Tran, Ninh Thi, wife of Nguyen Giap Ty, also worked as a typist for various American government agencies, including the defense attaché.

Tu, Tran Da, one of South Vietnam's most renowned novelists and poets.

Ty, Nguyen Giap, retired South Vietnamese Army lieutenant colonel, awarded the Bronze Star by American forces, was terminal manager at the Port of Saigon at war's end.

AMERICAN CIVILIAN LEADERS AND DIPLOMATS

Ford, Gerald R., President of the United States.

Francis, Albert, Consul General of Da Nang.

Kissinger, Henry A., Secretary of State of the United States.

Lehmann, Wolfgang, Deputy Chief of Mission, United States Embassy, Saigon.

Martin, Graham A., United States Ambassador to South Vietnam.

McKinley, Brunson, Ambassador Graham Martin's aide-de-camp.

McNamara, Francis "Terry," Consul General, Can Tho

Peters, Richard B., Consul General, Bien Hoa.

Spears, Moncrieff, Consul General, Nha Trang.

AMERICAN MILITARY

Babel, Sergeant Philip A., USMC, Marine Security Guard, Saigon, among the last eleven Marines to depart Saigon.

Bauer, Corporal Stephen Q., USMC, Marine Security Guard, Saigon, among the last eleven Marines to depart Saigon.

Bennington, Sergeant Terry J., USMC, Marine Security Guard, Saigon, among the last eleven Marines to depart Saigon.

Berry, Captain Gerald L., USMC, pilot of Lady Ace Zero-Nine, the Marine CH-46F helicopter that flew Ambassador Graham Martin from Saigon at 4:58 a.m., April 30, 1975.

Carey, Brigadier General Richard E., USMC, Commanding General of the Ninth Marine Amphibious Brigade and operational commander of Operation Frequent Wind.

Carlson, Lance Corporal Eric, USMC, Marine combat correspondent, photojournalist, assigned to 9th MAB, based at III MAF Public Affairs Office, Okinawa.

Carr, Staff Sergeant Joseph, USMC, Marine combat correspondent, III MAF Public Affairs Office, Okinawa.

Cook, Captain Doug, USMC, copilot of Swift Two-Two, the last American military helicopter to fly from Saigon.

Ebert, Sergeant Carl, USMC, Marine combat correspondent, III MAF Public Affairs Office, Okinawa.

Frain, Sergeant Robert L., USMC, Marine Security Guard, Saigon, among the last elveen Marines to depart Saigon.

Gevers, Sergeant Duane R., USMC, Marine Security Guard, Saigon, among the last eleven Marines to depart Saigon.

Gray, Colonel Alfred M., USMC, Commander of the Fourth Marine Regiment and Regimental Landing Team 4, American ground forces ashore in the evacuation of Saigon.

Hargis, Sergeant Gregory E., USMC, Marine Security Guard, Saigon.

Harp, Captain Tilford, USAF, copilot of C-5A Galaxy 68-218, which crashed shortly after takeoff from Tan Son Nhut Air Base in Saigon on the inaugural flight of Operation Baby Lift.

Hasty, Staff Sergeant Boyette S., USMC, NCO in charge of the Marine Security Guard detachment assigned to the United States Consulate, Can Tho.

Holden, Captain Tom, USMC, pilot of Swift Two-Two, the last American military helicopter to fly from Saigon.

Houghton, Major General Kenneth J., USMC, Commanding General, Third Marine Division.

Hughes, Sergeant Stan, USMC, gunner aboard Swift Two-Two, the last American military helicopter to fly from Saigon.

Johnson, Colonel John M., USMC, Assistant Chief of Staff, Operations (G-3), III Marine Amphibious Force (III MAF).

Judge, Lance Corporal Darwin D., USMC, embassy Marine killed in action at 3:58 a.m., April 29, 1975 by enemy 122 mm rocket, one of last two Americans killed in action in Vietnam.

Kean, Captain James H., USMC, Major selectee, commanding officer, Company C, Marine Security Guard Battalion, among the last eleven Marines to depart Saigon, stranded on the roof of the American embassy until the morning of April 30, 1975.

Madison, Colonel John, USA, senior member of the Joint Casualty Resolution Team.

McCormick, Sergeant Michael A., USMC, assistant NCO in charge of the Marine Security Guard detachment at Nha Trang consulate.

McMahon, Corporal Charles, USMC, embassy Marine killed in action at 3:58 a.m., April 29, 1975, by enemy 122 mm rocket, one of last two Americans killed in action in Vietnam.

Neeley, Chief Warrant Officer Robert, USMC, station manager and officer in charge, Far East Network, Okinawa, American Forces Radio and Television Service.

Norman, Corporal David E., USMC, Marine Security Guard, Saigon, among the last eleven Marines to depart Saigon.

Nystul, Captain William C., USMC, among last Marines killed in action in Vietnam, pilot of the Marine CH-46F that crashed at sea near the USS *Hancock*.

Painter, Staff Sergeant Roger F., USMC, NCO in charge of Nha Trang consulate Marine Security Guard detachment.

Poggemeyer, Major General Herman, Jr., USMC, Commanding General, III Marine Amphibious Force.

Schlager, Gunnery Sergeant Robert W., USMC, NCO in charge of the Bien Hoa consulate, among the last eleven Marines to depart Saigon.

Schuller, Corporal Steven T., USMC, Marine Security Guard, Saigon, among the last eleven Marines to depart Saigon.

Shea, First Lieutenant Michael J., USMC, among last Marines killed in action in Vietnam, copilot of the Marine CH-46F that crashed at sea near the USS *Hancock*.

Shelton, Captain Jerry, Third Marine Division Public Affairs Officer, III MAF Public Affairs Office, Okinawa.

Smith, Major General Homer D., Jr., USA, Defense Attaché, Saigon.

Sneed, Corporal Jimmie D., USMC, Marine Security Guard at Nha Trang consulate.

Sparks, Staff Sergeant Walter W., USMC, NCO in charge of the Marine security forces assigned to the United States Consulate in Da Nang.

Sullivan, Staff Sergeant Michael K., USMC, Assistant NCO in charge of the United States Embassy, Saigon Marine Security Guard detachment, among the last eleven Marines to depart Saigon.

Thurman, Gunnery Sergeant Russell R., USMC, Marine combat correspondent, photojournalist, and public affairs representative for the 9th MAB, based at III MAF Public Affairs Office, Okinawa.

Tingley, Sergeant Steven L., USMC, Marine combat correspondent, III MAF Public Affairs Office, Okinawa.

Tompkins, Lance Corporal Donald, USMC, administrative clerk and driver, III MAF Public Affairs Office, Okinawa.

Traynor, Captain Dennis "Bud," USAF, pilot of C-5A Galaxy 68-218, which crashed shortly after takeoff from Tan Son Nhut Air Base in Saigon on the inaugural flight of Operation Babylift.

Valdez, Master Sergeant John J. "Top," USMC, noncommissioned officer in charge of the United States Embassy, Saigon detachment of Company C, Marine Security Guard Battalion, among the last eleven Marines to depart Saigon.

Weyand, General Frederick C., United States Army, Chief of Staff.

Wood, Sergeant Christopher, USMC, crew chief of Swift Two-Two, the last American military helicopter to fly from Saigon.

AMERICAN CIVILIANS AND WESTERN JOURNALISTS

Arnett, Peter, Senior Correspondent, Associated Press, Saigon Bureau, from New Zealand, remained in Saigon after the Americans left on April 30, 1975.

Daly, Ed, flamboyant founder, Chairman and Chief Executive of World Airways, made the last evacuation flight from Da Nang aboard one of his company's Boeing 727 jetliners on March 29, 1975.

Davis, Neil, motion picture photographer under contract with NBC News, photographed the NVA tank crashing the gates at Saigon's Presidential Palace.

Dawson, Alan, Bureau Chief, United Press International, for both Vietnam and Cambodia.

Halstead, Dirck, photographer for *Time-Life.*

Healy, Ken, World Airways Boeing 727 jetliner pilot in command of the last evacuation flight from Da Nang.

Kennerly, David Hume, White House photographer for President Gerald R. Ford.

Lea, Jim, correspondent and bureau chief, Okinawa Bureau, *Pacific Stars and Stripes*, United States Information Agency.

Van Es, Hubert "Hugh," Dutch freelance photographer who received the Pulitzer Prize for shooting the famous photograph of the Huey helicopter hovering over the PanAm building rooftop in Saigon with people climbing a ladder to get aboard the aircraft.

Williams, Derek, CBS News sound man, began working in Far East in Cambodia and eventually wound up in Saigon.

GOODNIGHT SAIGON

Chapter 1

GOODNIGHT SAIGON

REPUBLIC OF VIETNAM—WEDNESDAY, APRIL 30, 1975

THE CHOPPER WAS nearly out of gas.

Just like the war.

Over. Except for this last act: the outbound flight of a single United States Marine Corps CH-46 Sea-Knight helicopter, call sign Swift Two-Two, a transport from Marine Medium Helicopter Squadron 164. Her departure off the rooftop of the American embassy in the heart of Saigon would forever symbolize the closing scene of a long and tragic play.

The fighting. The frustration. The nearly three decades of conflict. Done.

The more than ten years of American soldiers losing their limbs, hearts, and lives. Finished.

Lifting from that last acre of American concrete in the Republic of Vietnam, low-fuel warning lights blinking as its rotor blades turned through a cloud of tear gas and lost hope, this dull green bird—at 7:53 on Wednesday morning, April 30, 1975—brought down the Vietnam War's final curtain.

With Saigon disappearing behind the trees, the twin rotorcraft cast her fate on dwindling fumes, just as the people of this besieged country had done for so many weeks. Now the hopes of a fallen nation, the fate of its people, flew in the wind that spiraled with the twisters that danced along the chopper's blades.

Beneath the wash of wind and lost hope, inside the aircraft's belly, rode eleven tired Marines—the last American soldiers to depart South Vietnam.

Yet much more than these eleven passengers and aircrew of four journeyed with that helicopter on this final voyage from Vietnam. Aboard it traveled the hearts of millions: the wounded, the dead, the homeless, the families broken apart; people who had suffered the many years of this war; and nations who had divided themselves, ruined their innocence, and lost their children. Tired, bleeding memories and regret also rode on that shuddering green bird.

Grown men cried that day—men who had given their courage, their dedication, their blood to a cause now lost. They had zipped shut too many black bags filled with too many friends who had given their lives trying to win over there. For these, the flight of that last chopper out of Saigon represented despair.

"What did we die for?" they asked. "For what did we suffer and pay such a price?" And they shook their fists as they watched the helicopter race toward the sea. "We never lost a battle, so why did we lose the war?"

Other men cried that day—men who had given their courage, dedication, and blood. They also had pulled shut too many shrouds wrapped around too many friends who had given their lives trying to win this war. For them, the flight of that last American helicopter confirmed victory.

They waved flags and raised their fists triumphantly. They pointed skyward at this last vestige of American superiority and cried out to the world as the helicopter flew away. "You see? Do you see? We did finally prevail!"

On the streets, in the villages, inside shanties and chateaus, people hid, terrified. Their eyes too followed the helicopter, and they cried, "Why did you forsake us?"

They feared what lay ahead. This thing that had finally come would kill many of them and enslave more. And they shook outstretched hands angrily as the helicopter departed. "We believed in you!"

Aboard the ships, thousands clung to rails and watched in bewilderment as the chopper rushed toward them. Their world—home, wealth, country—had all shrunk to a spot the size of their feet on the deck of a ship that belonged to someone else. They raised their faces and cried, "Now what shall we do?"

Many, whose temples sprouted gray but had once bristled dark when they gave everything over there, defiantly proclaimed, "This is not our doing! We did not lose this war. Our brothers died for freedom's cause—for liberty!"

They angrily stuck their middle fingers skyward as this last chopper flew. "Those damned communist pig-fucking war protesters. They did this. Those damned communist pig-fucking congressmen and limp-willed politicians. They gave it to them. We won it, and then they gave it away!"

In Canada and on the streets of New York, San Francisco, and cities scattered between, others whose hair now shown gray but had once flowed darkly, woven with flowers when they had stood in objection, also watched the helicopter fly. Angrily, they raised their middle fingers too.

"We told you so," they heralded. "This illegal, immoral, terrible thing our country did. There was no other end possible but this. We were right. Thanks to us, it has finally stopped."

Men and women and children watched the television films of that last flight—those last Americans to leave this terrible war. And they breathed a sigh in resignation. "It is done. Now the healing can begin," they reassured each other.

These made up a tired America, a divided and deeply fractured America. They needed something good to come after enduring so much bad: assassinations, civil unrest, out-of-control inflation, drug abuse, gasoline shortages, Watergate. At least this war—one of the greatest tragedies in United States history—had ended. The last soldiers now headed home.

All who watched as that helicopter flew could at least agree on one thing: It was over. Finally.

As Swift Two-Two raced through sporadic ground fire toward the sea, those last American vets of Vietnam's war considered little beyond their small world. Symbolism, popular opinion, who was right didn't matter. Healing, victory, loss—it all spun in an indefinable cloud.

For them, reality raced beneath their feet, and its grime mixed with

sweat that dripped from their faces. Apprehension and fatigue dominated their world at the moment. They didn't know quite which emotion to grasp: whether to celebrate or whether to cry.

Two of their brothers had fallen. Killed by an enemy rocket one day
ago. Or was it now two? Brand-new kids, they were. Newbees. Just off
the boat. Whisked away to stand guard for the Defense Attaché's Office at some exterior checkpoint by the airport. Hammered with their
bowels still full of stateside chow.

When the rockets hit, way before dawn, two minutes before 4:00
a.m.—rockets always fall at odd times like that, 3:58 a.m., Hotel Saigon
time—nurses from the Tan Son Nhut Seventh-Day Adventist Mission
Hospital came to help.

They picked up the pieces: the battered husks that remained of Corporal Charles McMahon, Jr., of Woburn, Massachusetts, and his partner, Lance Corporal Darwin D. Judge of Marshalltown, Iowa. God
knows the women in blood-spattered white prayed for the two boys.
Christian nurses do that. Surely they did. The last two American souls
to depart this war by hostile fire for everlasting life with Jesus.

Looking over the door gunner's shoulder at the rising sun, these last
eleven who had finally gotten out of Saigon alive wondered. Undoubtedly someone at Dodge City had remembered to reclaim their two
brethren. Surely they did. After all, we do not leave our dead. Marines
never do that—absolutely never. Cardinal rule number one.

Safely below decks on the helicopter carrier, the United States Navy
Amphibious Assault Ship, the USS *Okinawa*, they scratched that itch.
Marine Corps Major Jim Kean, the boss of this last bunch out—technically the last commander of American forces on the ground in Vietnam—had to ask. After all, they were his boys. Never rest before you
count your chicks, leadership rule number one. He had to know.

However, McMahon and Judge still lay at rest in the morgue outside Tan Son Nhut.

Somebody from the embassy had called the mission. A nurse had
told that caller that someone else from Dodge City had grabbed the
body bags and gone. Spirited them home, already, she thought. The
nurse just tried to help. She really didn't know. Scared too, she was.
Lots of other dead. And wounded, her own people.

Nothing these last eleven souls could have done, anyway. Clear
across a town of chaos. Crazed people with guns, really hating Ameri-

cans at that point. These boys couldn't have done a damned thing but gotten themselves killed too.

They would have, though. Climbed the wall. Screw the major. Our buds need us. What's left of them.

"And been dead too," the major reminded his Marines.

Nobody left those two on purpose. Somebody got them, they had thought. Everybody thought. Besides, too many lives still needed saving. Too many living left to get free.

No room here for the dead. Not aboard these birds. No way to get them now, anyway. Impossible. But guilt still chewed on their hearts. Always faithful. *Semper fi*—do or die—kept turning in their heads. Never fear. Your buds are here. Don't look back, Mac.

And what about themselves? Had that same *semper fidelis* credo of never deserting your own—tattooed on the spirit of every Marine, blending the blood of this brotherhood stronger than Spartan will. Had this single most absolute belief of any Marine with breath in his sails given these final eleven cause for morose celebration? Their brother Marines had not forsaken them, after all.

TWO HOURS EARLIER

RETURNING TO SHIP from a search-and-rescue sortie somewhere over Vung Tao, Captain Tom Holden and his crew aboard Swift Two-Two heard the news. Eleven still waited.

"No fuel," he had told Captain Doug Cook, sitting at his right. Barely enough for a direct shot from the USS *Hancock* for the forty-minute flight to Saigon. But hardly enough fuel to get back to the ship. No more.

"Maybe more," the copilot suggested.

"We might go down," they both agreed.

But they were nearest. The best bet to save those stranded Marines. The only real hope to pluck those eleven tired men who sat while terror closed around by the second. A matter of life and death. The airmen knew it.

On the jump seat, by the door, crew chief Chris Woods blinked cold eyed at fellow sergeant Stan Hughes. But the gunner just shrugged as he leaned back, grasping the double-handle grip mounted on the butt of his M2, .50-caliber machine gun. No big thing, his emotions told. Don't sweat the gas. Take the chance—or go down trying.

SERGEANT TERRY BENNINGTON saw the chopper first, then Jim Kean, and the other nine. A speck in the sky. Hope on whirling wings.

Slowly the silhouette grew against the rising sun.

High above came the coursing sound of a navy A-7 Corsair attack jet, call-sign, Frito, fast mover escort, on station. Then another noise: beating blades. A Marine AH-1J Cobra, known on the radio net as Space Gun, turned a steep circle while Swift Two-Two made her descent.

"Pop the gas!" Kean ordered the men.

Sergeant Duane Gevers and Corporal Steve Bauer let go of the door behind which a hysterical mob choked from tear gas the two Marines had released. Big cans. Clouds thick as smoke. It had instantly covered the roof and filled the stairway to it. Nobody, not even the Marines, had gas masks.

Master Sergeant Juan Valdez jumped aboard last, just as Tom Holden lifted the chopper off its wheels. The pilot's eyes filled so full of tears from the gas that he had to set down and try up once more. Ahead of a swarm of frenzied people, who had now broken through the rooftop door, Swift Two-Two cleared the deck and raced southward.

Kean and Valdez, Bennington, Gevers, and Bauer watched the pad grow small. Steve Schuller, Bobby Frain, Philip Babel, Michael Sullivan, Dave Norman, and Bobby Schlager all looked too, taking one last glance at Nam. A final memory. A lifetime's thought. Aimless, hopeless, lost people crowded atop the embassy shrank in the distance.

"**GOD HAS FORSAKEN** us," Nguyen Giap Ty told his wife, Ninh, while holding her close to him. His once unshakable, soft-spoken voice now trembled. Their whole family had missed its chance to leave.

First, they had gone to the Defense Attaché's Office compound, all the way through the hubbub of Saigon to its northwestern corner near Tan Son Nhut Airport, then back across the chaotic city to the American embassy. But no one at either place would let them through the gates. Too many people jammed ahead of them.

None of the Nguyen family had slept, although the traveling they had done through the night had worn them beyond feeling. Only the oldest daughter, Tuong-Van, now closed her eyes.

Mentally disabled since birth, she understood little more than something bad now came, so terrible that it had sent her family fleeing in the night. This horrible thing had gripped her hard. She was tired and wanted to go home, but the panic had kept her family on the streets all night.

At home, now, curling next to her mother, her fear finally grew distant, and she slept.

For Tuong's sisters, Bich and Vanny, rest seemed impossible. Home was not safe any longer. The night sky had glowed orange as fires from the Communist onslaught ringed the city. Being teenaged girls, they understood what closed upon them. So they sat on the sofa and watched the sun rise.

This uncertain day struck them deeply, despite their father's soft voice. Always before, when things seemed too terrible, his quiet and confident words gave them courage. But each of those times, everything had ended as he had reassured them it would.

Today, he offered no answers. He dared not speculate. Even though his voice still sounded so quiet and so calm, the confidence was gone. He had lost it somewhere in that horrible confusion of Saigon.

The girls first noticed this after their failures at the gates of Dodge City. There they had seen despair creep on to his face.

"Sir, sir," Ty had said to a United States Marine. He clapped his hands together, as if in prayer, and bowed his head to the young man using his rifle to push people back. "I have documents. Please, sir, look at them. My family, we are here to evacuate. We have clearances."

The sentry pushed Ty with his rifle and ignored the handful of papers that the desperate man frantically waved only inches from his nose. The man's persistence irritated the Marine to the point that he finally slammed his rifle against Ty's hand, knocking the annoying documents away from his face.

"Please let us pass, sir," Ty asked again. "We have clearances! Please!"

The Marine said nothing, but put his rifle in Ty's chest and pushed hard. He had his orders: no more people, no exceptions, no matter what.

The girls heard desperation in their father's voice when he spoke quickly and sharply to the South Vietnamese soldiers at another checkpoint outside the DAO compound. He tried to show them the family's evacuation papers. The guards shouted back at him and pointed their rifles at him.

The people Nguyen Giap Ty had spent so many years supporting, for whom he had sacrificed all of his adult life, had now refused to even acknowledge him. The maddening irony overwhelmed him. His throat burned and tightened into a knot.

Ty fought hard not to break into uncontrollable sobs and tears as his family stood in the street and watched the last people board the helicopters at the DAO compound and leave. The Marines had circled cars and trucks to make a landing site. Now, the vehicles sat in a silent ring, their headlights shining until their batteries would go dead.

Despite having his heart crushed in the disappointment he felt by everyone he had trusted now turning their backs on him, Ty gathered his family and pushed back to the city, back to its center where helicopters still flew from the roof of the American embassy. Perhaps they might find a way out there.

Arriving late in the night, Ty shouted and pushed his way through the thousands of frantic people crowded outside the embassy while Ninh and their five children stepped close behind him. Too many other would-be refugees tried the same thing ahead of them. Fear now showed itself clearly on Ty's face as a sense of panic sent blood rushing inside his head, pounding behind his eyes and ears as though he might suddenly explode.

Ready to fight, ready to kill, Ty roared at the people around him. He clenched his fists and screamed out his frustration at what he had once thought impossible. This could never happen! Never! Not after what he had given his country. Not after what he had done for these people. Not after he had so loyally supported the Americans, risked his life for them. No, it could never happen!

When the Marines hurried away from the gates and locked themselves inside the embassy, Ty turned to Ninh and bowed his head. His heart swelled into his throat, and tears filled his eyes. Despair overwhelmed him.

He held Ninh close to his chest, her head under his chin, and he raised his face toward heaven and cried.

Son and Nam, Ty's two boys, shouted angrily at the Americans. This after they saw one especially big GI take a wooden beam, lock it behind his back with his elbows crooked around it, and start spinning at the people who rushed toward the embassy's door.

"Why would the Americans now want to kill us?" they screamed. Others shouted too and began throwing bricks and bottles.

Then from behind the Nguyen family, gunshots cracked the air. Some rapid fire and some single reports, all aimed at the embassy roof where a helicopter sat with its blades turning.

Ty took his two sons by the arms and pulled them next to him. Ninh and the girls held close at his back. He knew remaining here was now foolish. His many years as a soldier told him even the Communists would be safer for them than this crowd.

After walking several blocks, they found the streets eerily deserted. In fact, given the situation, they looked surreal: Lights on, people at home, an automobile now and then passing. Hauntingly quiet. Yet Ty knew this tranquility told a lie. A great storm would rage here when the Communists came.

"God has forsaken us," Ty said to his wife as they walked. She pulled hard at his sleeve, trying to encourage him and urge him to quit such sad talk, especially in front of his children, all in their teens and easily affected by his presence.

Yet he said it again and again, to himself more than to her, all the way home.

Everything had gone so wrong. Fairness was something that he had learned, early in life, was foolish to expect. Yet in this case, what he had expected went beyond fairness. It was a return of loyalty.

Ninh had worked through several days at the DAO, helping the staff there process out refugees. She accepted that her turn for departure must come at the end. She knew her job as a typist was important to the evacuation effort. Ninh trusted that the Americans would not leave without her and her family. So until her time to leave came, she worked.

Ninh's husband had retired from the army only one year earlier. He had spent more than twenty-three years in uniform and had risen in rank to lieutenant colonel. A tall, attractive man, born in Hanoi, Ty was an elite soldier—at one time a member of the Imperial Guard under Bao Dai, Vietnam's last emperor. After the treaty of 1954, he moved to the south.

From 1967 through 1971, he served at Chu Lai as Vietnamese liaison for the United States Army's Americal Division. The Americans greatly respected him, and he felt close to them. He even exchanged addresses with several officers and wrote them letters after they had gone home.

One day at a landing zone near the combat base, a squad of soldiers, sweeping the perimeter, walked into an enemy minefield. Hearing one explode, Ty hurried to the stranded squad. They were mostly boys, frightened and unsure of what to do next.

Ty shouted to the men to relax and remain still until he reached them. With his many years of dealing with Viet Cong mines and booby traps, he knew well the dangers and the signs. He knew these young men did not. His quiet, confident voice kept the soldiers calm. Slowly and skillfully he guided them out.

For his heroism, the Americans awarded him the Bronze Star with the combat V device, denoting valor, something rare. Very few of these sorts of decorations had ever been given to soldiers of other countries. Knowing this, Ty wore his Bronze Star with special pride.

But that was in 1968, a very different time.

When the Americans left Vietnam during the sixty days that followed their signing of the Paris Peace Accords, on January 27, 1973, Ty moved to Saigon where he sat as a representative of the South Vietnamese Army on the Bilateral Joint Military Commission. Their jobs as representatives of the warring sides, the Republic of Vietnam and the Provisional Revolutionary Government, was to enforce the peace, to review violations of the Paris Accords and issue sanctions against the violators. To sanction a violator required a unanimous vote by the members of the JMC, which never occurred. He found the politics shameful. Field duty was more to his liking, but rank kept him from that, so he retired.

For the past year, Nguyen Giap Ty had supervised cargo shipments in and out of Saigon for a company that serviced the American corporation, Sea-Land. He enjoyed the work, leading platoons of men again, even though they were longshoremen instead of soldiers.

Recently, as terminal manager at the Port of Saigon, he was busy. But instead of container boxes, he loaded people onto the variety of vessels tied to the docks. Like his wife, he had a job that came ahead of his departure. And like Ninh, he trusted that the Americans would not leave without him.

When Ty and Ninh finally realized that they would not get themselves and their family out, the irony of it all became nearly too bitter to endure. They had spent two days helping the thousands of others, but now there was no one left to help them. With so many of the leaders and administrators gone, the evacuation process turned into a shoving war.

Saigon had become impassable for anything but foot traffic. And there was Ty at the Port of Saigon, and Ninh with the rest of the family at the other side of the city.

When Ty had reached his wife and children at the DAO compound, it was already dark. The Americans had burned all the buildings, and they were letting no one else inside the gates. He could see through the fences, the cars parked in a circle with their headlamps turned on, and the helicopters, operating from that light, taking on the last lucky few.

By the time Ty and his family had reached the American embassy, well past midnight, the same confusion greeted them. Angry crowds. Pleading people waving papers at United States Marines who held the gates closed. No more refugees.

Now at home, an attractive, small villa near the outskirts of Saigon, the Nguyen family waited. Nam and Son, and Tuong-Van, Bich, and Vanny, sat in their house's living room, together with Ty and Ninh.

Holding to each other.

Wondering.

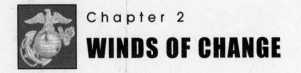

Chapter 2
WINDS OF CHANGE

DA NANG, RVN—THURSDAY, NOVEMBER 7, 1974

GNATS SWARMED LE Van Reung's face and mired themselves in the sweat around his eyes and mouth, waking the skinny Viet Cong soldier. Squatting on his haunches, he took the black-and-white-checked scarf that he carried tied in an overhand knot around his neck and wiped his face, shaking his head to free any insects that had crawled into his hair while he slept, hidden in a brush pile.

Combing his hair with his fingers, he watched the foliage around him shake and move as others in his platoon awakened from their day-long sleep. Their sentry, a boy from Phu Cat, smiled at him and then yawned. Reung did not return the smile, but only looked blankly at the young man, hardly more than fourteen or fifteen years of age.

Reung stared at the four small, cloth sacks at the boy's side, each filled with one or two pounds of high-velocity explosive, fused with pull-string detonators, sapper charges to blow holes in the barbed wire that always surrounded South Vietnamese defense positions. Several strips of old communications wire lay across the tops of the sacks.

In a few moments, this lad and twenty or thirty others like him would take that wire and tie it tightly around their upper thighs and around their arms, just above the biceps, restricting blood flow. That way, when they launched their attack and the South Vietnamese bullets struck their arms and legs, as they breached the defensive wire, they would not bleed out so quickly. They could advance a few additional yards, and make their lives and their crude satchel charges count for something more than if they dropped in their tracks with the first few shots that hit them.

Sapper duty. Suicide missions quite often. Like standing sentry watch, it represented the tasks performed by their lowest and newest, the most expendable. Reung had himself attacked fences and barbed wire barriers, his arms and legs aching from running with his blood flow tied off. Several bullet scars on his back and his legs reminded him that he had paid his dues. It was this boy's turn, so he should not feel bad about it. Yet he did.

He cared a great deal for his fellow soldiers, especially for the younger ones. They knew so little, yet did so much.

Tonight, many of them would die, perhaps this youngster who had smiled at him. Reung knew the intensity of fire they would face as they pushed their way up the big mountain on the western edge of Da Nang. A test of enemy resolve, and perhaps a chance to destroy a few communications and radar antennas, if they made it to the top.

They had never before made it to the top, not that he could remember, not even when the Americans had first come here, nearly ten years ago. But they had always tried, every few months.

Now, however, their attack held a greater purpose than harassing the enemy, destroying some equipment, and perhaps killing a few of their soldiers. They would spend their lives to test the enemy's defenses and assess their willingness to expend firepower. Somewhere high in the revolutionary government's leadership, military planners of something quite grand wanted to know this information. How intensely did the enemy fight today compared to previous times when the Americans had kept them fully supplied? Would he defend his ground conservatively or fight with full force? Were they in short supply? Were they becoming demoralized, as rumors reported?

Reung had heard the stories of corrupt South Vietnamese officers who hoarded munitions and sold their supply to soldiers who desperately needed the support of that firepower. Artillery shells, mortar rounds, even grenades all held cash value for these capitalistic traitors of the people.

He knew that such a thing would never happen among his army's leaders. Their cause was much greater than personal profit. Reung believed, with almost religious conviction, that all men and women who shared his rice and wore the red star, also shared his dream. One day, he could stop carrying his rifle and live at peace in his country, finally unified north and south.

For eight years he had fought as a full-fledged soldier of the people as a member of the National Liberation Front, and before that as a boy reservist. He could not remember the feel of a bed, only earth with leaves for a pillow.

It will end soon, he had told himself. He thought that nearly five years ago when the Americans started leaving. Yet it seemed to him to have only gotten worse.

The thought came to mind again two years ago that coming January when the Americans signed the Paris Accords and by March of 1973 had removed all their forces from Vietnam. This measure to bring peace allotted protected land areas for the National Liberation Front's Provisional Revolutionary Government, sanctuaries for the Viet Cong where the South Vietnamese forces could not come. But they did come, attacking villages with helicopters and rockets. Retaliation, they claimed. They boasted of their victories.

Land disputes occurred daily. South Vietnamese forces attacked villages held by the Provisional Revolutionary Government, claiming that the area belonged to the Republic of Vietnam. It was simply an excuse to attack Viet Cong forces where they lived.

Reung picked up his rifle, checked its chamber, and began the long walk with his comrades. They would attack at sunset, with the light in their enemy's eyes.

STAFF SERGEANT WALTER W. Sparks wiped dust from the lenses of his glasses and then looked again at the name etched on the sword's blade: Robert E. Cushman.

"It really does belong to the Commandant," he said to himself as he let the blade slide back into its nickel-silver scabbard trimmed with polished brass.

The seasoned Marine admired the weapon's Mameluke hilt and handle. Sultans of the Barbary Coast awarded United States Marine Corps officers the right to wear the Mameluke sword in honor of First

Lieutenant Presley O'Bannon's victory over the Barbary pirates. That band of early nineteenth-century Arabic outlaws had preyed on international merchant ships sailing from northwest African ports and had pillaged the villages along the coastline for many years, until O'Bannon and his company of Marines, in 1805, annihilated them.

"Exotic," Sparks said as he polished his fingerprints from the handle's brass crosspiece.

Albert A. Francis, the Da Nang consul general, had asked his old friend, the Commandant of the Marine Corps, to send his sword for the Da Nang security detachment's annual November 10 Marine Corps birthday-cake-cutting ceremony, which they would celebrate Saturday night, November 9. General Cushman regarded the invitation as a sincere honor and sent the sword with his blessings and his prayers.

That afternoon, Francis had called Sparks to his office and issued him a special charge, a duty, to a Marine, nearly as precious as that of protecting the Holy Grail.

Sparks immediately saw it lying on the consul general's desk. He recognized that the black leather case contained a sword, having one of his own, and he also noticed the initials R. E. C. imprinted in gold letters on its flap.

"You got a sword, sir," Sparks quickly said as he presented himself at attention before Francis.

"Not just any sword, Gunny," Francis replied. Even though Sparks was a staff sergeant, the consul general called him gunny. "This is the Commandant of the Marine Corps's personal sword."

"No shit, sir," Sparks said as Francis opened the top flap of the leather case, exposing the blue cloth sheath that contained the ceremonial weapon that symbolizes positions of military leadership.

"I have it on good authority," Francis said, sliding the cloth-wrapped piece halfway out of its container, "that General Cushman personally handed this sword to a C-130 pilot who flew it to El Toro and gave it to another C-130 pilot who carried it to Okinawa."

Francis untied the strings that held the cloth sheath fastened shut and slid it down, exposing the Mameluke handle, and then withdrew the sword from its nickel-silver and brass scabbard.

"I picked it up personally from Lieutenant General Herman Poggemeyer at III MAF headquarters and brought it back to Da Nang with me this morning," Francis said and handed the sword to Sparks.

"Guard it with your life, Gunny," the consul general said.

Filled with a sense of special duty, Sparks proudly carried the sword to his office.

Al Francis had done something exceptional for the Marines there, Sparks concluded and the Mississippi staff sergeant would remember the gesture with great warmth for the consul general for the rest of his life.

The man could have gotten any of the dozens of parade swords that Marine Corps Base, Camp Butler, III MAF, or Third Marine Division, had on supply back on Okinawa for their cake-cutting ceremony at the Da Nang consulate. But Francis had taken the extra step to get a significant sword for a special celebration, what would prove to be the last Marine Corps birthday observance in Da Nang, Republic of Vietnam.

Sparks had liked Al Francis the moment he first met him. The man was sincere and didn't act like a bureaucrat despite his long career in State Department service. Eloquent and polite, the consul general still, however, showed an edge, something common among many natural-born leaders. He carried a presence that spoke of honor, loyalty, and integrity. Marines pick up on these traits in a person very quickly because they so highly prize them. Sparks recognized the qualities in Francis immediately on the day he first shook his hand.

"Quite a guy," Sparks said to himself as he again admired the sword, unsheathed in his office, and began polishing its metal with a chemically treated cloth. He knew he must make sure that all of his men understood what Francis, as well as General Cushman, had done for them.

Sparks, a lanky, square-jawed Marine with a deep-South drawl, had arrived in Da Nang only weeks earlier with an infantry platoon sent to bolster the Marine Security Guard detachment protecting the United States Consulate there. Although well trained and equipped, no one in the platoon except the staff sergeant had ever experienced any level of armed conflict. Even Sparks' grass time was limited to that of a junior radioman operating off Hill 55, southwest of Da Nang several years earlier.

It worried him that his men had never before seen combat, had never yet looked the devil in the eye.

When Sparks had first come to Vietnam, he had the benefit of a transition to enemy fire. His battalion sent him on short-range, heavily armed patrols to introduce him, and other newbees like him, to combat. They did not just throw him to the wolves. However, for his men, their only benefit of transition would come in surviving an enemy's initial assault: getting rid of the shakes fast, controlling their fears, and staying focused while the world crashed around them.

Could they deal with it? Would fear make them choke? Would panic grip them at a decisive moment and cost them their lives? He could only hope that his Marines took their immediate-action drills and training seriously.

Meanwhile, intelligence reports and barracks talk kept the Marines and consulate staff edgy.

Colonel John M. Johnson, III Marine Amphibious Force G-3 (Assistant Chief of Staff, Operations), had briefed Sparks about the situation. Enemy aggression had grown exponentially in the mountains west and north of Da Nang since summer, corresponding directly with the significant reductions in American aid. Growing unrest among South Vietnamese forces, splintering from commands because of internal corruption and fear-mongering, left Americans in Vietnam and military forces in Okinawa feeling uneasy.

Recognizing the unrest, military commanders of forces that would have to carry out any Vietnam bailout missions began pushing and testing their troops. Business had suddenly become serious with a high operation tempo. Reaction drills became daily events. Rumors spread.

During the late summer of 1974, scuttlebutt among Marines based on Okinawa repeated these tales among their ranks. Stories of South Vietnamese forces selling their combat support to each other, bartering lives by the mortar round. Battery commanders charging cash by the shot for artillery fire to support frontline troops. South Vietnamese warlords hoarded stockpiles of equipment and ammunition, making themselves wealthy selling the booty left behind by the Americans to the troops on the front lines who were fighting for their lives.

When Walter Sparks returned to Vietnam in the fall of 1974 as the staff noncommissioned officer in charge of a virgin platoon of Marines, his instincts told him that this tour of duty would not last long. He only hoped that the lives of his men would endure longer.

Carefully sliding the Commandant's sword back in its cloth sheath and slipping that inside the leather carrying case, the Marine looked out his office's upstairs window. There he gazed at the peaceful flow of the river just beyond the street that passed in front of the consulate. He watched a lone man standing at the back of a small, flat boat, pushing

a long tiller from side to side, gliding it upstream. The man slowly an-
gled his craft to the water's far side where lights shone from the windows of a multitude of concrete block and stucco houses, densely
packed in neighborhoods. The city looked serene.

Turning his attention left, toward the center of Da Nang, the staff
sergeant could see radio towers, their red lights flashing as evening
grew slowly darker. Beyond the city, the silhouettes of the mountains
rose against the sunset. On their slopes he could see the crimson streaks
of tracers pouring from one position into another. Among them, orange
flashes burst, spraying fire skyward.

The veteran Marine unconsciously counted, "One-thousand-one,
one-thousand-two, one-thousand-three," waiting to hear the muffled
rumble of the artillery explosions on the mountainside. An old combat
habit, flash-bang distance estimating.

Calculating the time it took for the explosion's sound to reach him
after he saw the flash gave Sparks an idea of how far away from him
the round had struck. With sound traveling eleven hundred feet per second, each three seconds approximated one grid square on a map, or
one kilometer. The estimate's degree of accuracy depended on wind
speed and direction.

Atop the besieged mountain Sparks could see the many antennas
that used to mark the location of the III MAF headquarters. Freedom
Hill, some had called it, Hill 327.

General Lew Walt had commanded his I Corps Marines from that
post. Now Lieutenant General Ngo Quang Truong used the facilities
for the communications command center for his Military Region 1
forces in their duties of protecting Hue and Da Nang. It was only a mo-
mentary chopper hop from Truong's headquarters at Da Nang Air
Base, on the south side of Da Nang, across the Han River from China
Beach and the Marble Mountain Helicopter Base.

Sparks had met General Truong a few days earlier when he had visited the consulate to discuss current enemy activities with Consul General Francis and III MAF's Colonel Johnson. The general seemed to
contradict to the scuttlebutt about the South Vietnamese military leaders. This man clearly cared about his forces and pursued his mission
with an enormous sense of duty.

Watching the heavy machine gun fire, and the artillery and mortar
barrage intensifying on the south slopes of Hill 327, Sparks tried to
imagine himself there. He could feel the panic rising from his stomach.

He could smell the smoke and sweat. He remembered how he felt in the midst of just such a fight, a numbness sweeping over him, everything on automatic pilot, no time to stop, consider, or think. Just time to act. Immediate action. Yank and crank. Pour hot lead at them.

Only in the quietness after the battle did he ever start to think about what had happened, consider what he did, how many died, how close he came.

BELOW HILL 327, WEST OF DA NANG

SEVERAL BODIES LAY in the smoke and debris of what once had been a fence of barbed wire coils and crisscrossed steel posts when Nguyen Duc Cui crawled over the small rise that gave him a covered location from which he could watch the attack. A man with a radio on his back hugged the ground next to Cui while several other North Vietnamese officers lay a few yards away.

Nguyen Duc Cui, a stocky native of Hanoi, was younger than many of the other officers. Yet he had risen by his own initiative from lowly line soldier to communications officer for the entire division. He had suffered severe wounds in battle and now felt justly right watching the fight from his relatively safe position.

From the flashes of artillery and mortar explosions he could see the Viet Cong soldiers leading the charge up the slopes, behind them silhouettes of soldiers from his own unit, the North Vietnamese Army's 320th Division.

Cui's unit fought here, reinforcing the Provisional Revolutionary Government forces, in blatant violation of the Paris Peace Accords, just as this attack on the South Vietnamese communications site on Hill 327 was an open offense of rules established for the cease-fire, which had commenced January 28, 1973, as part of the accords. In the sixty days that followed enactment of the peace agreement, reached in Paris by chief negotiators Henry Kissinger and Le Duc Tho, North Vietnam sent home more than 150,000 of its soldiers from the battlefields of the south, in unison with the American withdrawal of its forces. However, as those 150,000 combat-weary NVA soldiers marched northward, another 150,000 fresh NVA troops marched southward, replacing the battle-worn forces on the front lines, supporting the Viet Cong. In the end, their numbers, totaling nearly

200,000 Communist soldiers opposing the more than 300,000 South Vietnamese, never changed. In all practicality for the North Vietnamese, the sixty days following the cease-fire allowed them an opportune time to overhaul their forces in the south, replacing nearly every unit with fresh combatants.

In the orange light from the fires and explosions, Cui could see men falling, his own men, struck by grazing machine gun fire from emplacements above them. Others were blown off their feet, running too near a mortar's impact.

Above the soldiers and through their ranks, thousands of tracers streaked red light and ignited small fires where too many of the burning phosphorus-tipped bullets had impacted together, setting the grass and debris ablaze. The whizzing, whispering sounds of thousands of other bullets cut through the air above Cui.

The NVA communications officer hugged himself close to the ground behind the knoll and listened to the radio traffic of the combined forces' commanders as they called for their own mortar and machine gun fire to suppress the enemy defenses.

Above him, a steady yellow light now flooded the whole southwest slopes of Hill 327, coming from flares suspended beneath small parachutes, illumination rounds fired by nearby South Vietnamese Army artillery batteries. One after another they lit the sky and danced slowly toward the ground, leaving trails of white smoke drifting above them.

Cui braced himself for the barrage of high-explosive artillery rounds that would surely follow the illumination. However, they did not come. Only the illumination rounds popped harmlessly overhead.

Then, in the distance, he heard the thumping of helicopter blades beating the air, and high overhead the coursing sounds of jet engines screamed toward him, louder and louder.

"Sound retreat!" his commander shouted a few yards to his right.

Cui snapped up the handset and put it to his ear, depressed the button on the side, and repeated the order, "Retreat! Retreat! Retreat!"

Police whistles cut through the air in front of him and at both sides. Forward commanders signaled their men to fall back, collect their dead and wounded, and evacuate.

"Yes, evacuate," Cui said to himself. The noise of the jet engines and beating helicopter blades raised his anxiety. Unless they moved quickly, the machine guns and rocket fire from the helicopters and the napalm from the jets would devastate their combined forces much worse than the defensive fire of the ARVN soldiers holding the hill above them.

WALTER SPARKS TOOK General Cushman's sword to the security locker and leaned it against the back wall. He shut the door, turned the key, and shook the handle. It would be safe there, even if a fire swept the building.

By the time the Marine staff sergeant got outside the consulate and flagged a cyclo-taxi to the curb, the fighting on Hill 327 had stopped. A few cars and trucks sped past him as his driver pedaled behind the open compartment where the Marine sat. Sparks preferred riding in a cyclo because it was serene. The few blocks' ride from the consulate to his apartment gave him time to relax, to feel the cool breeze off the river, to see the world unobstructed.

As the driver pedaled through the white light from the sodium lamps that lined the boulevard, Sparks passed several people on the street with now-familiar faces. He waved to them. Recognizing him too, the people along the sidewalk each smiled and waved back. Old women selling American sodas and cigarettes from their vendor carts. A one-legged man standing by an hibachi cart cooked meat skewered on kabob sticks, hopefully pork or beef, or possibly goat, but very likely black dog.

The Marine staff sergeant could smell the barbecue as he passed the man, and it made him hungry, so he asked the cyclo driver to pull to the curb.

"Beef?" Sparks asked the one-legged man.

"Yes," the man said, picking up one of the sticks containing several squares of meat on it.

"Pork?" Sparks then asked.

"Yes," the one-legged man said, still holding up the same stick and handing it to the Marine.

"Black dog?" Sparks asked.

"No, no," the man said and laughed, showing a smile with no front teeth. "No black dog. No, no."

"Okay," Sparks said and handed the man an American one-dollar bill. The man handed him three more sticks of meat, apparently four for a dollar, so the Marine gave two of the kabobs to the cyclo driver as they peddled away.

The meat was tasty and sweet, delicious barbecue, no matter what origin of the flesh, even black dog. However, savoring it, Sparks convinced himself it had to be pork.

As they neared his apartment, Sparks recognized the shapely figures of two young women who worked in the nightclub just up the block from where he lived. They wore ankle-length silk dresses and high-heeled shoes with open toes. Their black hair hung to their waists, combed straight and tied back with ribbons. False lashes caked thick with mascara made their eyes look large and round. Without their makeup, Sparks considered, a person might hardly recognize them as being the same girls.

"Suzie," he called to them, and they both waved and smiled at him. Bar girls in Da Nang usually adopted an easy-to-pronounce, American-sounding name like Suzie.

"You come out tonight?" one called back to him.

"Maybe for one beer, in a little bit," he answered as the cyclo pulled to the curb in front of his apartment. He stepped out and paid the driver, who then pedaled away.

Sparks waited by his gate and watched as the two girls reached the front door of the nearby club where they worked. They both stopped and waved at him again, smiling, and then they disappeared.

Inside his apartment, the Marine switched on his Sansui stereo system wired to a pair of three-foot-high Pioneer speakers, stripped off his clothes as he walked through the bedroom, tossing the dirty laundry across his double bed, and stepped into the shower. As a staff noncommissioned officer, assigned temporary additional duty to the Marine Security Guard Battalion, he rated certain privileges, among them a private apartment, which he had already made very comfortable in the few weeks he had lived there.

Sparks planned on eating a light dinner and then having only one cocktail or maybe two at the nightclub, making it an early evening. He knew that several of his Marines and perhaps some of the consulate staff would also be at the club, so he didn't want to make any bad impressions on any of them. Besides, he planned on getting to work early in the morning so that he could finalize his preparations for the Marine Corps birthday celebration in a couple of days.

In an hour, he stepped through the nightclub doorway, greeted by the sounds of a recording of Eric Clapton singing *I Shot the Sheriff,* blaring through a speaker system that would crack plaster. In the red lights of the stage, a young woman with waist-long hair, wearing a green, sequin-covered G-string, danced bare breasted to the music, pointing her fingers and pretending to shoot them like pistols at the several Marines and consulate staff members seated at tables that ringed a small dance floor.

Busy in booths that lined the walls and alcoves, girls in long gowns and high heels hustled drinks from a host of South Vietnamese soldiers on liberty and an increasingly dwindling number of Americans assigned to various posts in Da Nang. These days, however, several tables sat empty even on the best nights. The girls had to work twice as hard, often for half as much money, since most of their customers now were Vietnamese and knew the tricks. Thus, the girls highly prized an American customer, especially a serviceman, who usually bought plenty of drinks and gave generous tips.

For Staff Sergeant Sparks and many of the Marines under his charge, the club offered a refreshing change from what they had known in the bars in Hinoko, Kin Village, Ishikawa, Taragawa, and Koza, Okinawa. A dollar here went a much longer way, and nightclub acts could get fairly wild. Girls openly practiced prostitution without fear of police.

Next to the Philippines and Bangkok, liberty in Da Nang or Saigon still rated as the best and wildest for American soldiers in the Far East. A serviceman with five dollars in his pocket could have a long and happy night in the ville here.

Walter Sparks ordered his usual, Jim Beam and Coke in a tall glass with lots of ice. Before he could step from the bar and sit down, however, one of the Suzie girls who had waved to him on the street earlier locked her arm in his and accompanied him to the table where three other Americans from the consulate sat. He reminded himself that he would still make it an early evening.

THAT SAME NIGHT IN SAIGON

FOR YEARS, THE Caravel and Continental hotels in the heart of Saigon reigned as the primary watering holes of the Western press, foreign diplomatic corps, and South Vietnam's social elite. The Caravel's rooftop had often served as an attractive platform from which American television journalists filmed their reports on the war. Over their shoulders the cameras picked up the smoking hills, giving viewers the sense that the reporter faced eminent danger, while in reality he stood only a few steps away from the cocktail bar.

While the Caravel's rooftop featured islands of tables set among exotic potted palms on a system of multilevel risers and terraces surrounding a poolside-style outdoor bar, as well as an attractive enclosed rooftop lounge behind French doors, the Continental towered across the way. It overlooked Saigon's great white opera house and had its own unique character and polished woodwork cocktail center that Westerners had come to call the Continental Shelf.

Journalists tended to gather at the Caravel while diplomats, American contractors, politicians, and the local elite preferred the Shelf's social setting. Almost any night would find at the Continental bar a variety of CIA analysts, embassy staff workers, American military officers, and South Vietnamese aristocrats.

This evening at the Continental Shelf was no different. Several of the United States Embassy junior staff officers gathered near South Vietnam's former premier, former vice president, and current commander of the nation's air force, Air Marshal Nguyen Cao Ky. The mostly youthful group politely listened to his harangue about the resolve of the Republic of Vietnam's armed forces despite the inept leadership of President Nguyen Van Thieu, the crippling blows dealt to them by the latest United States aid cutbacks, and the ceaseless violations of the Paris Peace Accords by the Communists. He told how the Provisional Revolutionary Government, fronting for the North Vietnamese, only paid lip service to the accords and from the cease-fire's beginning had used the truce to their advantage to stop South Vietnam from thwarting the Viet Cong and illegal NVA buildups secretly going on.

"We act only in retaliation to their aggression," Ky insisted, spilling some of the Scotch whiskey from his glass as he shook the drink with his speech. He stroked his moustache and smiled at his friend, Vietnamese film star Kieu Chinh.

Kieu nodded in agreement with the former premier. She wanted to believe him. Like so many others in South Vietnam, she depended on his word that the Communists could never overwhelm the superior forces of the Republic of Vietnam. She hoped that one day soon they would defeat the Communists once and for all. Then she could return to her birthplace and home in Hanoi where several members of her family still lived.

As a girl, she had fled to Saigon where the Geneva Peace Accords and cease-fire of July 20, 1954, dissolved French Indochina and divided Vietnam at the seventeenth parallel, along the Ben Hai River, creating the infamous Demilitarized Zone and two separate Vietnamese nations. From the Viet Minh war to cast out French colonial control and overthrow its puppet regime under Emperor Bao Dai emerged Ho Chi Minh's continued campaign to ultimately unite all of Vietnam into a single, independent Communist state. For the Communists, the accords of 1954 and those of 1973 represented only steps in an unending effort, with only names and political labels changing. Their revolution never lost step.

Ho and many of his closest followers had seized upon their dream of a single Communist Vietnam even before the Japanese had invaded French Indochina in World War II. Then in 1946, with weapons, munitions, and funding provided to Ho Chi Minh's Viet Minh rebels by the allied powers, Ho launched in earnest his Communist rebellion. In 1954 the Viet Minh may have agreed to the terms of a formal cease-fire and peace accord, but like those adopted in 1973, they meant little. Their agreement paid only lip service to the accords simply to buy time, establish new boundaries, and enable the Communists to launch into a new phase of their protracted revolution. Although the political climate had changed from French to American, the Communist objectives had not changed at all.

In those twenty years since the first peace accords, Kieu Chinh had found widespread fame on the cinema screen and now enjoyed international notoriety as South Vietnam's most renowned star.

Today she boasted friendship with world-famous film and stage actors and with producers and directors in Paris, London, New York, and Hollywood. She accumulated wealth and status in Saigon and attended all the A-list social events, speaking on a first-name basis with her country's highest leaders, military officers, and foreign diplomats.

Yet she secretly worried. She knew that with so many things changing so quickly in her country, the test of its resolve and courage would come very soon. However, she told these thoughts to no one. She knew better. With the winds shifting so quickly, she spoke only with positive caution and hoped that what she heard her longtime friend, Air Marshal Ky, say was true.

However, these days the words of Nguyen Cao Ky meant little in terms of real political power. Today he mostly had only the reputation of a strutting peacock, fanning his flamboyant tail and boasting outrageously.

Unseated as Nguyen Van Thieu's vice president, Ky had built a formidable opposition to Thieu in an effort to claim the presidency for himself. However, in the 1968 Tet Offensive, vital members of Ky's camp were killed, badly crippling his political machine. Ky never knew for certain if these men had actually died at the hands of the Communists. His South Vietnamese political opponents could have just as easily used the Communist offensive as an opportunity to murder his allies and put his presidential hopes out of reach.

Thieu, meanwhile, enjoyed the favor of the American government, and with the CIA's help, he systematically eliminated Ky's remaining political foundation. Thieu's campaign proved so effective that all other opposition dropped from the race as well. Concerned that critics at home in the United States would question the legitimacy of Thieu's election, American agents in Saigon went to guilt-ridden extremes to cover up their dirty work. They even approached political moderate, General Duong Van "Big" Minh and offered him $3 million to stay in the race. Despite the handsome bribe, Minh nonetheless declined the offer, not wanting to lose face in a lost cause. Thieu won the 1971 election virtually unopposed.

A survivor, Ky recognized where the Americans stood with his political aspirations and wisely accepted his place for the time being. For now, he relaxed his grip on the political reins that remained within his grasp. However, he still enjoyed basking in the spotlight in his decorative but emasculated position as air marshal.

COLONEL BA SIPPED his tea and gazed at the night sky. Outside the walls of his villa he could hear the sounds of the nightlife, people laughing, cycle motors speeding past his gate, and beyond that the whine of jet engines at nearby Tan Son Nhut Air Base.

On the table in front of him, in the yellow light of a candle-lit lamp, he thumbed through a stack of papers and waited for his assistant to return with a plate of fruit. He blinked through his glasses and rubbed his narrow face, pondering the impact of what the documents represented.

Vo Dong Giang, commonly known among the Americans, the Western press, and South Vietnamese leaders as Colonel Ba, now enjoyed the status of diplomat rather than regimental field commander and intelligence officer in the North Vietnamese Army. Today he proudly held the title of deputy foreign minister, an official member of the Provisional Revolutionary Government, and enjoyed the attention from the Western journalists that it brought.

He sat as a member of the Joint Military Commission along with Commander in Chief of the Army of the National Liberation Front, the Viet Cong, General Tran Van Tra, his old friend and former field commander. Together, they spoke the Communist policies and positions of the Provisional Revolutionary Government on the commission. However, because of his command of English, Colonel Ba spoke to the world press for his nation.

"Sit, sit, sit," he said to his assistant as he set the bowl of bananas, berries, and sliced oranges on the garden table.

"Look at this," the colonel said, pushing the stack of papers toward his aide. "They have put it in writing. The politburo in Hanoi debates this as we speak. Next year we will either stand in control of our country, or stand behind bars, if we are lucky and they do not shoot us first."

Colonel Ba sat back in his chair, lighting a cigarette in a black, plastic holder, and studied the face of his assistant, a man not much younger than himself and a soldier of significant combat experience too. He trusted the man's opinions.

"I knew of this weeks ago," the aide said. "I worry that too many people now talk about it. Many of our soldiers."

"They know where their bread is buttered," Colonel Ba said and laughed, popping a slice of banana in his mouth. "Besides, we have nothing to say or do about it. General Tran only gave this to me so we could make our own plans."

"The politburo remains divided though," the aide said.

"Of course. The doves must be allowed to speak," Colonel Ba said arrogantly. "But we both know how it will end. Party First Secretary Le Duan and revolutionary hero General Vo Nguyen Giap still speak the voice of Ho Chi Minh. We will attack next year with absolute resolve. There will be no turning back. We will utterly win or lose this war."

The aide had never heard anything negative spoken by Colonel Vo Dong Giang, not in the battlefields west of Da Nang nor in the privacy of his colonel's home, until now.

"Lose?" the aide said. "Sir, how can you consider we could ever lose? Our revolution is without end until we succeed with unification of Vietnam."

"The revolution will always continue," Colonel Ba said, "but under what circumstances? Generals Tran Van Tra and Van Tien Dung, along with First Secretary Le Duan, himself, devised this plan with nothing remaining in reserve. All of our military equipment and resources are committed to the front line with this campaign. They must be in order to strike at once throughout the region. Thus their name for it, Campaign 2/75: The Blooming Lotus.

"Those dirty Russians will give us nothing more. We received our last shipment from them nine months ago. This while the South Vietnamese have the millions of tons of munitions and supplies left by the Americans, and the millions of tons of munitions and supplies the Americans shipped to them after that and continue to ship to them."

"We should wait, then," the aide said.

"For what?" Colonel Ba said.

"For a better time, when we have reserves," the aide said.

"The Russians do not have the money to keep giving us what we need," Colonel Ba said. "They have their troubles.

"No. The generals are correct with this plan. It has just come to this, our moment of truth."

Colonel Ba then took a newspaper and tossed it on top of the papers in front of his aide.

"Meanwhile, our friend Henry Kissinger tells the American Congress that those dirty Russians are giving us more, 150 percent more," Colonel Ba said. "That bastard Ford wants to increase aid and probably land troops too, if we knew the truth of it.

"We count on the American government, however, to help ensure our success. Consider that in 1973, when we enacted the Paris Peace Accords, the United States Congress authorized $2.2 billion in aid to South Vietnam. They have cut that aid by half each year since, which communicates their people's strong discontent. Their cutting aid now to $700 million for this fiscal year has had a telling psychological effect on South Vietnam's government and ultimately on its military forces. We see this and count on it."

Vo Dong Giang leaned over the table and pointed at the stack of papers. "Our army will make a proving strike somewhere on the border next month," he said. The colonel again studied the face of his aide, smiling at the look of enthusiasm his subordinate now tried to hide.

"If no one reacts," Colonel Ba continued, clenching the black plastic cigarette holder in his teeth, smoke puffing from his mouth with each word that he spoke, "our forces will make another probe, this time, much more deeply, and this time they will hold the objective, an air field, in January. If the Americans do not react, then we can gamble that they also will do nothing at all when we launch the campaign in the spring."

The veteran colonel sat back in his chair and turned his face up at the night sky, enjoying the cool breeze of the evening.

"For now, though," Colonel Ba said, "we should enjoy this peaceful moment."

Chapter 3
FIRST STRIKE

CAMP BUTLER, OKINAWA—SATURDAY, DECEMBER 14, 1974

A WARM AROMA OF coffee brewing greeted Steven Lynn Tingley at 6:30 a.m. as he stepped through the doorway of his workplace at Marine Corps Base, Camp Smedley D. Butler. The twenty-year-old corporal liked to start his routine in the central bureau and headquarters of the Joint Public Affairs Office, Okinawa, at least an hour early on Saturdays. The extra time allowed him a greater likelihood of completing chores by noon, when the shop regularly stood down for weekend liberty.

Tingley's office functioned as the official source of public information and internal communications for all Marine Corps activities on Okinawa, and the entire III Marine Amphibious Force, primarily composed of Third Marine Division, Third Force Service Support Group (formerly Third Force Service Regiment), and First Marine Aircraft Wing—approximately fifty-six thousand Marines and their equipment. Among its functions, the Joint Public Affairs Office published the *Okinawa Marine* newspaper and provided civilian press with news accounts, feature stories, and photographs of III MAF Marines in action.

The articles and images that the office released came from a small legion of approximately thirty Marine Corps reporters and photojournalists, called combat correspondents, assigned to key frontline units deployed throughout the Far East. These combat correspondents often reported and photographed initial engagements whenever Marine Corps units became embroiled in a conflict, usually long before any civilian media could arrive on the scene to cover the story.

The freshly made coffee's inviting smell raised a smile on Steve Tingley's face. Rarely did anyone ever arrive at work ahead of him, especially on a Saturday morning. Thus, seeing the lights on and coffee already in the pot surprised the young corporal, a tall, neat-freakish Marine from Matoon, Illinois, who oversaw the majority of the Joint Public Affairs Office's clerical administration. Although trained as a journalist, Tingley readily told anyone that he did a much better job managing correspondence, balancing budgets, maintaining a fully indexed, cross-referenced and color-tab-organized system of files, and helping out with community relations than he ever did writing news or feature stories. However, he did pride himself on his photographic skills.

"That you, Tommy-Guns?" Tingley called into the otherwise empty complex of offices and workrooms. He thought that perhaps the lance corporal who assisted him as clerk typist and van driver, Donald "Tommy-Guns" Tompkins, might have arrived early, something highly out of character.

"In here, Tingley," a familiar voice answered.

"Skipper, you're here awfully early today," the corporal said, recognizing that the response came from his boss, Captain Jerry Shelton, a man who had risen through the enlisted ranks to staff sergeant and then had advanced to lieutenant when he received a battlefield commission in Vietnam. Now a major selectee, the mustang captain who served as the Joint Public Affairs Office's operations officer and second in command, looked forward to pinning on gold oak leaves and entering field grade rank status. He had come a long way since growing up in Texas and working as a ranch cowboy until he joined the Marines as a boot private.

"Busy Friday night," Shelton said, pouring coffee for himself and a cup for the corporal too. "A Marine found murdered this morning, air winger from Futema. Someone slashed his throat and threw his body into the ocean. It washed up on the rocks near Torii Station. Naval Investigative Service says it looks like another dope killing."

"Lots of dope all over the place, Skipper. Smack, hash, Buddha, you name it. It's everywhere," Tingley said in a disgusted tone as he opened a briefcase and brought out a light green folder filled with the previous night's message traffic and laid it on the captain's desk.

"I stopped off at the communications center on the way up from the barracks, sir," Tingley said and then started laughing. "Last night, a Marine got his dick bitten nearly off at Camp Hanson."

"Come again?" Shelton said and laughed too.

"Yes, sir," Tingley answered, laughing more, now excited to tell the captain the entire ugly story.

The corporal had read the messages while at the communications center, including the Serious Incident Reports issued by each of the regiments and camps. At the top of the SIR list, a Marine nearly losing his penis to a jealous Okinawan bar girl in Kin Village, outside Camp Hanson.

"This turd from Fourth Marines," Tingley began, relaxing his butt across the corner of the captain's desk, reclining while casually sipping his coffee as he unwound the sordid tale, "he's taking his last night on liberty before he goes home. So he decides to finally tell his Okinawan girlfriend that he won't be seeing her anymore. She goes nuts in the bar where she works, but then seems to calm down. She makes an evening of it with the guy, soaking him for all the drinks he will buy.

"Well, sometime after midnight, when business is just about done, this girl talks the dumb shit into going home with her. Right off the bat, at her place, she goes down on the guy, to give him a fond-farewell blowjob.

"The guy is moving and grooving to it, you know, feeling the pleasure, and suddenly the girl clamps down on his rod. She does her best to bite it off.

"He comes undone, no doubt. Eventually, he manages to get what's left of his crank out of her mouth, but not until she had chewed all the way through it. His schlong is hanging only by a shred of skin on one side.

"Of course, he is bleeding like a stuck pig. So he panics and takes off running for the barracks. He hits the main gate at Camp Hanson, and by this time he nearly passes out from blood loss. Numbnuts tells the MPs that he got his dick caught in his zipper.

"The Ps know it's a lie right off because the asshole is wearing button-up Levis!"

Both Marines laugh so hard that tears stream from their eyes.

"In all seriousness, though, Skipper," Tingley added, catching his breath, "it was a pretty bad incident, and the Marine had to be taken to Kui Hospital. They sewed his tool back on, but who knows how the guy will be."

"Jim Lee, at *Stars and Stripes,* will love that one," Shelton said, still laughing. "It should be interesting to see how he manages to write it so that they will publish it."

"No way, Skipper," Tingley retorted and laughed. "They'll never put anything like that in the paper."

"Probably not," Shelton said with amusement. "But it won't be because Jim doesn't try. What else you have?"

"Marine in the barracks, also at Camp Hanson, damned near bought the farm after chugalugging a quart of vodka," Tingley said, pointing to the report. "His buddies found him in the rack, on his back, choking to death on his own vomit. This dumb shit, on a fifty-dollar bet, downed the whole quart in one long pull and then laid down. After a while, his buddies thought they better check on him. He was damned near dead. They managed to get him to the battalion aid station in time. He'll be headed for alcohol rehab at Long Beach, I imagine."

Captain Shelton thumbed through the stack of reports and said, "What about intel reps?"

"Sir," Tingley said in a low voice, "the confidential messages are there, in the classified folders. Two secret messages too. Information reports to the Commandant of the Marine Corps distribution list. Both pertain to the same thing. News from Vietnam."

The captain refilled his cup with coffee.

"Want more?" he asked Tingley.

"Sure, sir," the corporal said and walked to the coffee pot with his mug.

"So what's the scoop from Vietnam?" Shelton asked.

"Looks bad, Skipper," Tingley said. "One of the messages originated from the defense attaché in Saigon and the other from the Marine liaison officer in Da Nang.

"The NVA have crossed the border and attacked some little ville called Don Luan. They basically invaded South Vietnam, openly violating the Paris Peace Accords, like they're thumbing their noses at us. The messages say the assault was launched by the 301st NVA Corps made up of their Third and Seventh NVA divisions, some tank battalions, artillery, antiaircraft, and service support elements. Looks like a heavily manned and well-equipped invasion. Lots more detail in the messages."

"Of course, they're thumbing their noses at us," the captain said. "They know we won't do anything.

"Meanwhile, the big story in *Stars and Stripes* is how the ARVN kicked ass on the NVA, finally knocking them off Mo Tau Mountain on Wednesday, relieving the death grip from the Communist artillery positions that the NVA had used to shut down Phu Bai Airfield. I wonder how much of the NVA's incursion into South Vietnam, on Friday the thirteenth of all days, will make the papers?"

"You know the press, sir," Tingley answered. "If they report it at all, they will downplay it, of course. They damned sure don't want to say anything about the North Vietnamese violating the Paris Peace Accords."

"Motherfucking, cock-sucking, Communist whore bastard North Vietnamese!" Staff Sergeant Joe Carr bellowed as he stormed into the office complex, not knowing who, if anyone other than Corporal Tingley, waited inside.

"Joe!" Captain Shelton shouted from his office to the outer rooms where the staff sergeant had begun slamming furniture against the walls.

"Sir!" Carr responded.

"I take it that you have heard the news!" Shelton called to him.

"If you mean the fucking NVA have just reinvaded South Vietnam, and nobody in fucking Congress, the White House, or the whole fucking country gives a rat shit about it, then yes, sir, I have heard the news," the staff sergeant answered.

Carr had spent two tours in Vietnam as an infantry Marine and had served a tour on the recruit training field as a drill instructor, training Marines to fight in Vietnam. Light complected and blond haired, his emotions regarding what he held as America's long-standing obligation to the Vietnamese people showed itself in a bright red glow of heated passion on his face and balding head. He was a violently expressive man.

On Carr's heels, several other Vietnam War veteran Marines filtered into the office, each expressing similar sentiments about what the North Vietnamese Communists had done, but none quite as colorfully vocal as Joe Carr.

"No word on when we mount out, sir?" Carr asked the captain. "There is no way that we can just sit by and let those Communist cocksuckers waltz in and take over."

"Nothing so far," Shelton responded.

"Fucking III MAF has seen this coming," Carr said. "Nobody else wants to listen to them, but the division and the wing have been cranking everything up since last summer, getting ready to go back to war.

"Word I have is that the NVA has more men and weaponry positioned in South Vietnam now than when we were fighting the war. The day Kissinger locked us into that Paris bullshit peace-talks crap, the NVA started shipping all their shit and people south.

"I got friends at III MAF G-2, and they know the scoop, Captain. Believe me.

"They say the NVA has all kinds of SA-2 and SA-7 surface-to-air missiles, a whole network of radar air defenses, antiair artillery, plus a world of ground shit too spread all over I Corps and the Central Highlands, and some of it even sitting damned near in Da Nang.

"The Commies have 185,000 fresh combat-line troops and more than 107,000 support personnel standing at the ready in South Vietnam too. That's in addition to about 50,000 Viet Cong. The spooks tell me that the NVA even laid a 5,000 kilometer oil pipeline along the western border, plus built a whole new highway for their 600-and-some-odd new Russian T-54 tanks and all their other self-propelled artillery, ammo trucks, and heavy equipment to drive south. Assholes in DC have known this for months too, and they do nothing and say nothing. They just keep cutting aid to South Vietnam."

Captain Shelton knew that Joe Carr was correct in what he had just said. He had heard the same information repeated at the III MAF operations briefings during the past several months. In response, the Marine division and aircraft wing had heightened their training and had even begun putting armor plating in the bellies of some of the larger transport helicopters and fixed-wing aircraft. Several times weekly, Marines answered reaction drills, in which they reported to Kadina Air Base and Futima Marine Corps Air Station to mount out to South Vietnam at a moment's notice.

Several units from the Fourth and Ninth Marine regiments, Third Reconnaissance Battalion, and other Fleet Marine Force service and support elements operated at high alert. They stood ready to further reinforce the Thirty-first, Thirty-third and Thirty-fifth Marine Amphibious units and their reinforcements, which made up the Ninth Marine Amphibious Brigade, afloat on ships near the Philippines. Commanded by Brigadier General Richard E. Carey, the brigade had poised itself where it could react at a moment's notice to troubles that now appeared in Cambodia as well as South Vietnam.

"Joe," Shelton said in a calm voice, "the war is over. They gave it away. It's just a matter of time, so get used to it. Most of our planning now is evacuation. I would be very surprised if we landed any combat forces except to evacuate people."

Shelton knew the score, not just from what he had seen the operations planners doing and from what III MAF briefing officers had laid on the table. He knew it from simple political savvy. Congress would not stand for anything more in Vietnam except an evacuation.

"Motherfuckers!" Joe Carr grumbled, pouring himself a cup of coffee and lighting a cigarette.

"Gunny Thurman," Shelton called to the operations chief.

Gunnery Sergeant Russ Thurman joined the captain, and the two men walked outside to talk privately.

"From what I understand, this thing could get really bad very soon," Shelton told Thurman.

"I know," Thurman said. "I've sat in on briefings at Camp Courtney. They say if we land forces anywhere north of Vung Tao, the first battalion to hit the beach will virtually get wiped out—probably suffer a 90 percent casualty rate. That's if the Communists turn this into a full-scale offensive and we go back to fight."

"It won't happen," Shelton said. "All the plans I've seen call for evacuation programs. Anything involving offensive operations is purely for contingency purposes and in support of ultimate evacuation."

Both men stood quietly, sipping coffee and watching Marines scurry up the hill, reporting to their various duty sections for the standard half-day Saturday work schedule.

"You need to start thinking about people we can assign to cover this thing," Shelton said. "Whatever happens, I want you to deploy as team leader."

OUTSIDE THE WHITE House, the sun shone brightly, giving an illusion of warmth on the South Lawn. Meanwhile, cold, dry air gripped Washington, DC, on this sixth day of January 1975.

President Gerald R. Ford sat quietly at his desk in the Oval Office, taking a few moments to read situation reports sent by CIA Station Chief Thomas Polgar and the defense attaché in South Vietnam, Major General Homer D. Smith, USA. He wanted to have his thoughts collected regarding the current developments in South Vietnam before he listened to briefings on the situation from his national security staff during a meeting with Secretary of State Henry Kissinger, Secretary of Defense James Schlesinger, and CIA Director William Colby.

With the signing of the Paris Peace Accords on January 27, 1973, the Military Assistance Command, Vietnam (MACV), dissolved and essentially transformed into the Defense Attaché Office. It operated under the umbrella of the United States Embassy, much like the CIA station did, but limited any embassy operational influence or oversight to only such matters as public affairs and media information. Conducting business autonomously from the embassy, like its predecessor, MACV, the DAO remained an operational and reporting element of the Department of Defense, just as the CIA station was an operational and reporting element of the Central Intelligence Agency, with the embassy only handling its public information and news releases.

General Smith had replaced Major General John E. Murray, USA, in the fall of 1973, who had six months earlier begun formulating evacuation plans for South Vietnam. CIA Station Chief Polgar had assumed his post in Saigon in late 1972 when Henry Kissinger, then national security advisor and lead negotiator in Paris, finalized the peace accords with Communist Vietnam's Le Duc Tho.

As soon as the treaty was signed, the DAO and other experienced American strategic experts initiated the planning for the evacuation of South Vietnam, and not its defense, as the primary contingency. (If secondary contingencies that involved returning American forces to ground combat or similar defensive strategies even existed, no one has to this day ever taken credit for such planning, nor have they ever acknowledged that such plans existed. Thus one conclusion appears very clear: When Dr. Kissinger finally negotiated America out of Vietnam, the United States virtually conceded victory to the Communists and merely planned the means of getting the last Americans out of the country before the nation finally fell.)

Despite all of Kissinger's hopes in Paris, with the new year came the clear indication that the North Vietnamese had launched in earnest a major campaign. It had become obvious that the Communists had used the Paris Accords merely as a means to get the Americans out of their way so that they could mass their forces for a final thrust into the heart of South Vietnam and claim victory.

In a matter of only three weeks, the NVA had already driven their offensive to the city of Phuoc Long, crushing the ARVN forces that stood in their way.

Today's message from General Smith, who reported directly to Secretary of Defense Schlesinger, announced that North Vietnamese forces had captured the Song Be Airfield. With control of the airfield, the NVA culminated their offensive and now owned the entire Phuoc Long Province.

In the twenty-four days since their invasion strike began at Don Luan, the NVA had also captured Duc Phong, Bo Duc, and Bunard Fire Support Base. They had employed a strategy of infiltrating their forces inside the protective perimeters that defended the critical provincial villages and compounds. They commenced the primary thrust of their attacks from within the heart of each stronghold. The South Vietnamese defenses literally shattered in confusion and chaos.

Developed from the concept of airborne assaults used by American forces in the invasion of Normandy in World War II, the Communists called this strategy The Blooming Lotus, since the attack opened from the center like a blossoming flower. The Blooming Lotus of the North Vietnamese Army's 301st Corps had successfully taken, intact, the entire Phuoc Long Province. This was the first time since 1954 that a South Vietnamese province had fallen to the Communists.

Already in his heart, President Ford knew that South Vietnam's future rested in the hands of its leaders and the resolve of its fighting forces. No matter what he might present to Congress, he knew that they would not allow any intervention, especially with American ground forces.

From General Smith's report, and the success that the Communists enjoyed today, President Ford knew that the end of the war finally made its way to the fore. It was now simply a matter of time.

"YOUR CONGRESS HAS turned its back on South Vietnam. What makes you think that President Ford will go against their wishes and stop the Communists' attack?" South Vietnamese President Nguyen Van Thieu said, shaking his head as he spoke to the United States ambassador to South Vietnam, Graham A. Martin. "Their intentions are perfectly clear. Certainly, Hanoi knows this, or they would not have attacked us so boldly.

"In two years, the Congress has cut our aid from nearly $2.5 billion to a fourth as much, less than $700 million. Next they will cut our aid to nothing and let the wolves have us. Furthermore, I know of General Murray's and General Smith's evacuation plans, not attack plans. There are no plans for any defensive operations. So how can you sit there and tell me otherwise?"

Ambassador Martin stood in Thieu's plush office, towering over South Vietnam's president, his face long and his complexion matching his gray hair. "I cannot confirm nor deny what plans the military may have prepared at this point in time," he said. "Clearly, they would not be doing their jobs if they did not have a sound evacuation contingency established. However, I assure you, I give you my sacred word, the United States will not allow Saigon to fall."

Thieu smiled at the American diplomat. He knew Ambassador Martin believed what he had just told him. It was hard to imagine the United States indifferently turning its back on a ten-year-old commitment for which it had paid with more than fifty-six thousand American lives and countless billions of dollars. However, Thieu's intelligence network channeled information not only from deep within the inner circles of the United States Embassy, but from the Defense Attachés Office, American military headquarters in Okinawa and Hawaii, and the State and Defense departments themselves in Washington, DC. All those sources contradicted what Ambassador Martin had just stated. The United States would not, under any conditions, land forces anywhere in South Vietnam, except in relationship with evacuation operations, focused primarily to rescue Americans.

Graham Martin, however, argued angrily with anyone who suggested that the United States would allow Saigon to fall into Communist hands. He truly believed this could never happen. The aging diplomat's idealism had cast him into the light where many, including President Thieu, now regarded him as a Don Quixote caricature.

"If only the hearts of your countrymen were as true as yours, my good sir," President Thieu told Ambassador Martin. "But even you cannot make such a promise for your country. I know that they think little of betrayal, even to a well-meaning, loyal man like you. I hope you are correct in your promise but, I fear the worst and must plan for that event."

"MY BEAUTIFUL LADIES, I am home," Nguyen Thanh Trung called to his wife and trio of young daughters, three, five, and seven years old. A first lieutenant in the Air Force of the Republic of Vietnam, Trung had trained in the United States to fly the F-5 Freedom Fighter jet. Returning to South Vietnam, he passed along his skills to other pilots, as well as flying sorties against the Viet Cong and North Vietnamese Army.

This evening he had just finished another mission with three other F-5 jets in his formation. They had tried to attack new enemy positions in Phuoc Long Province, yet had to settle on secondary targets. Enemy air defenses simply proved too well established. So the flight of fighters dropped their bombs on suspected enemy emplacements west of Saigon, near the village of Cu Chi.

Trung knew their mission had simply wasted precious bombs, hitting no enemy positions, just trees and wrecked buildings demolished by previous bombings. He felt satisfied about it, though, since he had secretly joined the Viet Cong many months ago.

South Vietnamese ground forces had killed his father, calling him Viet Cong. He was simply an old man, not a soldier for anyone nor a politician. However, they had shot him, called him an enemy.

The soldiers had also arrested Trung's brother. They put him in prison because they had accused his father of treason and had killed him in the young man's presence. If the father was Viet Cong, so must be the son.

Trung hated the war. He detested politics too. Most of all, he wanted the killing to stop.

When he saw how corrupt the South Vietnamese leaders had become, lining their own pockets while the country and its people crumbled, he realized that President Nguyen Van Thieu's regime would surely fall. He knew that it was only a matter of time before the Communists finally triumphed. Then what would happen to his wife and three daughters?

It was not hard to join the Viet Cong. They were everywhere nowadays.

Once a member of the Communist Party, Trung discovered several others who had also turned coats. One man, a civilian architect at Tan Son Nhut Air Base, Dang Quang Phung, became his closest partisan.

For years, Dang had kept his Viet Cong contacts briefed on the layout and any engineering changes at Tan Son Nhut Air Base and the surrounding community, including the Americans' Defense Attachés Office compound.

Trung sat on the couch in his living room and sipped hot tea as he took a stack of papers from a manila envelope. Dang had handed the package to him as the two men met for drinks at the Tan Son Nhut officers club after work. Several other South Vietnamese flight officers had sat at the table with the two men and had seen Dang casually hand Trung the envelope.

Thus when Trung realized what the papers contained, the fright of it seized him so strongly that he struggled to catch his breath. Had any of the other officers seen what Dang had put in the envelope, both men would have faced a firing squad. Dang had given Trung a complete set of overhead printouts of the entire Tan Son Nhut Air Base and the DAO compound. Dang had even annotated exact distances and dimensions on each of the more than forty pages of drawings.

The unassuming architect who had worked as a trusted civil service employee at Tan Son Nhut for more than ten years had compiled drawings that clearly laid out the exact locations of every building, fence, sidewalk, and street, and their measurements. On many of the buildings, he had even included their functions, especially if they constituted strategic targets, such as ammunition storage or armories, barracks, or headquarters.

Trung read the small, handwritten note that Dang had taped to the top sheet of paper. "You will need these updated plans for your mission. Good luck."

Chapter 4

LOTUS BUDS

CENTRAL HIGHLANDS, RVN—THURSDAY, FEBRUARY 27, 1975

CLAPPING HIS BADLY worn sandals together, knocking loose the sharp pebbles and dirt that had packed in them during the day's long trek, Nguyen Duc Cui sat on a large, shady rock beneath dense, overhanging trees and dangled his bare feet in a narrow stream to soothe them. The clear, mountain water felt good on his sore soles and toes, now heavily calloused from so many years of walking.

The communications officer for the 320th NVA Division loosened his backpack's badly frayed straps from his shoulders and let the dusty haversack slide down his arms and fall behind him. Then he reached inside the canvas bag and felt for the flat can of American-made C ration cheese he had saved for the past two weeks and took it out. South Vietnamese soldiers on patrol near Da Nang had apparently discarded it on the trail, and Cui claimed the prize when his unit later crossed their path.

Turning it in his fingers, looking at the English words printed in black letters on its lid, Cui started to open the small, military green tin with his knife, but then he changed his mind. Other soldiers had begun cooking rice, and this cheese might taste better after he had rested and had filled his stomach.

The can, barely a half an inch thick and two inches in diameter, contained less than three ounces of pasturized, processed American cheese, hardly enough to satisfy anyone's appetite. However, it held enough of the delicacy for a person to enjoy, if he ate it slowly. Thus with a satisfied stomach, Nguyen Duc Cui could savor to a much higher degree each small taste of the creamy, sharp cheddar.

When he dug through his belongings, searching for the can of cheese, Cui had felt the pair of brown oxford shoes that he had kept tucked in the bottom of his pack, now, for nearly five years. He looked at his worn sandals, held together by salvaged American-made communications wire, whipped around braided hemp straps that had broken several times. The shoes in his pack had no wear at all on them. Their layered leather soles and laminated heels remained unmarred and clean. The brown, cowhide tops still retained their crisp, glossy finish.

For many, it seemed ridiculous for him to carry new shoes in his pack while such badly worn sandals covered his feet. However, for Cui, the brown oxfords held a far greater purpose than simply that of mere footwear. For him, they spoke a profound statement of this war. They also embodied an ironclad promise that he had sworn to keep.

His friend and companion from Hanoi, Nguyen Sinh Tuan, a documentary photographer with the 320th Division, understood why his friend did not wear the shoes. Few others knew the story, but Tuan had seen it happen. He had tearfully watched as his friend Cui inherited the unworn brown oxfords from another friend.

Adherence to proper etiquette and respect for Cui's privacy had prevented the photographer from talking with others about the sad event, including many men who had recently attached to the unit. Not knowing Cui's reasons, they scoffed at the communications officer for carrying new shoes in his pack while wearing worn-out sandals. Some of Cui's fellow officers openly made wisecracks to him while enlisted men joked privately among themselves. The photographer reasoned that if Cui wanted the reason explained to anyone, he would do that himself. For others to discuss it constituted gossip, and disrespect. It displayed poor character and ignorance to anyone who valued good manners.

Tuan had confidence that one day the soldiers who derided Cui would understand this protracted act of loyalty too. They would also feel rightfully embarrassed for their shameful conduct toward such a good and decent man.

Tuan sat on the ground near Cui and snapped his picture.

"Don't do that," Cui scolded. "You will be reprimanded for wasting film."

Tuan snapped another photograph of Cui and laughed, "I am doing my job, documenting today's events. Sore feet after a long hike."

"That is quite enough, now," Cui said quietly. "With those two pictures, history will fully comprehend today's walk. Please put away your camera. My head aches, my back hurts, and my feet throb. I do not need that thing clicking in my ears, adding to my misery."

"Give me your tin bowl," Tuan said, standing and taking his own metal dish from his pack. "I will bring your dinner to you. Should I also bring the wine list, sir, or will you just have your usual, water?"

"Oh, by all means, bring the wine list," Cui said, challenging his friend to follow through with the little joke.

"Ah, I just remembered, sir," Tuan said, "the wine that we have on hand is simply all wrong for the pork and rice on today's menu. May I suggest a quite lovely pot of tea instead?"

"Tea sounds wonderful," Cui answered as his comrade jogged to a clearing where several soldiers stirred pots of rice and pork, ladling it into the metal bowls of a long line of soldiers, all of them dusty, tired, and showing rings of sweat and salt on their drab green and khaki uniforms.

As Cui lay back, closing his eyes and resting his head on his pack, he felt the shoes pressing against his neck. He thought of how in a matter of perhaps a year or eighteen months, he might finally fulfill the dying wish that he had promised to keep.

Cui remembered how silly the idea had at first seemed when his best friend, Huong Chinh, bought the shoes in Hanoi, after their final class at the university. He recalled how he laughed and scoffed when Huong told him of his purchase.

"NONSENSE!" CUI SAID. "Romantic nonsense. What practical purpose can those brown oxfords truly serve, other than your wearing them?"

"Carrying these shoes will allow me to always see my goal and better hold onto it," Huong explained to Cui.

The pair of newly sworn army recruits sat on a bench in Hanoi's central park on a warm spring afternoon in 1968. While they talked of their futures, the duo gazed across the long, narrow lake with its ancient Buddhist shrine standing on a tiny island at its center. Across the water, swans and ducks cruised lazily. On the opposite shore, the two lads fixed their attention on a group of beige stucco buildings where a procession of schoolgirls filed through a set of high-arched wooden and wrought iron double doorways dressed in white dai, the traditional Vietnamese costume for young ladies, billowy silk pants and a silk top with long front and back panels that hang to the knees.

"And what is this goal that these shoes manifest?" Cui finally asked his friend.

"Our ultimate victory in the people's revolution, of course," Huong answered without hesitation.

"What do oxfords have to do with victory?" Cui asked, perplexed.

"Oh, the shoes have nothing to do with victory," Huong said. "However, I bought them to wear when we march in our victory parade in Saigon."

"Nonsense!" Cui again exclaimed to his best friend, a young man he had known since the pair had attended grade school together and had now advanced halfway through college, always side by side.

Nearly two years after that spring day in Hanoi's central park, the duo still remained united. Now, in the mountains northwest of Da Nang, near the Laos border, the young soldiers of the Socialist Republic of Vietnam anxiously hid beneath a canopy of trees. They huddled under the foliage, hoping that the crew of the American observation plane that climbed and dived overhead, banking in steep S-turns along the ridge, had not spotted their infantry company.

When the OV-10 Bronco finally departed to the east, the men shouldered their equipment and hurried eastward too. They sought to clear a safe distance from the probable target zone of the American B-52 bombers that nearly always came within minutes after one of these low-level reconnaissance aircraft had swooped and turned above these far mountains.

Sweat poured from Cui's and Huong's skin as they marched at a running pace. The two men kept their eyes constantly busy, surveying the surroundings. They looked for anything that could provide them sturdy shelter so that they could immediately take cover when they finally heard the faint roar of the big jets' engines high above, and the bombs dropped.

"I see one!" Huong cried to his comrades and pointed at white contrails in the distant sky overhead. Then, behind the first bomber, came the contrails of three more planes and the sound of their commander's whistle for the men of Cui's company to seek the deepest possible cover.

Huong wedged himself beneath the side of a huge log while Cui pushed his body inside a tight hole behind the upturned roots of the same fallen tree.

The wait seemed eternal. With each minute the men's dread increased. Finally, the earth shook with a terrible rumble as the first of many two thousand-pound bombs exploded.

Cui sighed with a sense of relief. The initial salvo had struck at a comfortable distance from them. The bombs had landed where the company had sat while the observation plane had flown overhead. However, he had no more than finished the thought and had only begun to sense the emotional relief when the showers of one-ton bombs from the other three B-52s began to explode. The second volley landed much closer, the third cluster even closer, and the last fusillade fell directly on top of them.

In a matter of seconds, the entire upheaval had begun and ended. However, for the men who lay in the fury, the seconds seemed to last forever.

Cui's body racked with pain from the concussion rendered by the explosions. The blasts released such force that they robbed the atmosphere of air, leaving the men who still survived, breathless. Each detonation uprooted three and four trees at once and blew craters in the earth twenty feet deep and forty feet across. Large chunks of metal, shattered from the bombs' thick iron casings, spun through the air at blinding speeds, ripping through anything that stood or lay within their line of trajectory.

With each burst, cries of agony mixed into the smoke and dirt that filled the air. Bodies lay in pieces, strewn across the ground, twisted in the brush, scattered and slung over the grizzled branches of the fallen trees. Heads, arms, legs, torsos. Strips of torn flesh, shattered bones, and shredded clothing. The gore dangled among splattered globs of blood, body fluids, and human entrails, and covered the hacked foliage, splintered wood, and churned earth in a gruesome decoration of carnage.

Cui could feel blood running from his nose, his ears, and his bowels, leaving the crotch of his khaki shorts wet and red. He felt tears coming from his eyes, bloody tears that he smeared across his face with the back of his grimy hand.

"Huong!" the soldier finally cried out, realizing that the bomb that had left so many of his body's small blood vessels and capillaries ruptured and bleeding had landed on the same side of the log where his best friend had sought cover.

Every tree and bush, large and small, in any direction that Cui looked, lay fallen or leaned severely, uprooted and fractured. Gray smoke and the heavy smell of burned cordite boiled thick in the air, swirling with the massive cloud of orange dust that rose skyward more than a hundred feet and drifted eastward on the prevailing breezes.

Hatred for this faceless enemy that had appeared as mere white streaks across the blue sky surged through Cui's heart as he saw Huong's bloody back and his twisted legs, bent at places where the soldier had no joints. The pain from the sight of his lifelong best friend stung Cui's skin, chewed through his stomach, and pounded in his lungs. His knees buckled, and he fell sobbing.

"He's still alive!" a soldier standing above Cui said, pointing to Huong, who now tried to roll onto his back. "We must help him. Hurry!"

Cui glanced at the soldier's face and saw his friend, Nguyen Sinh Tuan. Both men knelt by Huong, and Cui cradled his dying friend's head in his hands.

"Huong!" Cui cried, looking at his friend's eyes, which darted in confusion and then focused back on him.

"My pack," Huong said. "I stuffed it under the log."

"I see it, there," Cui said, pointing for Tuan, who then stretched beneath the downed tree and dragged out Huong's knapsack.

"Cui," Huong said, "take my shoes, the ones I bought in Hanoi, and put them in your pack. Promise me that you will carry them with you, always."

"I am doing it now, Huong," Cui said as tears streamed from his eyes.

"When we finally end this war, and you march victoriously through Saigon, then take out my shoes. If they do not fit your feet, then find someone whose feet match their size, and put them on. Walk with my shoes in your victory parade through Saigon. That is why I bought them. Even though I am not with you, my spirit will march with you, in these shoes."

"I promise you, I will, Huong," Cui said, sobbing. "I give you my pledge."

TEARS STREAMED FROM Nguyen Duc Cui's eyes as he lay on his back, remembering his friend and the sacred vow he had made to him as he died in his arms. Cui could feel the wetness dripping into his ears as his old friend, Nguyen Sinh Tuan, returned with their evening meal of pork, rice, and tea.

Seeing the streaks through the dust on Cui's face, Tuan said nothing of it, pretending to not notice.

"Extra pork," Cui said, surveying an ample amount of meat heaped in his bowl.

"Apparently, someone's pigs slipped through their fence and wandered to our camp," Tuan said, chuckling as he sprinkled over the top of his food a mixture of hot chilies and other spices in an oily concoction called *nuc mom* and then offered the pungent sauce to Cui.

As the two men ate their dinner on the edge of a stream in the hills southwest of Pleiku and northwest of Ban Me Thuot, they watched the sky turn orange and the shadows grow long.

Nguyen Duc Cui and Nguyen Sinh Tuan had walked with the majority of soldiers of the 320th NVA Division from the mountains west of Da Nang into Laos, where transport trucks then carried them southward down the newly constructed crushed rock and gravel roadway. The secret highway built by North Vietnamese Army engineers, along with a petroleum pipeline that paralleled it, followed Vietnam's border southward to a point where the new road terminated at the Y-intersection of Vietnam Highways 13 and 14 in Quang Duc Province, on the Cambodian border north of the provincial capital, Gia Nghia.

A hundred miles prior to reaching the highway's terminal, the 320th Division disembarked the transport trucks and then walked overland for five days, zigzagging eastward. Once in the densely covered mountains southwest of Pleiku and northwest of Ban Me Thuot, they consolidated their forces with the 10th and 316th NVA divisions and the regional cadre of Viet Cong, forming the 968th NVA Corps.

This new army held the important mission of breaking the enemy's back in the Central Highlands and then linking up with the 301st NVA Corps, which currently held Phuoc Long Province on the 968th's southern flank. The two armies would eventually merge on their eastern fronts with other Communist forces that, by that time, should have already campaigned well southward from Dong Ha, Hue, Da Nang, and Chu Lai, clearing the enemy from his strongly fortified enclaves throughout the coastal provinces, primarily following Vietnam Highway 1. Once the Communist armies had united, their combined forces would then victoriously culminate the war in Saigon.

On Saturday, March 1, their unit would commence preparatory strikes west of Pleiku to draw the attention of the region's primary defenders, the ARVN's II Army Corps, led by the notorious South Vietnamese commander, Major General Pham Van Phu. They hoped their diversion would leave only the understrength Fifty-third Regiment of the ARVN's Twenty-third Division to defend Ban Me Thuot, their initial objective for this region.

Then, on Tuesday, March 4, a sister unit would knock out the bridges on Highway 21 that linked Ban Me Thuot to the coast. Meanwhile, farther north, near Pleiku, other elements of the 968th NVA Corps would blockade Highway 19 at Mang Yang Pass and cut off that route of ARVN retreat from Pleiku and Kontum to Binh Dinh and the coast.

A week from Saturday, March 8, Cui and his comrades would take positions around Ban Me Thuot. The following day, elements of the 320th Division would cut off Highway 14, which connects Ban Me Thuot to Pleiku, the ARVN's last route of escape.

Then, before dawn, on Monday, March 10, Viet Cong sappers would initiate the primary strike from within Ban Me Thuot while Cui and his comrades closed from outside the city, and thus would begin in earnest the first battles of the Blooming Lotus, Campaign 2/75.

"Are you frightened?" Tuan said to Cui.

Cui laughed and set down his empty bowl and sipped hot tea from his tin cup.

"I cannot remember," Cui said. "I think that I became frightened the day Huong and I left Hanoi for training. I do not regard that I have ever ceased that fright. Over time, I believe that I simply learned to live with it always in my heart. So perhaps I am frightened. But since I am always frightened, I am accustomed to its presence, and it is now my normal life."

"I consider that is how I am too," Tuan said. "I don't feel frightened anymore, but I know that it is there."

"Panic, on the other hand, comes and goes," Cui said. "When the bombs land dangerously near, or a bullet surprises me, I feel panic. Not all the time, just when I step too close to death."

Tuan laughed.

"I had not considered fright and panic differently," Tuan said.

"Fright and anxiety seem to me the same things," Cui said. "I consider panic quite different. It we must always control. Panic can cost us our lives if we do not keep the upper hand on it."

"It can save you too," Tuan said. "Feeling it stir and reacting. I have had close encounters, and I can attest that had I not acted when panic struck me, I would not be here."

"Reflex reaction, perhaps sounds better," Cui said thoughtfully. "Panic and fear sounds somewhat cowardly."

Cui lay back on his pack, again feeling the shoes as he looked up at the stars in the clear indigo sky. The world lay quiet.

"COMRADE GIANG, I leave you with the politics and madness of the so-called Joint Military Commission and International Oversight Committee," General Tran Van Tra said with a smile, greeting his old friend and battlefield companion, Colonel Vo Dong Giang, now one of North Vietnam's deputy foreign ministers and the man that many Western newsmen had come to know as Colonel Ba.

"Of course, we know the priority of your departure," Colonel Ba said, "but, nonetheless, we will miss your spirited wit and inspiring, if not entertaining, leadership on the commission. The enemy still reels from your response on our seizure of Phuoc Long Province. What was it that you said? Our mere occupation of lands already our own pales in comparison to the thousands of attacks, in clear violation of the Paris Accords, committed by South Vietnamese forces against the Provisional Revolutionary Government? Your brilliance and wry audacity will be sorely missed by us, but I am afraid its absence celebrated by our enemy."

The general clapped his left hand over the shoulder of his friend and said, "I expect, Comrade Giang, they will be happy to have me gone from their presence, but I suspect they will do their utmost to discover the business that takes me away. I am sure their spies have us all under surveillance tonight, so we must act carefully."

"By all means," Giang responded.

"With my departure to the front line," General Tran said, "our colleague, General Trong Vinh, of course, will now become senior representative since he is the ranking military officer from Hanoi. However, I am trusting you, my dear friend, to remain our voice with the Western press. After all, they are the ears of the American people and their Congress."

"Yes. By all means, sir," Colonel Ba said, smiling as he carefully tucked a fresh cigarette tight in the silver tip of a black-plastic-stemmed holder. Then he clenched the devise in his teeth and lit the tobacco.

Drawing his lungs full of smoke, he added, "We have a very cordial relationship with the newspeople, including some of our own personnel among their ranks. The CBS News cameraman, Ha Thuc Can, works very closely with the reporter, Morley Safer, and is one of our loyal comrades, as is Ky Wahn, a photographer with the Associated Press.

"We have others like them, mostly drivers, clerks, and translators, but given these two men's status as journalists with the Western press, over the years they have provided invaluable intelligence for us. They have also proven very helpful in our propaganda missions."

Colonel Ba laughed and coughed, choking on his cigarette's smoke, and added, "The Americans trust these men without question. Good for us!"

Vo Dong Giang, Tran Van Tra, and Trong Vinh had joined another of South Vietnam's top Communist Party bosses, Tra Bach Dang and his close friend, Nguyen Xuan Ky, Saigon's regional Viet Cong commander, in the garden of Dang's villa, near Tan Son Nhut. They met for a social farewell for General Tran and a final coordinating conference for the Communist leaders.

In a few hours, General Tran, the commander in chief of the Viet Cong, would board a diplomatic flight to Hanoi. There he would meet with General Van Tien Dung, North Vietnamese Army chief of staff, and receive final briefings. Then, with orders in hand, he would secretly return south to his tactical field headquarters, currently located just across the Cambodian border, northeast of the Communists' newly controlled Song Be Airfield, at the border crossing called Tuy Duc, known under French occupation as Camp Le Rolland.

"Perhaps in a year or two, we will again celebrate together in Comrade Dang's fine home and toast our victory," Colonel Ba said.

"Yes, we shall, Comrade Giang," Tra Bach Dang responded, raising his glass. A tall, heavyset man with a large, round face and deeply receding hairline, Dang was the consummate politician. Likewise, as

Communist chieftain for the most populated and influential region of South Vietnam, he maintained a reputation of ruthlessness and viciousness. Even men like Tran Van Tra accorded the man a respectful and capacious standing.

"Salute," General Tran said and drank a sip of the Scotch whiskey in his glass. "All goes well."

"Tell me, sir," Dang said.

"Today in Hanoi, Party First Secretary Le Duan has succeeded in winning full support of the politburo for our planned offensive," the general said jubilantly.

"Then by all means, we must celebrate!" Dang said.

More than a year earlier, Communist Party First Secretary Le Duan had sat with generals Tran Van Tra and Van Tien Dung and others of the Communist military staff in Hanoi, and devised the Blooming Lotus, Campaign 2/75 plan.

Recognizing that the Soviet Union would no longer support their war and that with each passing day North Vietnam grew weaker from a supply and logistics standpoint, the Vietnamese Communist military leaders concluded that timing to launch a major offensive could only worsen by the day as they consumed their fixed tonnage of war materials. Conversely, with American aid now virtually cut off to South Vietnam, visibly demoralizing not only the military forces, but government leaders as well, the opportunity for the Communists to seize and hold the initiative, and even turn the balance of the war to their favor, could exist no better than at the present time.

Le Duan boldly concluded that in order for the campaign to succeed, however, the Vietnamese Communists must commit to the fight all military assets that they held. If they chose to take any other approach, conservative tactics of holding forces and supplies in reserve, their effort would likely fail. Such tactics would most likely lead to a long, slow decline in capabilities on both sides. Furthermore, since South Vietnam had greater stores of wealth and materiel, they held more favorable odds over the long course. Therefore, a decisive and overwhelming campaign launched immediately represented Communist Vietnam's best hope for winning the war.

To prevail, Duan and the generals concluded, they must mobilize all of their forces to the battlefront. Furthermore, since they held insufficient equipment and supplies to allow keeping anything in reserve, all bullets, beans, and Band-Aids must go to the front as well.

Like a gambler at the card table, with this campaign North Vietnam put all of its poker chips into the pot and wagered everything on this final hand. They had to either go big or stay home.

Thus, the opportunity to finish the war with Communist victory was literally at hand. Yet the risk of losing the war was equally as great.

South Vietnam had always fought well in defensive positions. They also had significant caches of ammunition and equipment stored within those defenses. General Dung and General Tran cautioned that should their forces become bogged down for any significant period of time, such as a month or more, the initiative could very well fail.

With no war supplies held in reserve and all their munitions depleted in a stalemated battle, they could easily find themselves retreating from a South Vietnamese counteroffensive with no stopping. South Vietnam could turn the tables, sweep across North Vietnam, and win the war.

Therefore, the generals all agreed that maintaining the initiative and moving at or ahead of their timetable was imperative. With no reserve, they had no room for error. Their futures, their nation, their very lives rested on the success of their plan.

Since October, Party First Secretary Duan had worked fervently to win support for the campaign in a sharply divided politburo. Despite reservations held by many party members, Duan had nonetheless authorized the initial probes and assessments that the plan had established in order to remain on its timetable. Now, with more than two months passed and the United States doing no more than condemning the North Vietnamese incursion at Phuoc Long, the Hanoi regime finally reached agreement.

"Once we achieved our victory at Phuoc Long," General Tran said, "and the Americans made no response, Comrade Duan has concluded, quite correctly I believe, that they will also make no efforts to repel this campaign. The United States has no more stomach for this war, at any level.

"Furthermore, our forces have never fought better. They can smell victory in the air. At Phuoc Long, our army defeated the very best forces that South Vietnam has fielded, their rangers. Many of these units are the very same that overwhelmed us so badly two years ago at An Loc. Loss of Phuoc Long, for many of these soldiers, represents a very demoralizing defeat. Much more so than many in South Vietnam or the United States appreciate.

"Today First Secretary Duan presented this very case to the polit-buro and has, at last, won approval for our timetable," General Tran said. "We will commence our campaign in a matter of days."

SWEAT ROLLED OFF Le Van Reung's face, arms, and back as he struggled behind a U-shaped handlebar that pulled a two-wheeled cart heaped with half a dozen sacks of rice, each weighing nearly 100 pounds. Beneath the burlap bags of grain, wrapped in brown-stained cellophane and looking like squared sticks of white modeling clay, 150 quarter-pound blocks of C-4 high-velocity explosive lay hidden, nestled alternately between layers of rice straw. Next to them rode a 10-pound roll of TNT-composition engineering cord, commonly called det cord; a box of 50 electrically triggered detonating caps; two 500-meter rolls of 18-gauge, twisted dual-lead, electrical fuse wire; Reung's Soviet-made SKS semiautomatic assault rifle, and two 500-round cans of 7.62-millimeter ball ammunition.

While the hard work of pulling the heavy cart generated much of Reung's perspiration, the emotional tension of hauling the highly sensitive blasting caps, hidden among so much explosive, churned a greater amount of sweat, and it soaked the guerilla's shirt and shorts. White salt rings crusted around his waistband and back. Even the conical straw hat that he wore showed a wide ring of wetness. There seemed no end to the ocean of perspiration that his jangled nerves sent pouring from his skin.

A two-way radio signal keyed too closely to the cart, an errant short circuit in the ignition system of a passing automobile, or even the mere discharge of static electricity generated from the rice bags rubbing together and then brushing something grounded could ignite any of the highly sensitive electrical detonators. Just one of the caps, exploding with hardly more than a firecrackerlike bang, would send Le Van Reung, his 600-pound cargo of rice, and his rifle and ammunition skyward in vapor-sized particles, as it set off the 47.5 pounds of high-velocity explosive that he negotiated through the streets of Ban Me Thuot.

Such a blast would certainly maim and kill a countless number of other people crowded in the traffic circle near Reung as he guided the load through the center of the city. It would also kill the nine other explosive-and-munitions-laden Viet Cong guerillas under his command, scattered among the people who bustled near him, and set off their cargos as well. Disguised as farmers and blending in with the masses of local citizenry who made their way along the busy main street, several of the soldiers pedaled and pushed bicycles, carrying explosives and ammunition-filled bundles similar to those hauled by Reung, stacked several feet high and strapped onto racks above the wheels, front and back. Other soldiers carried similar packages and boxes tied to the ends of long poles balanced across their shoulders.

Killing himself, the citizens of Ban Me Thuot, or even his comrades troubled Le Van Reung very little. However, such an event involving ten Viet Cong soldiers would clearly reveal that his unit had begun infiltrating the city for an imminent attack. It would immediately trigger South Vietnamese redeployment of forces to the Ban Me Thuot garrison. Such an action could prove a disastrous blow to the entire NVA and VC division's objective. More importantly, initial victory in Ban Me Thuot held vital importance for the overall Communist strategy. It provided them the momentum to roll the great campaign forward. It also held untold psychological value.

Although a poor peasant warrior, the thin little man possessed much more intelligence than his simple appearance revealed. As a seasoned, small-unit leader, he deeply appreciated the significance of the role that his men played in this historic moment. Thus sweat poured from Le Van Reung. His stomach churned and knotted with each step and bump.

Already, since he had guided his cart into the town of Ban Me Thuot and entered its busy main street, several well-meaning people had offered to help the wiry, bantam-sized fellow with his load. One person even gave him water.

After turning away several good Samaritans, a pair of young South Vietnamese soldiers dashed behind the two-wheeled wagon and started pushing. Reung began to shout at them and tell them that their assistance caused him more discomfort than ease. So they trotted around to the front of the cart, grabbed the U-shaped handlebar, and began pulling alongside the weathered and salt-stained Viet Cong guerilla.

A block before they reached the traffic circle, the two lads patted Reung on his tired shoulders, calling him grandpa, bid him farewell with his heavy load, and departed, jogging through the open gate of a small military compound on the left side of the roadway. A row of dark green jeeps with white stripes and black lettering painted below their windshields sat parked in front of the four-story, square-looking, metal-and-glass building, the local military police station.

Reung thanked the young soldiers graciously for their help. He paused for a moment while he watched them trot happily through the main doors, where other South Vietnamese soldiers wearing green helmets with white stripes painted around them walked to and fro. He boldly waved to the men, and they waved back. His heart pounded. Sweat seemed to run at high tide.

Even one checkpoint could have easily discovered the contraband explosives, weapons, and ammunition that he carried. Yet he had encountered none on his journey. Obviously, the South Vietnamese Army had focused its concerns of North Vietnamese Army activities farther north, beyond Pleiku, where the diversionary strikes had already taken place. The main force of the ARVN's II Corps now busied themselves with token firefights that held the attention of their infantry resources, but vanished like smoke once they engaged the enemy.

For Le Van Reung, it seemed almost too easy. Something had to go wrong. It always did. For the past two days, hundreds of his Viet Cong comrades had casually infiltrated Ban Me Thuot without incident or detection and now quietly hid, awaiting their moment to commence the attack. Nothing ever before had gone so smoothly. It made him sweat even more to think of it.

EVERY DIRECTION BUT one that Nguyen Manh Tuan focused his binoculars showed dust trails billowing skyward in the distance. South Vietnamese mobile artillery pieces, tanks, armored personnel carriers, trucks, and jeeps zigzagged on motorized patrols throughout the highlands surrounding Pleiku, trying to corner the enemy that had now struck several times to the north and east.

Every convoy that had departed Pleiku or Kontum on Highway 7, through Cheo Reo, or on Highway 19, over the high pass into An Khe, had turned back because of sudden and fierce enemy opposition. The NVA had, so far, successfully closed the primary routes that led to the sea, essentially blockading the main force of the ARVN II Army Corps.

For two days, NVA attacks had become increasingly frequent: mortars, some light artillery, but mostly direct fire with machine guns and rifles in ambushes. Clearly harassment.

Tuan quickly recognized the classic patterns, almost a cliché of

North Vietnamese harassment tactics that he had examined in detail while attending the United States Army Command and General Staff College. There he had studied alongside American majors and lieutenants colonel, learning operational planning and execution from a regimental and divisional level. Graduating at a respectable station in the class had put the tall, slim soldier on a track that usually led to high leadership, perhaps even a general's stars on his collar.

In the mid-1960s Tuan had first attended the United States Army Field Artillery School at Fort Sill, Oklahoma, beside Army and Marine Corps lieutenants. Two years later he returned to Fort Sill and completed the advanced artillery officers' school.

He had made many friends while at the sprawling army post on the northern outskirts of Lawton, Oklahoma. As he stood in his command bunker, atop a hill east of Pleiku, and gazed at the dust trails on all but the southern horizon, Tuan wondered about those old chums with whom he had spent so many hours sipping beers in the officers' club or dining with their families. He enjoyed living in America and particularly liked the people he had come to know there.

The seasoned South Vietnamese Army lieutenant colonel looked at his tactical map with its clear plastic overlays on which he had marked operational positions showing friendly units in black grease marker and enemy contact points with their suspected strengths scrawled in red. Above these, a second plastic overlay plotted his on-call targets with their grid coordinates. While the list of them grew, he had received few actual fire missions. The NVA always seemed to retreat after only a few volleys.

For so much enemy activity with such little consequence occurring in the Pleiku and Kontum region, it appeared to Tuan very strange and suspicious. The NVA's tactics seemed almost too obvious to him. It followed classic philosophy designed by the Vietnamese Communists' greatest military strategist, General Vo Nguyen Giap, plotted first against the French in 1954 at Dien Bien Phu and then against the Americans in the Tet Offensive of 1968.

Late in 1967, General Giap commenced a siege of the Americans' far western support base at Khe Sanh. He massed four full infantry divisions supported by two artillery and armor regiments at the heretofore largely unknown complex at the opposite end of Highway 9, the farthest compound away from most American or South Vietnamese principal enclaves. He purposefully made the presence of the more than forty thousand North Vietnamese troops highly visible to South Vietnamese and American intelligence gatherers.

The congregation of NVA forces immediately drew the attention of General William Westmoreland. He had, a few months earlier, begun development of the primitive Khe Sanh outpost into a materiel support base for his proposed operations in Laos. The supreme commander of American forces in Vietnam had deployed a battalion of Marines and a crew of United States Navy Seabees to develop and defend the base. They quickly turned to, bulldozing the ground and installing steel matting for a primitive airstrip and laying in stockpiles of ammunition and supplies for the proposed Laos operations.

Responding to the North Vietnamese action, Westmoreland ordered more than six thousand additional United States Marines to the distant and tactically unimportant base. In concert with the defense of Khe Sanh, Westmoreland also ordered commencement of massive air bombardment of the entire region that encircled the remote enclave, appropriately naming the aerial onslaught, Operation Niagara.

As the battle raged, President Lyndon Johnson vowed that America would not lose Khe Sanh. The President said this despite the fact that he had already scrapped Westmoreland's plans for border-crossing operations into Laos. His decision had thus rendered the Khe Sanh support base tactically useless.

Illustrating such intense enemy activity in this far northwestern corner of South Vietnam, Vo Nguyen Giap had succeeded in convincing General Westmoreland that the Khe Sanh siege supported a greater North Vietnamese effort to overwhelm South Vietnam's northern provinces. The American general envisioned a modern version of Dien Bien Phu about to occur. Therefore, he even resorted to asking President Johnson for permission to authorize a feasibility study to examine the possible use of tactical nuclear weapons to defend Khe Sanh.

Meanwhile, the onslaught at the distant outpost served the North Vietnamese general in drawing a significant amount of American attention away from the major enclaves in the seaside provinces north of Da Nang. As the Lunar New Year, Tet 1968 approached, Giap redeployed the majority of his forces from Khe Sanh and secretly sent them eastward, moving them in small bands. Then, during the end of January, he very effectively commenced a blitzkrieg of attacks on the coastal cities as part of the greater Tet Offensive, which sent mostly Viet Cong guerilla forces striking American army units in the southern regions while General Giap pitted his battle-hardened NVA regulars against United States Marines in the north.

The 1968 campaign mobilized Communist forces throughout South Vietnam, successfully hitting ARVN and American forces with complete strategic surprise. While the NVA general had enjoyed great success, surprising the Americans, he had badly underestimated their forces' capabilities. In the end, the Vietnamese Communists garnered a media coup with world headlines that proclaimed North Vietnamese and Viet Cong victories, but in most practical military terms suffered significant losses at all corners. Tactically, Tet 1968 may have begun as a successful offensive, but quickly turned into an abysmal failure for the Communists. For all their expense of lives, equipment, and weaponry, they had gained nothing but a scrapbook of press clippings.

To regain political face, Giap returned many of his forces to Khe Sanh and commenced draining more American resources at the strategically unimportant support base. The battle of prestige, however, soon became too costly for either opponent. Eventually, after more than two months of heavy fighting and severe losses of lives on both sides, the Communists and the Americans started pulling out. Determined to leave the enemy nothing, United States Marines destroyed every bunker and structure and even pulled up the steel runway matting that served as their airfield, symbolically turning out the lights at Khe Sanh.

Nonetheless, the diversionary tactics that Giap used to set up the initial strikes of his forces in the 1968 Tet Offensive proved masterful. For a brief time, General Giap had even controlled the ancient Vietnamese capital city of Hue. Indeed, during his early years as a Viet Minh rebel, drawing focus away from the intended target with an attention-gaining movement or assault was Vo Nguyen Giap's tactical signature. The legendary general seemed to always lead his main punch with a diversion.

Although the aging general, and prime adherent of the late Chairman Ho Chi Minh, had for most purposes retired, his legacy remained very much alive. It lived in the tactics and strategies applied by the Vietnamese Communists' reigning military leaders, who had learned their lessons at General Giap's knee. Just as a boxer will jab, jab, jab, draw a punch from his opponent, feint it, and then counter with a devastating overhand right, a cross, or an uppercut, so did Giap's brand of maneuvers.

For the South Vietnamese lieutenant colonel who stood solemnly in the headquarters bunker of his artillery command on a hilltop east of Pleiku, glassing the countryside through binoculars, the hit-and-run strikes of the past several days seemed hauntingly like jabs from the NVA's left fist. So much movement going on with so little consequence. The thought of it made his hair prickle as he watched the dust clouds on the northern and eastern horizons.

Nguyen Manh Tuan kept turning his gaze southward, though, along the eerily quiet Highway 14, which led to Ban Me Thuot. A single question repeated in his mind. Why so quiet there?

Chapter 5
THE LOTUS BLOOMS

BAN ME THUOT, RVN—SATURDAY, MARCH 8, 1975

"COMRADE TRAN, PLEASE come in," General Van Tien Dung said to General Tran Van Tra as he stepped from the shadowy, green-tinged light of a dense forest located several kilometers northeast of the Cambodian border village of Tuy Duc and entered a heavily camouflaged tent that served as forward-operations headquarters for the commander in chief of the North Vietnamese Army.

Tran, a stockily built, round-faced man with receding gray-streaked hair, removed his cap as he took two short steps inside the command post, bowed respectfully to General Dung, and then nodded to the NVA deputy chief of staff, Lieutenant General Hoang Minh Thoa.

"I hope you are not too perplexed with our bit of clandestine maneuvering from Hanoi," General Dung said.

"Not at all, sir. In fact, I found myself quite amused at chasing your shadow," General Tran responded. "I did fully expect to see you at headquarters, but when I received my briefings by members of the general staff, rather than you or General Hoang, I quickly made the correct assumption that you had secretly moved ahead and deployed to

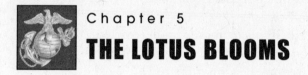

Chapter 5
THE LOTUS BLOOMS

"COMRADE TRAN, PLEASE come in," General Van Tien Dung said to General Tran Van Tra as he stepped from the shadowy, green-tinged light of a dense forest located several kilometers northeast of the Cambodian border village of Tuy Duc and entered a heavily camouflaged tent that served as forward-operations headquarters for the commander in chief of the North Vietnamese Army.

Tran, a stockily built, round-faced man with receding gray-streaked hair, removed his cap as he took two short steps inside the command post, bowed respectfully to General Dung, and then nodded to the NVA deputy chief of staff, Lieutenant General Hoang Minh Thoa.

"I hope you are not too perplexed with our bit of clandestine maneuvering from Hanoi," General Dung said.

"Not at all, sir. In fact, I found myself quite amused at chasing your shadow," General Tran responded. "I did fully expect to see you at headquarters, but when I received my briefings by members of the general staff, rather than you or General Hoang, I quickly made the correct assumption that you had secretly moved ahead and deployed to mosquito net flap. Two officers then entered the command post and took positions at each side of a large map mounted on a wooden easel with several transparent plastic overlays rolled over the back of the display.

"The gentleman to your right is Comrade Nguyen Thien Luong," Lieutenant General Hoang Minh Thoa announced, providing the two commanders in chief the benefit of introduction to their morning briefing officers. "General Tran, Comrade Nguyen is one of your subordinate commanders and has charge of the Provisional Revolutionary Government's forces attached to the 320th Division.

"Opposite Comrade Nguyen is Comrade Truong Quang Thi, commander of one of the 320th Division's infantry battalions. Their units have enjoyed a great success in accomplishing the mission of diverting and holding enemy attention to the north, in the regions of Kontum and Pleiku, while we finalize our preparations here.

"Gentlemen, if you please."

"Thank you for your most gracious introduction, Comrade General Hoang," Truong Quang Thi said, working hard to control his nervousness. He knew that his colleague, Nguyen Thien Luong, could never possibly master the moment, so it was up to him to take charge of the briefing, and hopefully Nguyen would support him by answering some of the questions that addressed Viet Cong activities in support of the 968th Corps's operations.

"The situation this morning continues to hold in our favor," Truong began. "The shadow headquarters at Duc Co, emitting inconsequential message traffic, continues to attract the ARVN II Corps command's attention, and the vast majority of their sixty-thousand-man force still maintains their defenses well to our north. Judging from their troop concentrations and activities, we believe that they remain convinced that our main forces and headquarters operate in the western reaches of Pleiku and Kontum provinces.

"Today, we have in place all elements of the 10th and the 316th divisions, along with their mass of heavy artillery and tanks. Tomorrow, our batteries of long-range guns will lay in their firing positions while the tanks and self-propelled artillery, the mortar and automatic weapons units, and the infantry will proceed eastward to the final coordination line and await departure, sometime after midnight or during the very early hours of March 10.

"Intelligence sources in Pleiku indicate that the enemy has full awareness of the 320th Division but assumes that they remain in their common area of operation, west of Pleiku. They also indicate that the enemy suspects the presence of the Tenth Division as well and, as we had hoped, place them at Kontum. Currently, our intelligence sources tell us that the enemy has no inkling that the 316th Division is here."

The three generals immediately began clapping, after which the other officers seated behind them clapped and cheered as well.

"Excellent news," General Dung said. "Do you see why I want to use the old sparking wires, setting the woods ablaze?"

Tran Van Tra nodded, fully agreeing with General Dung's logical thinking.

"Gentlemen, if I may continue," Truong spoke.

"By all means," General Dung said.

"For several days, guerrilla units from the people's forces have successfully infiltrated the enemy's lines and stand ready, well supplied with explosives and handheld weapons," Truong said and glanced at Nguyen, who stood locked in place, glass eyed and silent. "They now await the signal to launch their attack from within the city.

"In regard of noteworthy enemy activity, this morning, reconnaissance scouts have reported that a regiment from the ARVN Twenty-third Division has departed Pleiku, traveling south on Highway 14. Intelligence assessments indicate that the unit has the mission of establishing a flexible support position at the hamlet of Buon Ho. There, they remain available to reinforce units at Pleiku but enjoy less than an hour's convoying time to Ban Me Thuot, should the garrison there call for help."

General Dung stirred in his seat and then looked at General Tran.

"Do you have any thoughts on this?" Dung said.

"The enemy has obviously discovered information that leads him to suspect our true intentions here, yet he still remains unsure of them, thus the compromising position so typical of our indecisive adversary, Pham Van Phu," General Tran responded. "Clearly, we must cut the route to Ban Me Thuot without delay. Allowing this regiment to reinforce the city's garrison measurably reduces our superiority in strength. This additional force, if they successfully link up, could make Ban Me Thuot a mire for us."

"I fully agree," General Dung said. "Furthermore, once this regiment establishes its bivouac, it will certainly send out reconnaissance scouts. They could easily discover the massive size of our presence here, thus alerting the entire ARVN II Corps, and deny our forces the element of strategic surprise that we now enjoy.

"Currently, the 9th Regiment of the 320th Division stands in reserve for the strikes planned against the outlying Phung Duc Airfield, does it not?"

"Yes, it does," Lieutenant General Hoang said.

"Tomorrow, or possibly even tonight, the Ninth Regiment must move swiftly and establish a blocking position at Buon Ho, ahead of this newfound regiment, and must cut off Highway 14 at that point."

"It will be done, sir," Lieutenant General Hoang said.

"That is all of my information at this moment, gentlemen," Truong said and glanced at his able assistant, Nguyen, who remained frozen at muted and stoic attention.

"Well, comrades," Dung said, rising from his chair, striding proudly to the front of the tent where the map stood on the easel and turning to face the audience of staff officers, division commanders, and regimental and battalion leaders. "My last comment this morning regards our actions in the northern provinces. It is my pleasure to announce to you that the first two lotus buds of our great campaign have begun to bloom. Today, launching their assaults well before dawn, the people's forces, led by our comrades of the Forty-fourth Line Front, have successfully commenced attacks on our initial objectives north and west of Hue City and in Quang Tin Province, just south of Da Nang.

"Already, they have overwhelmed fifteen hamlets in southern Quang Tri and northern Thua Thien provinces, sending scores of frightened peasants fleeing to Hue, which will provoke chaos and cause our enemy no small measure of distress.

"In another two days, our whole lotus bed will surely bloom in great profusion."

"GUNNY, DAMN IT!" Deputy Consul General Terry Tull called loudly as she tramped across the Da Nang consulate's interior plaza, where at its hub stood a fountain and tall bronze, impressionist sculpture of a nondescript human's smooth-headed, gender-absent upper body with its arms held high and eyes cast toward heaven. The heels of her shoes clacked loudly with each hard step that she took, and the sound of her walking across the courtyard's hard masonry surface echoed against the edifice that surrounded her.

Styled in classic French colonial architecture, prevalent among Southeast Asia's public buildings, Christian churches, and palatial, European-owned coffee plantations, the compound's primary structure consisted of a double-deck horseshoe of white stucco offices connected by a continuous balcony that overlooked three sides of a concrete and cobblestone square, where the statue stood as the centerpiece. A series of rectangular columns, also covered in white stucco, supported the upper walkway and the overhanging shelter that extended from the roof. Bronze railings and fixtures, weathered powder green, and wrought iron–decorated banisters fronted the balcony that extended the length of the right and left wings. The building that stood at the rear bore a white concrete guardrail supported by four-inch-square, white stucco pickets set every ten inches. Similar concrete, bronze, and ironwork staircases joined the upper walkways at each end and corner.

A fifteen-foot-tall security wall built of white limestone blocks, each measuring two feet high by two feet thick by four feet long, topped with crisscrossed steel spikes and coils of razor wire, watched around the clock by Walter Sparks's detachment of Marines, guarded the consulate's sides and rear. At the front, the high rampart joined, at right and left, two stories of security stations, bunkers, and cells, similarly composed of white limestone blocks. This forward bulwark flanked a pair of wide, wrought-iron gates made of spear-tipped vertical bars, sheltered beneath a red-tile-roofed portal that also held two thick wood and steel, blast-resistant doors that served as the primary entrance to the facility.

Staff Sergeant Sparks sat on the low concrete wall that encircled the fountain and statue, enjoying the noonday sunshine while eating a tuna sandwich and potato chips and drinking Coca-Cola from a red-and-white, pull tab can. Seeing the consul deputy briskly walking toward him, the Marine set down his lunch and snapped to his feet.

"Gunny, damn it. I've been ringing your office for the past twenty minutes," Tull said in a lower voice as she came near him.

"Gunny Damn It's not there, ma'am," Sparks said with a wry smile to the most highly ranked female American diplomat in Vietnam.

"You're too cute sometimes, Staff Sergeant Sparks," Tull said and returned his smile with a good-natured smirk.

"I know, ma'am," Sparks said. "I try."

"Small talk aside, Gunny, we have a problem. The Communists have launched what I consider a troubling offensive this morning in Quang Tri and Thua Thien provinces, moving toward Hue, and here in our own area, just south, in Quang Tin Province," Tull said, taking a seat on the concrete wall and then snatching a pinch of potato chips from the paper plate where Sparks had laid his sandwich.

"Rumor mill about that started early this morning, ma'am," Sparks said, sitting down and picking up his lunch. "Our Vietnamese gate guards told me one version when I inspected the new watch, just after colors. I wanted to check out their story against what we have on the message board, but the read file hasn't made it to my office yet. According to their scuttlebutt, though, it seems like a whole division or more of NVA has begun hitting the outlying hamlets, driving people toward the cities."

"No rumor, Gunny," Tull said, nibbling the edge of a potato chip. "I have copies of several MR 1 alert messages routed to the field and higher headquarters from General Truong, and they corroborate that very idea. They even specify that the Second NVA Division and Fifty-second NVA Brigade have moved on Hau Duc and Tien Phuoc hamlets and likely threaten Tam Ky. That might very well cut off Chu Lai.

"Up north, every road and trail leading to Hue has refugees jammed on them butt to belly, all headed to the apparent safety of the city. Not a good situation at all.

"First on your agenda, we'd better get security here at the Alamo tightened down, now. Also, you recall those contingency plans that the station chief laid out for us last fall, when Colonel Johnson was here from III MAF?"

"Yes ma'am," Sparks said.

"Dust off your copy and bring it with you to my office this afternoon," Tull said. "I want everybody's input.

"With Al Francis out of pocket, I may have to start making some serious decisions, quite soon, without benefit of his presence. I am greatly concerned about the safety and security of our outlying consulate offices and their staffs, especially in Hue and Chu Lai, and also the few dependents we have with us here.

"Meanwhile, the station chief makes his case in one direction with his CIA assessments assuring everyone that the South Vietnamese forces are better fighters than we give them credit. However, my concerns about what we have begun to see now happening in the country-side push my thinking quite strongly the other direction. Furthermore, your fleet Marines over in Okinawa certainly don't buy the have-faith-in-the-ARVN argument either. They've been sharpening their spears for quite a few weeks now."

"Roger that, ma'am. Any word from the boss?" Sparks asked, referring to Consul General Albert Francis who had spent the past month in Washington, DC, recovering from a thyroid gland infection, and continued to remain there, recuperating.

"He's still quite sick," Tull said. "I think two more weeks at the very least before we see him anywhere near here. In addition, given the tenor of Ambassador Martin's don't-rouse-the-natives policy, wanting to avoid panic and reassuring the South Vietnamese of our commitment to them, Mr. Francis may not even be aware of how serious the situation here has truly become."

"That's hard to believe, ma'am, considering all the firefights in the Central Highlands," Sparks said. "I think that they would at least brief the boss on some of the intelligence reports I have read just in the past few days. We have captured prisoners talking about not regiments but divisions of NVA massing along the western borders down there. With the attacks up here this morning, on top of that information, it sure gets my attention."

"Mine too, Gunny," Tull agreed. "However, the powers-that-be at the embassy in Saigon, Ambassador Martin, and his loyal legion that followed him from Rome seem to have another take on the situation. They do not want reality to mess with their politics nor their agenda. They want everyone to stay convinced that all remains well. America still stands proudly with Saigon. And heaven help anyone who even suggests coordinating discussions about contingency planning or evacuation."

"Well, I guess it's lucky you, then," Sparks said, smiling. "You're the monkey in the barrel, and it looks like you get to deal with this Chinese fire drill pretty much on your own."

"You know it!" Tull said, smiling back. "But don't forget, you monkeys are rolling around in the barrel with me," she added, responding to the irony as she began to walk away.

"Half an hour, Gunny, in my office, with the intelligence and security people," Tull continued. "Also, in light of what I said about Ambassador Martin and the current embassy policy on this, please keep everything under your hat. The last thing we need is more friction."

"Not to worry, ma'am," Sparks said. "What's said here, stays here. I'll see you in half an hour."

A DAMP CHILL lay in the air and caused Le Van Reung to shiver. In the nighttime breeze, cooled by the downslope currents drifting off the neighboring mountains, he squinted to see the faint glow of the radium-coated hands and tick marks on the black face of the Timex wristwatch that he wore.

A pretty friend who had worked at Chu Lai's post exchange had given him the timepiece as a gift on the day before the Tet Offensive, in late January 1968. She was one of several spies that the Viet Cong had employed to work inside the American compound and glean tidbits of intelligence information from unsuspecting GIs who might speak freely to a sweet-faced young female.

The girl had surprised Reung with the gift just before sunset on the eve of the attack. Prior to that day, during various other secret meetings, when she passed information, she often chaffed him with light-hearted banter because he seemed to never know the time. He always had to ask someone or look for a clock somewhere. It had become their little joke, and it helped endear each to the other.

The day she surprised him with the watch, the girl delicately buckled the olive green strap around Le Van Reung's boney wrist, where it dangled and then slid up his forearm when he raised his hand, causing her to frown sympathetically because he was so skinny. Then she gently kissed his cheek and told him that his life could very well depend on him having a good knowledge of the time of day.

When the Americans left Chu Lai and ceded the PX to the South Vietnamese, the young woman went home to Hoi An, a fishing village a few miles to the north, near Da Nang. Le Van Reung never saw her again. Yet even after so much time had passed since their last meeting, she still remained dear in his more peaceful thoughts each day and night, and the memory of her soft, round face and her sweetness vividly lived in his heart.

Her gift to him, now worn seven years, like his feelings for her, endured. Surviving brutal combat and unrelenting weather, forgiving the scratches across its crystal and the frayed edges on its nylon band, the timepiece, like the soldier who wore it, still functioned exceptionally well.

"Nearly two o'clock in the morning," Reung whispered to a comrade who lay with him in the ditch across the street from the military police headquarters in Ban Me Thuot.

In the dim light, the two men could see a white, spherical structure composed of a multitude of triangular panels, conjoined to form greater geometric shapes, in a ratio of three pentagons per every five hexagons, making the thing resemble a gigantic soccer ball. Its builders based it on the geodesic dome design, patented in June of 1954 by its inventor, American engineer and philosopher Richard Buckminster Fuller. The futuristic-looking object stood on the back lawn, left rear of the five-floor building, surrounded by a second twelve-foot-high chain-link and barbed wire fence.

Reung estimated that great white ball stood at least twenty feet high on its concrete pedestal and had a diameter of no less than fifteen feet. Judging from the cluster of thick conduit and heavy, black cables that entered the ground beneath the thing, the pair of soldiers quietly agreed that it must contain some sort of highly technical electronic mechanism, perhaps an antenna that communicated through satellites in outer space. Maybe it held some kind of ultrahigh-frequency transmitter and receiver, or even a radar dish. Whatever it contained, the guerillas decided that they must put the strange device out of action very soon after the onset of their attack. It simply looked too ominous to allow to just sit.

While the large, mysterious dome pressed on their minds, the two machine gun emplacements that flanked the front corners of the military police headquarters and the automatic weaponry in the tower that stood ahead of a tree line near the rear fence caused Le Van Reung and the dozen comrades in his squad more immediate concerns. These three defensive strongholds controlled access to the headquarters compound.

Considering the dominance that the post held over the perimeter, Reung instructed four of his men to open fire at their maximum sustained rates on the three positions at the instant when he blew his whistle. Their hail of bullets would hopefully suppress the enemy behind his sandbag cover long enough for Reung and the eight remaining members of his squad to cross the roadway and run through the open gates without getting mowed down. Once inside the fence, they would attack the three positions with grenades and take out the machine guns. With these primary exterior defenses of the police headquarters disabled, an avenue would open for the other platoons in his company to follow his squad's lead and overrun the compound.

"Any moment now," Reung said quietly, looking up from his watch, holding his whistle near his lips, and searching the night sky for the flash of a green pyrotechnic that would signal the guerilla forces to commence the attack.

A soldier who lay in the ditch next to him nodded nervously and rubbed his hand up and down the forward stock of his almost-new, Soviet-made AK-47 assault rifle.

Reung watched his comrade and smiled. He and most of his men had gotten their old, badly worn Chinese SKS rifles replaced with the more reliable, fully automatic, Russian-manufactured Kalashnikovs just days before they began their migration into Ban Me Thuot. It had made them feel important, and appreciated, getting outfitted with some of the best available weaponry rather than the customary, heavily used hand-me-downs that they typically had received in the past.

"Tonight will be very special, historic," Reung told his comrades just as several gigantic, green star-cluster flares, shot from a battery of Tenth NVA Division artillery pieces now positioned on the outskirts of Ban Me Thuot, burst in the sky overhead. "Remember this moment well."

In the distance, Reung heard the booming voices of dozens more big guns, launching their munitions into designated targets, announcing that the attack had now begun. In the pale green light of the flares, the guerrilla saw the expressions of stress that stretched themselves across his men's faces as they awaited his signal. So without another second of hesitation, he took a deep breath and gave his whistle three hard blasts.

The sound of it cut through Reung's ears and sent his gut into a twist as he pushed himself up from the ditch with his hands and knees and tucked his rifle close to his hip. He felt his hair bristling on his skin while his eyes and ears pounded from a gush of adrenaline that surged through his body as he leaped onto the roadway with his AK-47 spitting fire. Quickly, the soldier focused his vision and his stream of bullets at the double doorways of the building where only a few days earlier the pair of young South Vietnamese soldiers who had insisted on helping him push his cart had gone. He tried not to think about the two boys and focused on advancing his men across the street without getting himself or them killed.

At each side of him, red tracer bullets arched into the two sandbagged machine gun nests and into the fortified tower. The guerrilla could not tell if the enemy had yet even returned fire.

Reung's confidence soared as he ran past the tall steel and brick corner posts at the front gate, in echelon with eight of his men. Slamming a fresh, banana-curved magazine into his Kalashnikov, he turned his rifle toward the nest on the left and opened fire, straight at the muzzle flash of the .30-caliber machine gun there that had now begun to belch a stream of red at his comrades who ran from the ditch and buildings, attempting to cross the street behind him. He knew that he had to silence this gun, or at least suppress its operators with his rifle fire, so that his comrades to his rear could join the rest of his men in their attack.

Suddenly, the world shone eerily yellow in the light from dozens of illumination flares that ignited overhead and then dangled beneath small parachutes that drifted across the black sky. South Vietnamese soldiers barracked in the squad bays of the upper floors of the headquarters had scurried to the building's rooftop and had launched the pyrotechnics with an array of mortars that they had hastily positioned up there.

Long shadows from the advancing Viet Cong danced across the lawn as the soldiers on the headquarters roof now opened fire with automatic rifles and heavy machine guns and hurled grenades at them. Reung could hear the hollow thump of mortar shells launching into the sky, and then behind him, among the buildings and along the ditch, the ka-chunking boom of the projectiles exploding.

"Attack! Attack!" he shouted to the men who ran alongside and ahead of him, urging them onward as several of them momentarily stopped and looked back at him, obviously surprised by the enemy soldiers atop the building.

Reung shoved his hand into a canvas satchel that he wore with its single strap slung across his left shoulder and the bag laid against his right hip. In it he found the clutch of hand grenades that he had put in the sack, along with several quarter-pound sticks of C-4 explosive, and took one out. Quickly yanking the pin that held down its trigger, he hurled the small bomb into the bunker, now only thirty feet in front of him, and then dove for the earth.

Orange sparks and gray smoke blew out of the sandbagged nest, and the machine gun went silent.

Not looking back nor hesitating to survey the damage, he and four of his men ran past the corner of the headquarters building just as mortars fired by his own company now exploded on the roof. In the shadowy, yellow light from the illumination flares dangling beneath the small parachutes overhead, Reung could see the great white ball looming in front of him.

Then his eyes caught the muzzle flash of the machine gun in the tower as it opened fire on the five Viet Cong. Two of his soldiers dropped to the ground and returned the volley, causing the men in the tower to duck behind their parapet of sandbags. Le Van Reung and the other two guerrillas dashed back to the side of the building and ducked past the corner, where they immediately opened fire on the tower so that their two comrades on the ground could maneuver back too.

Beyond the tower, through a space between a line of trees, the guerrilla squad leader noticed another tall chain-link and barbed wire fence. Behind it, he could see sodium vapor lights mounted on tall poles and the silhouettes of several men trying to climb the barrier while many others scurried frantically behind them.

"The stockade, do you see it?" he shouted to his comrades and pointed to the gap in the trees, the lights, and the fence with men now clinging to it. "This tower does not guard their back perimeter, but the entrance to their prison."

Feeling inside his satchel, Le Van Reung plucked out two hand grenades and clipped them by their long, spoonlike triggers to the waistband of his trousers. Then he looked at his men, who stood with their backs plastered flat against the wall to avoid the hail of machine gun fire that poured at them from the tower.

"When I run," he said, "you open fire on the tower, and do not hesitate for an instant until I am standing beneath it."

Then he looked at the young man who had lain next to him in the ditch, nervously clutching his new rifle, and said, "You must follow me to the tower. No more than a hand's width behind me."

Reung turned his eyes to the other three men of his squad who had followed him to the rear of the headquarters. "If we draw fire from the prison," he said in a calm voice, "you must divide your shots between it and the tower.

"If a substantial number of guards remain in the stockade, they will probably kill the two of us. In that case, you must immediately retreat and report what we have discovered.

"I suspect, however, that the guards have joined their comrades in the safe confines of the main building here. Otherwise the prisoners would not attempt to so boldly climb the fence, as they are doing. Unfortunately, even if they manage to get over the top of it, the guards in the tower will cut them down, unless we eliminate their position."

Reung gave his comrades a nod, then took hold of his partner by the shoulder and pushed the toes of his sandals hard into the sod, launching himself in a suicidal charge for the tower. Driving his legs with all his strength, he didn't look at anything except the four white uprights of the structure. As he ran, he could hear the heavy breathing of his terror-filled cohort pounding his feet in step behind him.

In that same instant the earth began to explode in front of the two men, where the bullets from the machine gun in the tower chopped a line across the ground toward the pair.

"Go right!" he shouted to the comrade who ran with him, while Reung sidestepped left and then dodged to the right.

The ground that they had just crossed only a few strides earlier ripped open, and clods of earth and lawn grass splattered through the air as the machine gun churned a deadly line chasing the men. Then it stopped for an instant and started again cutting in front of them.

Just as Reung turned to glance over his shoulder to see why his men had not yet fired their rifles into the tower, he heard their gunfire erupt. Then the trail of machine gun bullets began to splatter across the ground in an erratic pattern. The enemy had finally ducked his head.

A matter of hardly six seconds had seemed an eternity when Le Van Reung and his partner reached the legs of the tower.

"Aim your rifle up the ladder and fire bursts into the entryway; otherwise those soldiers up there will shoot at us or may even drop grenades down here," Reung said.

While his frantic partner sent sporadic, short sprays from his Kalashnikov into the tower floor, Le Van Reung quickly pulled several sticks of explosive from the satchel he wore strapped over his shoulder and hip. Then he tied them on each of the legs and linked them together with high-velocity explosive engineer cord, with which he also wound several wraps around the structure's four main supports and primary girders. In one of the white, claylike charges he shoved a shiny metal blasting cap with a six-inch length of fuse crimped in it.

"Now we must run for the trees!" Reung shouted to his comrade and took an old brass cigarette lighter from his pocket and ignited the fuse, which lit with a shower of sparks and a plume of thick, white smoke. "We have less than thirty seconds!"

When the three guerrillas who had given Reung and his partner covering fire saw the two men tumble behind the line of trees and shrubbery, they ducked back around the corner of the building. In an instant the explosives cut the legs from beneath the tower. The structure crashed onto the lawn.

When it hit the ground, it spilled out the pair of South Vietnamese soldiers and their machine gun. The two men cried for help and fought to get to their feet, but the three guerrillas at the corner of the building quickly silenced their voices and ended their struggles with two short bursts of 7.62-millimeter copper-jacketed lead.

When the explosion destroyed the tower, the concussion sent the men who were climbing on the fence tumbling to the ground. The remaining prisoners retreated backward, stunned and confused.

Before any of the confined men could again approach the fence, Le Van Reung took the two hand grenades from his waistband and rolled them at each corner of the stockade's front gates. As the two fist-sized bombs tumbled across the ground, he shouted, "Grenades!" and dove behind the trees with his partner just as the blasts sent debris and metal fragments through the air.

Instantly, a score of screaming prisoners charged at the damaged gates and pulled what remained of them off their hinges. They ran past the two guerrillas and charged across the lawn and parking lot at the front of the police headquarters. The newly freed men ran past several platoons of Viet Cong who advanced on the front of the building, firing at the South Vietnamese soldiers still shooting at them from the rooftop, and disappeared into the darkness.

For Reung, it seemed as if he had opened a birdcage and all the captive creatures suddenly flew away as hard as they could bat their wings. Not one of the men had stopped to thank him or his partner, or even acknowledge their presence, much less attempt to rejoin their comrades in battle.

"We may have only released a jail full of cutthroats," Reung said and began laughing with his cohort, who squatted with him by the trees, next to the entrance of the empty stockade.

Before dawn, Le Van Reung and his platoon destroyed the large, white geodesic dome and the electronics that it contained. The two dozen prisoners that he and his men freed apparently scattered into the city of Ban Me Thuot and disappeared. He never heard anything more said about them.

"ATTACK! ATTACK!" Nguyen Duc Cui shouted into the handset of his radio, repeating the words of the 320th NVA Division's commander, who stood ceremoniously among several of his key staff officers in the organization's combat operations and communications center.

Cui's friend from Hanoi, Nguyen Sinh Tuan, had anchored his camera on top of a stack of radio boxes in the command post and tried to photograph the momentous event. Although he had a flash unit tucked inside his equipment bag, he almost never used it. The light from even a small strobe could travel miles at night and tended to blind everyone nearby. So the photographer kept the powerful little light put away in a black leather pouch, zipped in a side pocket on the satchel with other things that he rarely used.

The dim glow from a string of three small lanterns suspended beneath the tent top seemed immediately absorbed by the dark green canvas above them and hardly rendered enough illumination to even trigger Tuan's low-grade black-and-white film at any of his twenty-year-old Leica M3's available preset shutter speeds and widest light openings. So he braced the camera as solidly as he could, closed the aperture back to f8 to allow at least a reasonable depth of field for the picture's focus, turned the shutter-speed dial to bulb, which would lock it open as long as he held down the release, and began to shoot.

With each frame, he pressed his finger on the button and counted slowly under his breath, guessing at the timing as he bracketed two-, three-, and four-second-long exposures. He hoped it was enough.

Even if the pictures turned out too poor to use, he would never lay fault on the trusty Leica, his favorite of the three cameras that he carried. If it could not make the photographs under this dismal available light, then nothing could, especially given the inferior quality and unpredictable variance of the Soviet-manufactured 35-millimeter film that he had to use.

He felt lucky, however, that he at least had such an excellent camera, no doubt appropriated from a captured Westerner and then relegated to him. His superiors would have never authorized the purchase of such an expensive and finely tooled piece of photographic equipment. Even in used condition, Tuan knew that the Leica would have cost the purchase price of more than two rifles, perhaps three, or possibly even more.

Made in Germany during the mid-1950s, the old M3, with its range finder–focus eyepiece offset to the left above its lens, took remarkably crisp and deeply sharp photographs. Tuan loved the camera too because it weighed only a few ounces, had a wonderful feel and balance, and possessed a shutter that operated so smoothly that he could hand hold remarkably sharp available-light pictures with exposure speeds as slow as one-eighth of a second. Most significantly for Tuan, the Leica's unique shutter made no discernable sound when he snapped a frame, perfect for subtly capturing an unposed picture of a comrade on a patrol or for recording on film timeless moments in a busy CP, where the noise of a clicking camera would certainly distract and irritate people.

Thus Tuan quietly worked in his small world, taking pictures with the little Leica, much like the great French master, Henri Cartier-Bresson, unnoticed. He had transformed himself into just another piece of furniture, out of the way and unimportant. Around him, officers and soldiers hurried in circles, buzzing quick words to each other and scurrying back and forth. Slowly and methodically, the unobtrusive photographer attempted to work magic, capturing the historic, nervous moments on his sorry film.

In the midst of this busyness, Nguyen Duc Cui sat with his head and shoulders leaned over a table piled with radios. There he worked, straining to hear the static-ridden, anxious conversations that flooded through his earphones. Since late afternoon he had labored, totally focused on his duties, with his friend Tuan's presence completely out of his thoughts.

He had no more than uttered the commander's signal to the division's units when bursts of artillery fire flashed from the masses of gun batteries stationed all along the horizon. In a matter of moments, the entire world seemed to rumble beneath his feet. The initial assault on Ban Me Thuot had begun.

Cui's unit held the primary mission of eliminating all enemy access to aircraft and air support. They sought to accomplish this by seizing control of the ARVN's L-19 landing strip, on the city's northeastern outskirts, and the South Vietnamese Army's much larger Phung Duc Airfield, located three kilometers to the west.

With North Vietnamese ground forces severing all overland routes for enemy reinforcement, resupply, or additional support, and with the two primary air bases under Communist domination, the ARVN's hapless Fifty-third Regiment, assigned to defend Ban Me Thuot and the surrounding province of DarLac, as well as neighboring Quang Duc Province to the south, stood virtually cut off.

To make matters worse, nearly all of the Twenty-third ARVN Division's regional force and popular force units, primarily composed of Montagnard platoons and expected to support the Fifty-third Regiment in defending Darlac and Quang Duc provinces, defected to the enemy.

Most of the Montagnard soldiers in the Ban Me Thuot region belonged to the separatist group, *Front Unifie pour la Liberation des Races Opprimees* (Unified Front for the Liberation of the Oppressed Races), and defected to the North Vietnamese Communists as a group under their FULRO banner. Weeks prior to the attack, their chief had met with political representatives from the politburo in Hanoi, who had promised him, in exchange for the Montagnard defection and guarantee of noninterference, the establishment of an independent, self-ruled Montagnard state. In their agreement, the Communists had pledged to cede to the Montagnards, at battle's end, the remote regions north and west of Ban Me Thuot, near the Cambodian border.

(At battle's end, however, the popular force and regional force defectors would suddenly find themselves at the bad end of a double cross by their new allies. When the shooting stopped, the Communists quickly turned their guns on the Montagnards and took them prisoner alongside the South Vietnamese soldiers who surrendered at Ban Me Thuot. Even the Montagnard chief who negotiated the deal with the representatives from Hanoi spent several years in a so-called re-education camp.)

Not only did the Montagnard soldiers betray their loyalty by laying down their arms against the Communists, but in many cases worked as reconnaissance scouts for the North Vietnamese, leading their units safely through South Vietnamese weak lanes and gaps so they could strike deep at the heart of the ARVN defenses.

With turncoat Montagnards showing the way, regiments from the NVA's 316th and 10th divisions closed a three-prong attack from the southwest while on the opposite side of the city the 320th NVA Division launched two fronts from the northeast, one at Phuong Duc Airfield and the other outside the L-19 airstrip. This tactic trapped Ban Me Thuot's defenders inside a ring of fire.

Four of the Fifty-third ARVN Regiment's battalions manned the Ban Me Thuot garrison and faced the brunt of the entire 316th NVA Division, heavily reinforced with tanks and artillery, plus an additional infantry regiment from the Tenth NVA Division.

Another Tenth NVA Division regiment struck the backside of a lone battalion of the Fifty-third Regiment, stranded south of the Phuong Duc Airfield, and hammered them against the anvil created by the 320th NVA Division attacking from the north.

Meanwhile, the remaining two regiments from the NVA's Tenth Division, reinforced with several battalions of tanks and mobilized batteries of self-propelled artillery, patrolled the eastern flanks of the battle area, ready to welcome any ARVN relief efforts.

A LONE SERGEANT wearing a white helicopter-crew helmet, decorated with orange, silver, and green strips of reflective tape, stood at attention by the side door of the UH-1N Huey helicopter, ready for the ARVN II Corps commander, Major General Pham Van Phu, to come aboard. Sweat rolled off the sergeant's nose and down his cheeks, but he did not move because he could see the diminutive, nearly boylike figure of the man for whom he waited standing at the window, watching him.

The early morning attack of Ban Me Thuot had not completely surprised General Phu. His deputy for operations, Brigadier General Tran Van Cam, had tried to persuade him two weeks ago to move more forces south of Pleiku and establish a stronger link to Ban Me Thuot.

General Cam, as well as members of the II Corps intelligence staff, had warned General Phu that they held strong beliefs that the NVA planned to attack Ban Me Thuot. Soldiers in the field had found a diary on the body of a dead North Vietnamese officer, and analysts had found that the booklet contained detailed notes that outlined the attack plan. The II Corps G-2 section had also compiled a comprehensive report based on information from several prisoners that they had interrogated, further supporting their belief that the NVA intended to attack Ban Me Thuot. Additionally, one captured prisoner defected and told the ARVN interrogators that his unit, the 320th NVA Division, had moved from the hills west of Pleiku and now stood poised to launch their attack on the airfields at Ban Me Thuot.

Pham Van Phu faced the dilemma of having to make a commitment of his forces either in the vicinity surrounding Pleiku and Kontum, where he envisioned the enemy most likely to strike, or at Ban Me Thuot, where intelligence said the enemy now planned to strike.

The Twenty-third Division represented II Corps's best fighting units, and General Phu had them already spread dangerously thin. In order to properly reinforce the regiment responsible for defending Ban Me Thuot and the greater areas of Darlac and Quang Duc provinces, he would have to reinforce them with at least two more regiments. To do that required stripping the units from the defenses surrounding Kontum and Pleiku. Doing that would leave the II Corps primary headquarters and principal garrisons vulnerable. Pham Van Phu angrily refused to even consider such a move as an option.

General Phu realized that the Communists had tried repeatedly to cut South Vietnam in half, and their current maneuvering supported his belief that they now prepared yet another effort at that goal. Pleiku and Kontum provinces stood astride the primary infiltration routes of the Ho Chi Minh Trail. If the Communists could take Pleiku and Kontum, they could control the Central Highlands and, using Highway 19 as their principle route to the coastal city of Qui Nhon, finally succeed in this long-sought mission.

He would rather lose Ban Me Thuot than go down in history as the man responsible for allowing the North Vietnamese to cut South Vietnam in half. Should they gain such a foothold, then from it they could very likely overtake the entire country.

The general then defended his position by reminding the officers who briefed him, warning of the Ban Me Thuot attack, that their own intelligence sections had intercepted significant numbers of North Vietnamese radio communications emanating from the area of Duc Co, the Communist-held territory along Highway 19, near the Cambodian border. Most of the message traffic had the 320th NVA Division signature. Phu reasoned that if the 320th Division operated there, that the prisoner who had told of their movement toward Ban Me Thuot had very likely lied. Furthermore, planting a detailed counterfeit plan on a dead officer seemed to him a likely ruse the enemy might use to add credibility to misinformation spread by the enemy soldier who fell captive to South Vietnamese forces.

Since he did not have enough forces to adequately cover both areas, he chose to compromise and send an additional Twenty-third Division regiment halfway to Ban Me Thuot, an absurd token gesture from a confused and frustrated commander.

That same day he had called on his superiors at the Joint General Staff in Saigon, asking their advice and help. He begged them for additional troops or at least more supplies and equipment. However, his pleas fell on unfriendly and skeptical ears.

His friends and fellow senior officers, while smiling sympathetically to his face and sharing in his frustration, generally held contempt for Phu behind his back. To them, he was an old warhorse whose imagination and initiative had long ago withered. They believed that the only way to motivate Phu to lead his II Corps soldiers to hold the Central Highlands and keep open Highway 19 was to leave him spread thin and short. With ample supplies and forces, they thought him likely to hole up at Pleiku and Kontum and let the enemy have the highlands and the route to the sea.

They remembered that when the French fell at Dien Bien Phu, General Pham Van Phu had fallen with them. The Viet Minh took him prisoner and tortured him. He had no stomach for ever coming close to repeating such a horror.

Leaving him in a tight spot would motivate General Phu to hold the Central Highlands and keep his lifeline, the road to Qui Nhon, open.

Yesterday morning's news, the predawn attack on Ban Me Thuot, had sent a shockwave through the Joint General Staff. Outwardly, Pham Van Phu expressed determination to hold the Central Highlands to the last man and assured his superiors that II Corps would not lose the capital city of Darlac Province nor its southern neighbor, Quang Duc Province. When the general laid the telephone back in its cradle, he slumped in his chair. He realized that he had been terribly wrong in his judgement, and now he could lose everything.

He also felt deeply embarrassed. For more than a week his forces had lost all contact with both the 10th and the 320th NVA divisions. No matter where his reconnaissance scouts searched, they could find no trace of them. Their sudden appearance outside Ban Me Thuot left him feeling foolish.

In a last-ditch attempt to save face, as well as Ban Me Thuot, Darlac, and Quang Duc, which represented a third of the area that Military Region 2 covered, General Phu hurriedly organized a counteroffensive that would launch from the air and have ground forces follow on. Now, as news of failure came in the afternoon message traffic, the hopes he had tied to this initiative drifted like feathers in the wind.

A pattern of sweat spread across the back of the old general's shirt as he twisted his wire-frame glasses in his fingers and looked at the sergeant standing by the helicopter. From his office window, Phu watched as the light westerly breezes lifted the main rotor blade up and down, causing it to shudder against the lanyard that had it tied to the nose of the Huey, near a red placard with two white stars painted on it. Inside the aircraft's cockpit, the pilots sat patiently, also waiting like their crew chief.

Inside the general's office, Tran Van Cam sat on a large green leather chair opposite the corner of Pham Van Phu's desk. At the other corner, seated in a similar chair, II Army Corps chief of staff, Colonel Le Khac Ly, scanned a stack of messages and unconsciously shook his head and pursed his lips at what he read. Together, the three officers waited for the first situation reports from the second wave of the airborne assault initiated this morning against elements of the Tenth NVA Division sighted by reconnaissance aircraft at Phuoc An, approximately twenty-five kilometers southwest of Ban Me Thuot.

At dawn, he had filled the sky with helicopters lifting the entire Forty-fifth Infantry Regiment, reinforced with elements of the Twenty-third ARVN Ranger Group, in an airmobile counteroffensive. This first wave had met with complete disaster.

The troop-laden helicopters literally flew into cones of fire. In them the airborne forces suffered total annihilation. Soldiers perished by the hundreds.

Several battalions of tanks and artillery of the Tenth NVA Division, working as a rear guard for the main body of the 968th NVA Corps, had lain in wait for the ARVN airborne assault on the fringe of their primary forces that now focused heavy fire on Ban Me Thuot and Phuong Duc Airfield. As the ARVN choppers settled toward their intended landing zones, the NVA guns blew them out of the sky.

Of the few aircraft that made it to the ground, the Twenty-third Division soldiers that leaped from them found themselves in the center of a huge killing zone, with no way out. Five artillery battalions bolstered by a full infantry regiment firing all levels of automatic weapons, rifles, rocket-propelled grenades, and mortars chewed the hapless ARVN to bits.

Suddenly, the telephone on the general's desk rang, shocking the silence that prevailed in the II Army Corps commander's office. Colonel Ly snapped his head up and dropped his lapful of papers. Pham Van Phu did not turn his face from the window, but listened.

"Sir," Brigadier General Cam said, placing the telephone handset back on its cradle, "the second attack has also encountered heavy losses from antiaircraft fire."

"I expected as much," Phu said and turned from the window.

"However, recognizing the fire," Cam said, "a number of the helicopters in this wave managed to turn and have successfully landed troops at alternate sites away from the enemy. Those forces have now consolidated on the ground and initiated an advance, attempting to engage the enemy."

"We can only hope that they gain a foothold," Phu said, but knew in his heart that the army his soldiers faced had his Twenty-third Division and entire II Army Corps, for that matter, outstripped. Unless the Joint General Staff took immediate action to reinforce his command, Ban Me Thuot, Darlac, and Quang Duc would fall to the enemy in a matter of days.

"General, sir," Colonel Ly said, "what about your helicopter? Will you join the rangers and Colonel Pham Van Tat this evening after all?"

Pham Van Phu said nothing, but merely shook his head slowly from side to side and returned to the window. He watched the sun disappearing behind clouds that formed thunderstorms above the western horizon. A soldier ran across the lawn in front of his headquarters and shouted in the ear of the sergeant who wore the white helmet decorated with the orange, silver, and green strips of reflective tape.

He watched the young aircrewman run to the nose of the helicopter, unhook the lanyard from the rotor blade, and then motion to the pilot to start the aircraft. In a few seconds, the rotor spun rapidly above the dark green aircraft, thumping the air as it generated lift.

Even from the distance of his office window, the general could sense the relief felt by the helicopter crew, simply by the way the sergeant hurried through his launch chores. The young man nearly skipped as he lightly danced around the aircraft, preparing it for flight.

With a small red light flashing beneath its belly, the Huey lifted from the II Army Corps headquarters landing site. The general looked at the sergeant seated inside the helicopter, looking back at him.

As the sergeant squinted his eyes at the window, slowly growing smaller as the aircraft pulled away, he could see the general still standing there. It appeared as though the man had waved just as the chopper had lifted off. The sergeant raised his right hand, covered in a green cloth glove trimmed in gray leather, and waved back.

Chapter 6
FATAL PANIC

NHA TRANG, RVN—FRIDAY, MARCH 14, 1975

"WHAT HAVE YOU allowed to happen!" South Vietnamese President Nguyen Van Thieu said, straining his voice on the verge of shouting as Major General Pham Van Phu formally presented himself, snapping his heels together, his body locked straight, his thumbs pressed tightly at the seams of his trousers, and his eyes fixed ahead.

"Sir," Phu said, pausing to carefully choose his words while restraining his own frustrations. "One could better place that rhetoric at the feet of the Joint General Staff. Had they provided the II Army Corps the supplies and reinforcements that I requested weeks ago, Ban Me Thuot, Darlac, and Quang Duc would not now stand in jeopardy."

"Jeopardy?" Thieu snapped. Then in his typical supercilious manner, like a lordly peacock with feathers fully spread, he strode across the room to a pair of opposing sofa chairs. There, he glanced at the demure little man standing rigid as a statue and tossed his head back and laughed sarcastically, forcing out several insulting huffs at his humiliated subordinate's claim.

"As always," he droned with a lofty nasal whine, projecting his disdain, "you fail to recognize the obvious. My dear general, those places have long since fallen beyond all hope of salvation. Besides, where, pray tell, would the Joint General Staff have obtained these precious supplies and reinforcements that would have made all of this difference? Do you not realize that the provinces surrounding Da Nang and Hue also lie under siege? Should we have redirected those forces to you? Oh yes, we could have simply stripped them from the defenses at Saigon and provided you those troops as reinforcements."

Pham Van Phu held his wooden stance for a silent moment, taking several calming breaths, but then he turned his head and looked the South Vietnamese president directly in the eyes and spoke. "Sir, if the Communists divide the Central Highlands, then they also succeed in dividing the Republic," he said and then paused thoughtfully. "That places them one step away from winning this war."

Phu again stood silent for several seconds, letting his words find weight with his president.

"Stopping the Communists at Ban Me Thuot," the general continued, "is very well worth the cost of redeploying whatever forces and supplies necessary. The alternative hands our enemy ultimate victory."

President Thieu fell into a sofa chair and pointed to the one opposite of him, motioning for General Phu to relax and to sit.

"If you believe that, why did you not redeploy your own forces to Ban Me Thuot?" Thieu said, now using a more civil tone, but still tinting his voice with a mordant edge.

"That would have left Pleiku and Kontum unguarded," Phu responded, holding fast to his original beliefs. "We can isolate Ban Me Thuot, along with Quang Duc Province and the lower half of Darlac, and hold the enemy in check where he now stands. However, I cannot do that with only the two infantry regiments that remain of the Twenty-third Division and what we have left of the three ranger groups assigned to them, perhaps twenty-thousand troops."

"You also have the Twenty-second Infantry Division, the Second Armored Brigade, and four additional ranger groups supporting them," Thieu said casually. "What are there, ten battalions in those four ranger groups? Ten out of the seventeen battalions of rangers that you have in total? With the forces in the Twenty-second Division and the Second Armored Brigade, that gives you what? Something like sixty-thousand additional troops? Plus, that goes without mentioning that you can also draw from a sizable reserve of Montagnard popular and regional force militia."

"Do you not realize that we face three full infantry divisions heavily reinforced with tanks and artillery moving on Ban Me Thuot?" the general retorted, without actually addressing President Thieu's observation that his forces numbered closer to eighty-thousand than twenty-thousand. "I estimate their strength at more than one hundred thousand seasoned and well equipped veteran soldiers."

"I suspect an even greater number," Thieu admitted in a low voice, "perhaps half of the more than three hundred thousand North Vietnamese troops currently deployed south of the DMZ. Probably even more. We have no way of knowing how many additional divisions that the enemy may have secretly transferred here since their attack at Don Luan in December. In any regard, General Truong and his Military Region 1 army and Marine Corps units no doubt face what remains of those enemy forces not presently striking the Central Highlands."

"Where we break our ranks," Phu warned, finally taking the seat across from President Thieu, "they will pour through the gaps. Clearly they intend to divide and then conquer."

"I agree," Thieu said. "The Communists obviously seek to disjoin our forces and overwhelm us from multiple fronts. That is why I have reached certain conclusions and now propose a resolution that will position our forces so that we can at least save Saigon and negotiate a cease fire."

"You mean to abandon our northern provinces?" Pham Van Phu finally asked after sitting in shocked silence for several seconds.

"Yes," Thieu said. "My plan establishes a new demilitarized zone north of Nha Trang Bay, where Highway 21 joins Highway 1 at Ninh Hoa, extending from there to the western border. If we fail to hold that position, then we will fall back to a similar line at Vung Tao, along Highway 15."

The South Vietnamese president then looked out the windows that opened to the blue sea that washed the snow-white crescent beach wrapped along the shore that embraced Nha Trang. Just beyond the breakers, tall volcanic rocks that formed tiny islands covered with thick vines, bushes, and small trees, giving them a visual texture of lumpy, green velvet, jutted fifty to a hundred feet above the clear water. Below the emerald peaks, swarming in the currents that flowed through lava and coral grottos, colorful fish and giant prawns teemed. It looked like a picture from a postcard, a warm and tranquil place, beautiful.

Pham Van Phu cleared his throat, breaking President Thieu's lapse.

"It would be such a shame to lose all of this to people who could never truly appreciate it," Thieu said in a soft voice, now speaking from his heart.

The general looked at the sight from the open windows: the giant, white marble Buddha towering above the trees on the hillside across the bay, overlooking the bright blue sea and white coral beaches. Beneath the tall salt cedars that lined the boulevard and walkway bordering the strand, he saw old men seated at concrete tables, playing chess. Throughout the sandy stretch that curved along the length of the city, fading into a rocky peninsula at its northern limit, he observed a colorful array of countless parasols with people lazing in their shade, reclining on towels. He too enjoyed the beauty and the life that Nha Trang afforded and agreed with his president's view about it, nodding to him with a sad smile.

"We cannot allow that to happen, can we?" Thieu said, sighing.

"It will not happen, sir," Phu said in a stronger voice, trying to rescue both of their spirits from the doldrums.

President Thieu then clasped his hands together and pressed them to his forehead, as if in prayer, bowing his head slightly. Then, putting his hands back in his lap, he looked squarely at General Phu.

"When I held my field command, you served me well," Thieu said, smiling. "In all the years that we have known each other, I have never questioned your loyalty to me. Today, I must call upon that long friendship because I need your unequivocal faith in support of my strategy to save our nation."

"Sir, without question," Pham Van Phu said, seizing the opportunity to endear himself, and leaned forward in his chair to carefully hear his president.

"Most of the other regional commanders and the entire Joint General Staff disagree with my assessment of this situation," Thieu said. "They support the CIA's and Ambassador Martin's positions that our forces outmatch the Communists when we stand in defense and that from the fortifications at our key enclaves we can ultimately stop this offensive. I disagree."

"Respectfully, sir," Phu said, "may I address this matter with candor?"

"Certainly," Thieu said, forcing a smile. "That is why I asked you to speak privately with me. I greatly respect your thoughts about this crisis."

"Sir," Phu continued, "I believe that in most situations, apart from that which we presently face at Ban Me Thuot, our forces will prevail in defense.

"We do not have the cache of munitions and stores, nor the fortresses, at Ban Me Thuot that all of our other principal enclaves possess. That lack of adequate fortification and supply represents the two greatest reasons why we now suffer the loss. However, our forces at Pleiku and Kontum, and to a greater extent at Da Nang, Chu Lai, Hue, Phu Bai, Dong Ha, and even here at Nha Trang and Cam Ranh Station, have very adequate hardened positions controlling the high ground and ample hidden stockpiles. The Americans abandoned much of these stores as so-called junk for us to reclaim, taking advantage of a loophole in the Paris Accords.

"You have my loyalty, sir, but I must hold faith with what the other generals have advised you."

"No!" Thieu shouted, lurching from the chair. He rushed to a table where he picked up a pale green, manila folder stuffed with papers and shook it at General Phu. "These reports indicate that we have depleted the greater majority of those very supplies and munitions."

"Sir, I have seen with my own eyes what we hold in many of these caches," Phu said, rising from the chair in a respectful response to the president abruptly leaping to his feet. "We drafted those reports in hopes of gaining additional American support. Just as when we submitted our budgets, the truth that they tell represents a different set of circumstances and realities."

"Our forces, thus far, have stood no match against the North Vietnamese," Thieu snapped. "You lost, what, two regiments already? Or is it now three? Annihilated! Sixty percent of the men killed before they could even land!"

"This is not the same situation, sir," Phu said in a soft, conciliatory voice, hoping to ease the tensions that had sent President Thieu into such an explosive tantrum. "That is one battle, not the war, nor does it represent the whole country. We must now resolve to isolate the enemy's forces and contain them where they presently stand."

"I have solid information, documented in a top secret intelligence report from a very reliable American military source, that tells me that while the United States withdrew their support of us during the past two years and cut our aid to a fraction, the Russians have covertly shipped no less than seven hundred million long tons of new military equipment, ammunition, and supplies to Hanoi in preparation for this very campaign! They blatantly violate the Paris Accords, just as the North Vietnamese now ignore its rules with this invasion!" Thieu preached, his voice crescendoing to a shout as his face flushed dark red and blood veins pulsed outward on his forehead and temples.

Pham Van Phu said nothing, waiting for the president's rage to subside. He deeply suspected that no such intelligence report ever existed, nor had any of the American military staff shown Nguyen Van Thieu anything even similar to the document he described. It contradicted everything that the Americans had otherwise said.

Furthermore, General Phu's old friend, "Charlie," an American general assigned to the CIA in Saigon, had visited him only weeks ago. When Phu asked him for advice, Charlie had refused because he claimed that the Paris Accords prohibited him lending such help. Not even advice from an old and trusted friend. Who would have known? It was only the two of them, yet Charlie, still, had said no.

Nguyen Van Thieu had no real friends within any of the American diplomatic, intelligence, or military communities. Ambassador Martin merely tolerated the man because his job required of him a minimum of such conduct. No one, in Phu's mind, would have given President Thieu such incredible news.

"The Communists clearly hold the upper hand," Thieu roared, continuing to bluster as he walked back to the table and threw down the green folder on a stack of others like it, toppling them across several cardboard tubes that contained charts and maps. "America has turned its back. Deserted us in the breach! How do we stand in defense against such forces when they can now so easily overwhelm us?"

"How can we withdraw our units from their defenses without placing them and the republic at far more risk?" Phu said, now courageously pleading for the president to simply consider what nearly any military strategist finds immediately obvious and most basic. "Forces in movement face the greatest vulnerability of all situations.

"On the march, our soldiers will have no defenses and can rely only on the equipment, ammunition, and stores that they carry. In such a massive retreat, they will have highly inadequate armor and artillery defenses, and even those that they can deploy cannot respond rapidly enough to an attack. They cannot count on air cover, either. The Communists now have widespread antiair defense missiles deployed throughout the northern provinces and Central Highlands, making our pilots very timid to fly into these hostile zones. A reinforced enemy lying in ambush will find such an army in movement an easy prey indeed.

"Remaining in defense, our forces will have the advantage of holding high ground fortresses, heavily supported by artillery and armor, with ample provisions. Placed in movement, the army must desert these fortifications and the greatest majority of their supplies and munitions. They are simply too vast to carry with us. What of them?

"Furthermore, consider the reaction of the people when they see the massive movement of our units. They will surely panic and crowd the highways, following the retreating forces to safety, and thus choke traffic to a crawl. Already, I have heard reports of civilians flooding into Hue, fleeing the attacks in those outlying hamlets. Certainly they will make an exodus at the sight of our retreat.

"Sir, abandoning the Central Highlands and the northern provinces to establish a new DMZ appears to me a recipe for disaster."

"You have no choice in the matter, General Phu," President Thieu snarled. "We will sacrifice those forces necessary to protect the redeployment so that my plan does succeed. I have already ordered such units to fight to the man. It is the republic's only hope."

Pham Van Phu said nothing more and turned his gaze to the ornate design and dark colors of the Persian carpet spread across the floor. He realized that President Thieu had now let fear dominate his thinking, and panic, driven by the defeat at Ban Me Thuot, his loss of faith in the fighting abilities of South Vietnam's armed forces, and the absence of hope for any American support, obviously guided his decisions. Clearly, the president's resolution to the crisis, if executed, spelled the end for the Republic of Vietnam.

The general now began to consider his own safety and what he must do to stay alive and free. He had endured captivity and torture by the Viet Minh in 1954 and felt certain that he could not again survive imprisonment under the Communist hand, especially considering his rank and his age.

Pham Van Phu stepped back to the sofa chair and stood, waiting for his nation's leader to return to his seat and spell out details of his plan. The diminutive general resolved to say no more about the matter and only to listen dutifully. Seeing the president so demoralized and now consumed with such trepidation that it warped his thinking, General Phu concluded that more words would only serve to further inflame President Nguyen Van Thieu.

THE WHITE HOUSE, WASHINGTON, DC

"DAVE, PUT DOWN your camera for a minute and talk to me," President Gerald R. Ford said to White House photographer David Hume Kennerly.

"What is it, sir?" the young photojournalist said, lowering his camera and casually walking to the President of the United States's desk in the Oval Office, where Kennerly had worked through the placid afternoon, snapping candid pictures of America's leader quietly reading a stack of memoranda and their accompanying documents.

"What do your friends in the press corps say about all this mess in South Vietnam?" President Ford asked.

"A lot of them think that this is the beginning of the end," Kennerly said in a matter-of-fact tone.

"What do you think?" the President then said.

"You know the press, sir," Kennerly answered and shrugged. "Lots of rants and raves over dinner. Lots of opinions, both informed and uninformed. Honestly, sir, it does sound bad to me, based on what we know here."

"The Secretary of State wants General Fred Weyand to return to Saigon with Ambassador Martin and make an assessment for us. I told Dr. Kissinger to give him *carte blanche* on his recommendations. Whatever he believes is necessary to save South Vietnam, I want him to tell me straight out. Whatever it takes.

"He will have a couple of our smartest military analysts advising him, George Carver and Ted Shackley, and Secretary of Defense Jim Schlesinger's best logistics man, Erich Von Marbod, looking at the situation too. We need to find out what we can do to save the country," President Ford said, watching the photographer's face as he spoke. Before he had finished the sentence, he realized none of it came as any surprise to Kennerly, a man who seemed to know anything about everything that went on at the White House.

"I could give you an objective opinion, if you sent me too," Kennerly said. "Those guys are the experts, but they also have long-held interests that may bias how they characterize what they see."

"Right," President Ford said, leaning back in his leather chair and lacing his fingers behind his head.

"I don't mean to suggest that they would consciously misjudge things or intentionally misguide you," Kennerly added, "but with the years they spent there, working to help the South Vietnamese, I think a bias in that way is a fair call."

"Oh, I understand what you say, Dave," the President said, still leaning back in his chair. "I have to weigh in that factor when I see their report. I am just considering your suggestion of going with them, as an additional observer. You could possibly help to give me that balance."

"I think that I would give you a picture of the facts without any tilt to them," Kennerly said. "I could report what I see, straight to you. Give you a fresh perspective, something to compare."

"I am thinking about that, Dave," President Ford said. "May not be a bad idea. Besides, you could make a historical record of this with your camera. I think that it is important that we have a good record."

"Just say the word, Mr. President, and I will pack my bags," Kennerly said and walked back to the couch to resume taking photographs of President Ford, seated at his desk with the afternoon sun streaming through the three tall windows centered in the curved wall behind him.

"I need to talk to the Secretary of State about the idea and consider his opinion of it, but right now I can't see where it would hurt anything to have you along," President Ford said and then quietly turned his eyes back to the stack of papers that he had earlier begun to read.

David Hume Kennerly raised his camera, and through its wide-angle lens he studied the way the brightness from outside reflected off the President's back, producing a kind of halo along the lines of his head and shoulders. Then the photographer took a quick glance at the needle on his spot meter, checking the various illumination levels that it read.

To eliminate excessively dark shadows, Kennerly had set up an umbrella strobe on a stand behind the coffee table. Triggered by his camera's shutter release, it would bounce a subtle kick of soft flash to fill in the foreground, but not so strong that it would become noticeable or reduce the embracing effect of the natural, rim lighting that streamed from the Oval Office's three tall windows.

Satisfied with the look and content that his exposure settings still held true, the photographer began snapping more pictures of the American leader at work.

ARVN II ARMY CORPS HEADQUARTERS, NHA TRANG

PRESIDENT NGUYEN VAN Thieu sat at the head of the long conference table at the Nha Trang garrison headquarters. He listened as members of the Joint General Staff and representatives of South Vietnam's military regions offered their assessments of the crisis as a prelude to the presentation of his redeployment plan.

Thieu felt deserted and alone. He had to chide and pressure his only ally, Major General Pham Van Phu, into supporting his position. He knew that Phu did it because he had no other choice. His losses at Ban Me Thuot had essentially emasculated him. Now the man just sought a way out, not merely out of the situation, but out of the country.

Already rumors had begun to surface that the former premier of South Vietnam, at one time Thieu's own vice president, and currently the supreme commander of South Vietnam's air force, the flamboyant Air Marshal Nguyen Cao Ky, had begun talk of staging a *coup d'etat*. According to the gossip, Ky had already approached several American leaders at the Defense Attaché's Office and had even discretely suggested the idea to some of the Joint General Staff.

Who at this table could he trust? Pham Van Phu? A small man, who today, seated in the large, leather conference chair behind the great mahogany table, appeared even more dwarfish than ever. His only ally?

He had no idea who the heavyset, round-faced General Nguyen Van Toan truly supported, nor where his real loyalties lay. Toan had the reputation of a man easily swayed with a dollar, or promise of power. He held no qualms in getting what he wanted by any available means, inside or outside the law or command structure. Toan wielded his muscle in Saigon and Military Region 3 more as a warlord than as a uniformed commander of forces.

However, Thieu felt confident that General Toan would stand with him, since the president's plan also benefitted the general's own self-serving interests.

Thieu's only openly defiant critic, Lieutenant General Ngo Quang Truong, commander of Military Region 1, did not attend the Nha Trang meeting, nor did he offer any excuses for his absence. He regarded the entire conference as merely an exercise in procedure, a game of smoke and mirrors, and totally a waste of his time. President Thieu already had his plan. Today's commentary simply shuffled more papers for no good reason other than to satisfy bureaucratic egos.

Two days earlier, Nguyen Van Thieu had ordered General Truong to redeploy the entire Airborne Division from the defenses of Hue and Da Nang so that he could move them into position to reinforce units that his plan had established to cordon off Saigon and at least save that city. The president did not even have a specific mission for the Airborne Division, other than they should report to MR 3 at once and that they would fill in where General Toan needed them.

At the onset of President Thieu issuing his order to redeploy the force, which represented more than a third of the defense of Hue and Da Nang, General Truong had emphatically refused and had vehemently pled for his commander in chief to reconsider.

That following morning, March 13, General Truong flew to Saigon to argue his case, face to face, with President Thieu.

BURLY AND SWEET smelling, Lieutenant General Nguyen Van Toan did not bother to stand as his senior-ranking protege, Lieutenant General Ngo Quang Truong stepped through the conference-room doorway inside the Presidential Palace, where the two men awaited their audience with President Thieu. The thin-faced general from Da Nang glanced at Toan and then at Toan's aide-de-camp, who had leaped to his feet when Truong entered the room.

Scowling now, General Truong sat in a leather armchair at the opposite end of the conference table from General Toan and dismissed the disrespect as another quality in the man's gangsterlike demeanor. In January, President Thieu had relieved the former MR 3 commander who had lost an entire regiment, more than three thousand men from the Fifth ARVN Division, attempting to defend Phuoc Long Province. Toan had stepped into the commander's billet and immediately boasted that his three divisions, armored brigade, and five ranger groups would lose no more ground.

"I hope you had a smooth flight from Da Nang," Toan said casually, trying to cut the ice with small talk.

General Truong simply looked at his colleague and nodded. He had few indulgent words for anyone today.

More than forty-five minutes passed before President Thieu finally entered the conference room. General Toan had fidgeted and chatted nervously with his aide-de-camp, while General Truong had sat quietly, jotting notes and studying a thick stack of battle-planning documents.

"Please remain seated, gentlemen," Thieu said as he breezed into the room and took a seat in the leather armchair at the right of General Toan.

The distance of the conference table looked like a long mahogany highway to Ngo Quang Truong. Clearly he had no advantage, and he immediately realized that his bumpy flight to Saigon this morning had only wasted his precious time. He felt suddenly sick at his stomach, and for the first time in his life he genuinely feared for his country, and for his fellow soldiers, whom he greatly loved.

"With all due respect, Mr. President," General Truong said with a sharp edge in his voice, "I had hoped that we could discuss this matter privately."

"My decision to redeploy the Airborne Division from Hue is a matter of direct importance with Lieutenant General Toan," Thieu said, "since I am reassigning that force to his command."

"And what of Hue City?" Truong asked.

"Those army and Marine Corps units that I have allowed you to keep there will defend that citadel to a man," Thieu said. "We have already had this discussion, Lieutenant General Truong. You must obey my order."

"No, sir!" Ngo Quang Truong snapped and stood defiantly.

Nguyen Van Thieu remained seated and smiled. Nguyen Van Toan leaned back in his chair and glared at General Truong.

"You will bring the whole nation to ruin with this insanity, sir," Truong said, his pent-up rage beginning to boil in his voice.

"That is quite enough, General," Thieu said, still keeping his seat.

"What is the purpose of this lunacy?" General Truong said. "Abandoning our cities makes no sense. Deserting our fortresses and our stockpiles hands the enemy victory.

"You order my soldiers to stand and die, for what? So that you and your cronies can cut and run? Meanwhile those units that you order to redeploy will be slaughtered on the highways. The timing is too late. The enemy is in place! Do you not realize this?

"Pulling such a force from Hue will cause its utter destruction overnight. Those soldiers left to fight will quickly lose heart. Those who actually remain at their posts, and do not desert, will surely die or fall prisoner to the Communists.

"Once Hue falls, refugees will flood over the Hai Van Pass into Da Nang, and with inadequate defenders there, it will quickly collapse too.

Then Chu Lai will topple, and an unstoppable tidal wave will come crashing down Highway 1 through Qui Nhon and Nha Trang, and straight into Saigon.

"I will not do it!"

"You will send those forces I order, and you will send them immediately," Thieu barked, now standing and walking around the conference table to meet General Truong face to face.

"Relieve me! Shoot me for insubordination! But I will not obey such an insane order, sir!" General Truong said, looking the president squarely in the face.

"I have already transmitted orders to your subordinate commanders and the Airborne Division," President Thieu said, turning his back on General Truong. "You will return to your command post, and you will fight and defend Hue and Da Nang and Chu Lai to the last man standing. Is that clear? You may not surrender!"

"History will bitterly remember you, Mr. President! Our people will come to scorn your name," General Truong said, snapping his satchel filled with working papers under his arm and marching defiantly out of the room.

On the other hand, General Toan did not even wince when President Thieu ordered him to abandon his positions at An Loc, the capital of Binh Long Province, and redeploy those forces to Saigon. General Truong had no more than stormed out of the conference when the president turned toward Toan and told him of his decision.

Thieu had fully expected a reasonable and strong argument from the general, because of the significance of An Loc, not a simple shrug and nod from the man. Such indifference and casual agreement at giving up a stronghold that was perhaps the most symbolically important among the rank-and-file of the South Vietnamese armed forces had even caused Nguyen Van Thieu to pause and wonder where the burly general's true loyalties really lay.

Giving up An Loc without a bullet fired would sit hard among South Vietnam's armed forces. Especially among the ARVN rangers who in 1972 successfully defended the fortress city against a ninety-five-day siege and forced the badly battered NVA divisions to retreat into Cambodia to lick their wounds. The ARVN victory greatly bolstered self-confidence among all branches of the South Vietnamese armed forces. They had, after all, beaten the best efforts of the North Vietnamese, and had done it without American assistance.

In this one instant, President Nguyen Van Thieu had literally reversed the Army of the Republic of Vietnam's greatest victory, and General Nguyen Van Toan hardly raised an eyebrow, agreeing to the order with a mere shrug and nod.

As Nguyen Van Thieu sat in the darkened conference room in Nha Trang, he thought of General Toan's indifference and questionable loyalties. The worry of it gnawed at him as he listened to the operations officers from his general staff explain the details of his plan and its timelines to the regional commands and Joint General Staff, all seated at the table. Even above the drone of the air conditioners, the president could hear the heavy sighs at the announcement of his casting An Loc to the enemy without a fight.

Then, when the briefing officer addressed the redeployment of the entire II Army Corps from Kontum and Pleiku to Nha Trang, the sighs grew to moans and loud coughs. Even to the lower ranking clerks and aides, the impending disaster appeared very clear.

"I think that went as well as one could expect, General, don't you?" Nguyen Van Thieu said to Pham Van Phu following the briefing.

"You could say that, sir," General Phu said, taking a seat in the sofa chair opposite the president, once again in the privacy of the office where the two men had talked prior to the formal conference.

"Unfortunately," President Thieu said, sipping a cup of tea, "I have further orders for your forces. While your forces will redeploy to the coastal lowlands and form defensive perimeters around the major cities, you must also do likewise for Ban Me Thuot."

"Sir?" Phu said, unsure of what he had just heard.

"You will retake Ban Me Thuot," President Thieu said. "We cannot allow Darlac Province nor its capital to remain in enemy hands."

Pham Van Phu lowered his eyes and looked at the age that showed itself on his hands. He thought of the horrible months he had spent in captivity, tortured and threatened with death by the Viet Minh when Dien Bien Phu had fallen and he had surrendered to the Communists along with his French leaders. Hundreds had died in their prison. He had survived by pure will.

"As commander of the II Army Corps," Phu said, "I must remain at a position where I can command all the forces. Correct, sir?"

"Yes, that is correct, General Phu," Nguyen Van Thieu said. "However, I regard the counterattack and reclamation of Ban Me Thuot as one of your highest priorities. Success of my overall plan for saving Saigon and our southern regions depends on your success there."

"Agreed, sir," Pham Van Phu said. "Yet Ban Me Thuot means little if the coastal lowlands fall while I am preoccupied in Darlac."

"What do you propose?" President Thieu said.

"The commander of our rangers, Colonel Pham Van Tat, has proven himself quite a capable leader," Pham Van Phu began. "He can provide that forward-area command presence while I am able to manage all these operations from our new headquarters in Nha Trang. I propose that you promote Colonel Tat to brigadier general so that he can command the forward regiments directly."

Nguyen Van Thieu laughed, shaking his cup and spilling tea in the saucer.

"Very well, General Phu," the president said. "Consider Pham Van Tat promoted to brigadier general. I agree with you that he is a very capable and strong-willed commander and a good choice to take charge in the forward areas. However, the obligation of retaking Ban Me Thuot remains with you. I will look to you for answers. You cannot fail, or all is lost."

"Thank you, sir," Pham Van Phu said, feeling great relief.

In his heart he knew the entire plan held together like feathers in a torn pillow. One good shake and everything would fly to the four winds.

Chapter 7

WHIRLWINDS

CAMP BUTLER, OKINAWA—MONDAY, MARCH 17, 1975

"SKIPPER, WHAT ABOUT these front-page pictures," Corporal Steve Tingley called to Captain Jerry Shelton as he stepped through the doorway at the Joint Public Affairs Office, shortly after 10 a.m. "Looks like some heavy shit breaking out in Vietnam, all these people jamming the roads to Hue."

"I know," the captain said as he poured coffee and then began thumbing through a stack of messages. "Have you seen Gunny Thurman this morning?"

"He called at about 7:30 from Camp Courtney," Tingley responded.

"Good," Shelton said. "He must have gotten word about the operations briefing at III MAF."

"Yes, sir, he did," Tingley said. "The gunny told me he would be here as soon as he got finished with it."

"Lance Corporal Carlson with him?" Shelton asked.

"Yes, sir, I think so. Either that, or Eric is still at his office at Camp Hanson," Tingley said and then walked to the captain's office and shut the door.

"These pictures on the front page of *Stars and Stripes*, sir, what do you think? Seriously."

Shelton looked at Tingley.

"Don't put more into them than meets the eye," the captain said. "Granted, the NVA have increased their activity over the past year, and we have watched their buildup as an indicator that they will probably launch a major campaign this spring. However, every time fire breaks out, a gaggle of peasants seems to flood the highways into Hue and Da Nang, trying to get away from fighting at one place or another. Nothing new about it."

"Well, sir, the whole MAF mounting out," Tingley said, "that's new. At least that's scuttlebutt in the barracks."

"Granted, we have additional units mobilizing to reinforce the Ninth Marine Amphibious Brigade, but that's hardly the whole Marine Amphibious Force," Shelton said. "What's the point?"

"All the shit that's going down, sir," Tingley said. "Gunny Thurman and Lance Corporal Carlson, for example. They are mounting out, aren't they?"

"Look," Shelton said, "most of you guys will probably sit this one out. So loosen up your pack straps.

"Right now, Russ Thurman and Eric Carlson occupy the only two boat spaces that we could squeeze out of General Poggemeyer, and we are lucky at that to get them launched. Carlson has worked hard as Fourth Marine Regiment's correspondent, and as a result, Al Gray has adopted him as one of his boys. Gunny Thurman has combat experience, talent with a camera and a typewriter, and Colonel Gray likes him too. So we really had the choices of whom to send pretty much made for us."

Then the captain opened that morning's edition of *Stars and Stripes*, spreading it across his desk, and pointed to a one-column story on page three.

"Cambodia," Shelton said. "With the activity in Vietnam, the Khmer Rouge have decided to not be outdone. It looks like that situation, to no one's surprise, is rapidly going south. If the Khmer Rouge shut down the airfield, as they have threatened, we will have a host of Americans then stranded in Phnom Penh with little to no way out, except on our bloody backs. All the hubbub this morning has more to do with that potential evacuation, Operation Eagle Pull, than with anything going on in South Vietnam. Although the goings-on in Vietnam still ride high on the radar scope."

"What if Gunny and Carlson get busy in Phnom Penh, and all kinds of shit breaks loose in Vietnam?" Tingley asked.

"In that case, I am sure we will have no problems getting you boys over there," Shelton said, smiling.

THAT NIGHT IN OKINAWA CITY

RED NEON AND Christmas lights reflected in the mirror behind the bar at Mama Wolf's, an out-of-the-way nightclub on an alley-wide backstreet of Koza, Okinawa City's bar and brothel district. The smoke from a dozen burning cigarettes, inhaled by the usual crowd of older Marines and sailors who frequented the dark little den on the less traveled side of central Okinawa's tenderloin, lay in a crimson haze and swirled behind Chief Warrant Officer Bob Neeley as he hurried back to his table, carrying a large bottle of Orion beer, Okinawa's local brew, in each hand.

"*Toxon Orion, desu ne?*" Neeley said in GI-slang Japanese, describing the size and brand of the two beers as he slid across the red vinyl seat in the booth where Jerry Shelton sat.

"*Hi dozo,* and *domo* alligators," Shelton said, humorously substituting the amphibian reptile for the Japanese word for thank you, *arrigato*.

"Don't touch my moustache," Neeley said with a laugh, playing off the Japanese language response of you're welcome, *doi touchi musta*.

Although a Marine, Neeley worked at Kadina Air Force Base, managing the Far East Network radio and television station located there. He and Shelton had a long-standing friendship that began in Vietnam when they served as junior enlisted combat correspondents working in the Da Nang press center nearly ten years earlier.

The stocky, round-faced warrant officer had just begun pouring his beer into a water-spotted glass when a wide smile broke across Shelton's face. Neeley then looked over his shoulder and saw *Pacific Stars and Stripes* correspondent Jim Lee sauntering past the bar with a pair of likely suspects in tow. Following closely behind the reporter, like novice monks in trace of their kung fu master, Steve Tingley and another Marine from the public affairs office, Sergeant Carl Ebert, apprehensively searched the darkly lit room for comrades and beamed happily when they finally saw the familiar faces of Neeley and Shelton.

"Oh shit," Neeley said, laughing wryly, "he's corrupting the troops again. We're going to be here all night."

"Not if I can help it," Shelton said, waving at the trio.

Short, heavyset, his black hair combed slick in an oily ducktail, and wearing black plastic sunglasses, black slacks, and a predominately black silk Hawaiian shirt with pink, purple, and green flowers printed on it, Jim Lee, a native son of Monroe, Louisiana, had lived in Okinawa for years, kept intimate acquaintances at all the local watering holes, and spoke fluent gutter Japanese. He immediately found Mama Wolf, bear-hugged the burly woman, who stood nearly two inches taller than Lee, and began laughing and yammering in colloquial Okinawan dialect with the club's female proprietor.

Shelton and Neeley smiled knowingly as they watched Lee then lead Mama Wolf to the two young Marines that the reporter had brought to the club and introduce them to her as "Okinawa cherry boys."

Carl Ebert put out his hand for the woman to shake, but instead, the hefty *Mama-san* immediately embraced the Marine in a suffocating squeeze with her massive arms and buried his face deep in the perfume-rich, jiggling-fat cleavage between her watermelon-sized breasts. Then she lowered her hug, reached behind the sergeant, and clamped both cheeks of his buttocks in her palms, squeezing hard.

Ebert immediately rose to his tiptoes and cried out.

Everyone in the bar erupted, laughing.

Showing her large, gold teeth in a wide smile, Mama Wolf then turned toward Tingley, who took a long step backward and offered the woman his hand at a stretched-out distance, cautiously avoiding her clasp. However, rather than grasping his dangling paw, Mama Wolf shot her arm past it and straight into Tingley's groin, where she clamped her ironlike grip onto his testicles, jolting the Marine to virtual levitation.

Patrons of the bar laughed even louder while Tingley screamed and danced, and Mama Wolf paraded him in a circle as he wailed on his tiptoes.

"I see you boys have now joined the Wolf pack," Shelton said after Tingley and Ebert had bid Mama Wolf *adieu* and now slid to a happy landing in the captain's booth.

"You got the classic Wolf kiss, Sergeant Ebert," Neeley said. "Tingley, however, found out the hard way what one gets when one tries to avoid the Wolf kiss."

"What kiss?" Tingley said loudly, still laughing. "It seemed to me more like groped ass and scrambled balls. Gunner Neeley, her lips never even puckered. She just smiled that mouth full of Hong Kong gold and filled her hands."

"Consider yourselves now members of the club," Shelton said, raising his beer toward the two sergeants.

A young woman dressed in a long, clingy, green silk gown, embroidered with yellow dragons and peacocks, followed Jim Lee to the table, carrying four large bottles of Orion beer that she set in front of Tingley and Ebert.

"You two guys' drinks are on the house, courtesy of Mama Wolf," Lee said, pulling a chair to the end of the booth and setting down his glass of Johnny Walker Scotch and ice.

"What brings you to the ville on a Monday night?" Shelton said to the newsman.

"Don't ask me," Lee said. "Talk to your two knuckleheads here. They showed up on my doorstep before sunset, begging me to go have a drink with them."

"So, what's in the funny papers tomorrow?" Shelton asked the reporter, making small talk.

"Cambodia," Lee responded. "Place has steadily gone down the shitter for the past year. Your guys had a briefing about it today. I think General Lon Nol and his gang are history. Just a matter of weeks now."

Shelton nodded and said nothing.

"Why do you say that?" Tingley asked.

"Let's see," Lee said. "For starters, the Communists have now controlled the Mekong River for the past month or so, cutting off that supply route, in addition to all the highways. The Khmer Republic has a navy base at Neak Loung, on the river near Banam, about halfway between Phnom Penh and the South Vietnam border. However, those guys have no way out. Totally cut off, and no way to get supplies. So check them off the list.

"Until now, the Mekong River was the principal supply line for what was left of Lon Nol's government. With the highways long since owned by the Khmer Rouge, Pochentong Airfield, the air base outside the capital, is now the only way in or out. Bird Airways, Cambodia's version of Air America, has a bunch of what the CIA calls surplus

American C-130s and three DC-8s making fifteen to twenty supply flights per day into Pochentong. However, it is just a matter of time before the Khmer Rouge move back and start shelling the runway and aircraft operations again."

"Kind of like the Berlin airlift," Tingley said.

"Except under rocket, small arms, and antiaircraft attack going in and out," Shelton said.

"Actually, they have not had any rocket attacks for quite a few days because the Khmer Rouge got kicked out of their firebases at Toul Leap, northwest of the air base," Lee said. "But like I mentioned before, that won't last long. Like mold, they'll creep back in the cracks."

"So we have basically chalked off Cambodia too," Sergeant Ebert said quietly.

"They don't have a prayer," Neeley said.

"What's the Marine Corps going to do about it?" Lee asked.

"Can't say," Shelton said and looked straight at Tingley, who started to open his mouth, but closed it on seeing the captain's eyes.

"People say that you guys are going in there to roll up the rugs, shred the secrets, and get the hell out of Dodge," Lee said. "At least that's according to the guy on the third shitter from the right and pretty much common skinny on the streets."

"Like I said, I can't say," Shelton said and sipped his beer.

"Well, I will tell you this," Lee said. "We wouldn't be sitting here dribbling in our suds, talking about doom had Nixon told the truth."

"Watergate?" Tingley said. "What does that have to do with anything here?"

"Fuck Watergate," Lee said. "Nixon has lied since the day he took office. I'm talking about the crock-of-crap Nixon Doctrine and his bullshit denials about our combat operations in Cambodia and Laos."

"True," Shelton said, sipping his beer.

"Damned right, true," Lee said. "I will never forget the day Nixon went on national television. Lon Nol had just overthrown Prince Sihanouk and sent him packing to Paris. Of course, the CIA set up the operation. Sihanouk got on television in Paris and cried foul, and Nixon said, 'Who, me?'

"Anyway, Senator Frank Church and a bunch more head-hunting Democrats from both the House and Senate flat out asked Nixon if there was any truth to what Sihanouk said. Nixon very cooly denied any involvement. Then like the guilty dog that he is, Nixon goes on national television and says that the United States has no ground forces in Cambodia, no military advisors, nor has the United States any air assets supporting any actions in Cambodia. He says, and I quote, 'Cambodia is the Nixon Doctrine in its purest form.' "

"Bullshit, I remember that boot full of paddy scum," Neeley said. "I remember thinking, what a lie."

"Every junk monkey in any of the armed forces who ever cranked a bolt and saw past the smoking shitters knew it was a lie," Lee said. "Hell, half of Congress knew it at the time, until the truth raised its ugly head in the newspapers, which it finally did, and set off Senator Church, all the Democrats, and a number of survival-oriented Republicans, on the political warpath."

"So we wound up with the infamous Case-Church Amendment, shutting off air and ground combat support in Southeast Asia, including Cambodia and South Vietnam?" Ebert said.

"Give the man a cigar," Lee said.

THROUGHOUT MOST OF the years of United States involvement in South Vietnam, although Cambodia proclaimed a nonbelligerent, neutral status, it actually supported the Viet Cong and North Vietnamese forces by providing them refuge, primarily in the Parrot's Beak region along the Mekong River, hardly more than fifty kilometers west of Saigon. In this so-called neutral territory, Communist forces successfully escaped American and South Vietnamese pursuit and rested and recuperated between commitments to combat operations. In this Cambodian haven, they also stashed large caches of weapons and supplies ferried over the notorious Ho Chi Minh Trail, which crossed through Cambodia at several points, exiting into the Mekong region and the Central Highlands.

In March of 1970, Cambodian Marshal Lon Nol led a pro-Western coup, supposedly engineered by American CIA operatives and military advisors, and ousted Cambodia's recognized leader, Prince Norodom Sihanouk, who then fled to Paris and openly accused the United States of his ouster. The coup created the Khmer Republic, led by Lon Nol.

In less than a month, United States and South Vietnamese forces launched a clearing operation into the Parrot's Beak and other areas of Cambodia that served as sanctuaries for North Vietnamese and Viet Cong forces. The operation also helped to bolster Lon Nol's regime against the Khmer Communists, who became known as the Khmer Rouge.

As American air and ground forces swept through Cambodia during April of 1970, President Richard M. Nixon, when confronted with press reports of the United States–led aerial bombing and ground combat operations there, addressed the issue in a nationally televised speech. President Nixon directly stated that the United States had no advisors on the ground in Cambodia, had no American military forces involved in any actions in Cambodia, and had no American military air assets supporting any action in Cambodia. He said, "Cambodia is the Nixon Doctrine in its purest form."

President Nixon's blatant lie set off a congressional firestorm and did more to cripple assistance in South Vietnam and Cambodia than anything else.

For the next three years, United States military air assets attacked the Cambodian links on the Ho Chi Minh Trail and in Viet Cong and North Vietnamese refuges, and executed air strikes and bombing missions on the Khmer Rouge in support of the Lon Nol, Khmer Republic forces.

Responding to the overthrow of Prince Sihanouk and the United States presence in Cambodia, the North Vietnamese (despite long-standing differences based on tribal and social conflicts) began significant support of the more than sixty-thousand-strong Khmer Rouge. This support included training cadres of Cambodian Communists at facilities in North Vietnam and providing a conduit and flow of military supplies and weapons from China and the Soviet Union.

During this same period, and despite an active South Vietnamese and United States presence, the Khmer Republic army remained poorly equipped and badly lacked formal military training. Called the FANK (*Force Armee Nationale Khmer*), the Cambodian Republic army did, however, manage to hold the Communist guerrillas at bay, in large part due to continued American air support.

Fighting generally took place during the dry season, the months from early January to mid June, after which monsoon torrents resumed and flooded much of the region for the remainder of the year. With each dry season, the Communists slowly began to gain more and more control of the rivers and roadways leading to Cambodia's capital city, Phnom Penh.

Given the military investment in Cambodia, its impact on the war in South Vietnam, and the Communist gains made in the Khmer Republic despite American military support, in April of 1973, the United States Congress sent a fact-finding team to Cambodia to examine the situation. James G. Lowenstein and Richard M. Moose headed the team and issued the report from the mission to Missouri Senator Stuart Symington, who chaired the Subcommittee on US Security Agreements and Commitments Abroad.

Lowenstein and Moose reported that to offset Communist guerrillas' increasing successes in gaining control of key territory, the United States had increased its air support of Cambodian republic forces to ensure the survival of the Khmer Republic. The report cited that the fighting would continue indefinitely since the Khmer Rouge and their North Vietnamese, Soviet Union, and Chinese Communist allies were clearly not interested in any cease-fire options. The report further stated that even if the Communists might agree to a cease-fire, it would no doubt hinge on the condition that the United States stop all of its support to Cambodia, similar to the stipulations laid out in the Paris Peace Accords. The report concluded that without American support the Cambodian republic could not last very long.

Most significantly, once Cambodia fell, then South Vietnam would face its worst nightmare: North Vietnamese Army forces poised on its western flank with no American air support.

The Lowenstein and Moose report virtually laid out a set of no-win options for Congress. Continued support of Cambodia would potentially mire the United States in another war much like the one in South Vietnam. The alternative literally gave away Southeast Asia to the Communists.

On June 29, 1973, two months after Lowenstein and Moose's report, Congress placed a rider on the 1974 budget authorization bill that required a halt to all combat air operations in Southeast Asia. Idaho Democrat Senator Frank F. Church and New Jersey Republican Senator Clifford P. Case authored this amendment, which bore their names.

To seal out all American involvement in any combat in Laos, Cambodia, and Vietnam, Congress passed yet another amendment. This measure, a shirttail rider attached to the December 1973 foreign aid bill, forbade any funding of any military operations anywhere in Southeast Asia.

Senator Church and other members of Congress were so angered by President Nixon openly lying about United States military involvement in Cambodia that they immediately took action to begin cutting funding for the war.

The first volley in Congress came in 1970 when Senator Church and Kentucky Republican Senator John Sherman Cooper authored a bill that cut off funding of all military activity in Southeast Asia. That measure narrowly failed in its original form. However, on December 29, 1970, as a shirttail amendment to the defense authorization bill, a watered-down version of the measure finally passed. That version of the amendment only barred the introduction of United States ground forces in Laos and Thailand.

"NO MATTER WHAT happens in Cambodia or South Vietnam," Lee said, crunching a mouthful of ice as he spoke, "we have several mandates passed by both houses of Congress and signed into law by the President that say we can only watch while Southeast Asia goes down the tubes. We can land no ground forces. We can send no air support. We can provide no military advisors nor any military aid."

"So we just let all that we fought for, everything that more than fifty-six thousand Americans died for, all just float down the *binjo* ditch?" Carl Ebert said. "We're doing nothing but running a fucking Chinese fire drill."

"Why do you think I get so frustrated when I hear guys like Staff Sergeant Carr chomping around the hootch, telling you guys to get your pack straps tightened up because we are going back to war?" Shelton said. "Its just hot air and sparklers. We're pushing the envelope even if we end up only going back to evacuate."

"So, Skipper," Tingley said, "what happens if we go to get our people out and the bad guys start shooting at us?"

"Good question," the captain said. "According to what we can and cannot do, we are supposed to only act as humanitarian relief, noncombatants."

"So, when Gunny Thurman came back from his briefing today and said that the forecast casualty rate for First Battalion, Fourth Marines, if they lead our landing forces back into South Vietnam for combat operations, would be 90 percent, what was that all about?" Tingley blurted.

Jim Lee sucked on an ice cube and pretended to not hear.

Bob Neeley blinked at the captain.

Jerry Shelton drank more beer, said nothing, and looked squarely and coldly at Steve Tingley.

Carl Ebert spread a white, toothy smile beneath his black moustache and then slapped his hand over his mouth and laughed.

"Now we gotta kill ya," Ebert said in his thick New Orleans drawl.

PLEIKU, CENTRAL HIGHLANDS, SOUTH VIETNAM

"WHERE CAN THEY be? Surely they did not leave without allowing me to tell them goodbye?" Lieutenant Colonel Nguyen Manh Tuan frantically asked himself as he yanked hard on the parking-brake handle, slamming his car to a stop in the driveway of his home, and saw no one there. Obviously, his wife and sons had already joined the hundreds of other frightened civilians who had begun crowding the streets of Pleiku in a panicked exodus upon a heretofore abandoned roadway leading them toward the coast, and hopefully to safety.

The South Vietnamese Army artillery commander ran through the front entrance of his house, letting the screen door slam, and found his suitcase and a duffel bag already packed and lying on the bed for him. His eyes shifted through the bedroom, and then he took a quick look in the bathroom to be sure that his wife had forgotten nothing vital when she packed his bags. Then, in the kitchen, he looked in the refrigerator and found a six-pack of colas in cans and shoved it under his arm, holding his suitcase in one hand and his duffel bag in the other.

Tuan did not bother to shut his front door or even switch off the kitchen light, which he left burning. No need. In a matter of hours, no more than a day at the most, he felt certain that the Communists would take possession of everything. His house, his furniture, his stereo system—they would take everything, and he would only have what he could carry with him.

The tall, stately officer had called his wife on the telephone the moment that he had departed the commanding general's briefing in which Major General Pham Van Phu dictated his orders to redeploy the entire II Army Corps to Nha Trang and the coastal lowlands and from there to retake Ban Me Thuot. Tuan had sat in disbelief, as did many of the other officers, while the general told them that they would load all the weapons and ammunition that their trucks and trailers could carry, and that they would evacuate their forces and families from Pleiku and

Kontum to the coastal plains, where they could regroup and counter-attack the Communists.

"Our regiment has fifty trucks that can pull artillery pieces," Tuan had whispered to the colonel seated by him. "However, our regiment has more than 150 howitzers, accompanying spare parts, and ammunition that I estimate could support our defenses here for three months. This means that we must abandon fully two-thirds of our weapons and an even greater proportion of our stockpiled munitions and supplies. We have organized our forces for defensive and offensive operations based on our fixed garrison and stockpiles remaining here. We do not have the logistical strength to redeploy our entire force! How can we simply leave so much of our materiel behind? What is going on?"

"We are cutting and running from the battle," the colonel had whispered back to Tuan.

"What of our cache of weapons and supplies that we cannot carry with us?" Tuan asked.

"Blow them in place," the colonel had suggested, "if you want to take the time to risk capture by doing such a thing. However, I think that we should be with our units, loading our trucks and running, rather than sitting here at this very moment, listening to this fool talk nonsense. If we can make it to Nha Trang, I intend to keep traveling south, to Saigon, where I will buy myself and my family airplane tickets to Australia or America."

Tuan slammed the palms of his hands against his car's steering wheel as he started the engine. He screamed in frustration and began to sob. Tears streamed from his eyes as he desperately wished that he had gotten home in time to say good-bye to his family.

Now, he could only return to his artillery battery and get his men and machinery on the road to Nha Trang. Already, the sun stood straight overhead in the sky, and he knew that he had only a matter of hours to complete everything and join the convoy eastward.

PHAM VAN PHU had already sent his family to Saigon when he briefed his staff about their redeployment a day ago. He had called his kinfolk from Nha Trang and had told them to take all their money and what things of value that they could carry and to leave nothing precious to them behind, but that above all else, to depart Pleiku with all haste. He had even told them to consider flying to America for a vacation, until matters became resolved in South Vietnam.

Even before he had returned to Pleiku to effect the withdrawal, redeployment of forces, and what he considered the suicidal attempt to retake Ban Me Thuot, Pham Van Phu had begun trying to formulate a plan that promised at least a degree of success.

Communist forces had fully blocked and now controlled the two best thoroughfares leading from the Central Highlands: Highway 14, which extended southward from Pleiku and intersected with Highway 21 just northeast of Ban Me Thuot, which led eastward to Nha Trang, and Highway 19, which extended due east from Pleiku, traveling over the An Khe Pass, where Phu recalled the Viet Minh had decimated the French in 1954 in a virtual massacre there.

Phu had studied reconnaissance photographs of the roadways leading from Kontum and Pleiku and found that the North Vietnamese had apparently overlooked one road, the abandoned Interprovincial Highway 7B. Although still paved in a few stretches near Pleiku, the old road had now decayed mostly to rocks and dirt. II Army Corps engineers had informed the general that all of the bridges on the route had fallen in disrepair, rendering nearly all of them unsafe for anything except bicycles and foot traffic, and in several locations the bridges had even collapsed.

"We can ford the rivers, and our heavy equipment can cut new pathways down the embankments," Phu had told his staff, after he had decided to use the dilapidated roadway and now briefed them of his plan.

"The Communist forces will not look for us on Highway 7-Bravo," he had said, correctly. "With the bridges in disrepair, and many even missing, we can move with surprise and catch the enemy not looking. Our forces can cross the 135 miles to Nha Trang in one day's time if all goes well. Two or even three days, encountering a few difficulties."

"General, sir," Tran Van Cam, the one-star general who headed Pham Van Phu's operations staff, said in a low voice while rising to his feet. "What about the mines?"

"What about them?" Pham Van Phu said, taken somewhat off guard.

"Once our traffic succeeds getting past these bridges, rivers, and gullies, and enters the coastal plains," General Cam said softly, "they will find that the enemy has heavily mined Interprovincial Highway

7-Bravo. Clearing those mines will take time and will bring our traffic to a halt."

"Put armored vehicles with mine plows on them at the lead," General Phu told his deputy for operations. "Honestly, sir, we have no other route available with even a fraction of the promise for any degree of success that we have with Highway 7-Bravo."

"You make a valid point, sir. However, I believe you have an overly optimistic timetable. It will take one or two days simply to mount our forces and several more to transit the highway, given the difficulties that I anticipate," General Cam said and returned to his seat.

"To help assure that we deploy with an element of surprise," Pham Van Phu continued, "I have ordered our regional and popular forces commanders to have their units screen our departure. They will begin maneuvers down Highway 14, drawing the enemy's attention away from us. Hopefully, our column can then travel a reasonable distance before the North Vietnamese command realizes our movement. If we move quickly, we can perhaps enter the coastal lowlands before the enemy can begin to ambush our forces."

With the afternoon sun streaming through his office window, Pham Van Phu looked at the dull green UH-1N Huey helicopter sitting on his command headquarters lawn, its blade tethered to its nose, and the sergeant wearing the helmet covered with reflective tape standing by the aircraft's side door. A red placard displaying two white stars sat in its carrier by the pilot's door. Phu's aide-de-camp had already loaded the general's two large canvas valises and his hanging suit bag aboard the chopper.

As General Phu had instructed the aide, he had also taken off the baggage belonging to Chief of Staff Colonel Le Khac Ly and II Army Corps Deputy for Operations Brigadier General Tran Van Cam. The two senior officers' belongings sat ominously on the lawn a few yards away from the helicopter.

"I thought we would fly out on the same aircraft, General Phu, sir," Colonel Ly said, seeing the suitcases piled together.

"Change of plans, Colonel," Pham Van Phu said, taking his briefcase in hand and walking from behind his desk. "Since General Tat is so new in command, you will remain with him to assist in effecting the withdrawal from Pleiku and Kontum."

"Sir, all members of your staff have departed," Brigadier General

Tran Van Cam said. "Your aide-de-camp has apparently removed my baggage from your helicopter too."

"Yes, General Cam," Phu said, walking to the door and handing his briefcase to his aide. "Given the importance of retaking Ban Me Thuot, I have decided that your operational expertise will serve the command much better from the front line. You will keep me informed.

"Now, gentlemen, time is of the essence, and I must get started to Nha Trang. We will plan to retake Ban Me Thuot from there."

Chapter 8
CHEO REO

CENTRAL HIGHLANDS—TUESDAY, MARCH 18, 1975

THICK BILLOWS OF dust, ground from the rocks and soil that covered Interprovincial Highway 7B, pulverized flour-fine and churned into the air by the slowly rolling wheels of thousands of trucks and cars and bicycles and carts, driven and pushed by more than 160,000 people fleeing Pleiku and Kontum, who intermingled with the 60,000-man mass of retreating forces of the II Army Corps, filled the sky. The dull orange pall rose two hundred feet high and lay more than fifty miles long. It drifted far above the Central Highland's green hills and settled a filthy shroud on everything beneath the acrid plume. This mantle of engine exhaust and dirt rolled and boiled above the entire length of the elephantine exodus of newly begotten refugees who jam-packed the roadway from the intersection of Highway 14, on the eastern outskirts of Pleiku, all the way to Cheo Reo, the capital of Phu Bon Province. Like a red hailing flag, the prominence of the cloud signaled the migration of this massive mob of a quarter-million souls to anyone who might glance in its direction.

In the midst of the mayhem, near the front of the column, an olive

drab neckerchief tied over his mouth and nose, Lieutenant Colonel
Nguyen Manh Tuan stood on the passenger seat of his jeep as it inched
forward. The tall and lanky artillery commander rode at the head of his
battalion's convoy of six jeeps and twenty-four trucks. Each of the two
dozen tactical cargo vehicles pulled a 105-millimeter howitzer and had
its six-ton capacity bed filled to the top of its canvas cover with ammunition for the fieldpiece that it towed. Along both sides of the caravan, soldiers from Tuan's unit trudged wearily through the haze of
exhaust fumes and airborne dirt. The men toiled under the burden of
heavy field transport packs, stuffed tight with bandoleers of small-arms
rounds, grenades, and other low-echelon weaponry, along with bits of
their personal belongings, strapped to their backs, and rifles slung
across their shoulders.

Despite traveling on this slow road for two days now, Tuan still
searched relentlessly among the sea of cars and countless faces that surrounded him, looking for his family. Silently, as he unceasingly shifted
his eyes, looking rearward and forward, he hoped that his wife and
sons had somehow managed to drive their car well ahead of this rolling
traffic jam. He prayed that by some miracle they now waited for him
at the seacoast, where Interprovincial Highway 7B ended, in the town
of Tuy Hoa.

From time to time, throughout the past two days, he had noticed
uniformed reservists from the local militia, members of the Pleiku and
Kontum popular force and regional force, walking with their rifles on
their shoulders and their families in hand, randomly scattered among
the endless flow of civilians. Finally, recognizing one captain from the
regional force, Lieutenant Colonel Tuan asked the man why the PF and
RF units had not executed the screening movements up and down
Highway 14, as General Phu's plan had provided.

"No one ever issued such orders to us," the captain had replied.
Then he smiled and added, "These men would not have done it anyway. You know they still would have taken their families and fled with
everyone else."

Tuan laughed and waved the captain forward. Such a failure in
communications did not surprise him at all. Nothing in this mission
had gone right. Confusion had only grown worse since the operation
began. At the redeployment's onset, even before many of the units had
assembled in the column, senior leaders had mysteriously evaporated

from the scene, scattering like cowards. Most of them had caught the last helicopter flights to the safety of the coast, leaving responsibility for the actual movement of their forces, and the risk, to their subordinate field staff and unit commanders such as himself. To a man, the generals had all disappeared well before the first trucks had even begun to roll.

TWO DAYS EARLIER

"I HAVE AUTHORITY here, not that tyro," Brigadier General Tran Van Cam growled at Colonel Le Khac Ly. The chief of staff stood wide eyed, almost speechless, and now more confused than ever, hearing the command's deputy for operations vent his indignation while the lead vehicles of the convoy sat with their engines running, prepared to depart and thus initiate the redeployment of the II Army Corps from Pleiku to the coastal plains. "Colonel, or rather should I say the recently promoted Brigadier General, Tat remains my junior. I will not take orders from any subordinate, especially not from a newly pinned brigadier!"

"General Cam, sir," Colonel Ly said politely, "I do not believe that General Pham Van Tat has issued you any orders. Therefore, I do not understand your anger."

"It is not your concern, Colonel," General Cam snapped.

"Sir," the chief of staff responded, "I am doing my best to execute Major General Phu's orders. I believe that General Tat merely reminded you that General Phu had left you behind to jointly oversee our redeployment and to coordinate with General Tat regarding our counteroffensive of Ban Me Thuot. I beg your pardon, sir, but General Phu did not hand sole command to you."

"Colonel Ly, I should charge you with insubordination right now," General Cam growled. "By virtue of my rank, I hold sole command. I share that with no one!"

"Yes, sir," Colonel Ly said respectfully.

"I cannot waste any more time standing here," General Cam fumed. "I will establish my headquarters at the point where this pitiful highway reaches the coastline, at Tuy Hoa. Unless you have something further to say to me, I am now leaving on my helicopter."

"No, sir, and good-bye, sir," Colonel Ly said, deeply relieved to see the difficult brigadier depart, and watched as the deputy for operations boarded the Huey and flew away.

"Where, pray tell, is General Tat?" Colonel Ly said, turning to the sergeant seated behind the steering wheel of the chief of staff's jeep.

"Colonel Ly," a ranger lieutenant spoke, standing by the jeep.

"Yes, lieutenant," the colonel said. He recognized the junior officer as a subordinate aide recently appointed by the newly promoted ranger brigadier.

"Begging your pardon, sir," the lieutenant said. "Brigadier General Pham Van Tat has flown to Kontum, where he has begun reorganizing the seven-thousand rangers that we have currently deployed there. Respectfully, sir, the general told me to convey his instructions that you should immediately proceed with the deployment, placing the Twentieth Combat Engineer Group at the head of the column. General Tat will execute a rear guard movement with his rangers protecting the convoy's back and flanks."

"Very well, lieutenant, but when did you last see General Tat?" Colonel Ly asked.

"Hardly more than an hour ago, on his way to Kontum," the lieutenant said. "General Tat sent me here to act as an aide for you and to serve as his fire support liaison."

"Advise the commander of the Twentieth Combat Engineers to pull his trucks forward and lead off the column," Colonel Ly said to the communications officer seated by the radio mounted in the right rear corner of his command jeep.

ON THE HILLS OVERLOOKING CHEO REO

NOW TWO FULL days on the dusty road, crawling along while even foot traffic passed by his unit's trucks, Nguyen Manh Tuan thought of General Pham Van Phu's optimism, suggesting that the redeployment along the 135-mile trek to the coast should take only one or two days. Cheo Reo, a town of Montagnards and peasant farmers and the seat of government for Phu Bon Province, stood just a few miles ahead of his trucks, below the long, gentle slope of Ban Bleik Pass, the last set of rolling hills west of the rural provincial capital before the land fell away to the coastal plains. The hamlet lay far from their goal at Tuy Hoa, nearly a hundred miles away, the point where Interprovincial Highway 7B terminated into Highway 1.

Almost since the onset of the movement, problems had emerged. Even at the moment that they departed Pleiku, Viet Cong guerrillas had begun sniping at the rangers who patrolled the column's flanks. The harassment and the losses had grown worse by the hour.

Meanwhile, adding to the friction, every damaged bridge or small water crossing seemed to present issues to the engineers who argued about how best to deal with each obstacle that they encountered. Rather than simply lowering the blade of a bulldozer and grading off a slope so that the rolling stock could bypass the problem spot, the officers had to discuss options. Where to grade? How much to grade? How deep or how steep to cut the detour? Compounding their debates, enemy mines lay in random patterns along the roadside too. Venturing off the solid track carried with it significant risk. Thus the column could only inch forward, stopping at every rise, turn and dip. They got nowhere very fast.

Now Tuan had begun to feel his intestines writhe with the onset of colic. His stomach had burned since day one of the redeployment. At first he simply dismissed the discomfort as jangled nerves. Even before departing Pleiku, he anticipated that the huge column could not go far down this road before the enemy moved on them with substantial numbers. His worry underscored why he had ordered his battalion to carry weaponry rather than personal belongings.

Whether caused by stress or a bug seemed academic to Tuan; sickness now held him firmly. His bowels rumbled and his stomach boiled.

Feeling ill troubled Tuan, not only because of health issues, but how would it affect the confidence of his men? Seeing him throwing up or worse would certainly unnerve his battalion. So Tuan kept his neckerchief pulled high on his face and worked hard to conceal his infirmity. Behind his bandana mask, he kept his disease, and his fear of imminent attack and ultimate capture or death by the enemy, cloaked.

Adding to his internal distress, Tuan's caravan of trucks, howitzers, and support jeeps had now ground to a complete stop, had shut down their engines, and had not moved for more than two hours. The bridge that crossed the wide river that stood between the final grade of the Ban Bleik Pass and Cheo Reo had much of its superstructure missing. In areas, only topless concrete columns now stood in the wide, rocky riverbed and the several narrow channels of water that flowed among the stony bars. Engineers would have to rebuild much of the structure, and the two other spans that lay just beyond it, before any vehicles could move farther.

HIGHWAY 19 AT AN KHE PASS

"SUICIDE!" Truong Quang Thi said, reading the one-page, handwritten transcription of a flash radio message. It ordered him to immediately redeploy his North Vietnamese Army light infantry battalion from its blocking position at An Khe and move southward without delay, overland along the ridges above the Song Ba and Ea Pa rivers to Ban Bleik Pass, overlooking Cheo Reo. There, his unit would attack the northern flank of the advancing II Army Corps' retreat along Interprovincial Highway 7B.

"Sir?" the administrative aide who had brought him the message said. "Suicide?"

"No, not us," Truong Quang Thi said and laughed. "I am sorry, not us. No, the enemy. It appears that they have committed suicide. They have decided that rather than standing and fighting from their well-placed, hardened defenses at Pleiku and Kontum, they will flee down a road with no bridges that eventually only leads them into a minefield. Utter suicide!"

"Ah," the soldier said and smiled.

"This message is from Lieutenant General Hoang Minh Thoa, commander of the Central Highland forces," Truong said proudly. "I had the honor to brief him, General Van Tien Dung, and General Tran Van Tra recently. General Hoang has chosen our battalion to lead the main attack. We will annihilate Pham Van Phu's army. Do you realize what significance this can have?"

"Very good luck, sir," the aide said, minimizing his words and keeping his response broad and positive so that he did not appear ignorant to his commanding officer.

"Very good luck indeed!" Truong said. "The enemy's blunder has embarked their entire force onto a great killing field that provides them no means of escape. They can now only surrender there, at Cheo Reo, or die."

JUNGLES WEST OF BAN BLEIK PASS

NGUYEN THIEN LUONG hugged the backside of a four-foot high boulder, taking cover from the sporadic fire of the company of ARVN rangers who now pursued a platoon of guerrillas from his Viet Cong battalion. For two days his soldiers had harassed the rear and flanks of the massive column of enemy troops and fleeing civilians, taking potshots to draw their security patrols away from the protection of the main force. Like a pack of hounds chasing a slow-running fox, the ARVN Rangers invariably followed the easy trail of the retreating soldiers into the crux of an ambush set by one or more of Luong's four infantry companies.

With each succeeding attack, the ranger force that had responded and pursued them had subsequently grown larger and larger. The enemy had strengthened the initial squad-sized patrols eventually to full platoons. Now, a heavily reinforced rifle company of more than four hundred ARVN rangers chased Luong and a handful of his men into a narrow, dead-end valley where the remainder of his battalion had quietly converged along each side and atop the canyon's terminal point for an afternoon slaughter.

Near the crest of the hill that Luong and his men had begun to climb, just above the place where the guerrilla commander now took cover behind the large rock, Le Van Reung lay quietly with his shoulder snugged against the butt plate of a .30-caliber machine gun that his platoon had captured in Ban Me Thuot a few days earlier. Reung and another soldier had set up the weapon inside a blind of branches and grass that served as a key firing point in today's ambush.

The two guerrillas with the machine gun could see Nguyen Thien Luong flattened against the large rock, looking up the hill at them, holding one hand with his palm showing outward, signaling the battalion to continue holding their fire. The Viet Cong commander wanted the whole attacking company of ARVN rangers fully within the ambush's killing zone when the butchery commenced, and his retreating squad of VC guerrillas safely past it.

From the vantage points of the bluffs above each flank of the valley, and from the crest of the ridge at its end, the Viet Cong battalion dominated every inch of terrain below them. They left no spot, no dead space, where even a single enemy soldier could find cover from their fire. In Le Van Reung's mind, this constituted the ideal ambush, quick and certain death to the enemy.

"They will first dive for cover," Reung whispered to his assistant, who would soon feed the belts of ammunition into the machine gun and help clear any stoppages that might occur. "Quickly, they will realize that they have no place to hide, and the more seasoned veterans will try to fight back and attack our positions. When we start killing those men, the rest of their company will disband in panic and try to run."

"Even if they do try to turn their fire into the center of our ambush and counterattack us, they will have no chance," the assistant said, reassuring Reung.

"Very true," Reung said, watching the retreating squad of Viet Cong decoys finally run past the line of their ambush, leaving only Commander Luong and the pursuing enemy company within the killing zone.

"Did you ever see a Montagnard slaughter a pig?" Reung then asked.

"No," the assistant said.

"They run the animal into a small pen," Reung said, "and they catch the pig by its hind feet and tie them to a sturdy post. Then, with an ample club they bludgeon him. They hit the animal on his head again and again. A pig has a very hard head, so this takes a little time. He fights for his life and screams violently and tries to bite his killer. He has no chance. Soon, the pig just collapses and lies still while the Montagnard cuts his throat."

"I have heard pigs slaughtered that way," the assistant said. "They scream horribly."

"These men will soon die much like the pig tied in that Montagnard's pen," Reung said. "They too will scream horribly."

Seeing his squad find safety behind the ambush line, Nguyen Thien Luong put his head down and bolted up the hill, pumping his legs as hard as he could push them. Just as he had lunged from the boulder's cover, he dramatically pointed downhill at the pursuing company of ARVN rangers, signaling his men to commence firing.

The Viet Cong commander ran a zigzagging pattern up the hill that led him no more than a step to the left of Le Van Reung and his machine gun. Bullets grazed past his churning legs, zipping through the grass and twigs only a few feet to either side of him. He had literally gambled his life on the accuracy of his men's gunfire and their discipline of remaining within the limits of their sectors of fire, allowing him just enough of a gap to escape the killing field.

On the slopes and in the ravine below him, Luong could hear the screaming and chaotic firing of the desperate South Vietnamese soldiers caught in the gristmill. From second to second, a sporadic enemy bullet hissed past his ears or popped into the mud on the slope ahead of him. Similarly, the bullets sent downhill by his men whizzed farther out from his sides, snapping and popping as they clipped branches and grass. Among the loud cracks of supersonic lead and longing whines of the ricochets came the telltale thuds accompanied by anguished cries as other projectiles found their deadly marks in the flesh and bone of men who scrambled for their lives.

Smoke from smoldering hot oil that coated Reung's gun barrel rose in white curls as he exhausted the first belt of .30-caliber bullets and ceased firing for a few seconds to lock a fresh string of linked ammunition into the weapon's breach. Even holding bursts at four to six rounds, the chains of ammo seemed to fly from the metal boxes that had contained them. In the course of only a few heartbeat-paced minutes, that to Le Van Reung seemed compressed into milliseconds, the Viet Cong guerrilla had blazed several hundred rounds downhill into the writhing mayhem of enemy troops.

Along both sides of the valley, Viet Cong soldiers poured machine gun and rifle fire into the ARVN company, filling the air with gray smoke and the smell of cordite and blood. At the same time, mortar rounds and claymore mines exploded at the rear of the enemy unit, driving the doomed rangers even more tightly into the pocket of the ambush, where the interlaced hail of bullets chewed at them like the spinning blades of a meat grinder making sausage.

In seconds, bodies piled on bodies, and the hammered men's gore spread over the rocks and drizzled into the ravine. Some soldiers threw down their rifles and raised their hands to surrender, only to fall dead as bullets ripped through them without regard. Others tried to fight back, while many more turned and ran, trying to escape the massacre.

White smoke poured from the breach of Reung's machine gun as he once again popped open the black, hinged plate that covered the weapon's receiver and bolt, and he readied it for a new string of cartridges. His assistant blindly tossed another empty, green metal box clattering down the slope in front of them as he pulled a fresh chain of rounds from a full ammo can and laid it in place, slamming shut the breach over the top of the belt.

One quick pull of the machine gun's charging handle, and Le Van

Reung sent a fresh dose of copper-jacketed, hardball death into the valley.

In minutes, the narrow ravine that cut along the bottom of the canyon clogged with ARVN dead. Bodies scattered up the slopes on each side, where men had desperately tried to escape. Only a fraction of the enemy company, less than one-quarter of their original strength, succeeded in fleeing the killing field, braving their way through a barrage of 60- 81-, and 120-millimeter mortar fire, and managing to survive a high-velocity hail of deadly ball bearings blasted at them by the exploding claymore mines that lined the route leading out. More than three hundred rangers lay dead when Nguyen Thien Luong finally commanded his battalion to cease fire.

The sudden silence startled Le Van Reung. Then came the moans and cries from the dying. Reflexively, trying to bury his emotions and move his mind from the horrible presence, the guerrilla began to hum a song about fishermen that his mother used to sing. The sight of such massive slaughter made the soldier's stomach turn, and the hardened veteran of more than ten years of close and ugly fighting had to shift his eyes from the gory scene below him and turned their attention to his smoking machine gun. He said nothing to his assistant. He wanted to make no impressions at all. So he simply busied his fingers as he hummed the old song, checking the weapon, careful to not burn his hands on the hot metal. While death came in his life almost daily, he had never celebrated killing.

BRIDGE REPAIRS AT EASTERN EDGE OF CHEO REO

THE SHARP TASTE of vomit stayed on Nguyen Manh Tuan's pallet, like red wine stain on a white shirt. He could not rid his tongue of its nastiness no matter how much he spit. Acid fumes from the foul spew seemed to color the smell of everything that entered his nostrils too.

While only vacuous liquid had refluxed this time, it had burned his throat and sinuses much worse than when the lieutenant colonel had upchucked the greater portion of his lunch just a half hour earlier. Drizzling water out of his canteen, he soaked the green bandana that he had previously worn tied across his face to stop the road dust and now wiped his brow, eyes, cheeks, and nose with it. The cool wetness against his flushed skin felt good. Then he spat again, trying to clean from his mouth more of the bad-tasting, sick-stomach residue.

He had just finished taking yet another short stroll, one of several already this day, among the bushes and brushy mounds that spread on each side of the road west of Cheo Reo, where he had surreptitiously cleared his bowels and his stomach. As he meandered back toward his stalled unit, rubbing the damp kerchief on his throat and neck, he noticed a familiar figure among a group of soldiers, plodding along the traffic-jammed roadside.

"Colonel Tuan, when you have finished your business, come speak to me," Colonel Le Khac Ly said to the approaching artillery commander, sighing as he collapsed onto the passenger seat of Nguyen Manh Tuan's parked jeep and then unlacing his hot and dusty boots.

"Sir," Tuan said as he wiped his mouth with the wet bandana and then spread the green cloth on the hood of his jeep to dry. "I am pleasantly surprised to see you."

"Thank you, but it is not a pleasant mission that brings me here, Lieutenant Colonel Tuan," Ly said, stretching his legs while still seated and letting his socked feet dangle and cool in the breeze. "I have walked nearly thirty miles in the past day and a half, working my way up here to take charge of the madness that has caused our column to sit still and fester while the enemy increasingly harasses our flanks and surely closes on us at this very moment."

"That is why I am pleasantly surprised to see you," Tuan said. "The engineers' endless conferring with no real action initiated needs the decisive foot of leadership placed squarely into their endless discussions."

"At the very least, my friend," Ly said and smiled, clearly agreeing with the observation. "I sent a captain and two lieutenants ahead of me, to the bridge work, to convey my displeasure at this chaos and to announce my presence here. Perhaps, by the time I get my boots laced back on my feet and walk these last few hundred steps to the river, the engineers will have finally concluded on a plan, and we can get on with crossing this bloody river. Right now, we are like the man lying in hospital, dying with a bullet lodged in his stomach, and the surgeons reluctant to take it out for fear that their operation will kill him. Immediate action just might save the poor wretch. Delay will only assure his death."

"Sir," Tuan said quietly, "I am deeply concerned that the enemy will attack us while we sit. We have poor defenses here and little room for countermeasures. While these low dunes and scrub thickets offer us no real cover, they do present a large enough blind to allow the enemy a means for rapid maneuver in an assault. I have tried to deploy my guns and have managed to get a few placed along the roadside here, to give us some flanking cover. In all practical terms, however, where we stand now, my guns provide us little more than a boost to our troops' morale. Positioned at a narrow point on the low ground, surrounded on three sides by much higher terrain, represents very poor tactics and an unenviable set of circumstances. If we can just get across this ford so that we can deploy my artillery in a more appropriate fan and give this column some decent fire support, we might then have a glimmer of hope."

"Feathers in the wind, my dear colonel. Spinning feathers, flurrying in a gale. I am afraid that what little hope we held at the beginning of this foolish parade has now dwindled to nothing, your artillery fan withstanding," Colonel Ly said in a hushed voice, sighing as he spoke. "General Tat and his rangers have repelled constant harassment by the Viet Cong, and it is only a matter of time before all of the NVA divisions in this region converge a full-scale attack on us. On my way here, I ordered the Twenty-third Ranger Group to immediately deploy their forces into guard positions above us on Ban Bleik Pass, where I expect that the enemy will initiate their main infantry assault. I also suspect that they have reserve forces and artillery converging beyond the far side of Cheo Reo, with the objective of establishing blocking positions there, to hold us here while their units staged on the high ground annihilate us. Hopefully, the Twenty-third Rangers can buy time so that these engineers can finish repairs on this crossing. If we can manage to bridge the river before those NVA blocking forces get in place, then some of these people might succeed at making a run for the sea. Beyond here, the terrain improves, and so does this road. However, like you, I am confident that the enemy sees this too and moves fast upon us."

TRUONG QUANG THI awoke with a jerk, hearing the thunder from the predawn barrage striking below him, on the lower slopes of Ban Bleik Pass. He smiled as he raised his head and leaned on one elbow to see the impact of the exploding shells launched by artillery batteries of his own 320th NVA Division and sister batteries from the Tenth NVA Division. They had maneuvered their guns through a day and a night into blocking positions east of Cheo Reo, effectively closing the highway there. From those firing emplacements, they now converged their bombardment on the South Vietnamese rangers, who had until this moment successfully repelled the infantry assaults of Truong's battalion.

Rather than waiting for coordinating forces the previous day, Truong had begun his attack early, on his own initiative, once he saw the II Army Corps begin movement across the bridges that they had finally repaired. His hit-and-run tactics succeeded in distracting and, thereby, stalling much of the column, while only a handful of vehicles and people managed to trickle past the bridges and flee eastward.

While the rangers had chased his illusive forces, he watched, in the dimming light of that evening's setting sun, as many of the people still trapped on the roadway had celebrated their small victory. Among them, Colonel Le Khac Ly reluctantly accepted congratulations from Lieutenant Colonel Nguyen Manh Tuan.

"I think we may finally reach the coast," Tuan had said happily, intoxicated by the jubilance that now surrounded him.

"Yes, as long as our rangers show such fierceness to the enemy, he may think twice about attacking us again in such a way. We surely do have good fortune presently on our side," Colonel Ly had replied, knowing well that his words only offered false hope.

"I wish that we could move the traffic more rapidly across these narrow bridges," Nguyen Manh Tuan told the colonel, looking at the creeping jam of vehicles and people waiting a turn to finally cross the rivers to apparent freedom.

"Unfortunately, that will be a task that you and other battalion commanders must oversee on your own," Colonel Ly said in a low voice.

"What do you mean, sir?" Tuan said, a sudden sense of alarm seizing him. "Your decisive leadership has saved the day for us! Will you now leave?"

"Yes, Colonel Tuan," Ly said. "General Pham Van Phu has ordered me to join him at Nha Trang, since it appears that we have overcome this last obstacle and the remaining task seems only to press this column forward to Tuy Hoa. The commander requires my services in his planning for the recapture of Ban Me Thuot."

*   *   *

IN THAT SAME evening light, but from a rock face overlooking Cheo Reo and the long, slowly moving column of traffic, the North Vietnamese battalion commander, Truong Quang Thi, watched a solitary South Vietnamese helicopter land by the bridges where one man then climbed aboard the aircraft and departed. Truong confidently suspected that the aircraft had taken with it the last of the enemy force's senior officers, abandoning their subordinate, expendable leaders and the bulk of their forces to the Communist onslaught.

Now crouched by a small breakfast fire in the shadowy grayness of predawn, sipping hot tea and eating a warm bowl of rice, Truong rocked on his heels as artillery shells exploded in the heart of the ranger positions and stalled line of traffic on the ridges and roadway below him. At first light, his infantry forces would again move forward, but today they would attack with a determination fed by the blood scent of certain victory.

DIRT CAKED NINH'S eyes, clogging them shut with grit that bit with searing pain into their soft flesh. She whimpered, but no one answered her. What little she could see hid in blackness.

When the tiny girl tried to breathe, the weight of the metal debris and broken wood from what was once the handcart and its heavy cargo that her mother had pulled pressed against her lungs, causing severe pain. It cut short her breathing, and she tried to cry. However, the daughter of the two peasants who now lay dead in the roadway could manage only choppy gasps. Desperate, she finally sang out a pitiful pule in what sounded to Nguyen Manh Tuan a dying child's voice.

"Mama!" the three-year-old Ninh Ca sobbed as the tall, kind man who had found her under the wreckage of her family's only possessions held her close to his heart. Tears rolled from the lieutenant colonel's eyes as he comforted the lone survivor of the nearby blast of a 120-millimeter mortar.

"Hold tight to me, daughter," Tuan whispered to the baby, sheltering her head under his chin. "Hold to me as tightly as you can."

Just then, several more 120-millimeter mortar projectiles exploded in a salvo that began landing only fifty yards ahead of him, and the lieutenant colonel dove off the roadway, skidding down the rocks and dirt on his shoulder, clutching the baby girl at his breast. Thick dust, stones, and more debris showered over him as he cupped his hands over the child's face, protecting her from the fallout.

Calmly Tuan whispered, "This will soon stop, and we will leave this place and find your family. Until then, I will keep you safe with me. For now, little daughter, keep your head close to my chest."

The countless fires ignited by the explosions lit the smoke-filled morning darkness bright orange. Tuan had barely escaped the first strikes of the Communist artillery bombardment as his entire convoy of trucks and the howitzers that they towed took direct hits. The ammunition the trucks carried detonated in secondary blasts, leveling everything and everyone near them.

Shrapnel from the truck exploding immediately behind his jeep had killed his driver instantly, blowing a ten-inch-wide hole completely through the soldier's back and out his chest. Another foot-long chunk of iron smashed between the driver and passenger and drove the vehicle's dashboard into its engine. In that same split second, Tuan had leaped from his seat and felt himself propelled through the air by the concussion from the secondary detonation of the truck's cargo.

Lying on his back, choking on the smoke and dirt that engulfed him, Tuan quickly realized that his command had suddenly terminated. If he wished to live, he should now focus on taking care of himself.

Tuan found a nearby ravine where he snuggled until the barrage moved to targets away from him. Then he crept out of his hiding place and ventured back to the roadway to see how many of his men had survived.

As he worked his way up the trail of wreckage that had once represented his artillery battalion, dead bodies and utter destruction greeted him. Cries of badly wounded soldiers and civilians surrounded him. If any of his men had survived unscathed, they had, like him, dashed for shelter off the roadway, but he could find none who had returned.

The lieutenant colonel felt the grip of fear tightening in his throat, and he too wanted to run. He wanted to join those who now sought escape through the thickets of low bushes and dunes that spread from the hills above Cheo Reo and stretched across the wide, dark landscape. However, Nguyen Manh Tuan abdicated his fear to a stronger force that had burned within him since his youth, a quality he had cultivated at the United States Army Command and General Staff College and at artillery school at Fort Sill, Oklahoma: his sense of integrity. His very honor.

This dusty, disheveled, badly broken soldier believed that in life others can take virtually everything from a person, money, home, even the person's life, except for one thing, one's honor. For a man to lose his honor, he must give it up by his own will.

In the darkness he could see peasants beginning to dig in the rubble, looking for their loved ones. He could hear the moans of the wounded, who needed his help. He knew that he could not abandon these people now. How could he otherwise live with himself? As badly as he wanted to survive and live free, cowardice did not exist within Nguyen Manh Tuan.

The enemy at the very least would imprison him, perhaps for the rest of his life. They even might execute him, because of his rank. However, Tuan knew that they could never take his honor. So he decided to stay and help his people and face his fate.

Tears streamed from his eyes as he pulled the twisted steel and broken bits of wood from atop the little girl whose tiny, weak voice had caught his ears. When he finally had wrenched her from the debris, he held her to his heart because she represented the cause for which he had dedicated his entire life. This unknown child to him now meant the world, and he loved her.

"PASS THE ORDER for the battalion to advance on the enemy," Truong Quang Thi told his radio operator.

Suddenly, along the lower slopes of Ban Bleik Pass, bugles from his companies echoed, and men shouted war cries as they charged forward.

In the golden light of the early morning, as far as he could see, lines of several thousand North Vietnamese and Viet Cong soldiers rushed across the landscape. It was a sight even Truong could never have imagined in even his most far-fetched dreams.

Other battalions had joined the line with his and now moved in a final thrust on a defeated enemy. In front of them, soldiers ran or threw up their hands. The few who tried to make a stand died.

Three days of bombardment now ended. Truong knew the fighting would end by sunset this day, March 21, 1975.

The bugles' sounds caught Nguyen Manh Tuan's ears, and he straightened his back, holding Ninh Ca crooked in his right arm. Several other newly orphaned children followed close to his side, and a growing crowd of fearful adults stood behind them with what remained of their families.

"We must try to maneuver around their lines and strive to make it to the coast," Tuan told the people who gathered in rapidly increasing numbers behind him. "Their infantry has now launched their assault and will catch us here if we do not hurry."

With the sun rising rapidly, spreading bright daylight across the bushy landscape, Tuan saw his chances to slip past the encircling enemy lines diminishing. Perhaps if only he and the little girl could move alone, they could still slip through. However, with a half dozen waifs clutching his sides and a throng of panic-stricken peasants running close with him, the attacking soldiers would quickly take them down.

Tuan had led the people hardly more than a kilometer when he saw the line of black-clad soldiers.

"*Chu hoi*," Tuan shouted to them and held his left arm high above his head, while still clutching Ninh Ca. "Please, do not shoot us. I am only trying to protect these children. Please allow them to live."

"Stand still, then," Nguyen Thien Luong growled at the tall ARVN officer who held the child. "We do not intentionally harm children, as I have seen your soldiers do."

Tuan bowed his head respectfully to this man who obviously held a significant rank, commanding a company or even a battalion. He knew to keep his mouth shut and not argue the truth that he also knew, seeing the bodies of children shot by Viet Cong in their attacks on villages sympathetic to the South Vietnamese government.

Seeing the enemy force, many of the people who had followed Tuan turned and ran. In an instant, shots burst from the line of black-clad soldiers, dropping several of the fleeing peasants.

"Please, sir," Tuan begged, "these people have no place to go. They cannot escape you. Please, sir, do not shoot them."

The Viet Cong battalion commander nodded to a nearby soldier and said, "They are unarmed. Just gather them up."

A company then swept in a closing circle, firing intermittently in the air to halt the peasants.

"Now, what is your name, Lieutenant Colonel?" Nguyen Thien Luong said in a stern, commanding voice.

"I am Nguyen Manh Tuan," Tuan responded, still bowing his head respectfully.

"Your unit?" Luong then asked.

"Destroyed, sir," Tuan answered.

"What of these people?" Luong then asked.

"Peasants and orphans," Tuan said. "After losing my command, I set about trying to keep these children safe. The peasants merely followed me, believing that I might deliver them also to safety."

"This child that you carry?" Luong asked.

"A baby I found buried beneath a cart," Tuan said. "Her parents lie back there on the road. I hoped to find her kin who might take her."

Ninh Ca clutched tightly to Tuan's neck and looked fearfully at the growing crowd of black-clad men and women who looked back at her. Some of them smiled at her, but the terror of the past two days left her stoic.

Then, among the crowd of faces, one familiar man began to laugh and clap his hands. Ninh's eyes brightened seeing him, and she smiled too.

The little girl had said nothing after crying for her mother when Tuan had found her, but now she found her voice.

"Uncle, uncle," she said and put out her hands toward the familiar man.

"Sir, sir," the man stepped forward, bowing to his battalion commander, Nguyen Thien Luong. "This baby is my sister's child. Her family were farmers who lived north of Pleiku."

"We cannot take children this young with us," Luong reminded the soldier. "She will be safe in the compound with the other peasants."

"My wife is nearby, sir," Ninh's uncle then offered. "I need only one day to take her there."

Luong thought for a moment and then looked at Ninh. Her dark eyes and innocent face weighed heavy on his heart, and he smiled at her.

"Take her, then," he said. "Move to the rear, and depart when you can safely do so. Report to me personally tomorrow morning that she is safely with your wife."

Tuan smiled at Ninh and kissed her cheek as he passed the little girl to her uncle. He looked at the half dozen other orphans and then at Luong.

"We will care for these children, Lieutenant Colonel," Luong said. "Do not concern yourself for them any longer. I hope that you will now concern yourself with your own prospects. Cooperate, and we will treat you appropriately well. Refuse, and we will shoot you. Quite a simple proposition, I think."

That day Nguyen Manh Tuan began what would be eight years of imprisonment and "re-education." He would not see his wife nor his two sons until after those eight years in prison had ended and he found himself living as a homeless man, begging on the streets of Saigon, fixing bicycles for pennies a day, with no tools except his fingers and what he could borrow from his clients. While he was in prison, his wife had renounced him and had remarried. His sons later emigrated to America.

For twenty years Nguyen Manh Tuan struggled, yet he again rose to greatness, founding a scissors-manufacturing firm, building it from scraps he scavenged in Saigon's garbage dumps.

Ninh Ca grew up in her uncle's and aunt's care and became a secretary in the Communist government office in Pleiku.

Forces from the 10th and the 320th NVA Divisions killed unknown thousands in the three days of artillery bombardment of the retreating ARVN II Army Corps and the civilians who fled Pleiku and Kontum with them. Estimates of the retreat range from 160,000 to 250,000 people. Of that exodus, only a handful of civilians ever reached the coast. More than 90 percent of the strength of the II Army Corps and the Fourth, Twenty-fifth, and Twenty-third Ranger Groups fell or were taken prisoner. Fewer than 900 of the ARVN rangers ever made it to Nha Trang, and less than 5,000 other soldiers of the II Army Corps escaped death or capture. None of those nearly 6,000 survivors of the massacre at Cheo Reo were in any condition to fight.

The loss at Cheo Reo ended any hope that President Nguyen Van Thieu held for retaking the Central Highlands and Ban Me Thuot.

In less than ten days the Communists succeeded in capturing all six provinces that comprised the Central Highlands. The North Vietnamese and Viet Cong divisions then turned their strength to the remaining ARVN forces protecting the coastal provinces and quickly captured them with little resistance. Only the Twenty-second ARVN Division in Binh Dinh Province, defending their stronghold at Qui Nhon, and the ARVN Third Airborne Brigade at Khanh Hoa stood and fought against the overwhelming Communist forces. However, those units fell quickly, and in a matter of days following the annihilation of the ARVN II Army at Cheo Reo, the entire central region of South Vietnam had fallen, now dividing the nation and cutting off the northern provinces.

Cities such as Hue, Da Nang, Dong Ha, Phu Bai, and Chu Lai now stood on their own and could hope for no help of reinforcement from units remaining south of Nha Trang.

Chapter 9

A COUNTRY APART

AN HOUR BEFORE dawn, Lieutenant General Ngo Quang Truong sat on the corner of his desk at MR 1 headquarters, at Da Nang Air Base, looking at the immense tactical map of South Vietnam that he had displayed on a pair of three-legged stands in his office. The general did not sleep much these days, usually no more than three to five hours after working until midnight most nights. His staff fared little better, just as the skeletonized army that he led. Despite the apparent blindness of his seniors, Truong clearly saw the tea leaves in the bottom of the cup, fearing the worst while fighting the Communist enemy on one front and the ineptitude of his own government's leaders on the other. A good night's sleep represented a luxury that today no one under his command could afford.

Red grease-pencil lines and boxes and paper-flag pins marked positions of Communist forces and the suspected locations of their command posts. Clearly, even a schoolboy could conclude from the crimson swath on the acetate overlay, covering the Central Highlands, that the whole nation now stood in jeopardy.

The Latin phrase, *abscidi dissaeptum debello*, "divide and conquer," repeated itself again and again in his mind. He had first heard the words in secondary school, learning of the classical battle tactics employed by the Roman legions.

"They have divided us; now they will strive to conquer," he said between sips of warm tea.

"Sir?" his senior aide, a major, said to him while standing in the general's office doorway.

"Oh, just talking to myself," Truong said and smiled.

"Sorry, sir," the major said. "Understood. However, I have President Thieu's secretary holding on the line for you. When you are ready, he will connect your call to the president, who will speak to you shortly."

General Truong walked behind his desk, sat, and opened a large note binder where he had written a short list of discussion topics that would efficiently guide his conversation and ensure that he did not overlook any important points. The first item addressed the disastrous events currently unfolding at Cheo Reo with the II Army Corps. The second posed the question as to which direction the Communists would attack once they had secured the Central Highlands.

"Sir," General Truong said as President Nguyen Van Thieu answered the telephone.

"Do not lecture me, General," Thieu snapped before the Military Region 1 commander had hardly spoken to him.

"I do not lecture my commander. I advise him, sir," General Truong answered. "What currently befalls our forces deploying from Pleiku and Kontum cannot now be undone. My duty this morning is to address what we can do today to defend against what surely descends upon us tomorrow."

"Well spoken, General, and I take your comments to heart," President Thieu said in a voice softened with the humiliation he felt from his losses in the Central Highlands.

"With three full North Vietnamese infantry divisions, supported by unknown legions of tanks and artillery, pressing upon our II Army Corps, I anticipate their demise at Cheo Reo in one or perhaps two more days," Truong began.

"Painfully, I agree with your assessment of that situation," Thieu answered.

"You have already deployed General Toan's forces from An Loc to the Saigon defense area. From my command here, you have also deployed to emplacements south of Vung Tao all of the Airborne Division except for the remaining First Airborne Brigade, which will deploy to Vung Tao today, unless you reconsider your original order in light of what we may soon face of the enemy coming from the Central Highlands," General Truong said.

"That is correct, General," Thieu said. "What do you propose?"

"Sir, that you reconsider and allow the First Airborne Brigade to remain here," General Truong said. "I also beg that you will redeploy the Airborne Division back to their posts here.

"Please consider that once the Communists have finished their tasks in the Central Highlands, I anticipate that they will most probably turn their full attentions to our positions here in the north. At the very least, they will use a portion of those forces to block us here and to reinforce their operating divisions in my area. Once Military Region 1 has fallen, they can then most easily close their combined forces on Saigon from the north, west, and east.

"Already we have suffered significant losses in and around Hue, and the attack tempo there increases by the hour. The buildup of tanks and logistics that we detected three months ago in the western mountains have now fully deployed toward our coastal enclaves.

"I fear that the boost of morale and the additional strength of captured arms that the Communists gain in their victory in the Central Highlands will enable their army to overwhelm us in a matter of days, unless we receive immediate reinforcement.

"Morale among my forces falters. Already, just this morning, I have received messages that our units all along the Demilitarized Zone, in Quang Tri City, and throughout Quang Tri Province have begun abandoning their posts with first sight of enemy forces massing in their presence. In instances, they have fled without firing a shot. Tonight, on your map, you can paint the entire Quang Tri Province red. It will surely fall to the Communists unopposed before the day ends.

"Day and night, our forces at Quang Ngai and Tam Ky fiercely defend their strongholds against increasing numbers of enemy units. Likewise, our soldiers, rangers, and Marines defend Hue and Hoi An. This morning Chu Lai has begun receiving fire. Meanwhile, here at Da Nang, the attacks have steadily grown in numbers and frequency since January. The enemy currently prepares us as a softened piece of steel, lying on his anvil, awaiting his hammer.

"Sir, Mr. President, please hear me. Unless you leave the forces here in place, and unless you reinforce these units before the enemy strikes with his main offensive, the northern provinces will join the Central Highlands in defeat before this month ends."

"Nonsense!" President Thieu fumed. "How can you speak of defeat? I order you to hold Da Nang to a man!"

"Sir," General Truong said, "to a man we will fight, and we will hold our ground, but once we are dead, we can fight no more. The enemy will hold our ground. Once we are dead here, you must ultimately face the whole of the enemy there.

"It is urgent that you redeploy the Airborne Division to Da Nang and Hue. I further ask that you also draw for us reinforcements from among the ample reserve forces that you have currently garrisoned at posts surrounding Saigon."

Nguyen Van Thieu said nothing for several seconds, considering what he had just heard from one of the nation's most revered frontline commanders.

"General, I will grant you this," President Thieu said angrily. "You may hold the First Airborne Brigade at Da Nang, but that is all that I will yield.

"Furthermore, in light of your concerns, I suggest that you seriously consider redeploying to Da Nang and Hue the many Marine units that you currently have scattered over the four winds in MR 1. However, all reserves and standing forces now in MR 3, including the majority of your Airborne Division, must remain here to protect Saigon. Saigon shall not fall. No matter what the cost, Saigon must endure!

"Unless you have something further to discuss with me, I have more pressing matters than your overly stated, dramatic tales to attend."

Before the general could even respond, President Thieu had hung up. The click of the suddenly broken connection and the hum of the dial tone that followed left Lieutenant General Ngo Quang Truong feeling hopeless, bewildered, and speechless.

The small man sighed deeply and laid his telephone receiver back in its cradle. He stood and then walked slowly to the large map of South Vietnam. On the clear plastic overlay the general began to draw with red grease pencil a series of narrow, parallel lines, using them to shade the entire area that represented Quang Tri Province. He wrote a large, red X over the provincial capital, Quang Tri City. Then he artfully drew three long, wide, arching red arrows, representing each of the three North Vietnamese Army divisions now operating in the Central Highlands and pointed them toward Hue, Chu Lai, and Da Nang.

MAI THAO VILLA IN NORTHWEST SAIGON

"COME INSIDE, MY beautiful flower, sit, and have a cocktail," Mai Thao told Kieu Chinh as he pushed open the iron gate to his villa's courtyard. "Tran Da Tu and Nha Ca will arrive momentarily. I look forward to a wonderful evening with three lovely friends."

Kieu blushed as she stepped past her longtime confidant, South Vietnam's leading novelist who had authored forty books in little more than twenty years of writing professionally, during which time he had also served as publisher and editor in chief of several major newspapers. Flamboyant and outspoken, Thao, a staunch supporter of the American-allied government and a longtime friend of former Premier Nguyen Cao Ky, lived in a plush French-style home surrounded by high stone and stucco walls, located in the northwestern district of Saigon, near Tan Son Nhut Airport.

Respected as a national treasure, Mai Thao often hosted elegant parties for small gatherings of his closest friends, such as that tonight, which included South Vietnam's leading international actress, Kieu Chinh, and two of the nation's most renowned authors, poet Tran Da Tu and his wife, novelist and poet Nha Ca. Most recently writing about the political executions, massacres, and other atrocities committed by the Communists when they overran Hue in the 1968 Tet Offensive, Nha Ca achieved national acclaim and received accolades for the work by the Saigon regime while leaders in Hanoi denounced her writings and labeled her an enemy of the people.

"Terrible business today, news of what has happened in the Central Highlands," Thao said, following Kieu across his home's richly polished mahogany floors to a long, jade green and golden silk embroidered couch where she sat.

"Martini?"

"Yes, thank you," Kieu said, taking a cocktail from an assortment of a half dozen freshly made drinks joggling in elegant crystal stemware on a silver tray held by Thao's white-jacketed houseboy.

"We will eat dinner as soon as our two wayward poets arrive,"

Thao said, taking a glass from the servant and sitting on a white-on-white silk brocaded armchair across from Kieu. "Meanwhile, thanks to their tardiness, we can have a quiet, intimate chat, and you can tell me all about your stardom and this new motion picture that you are making in Singapore."

"As a matter of fact, I fly back to Singapore on Sunday," Kieu said. "We resume shooting on Monday, and I doubt that I can come home again until mid-May at the very earliest. The producers have just now fully funded the budget, and because of it, they put us on a very ambitious schedule. We will film day and night with hardly a moment allowed for relaxation."

"Oh, so much work, it will make you old before your time, my flower," Thao said. "Perhaps I should fly to Singapore with you, to manage your daily affairs?"

"Or to have an affair? You would only serve to corrupt me, dear," Kieu said and laughed. "Your reputation precedes you, I am afraid."

"Lies, all lies," Thao said, gulping the last of his cocktail and then popping the olive into his mouth. "I drink too much, that is all. Otherwise, I behave myself quite respectably. You would not be here tonight if I did not, would you?"

Kieu Chinh laughed while her old friend gracefully swept up her hand and kissed it as he stepped to a black lacquer side table, where the houseboy had left the silver tray, and took another martini from it.

"What is this news that you spoke of earlier, this thing that has happened in the Central Highlands?" Kieu asked innocently.

"Perhaps I overly concern myself with the current events because they seem so terrible to my American journalist friends," Thao said. They have gone quite abuzz about this latest situation.

"According to their reports, it seems that our army has suffered a massive loss on an obscure roadway near a Montagnard village somewhere east of Pleiku. A large number of military units moving to the coast, along with a multitude of civilians fleeing with them, attacked and annihilated."

"Oh, yes, I saw a news report on Saigon television this afternoon, but they hardly mentioned any detail about it," Kieu said. "Besides, that place is quite a long way from Saigon. I do not understand the panic. This is not such an unusual thing, is it? It seems these sorts of things happen all the time."

"Oh, yes, tragically, they do, and to both sides," Thao said. "However, we should not fret. The armies all apparently weather the storms, as do we. Another cocktail, my dear?"

UNITED STATES CONSULATE, DA NANG

STAFF SERGEANT WALTER Sparks whistled happily as he jogged down the stairs from the second-deck balcony at the rear of the consulate's courtyard. While he liked and respected Deputy Consul General Terry Tull, the comfort of now having Consul General Al Francis again at the helm in Da Nang boosted the Marine's confidence.

Still whistling, Sparks joined an invitation-only gaggle of a half dozen members of the consulate staff, both senior and junior in rank, loitering outside the conference room doorway, coffee mugs and armloads of files and binders in hand. They waited on the outdoor walkway, mingling and talking nervously prior to the unusual early morning meeting.

The consul general had handpicked each of these people, not as a matter of political propriety or by their status in the hierarchy, but as a matter of potential life or death, liberty or incarceration. Each person possessed special qualifications that Al Francis regarded as vital to the successful evacuation of Da Nang. In light of the circumstances, it did not matter to him what rank or billet any of them held. To prevent confusion, miscommunication, and inefficiency from the normal bureaucratic layers of staff clearing other staff, he had pared the number of individuals he chose as key players down to this crew of six.

Francis had spent the prior day, while en route to Da Nang on his return flight from Saigon, dropping in on what remained of the consulate's outposts at Hue, Tam Ky, and Quang Ngai. At each location, the situation seemed to grow more desperate by the hour. Refugees from the outlying countryside now choked the cities' streets. Chaos predominated throughout the region. All things considered, he was thankful for his deputy's foresight and the precautionary actions she had taken in his absence.

Despite Ambassador Graham Martin's directive that no one should do anything that might provoke a lack of confidence among the population, Terry Tull had quietly withdrawn the bulk of the consulate staff from the outlying offices. This reduced the personnel numbers at those sites so that if and when the time came to bug out, it would take only one or two helicopter flights to evacuate the people who had remained to keep the stations functioning.

Additionally, during the past week, Tull had directed that the staff members who kept the consulate branch open in Hue had to spend their nights in Da Nang, commuting daily over the Hai Van Pass. Now with the crush of refugees flooding the old imperial capital, and enemy forces increasing their onslaught at the city gates, the Hue office had virtually closed for most practical purposes.

"Come inside and have a seat, gentlemen," Al Francis said, stepping briskly down the walkway and into the conference room.

Walter Sparks found his typical seat, against the wall, next to the door. Francis gave him a quick look and said, "Gunny, I need you here at the table with the rest of us."

The staff sergeant smiled, feeling suddenly legitimized in his presence, designated as one of the half dozen key people to deal with this crisis, chosen from among the more than fifty-member mix of intelligence, security, and embassy staff based at the consulate.

"It goes without saying," Francis began, "our discussions at this table today, and those related hereafter, cannot go beyond this inner circle, what I have code named the Black Box. Wolfgang Lehmann, our ambassador pro tem, assures me in our daily chats that South Vietnam shall stand. In those conversations, he reminds me that we must do everything possible to reassure the Vietnamese nationals that the United States will remain standing tenaciously alongside them during these uneasy times. In other words, any precautionary actions that we take must remain secretive so that we do not panic the natives."

"Sir," a junior CIA logistician said, "my colleagues in Washington tell me that Ambassador Martin has gone on record, assuring everyone that by next year South Vietnam will again control Ban Me Thuot. He has even invited some people on a tour there next spring. In light of what we see around us here, and now our preparations for possible evacuation, don't you find it a bit presumptive?"

"I hope that the ambassador is correct in his projections," Francis responded. "Our work today is simply preparing for the worst, while hoping for the best. I still have confidence that the ARVN may rally and turn the tide. Granted, this is the most serous aggression since the 1968 Tet Offensive, but I still share the ambassador's hope, presumptive or not."

Walter Sparks had heard the same story about Ambassador Martin's boastful prediction and his stubborn insistence that things were not nearly as bad as they seemed. The Marine, however, did not share even the slight hope that Al Francis still claimed to harbor. Sparks believed that the consul general simply acted out of loyalty to his longtime colleague, the ambassador. Stories that Sparks had heard, however, convinced him that Graham Martin had shut his mind to the obvious and had begun to actually believe his own wishful rhetoric. Contrarily, Sparks, as well as a growing number of the consul staff, now held strong concerns that the end for Da Nang loomed, perhaps in a matter of days.

Most recently, in the face of this impending doom, the ambassador had told several members of the national press corps, based in Washington, DC, that South Vietnam's northern provinces, including the ancient imperial capital of Hue and the city of Da Nang, in pragmatic terms, amounted to hardly more than a trifle. Despite the loss of land and natural resources, and the predominantly rural populations of mostly peasants who dwelled there, it meant very little in a national context, both socially and economically. He had said that these regions represented a far greater liability to the government of South Vietnam than an asset for them. Martin had offered that even with the possible loss of Military Regions 1 and 2, which he emphatically discounted, the nation in the larger scheme would suffer little impact.

Such a comment stirred the staff sergeant's anger to a rolling boil. After all, these northern provinces represented the land for which countless Marines had fought and bled to hold secure. I Corps had, until now, represented an important enough asset for America to spend tens of thousands of its sons' lives defending.

With those thoughts turning in his head, Walter Sparks unconsciously chewed a ragged path around the yellow pencil he had brought for note keeping, while the junior officers' small talk rambled. As he mindlessly gnawed the pencil's wood, he noticed an expression of irritation begin to creep across Al Francis's face. The staff sergeant cracked a smile, recognizing the look and awaiting the potentially sharp reaction. The consul general saw the spreading grin on the Marine's face and smiled too, letting out a sigh and a halfhearted laugh.

"Gentlemen," Francis said, "the gunny and I have some important matters to discuss. So, shall we leave the political opinion letting at the coffee bar?"

With the comment, Francis tossed on the table, toward the young, blushing CIA logistician whose commentary had momentarily side-tracked the meeting, a thirty-six-page stack of typewritten papers, stapled in three places down one side, like a small-town telephone book.

"First of all," the consul general said, "boil this evacuation plan down to one or two pages of bulleted topics. Stick with the main objectives, and forget the minutia. If we have to use it, we'll probably end up improvising the whole thing anyway. You have twenty-four hours to get it done.

"From this moment until I say otherwise, we at this table will remain on call, around the clock. Do not put yourself out of pocket.

"One does not have to be a Yale graduate to appreciate the magnitude of the task, should it come, of evacuating the consulate, other Americans, other foreigners, and friendly nationals whose lives would be in jeopardy if they fell into enemy hands. When we count noses, our people here and the plethora of American contractors in Da Nang, and we include as well the American military deserters in our area, the number quickly surpasses ten thousand people. This does not include those friendly foreigners who could represent another several thousand. At this point, I cannot come close to even estimating the number of local nationals we may desire to evacuate. Conservatively, I would calculate that their numbers could easily double ours. So the message seems clear to me: If we evacuate, it will be absolutely chaotic and very dangerous for everyone concerned.

"While we have ample United States Navy ships sailing offshore, and we had hoped to use their helicopter lift capabilities to serve as our principle transport, it appears that we cannot count on them to come get us after all. At least that is the present word from Saigon. They have concerns that using American military assets may violate the congressional mandate prohibiting the use of any and all United States military forces in Southeast Asia. In light of that interpretation, the defense attaché has suggested a work-around solution: American civilian maritime shipping. Albeit they remain under control of the navy, the vessels are still technically civilian ships and are therefore not affected. So we may well be looking at Sea-Land Express as our ticket out.

"Our intelligence staff and I have had some progress lining up Air America to transport the consulate personnel to safety, but they do not have aircraft assets to handle the greater numbers of Americans, friendly foreign nationals, and qualified Vietnamese. So the by-sea option seems the most plausible for them.

"With that consideration, I think that our immediate objective will be to line up a flotilla of vessels upon which we can transport as many as thirty to fifty thousand people from the docks across the street, down the Han River, and out to sea and the awaiting cargo ships. Gunny Sparks, we might call it a Marine Corps amphibious landing, in reverse, so to speak.

"With that said," Francis concluded, "I will take a helicopter trip to Hue, later this morning, escorting the American press who have gathered here for the grand bloodletting, and I must try to convince them that all remains well. Hue still stands, and the sky is not falling."

DENSELY FORESTED HILLS NORTHWEST OF BAN ME THUOT

"GOOD AFTERNOON, TRAN," General Van Tien Dung said to his colleague, General Tran Van Tra. "Please join me, and have a cup of tea."

The two Communist commanders sat on metal folding chairs at a small, square folding table beneath a camouflage net at the North Vietnamese Army field headquarters near Ban Me Thuot.

"I have excellent news to tell you," General Dung said, while pouring hot tea in a small clay cup for Tran Van Tra. "Hanoi has agreed that we must step up our operations and take full advantage of the initiative now established by our forces. We must think of this campaign not as a step toward ultimate victory, but as the final thrust for victory itself!"

Tran Van Tra smiled quietly, taking off his glasses and cleaning their lenses with his handkerchief. The round-faced, balding man thought of the long endeavor that he began as hardly more than a boy alongside Ho Chi Minh, first fighting the Japanese. After that, he joined the Viet Minh to combat the French. Then came the Americans and their puppet regime in the south.

As he wiped the lenses of his glasses, he thought of how he had spent his entire life in battle. How odd it now felt to consider the prospect of finally enjoying peace after a lifetime of war.

"You have nothing to say?" General Dung asked proudly, since it had been his own idea and his urging that had moved Hanoi to agree that the campaign should be now waged full out to victory.

"Perhaps my first question regards what plans we will now change? When we began, we had hoped for this outcome, but we had planned on a more protracted evolution that would last two or more years, a series of initiatives and retracements. What unfolds before us now clearly goes beyond our most enthusiastic hopes, and quite understandably taxes our maneuverability to the extreme," Tran Van Tra responded.

"Correct, General Tran. That is why I have concluded that since we must now push for a final victory, we must focus our attentions on Hue," General Dung said, rising to his feet and walking to the map board that stood on a tripod beneath the far edge of the camouflage canopy, outside the door of his adjoining command tent.

"I thought that our intention was Saigon?" General Tran asked.

"Ultimately, yes," General Dung answered. "However, our spies, including one very good agent inside Nguyen Van Thieu's own inner circle, have disclosed that our nemesis has ordered his division of Marines and the ARVN First Division at Hue, along with the ARVN Second Division at Chu Lai, to consolidate with the remaining forces around Da Nang. We cannot allow those units to join their counterparts in Da Nang."

"What would they matter if we seized Saigon instead?" Tran asked.

"If we turn our main forces toward Saigon," Dung said, "then those Marines and ARVN divisions at Da Nang could quickly move by transport aircraft or sealift to Saigon and reinforce General Toan's army there, which is now quite large and surrounds Saigon.

"We must first cut off and destroy the Marines and the First ARVN Division at Hue and do likewise with the Second ARVN Division at Chu Lai."

"Have you considered the Americans?" General Tran asked. "When we mobilize our offensives, crushing Hue and Chu Lai, and threaten Da Nang, they could land American Marines there."

"The United States at this point appears completely impotent," General Dung boasted. "They will not intercede, I assure you. Their people will not stand for another dead soldier. They have already shown their hand. All they can do is perhaps increase aid to South Vietnam, and even if they do that, they will not be able to rescue their puppets from the impending collapse that awaits.

"Now, my friend, would you like to hear something that I am confident will make you laugh?"

Tran Van Tra smiled and said, "I certainly would enjoy hearing something humorous today."

"I received a communique from our good friend, Colonel Vo Dong

Giang," General Dung said. "He reports that in response to the losses South Vietnam suffered at Ban Me Thuot, and now our northern on-slaughts, the thugs in Saigon have cut off the water supply and elec-tricity to the Provisional Revolutionary Government compound and at his home."

"How unfortunate for the poor diplomats and Colonel Vo," Gen-eral Tran said, smiling. "Is there more?"

"Ah, yes," General Dung said. "While Nguyen Van Thieu and his gang protest and cut off Vo's water and lights, the underlings of the puppet government come knocking on our good friend's back door, under the cover of night, and beg for lodging in his basement. It seems that many of them now embrace our cause and want to join us!"

"Of course he turns them away," General Tran said.

"Of course," General Dung responded. "Unless one can bring something of value for our consideration, then the good colonel may offer that person a damp room with no windows nor toilet."

"That is humorous," General Tran said, walking to the table and pouring more hot tea into his cup.

"Colonel Vo tells me that he has ample stores, a generator, and can-dles if need be," General Dung said, holding his cup out for more tea. "He related the action to the day our delegation arrived for the open-ing session of the Joint Military Commission and International Over-sight Committee, when they held them on the plane at Tan Son Nhut for a day in that awful Saigon heat. Such a silly and pointless antic, like a spoiled child on a schoolyard, yet so typical of Mr. Thieu."

OUTSKIRTS OF TAM KY, SIXTY-TWO KILOMETERS SOUTH OF DA NANG

HIDDEN BY DARKNESS, Colonel Hoang Duc The, commander of the Thirty-eighth Regiment, Second NVA Division, sat on a hillside at the edge of the gravel roadway designated Provincial Highway 333 and, through his binoculars, quietly watched the bustle of panicked refugees jamming the thoroughfares where the roadway intersected with High-way 1, in the city of Tam Ky. The chaos of terrified peasants had al-ready stripped the city of order. By the hour, policemen and soldiers deserted their posts and fled southward on Highway 1, shedding their uniforms and mingling with the fleeing civilians.

For two weeks, his unit had moved eastward from the western mountains, as the assault on Ban Me Thuot began and ended. As the Second NVA Division had built its momentum, sweeping toward Tam Ky, a growing tidal wave of frightened people ran ahead of them. This mounting surge of panic-stricken civilians and ARVN deserters served The's army well, breaking the enemy's hold on order and discipline and splintering their capacity to govern the people and defend its territories.

Earlier in the afternoon, The's Thirty-eighth Regiment had finally linked its forces with those of the First and Thirty-first regiments and now stood at their line of departure, ready to launch their main offensive against the remaining defenders of Quang Tin Province's capital.

For the North Vietnamese Army, Tam Ky represented a vital link in their greater objective of isolating and conquering Da Nang, only sixty-two kilometers to the north on Highway 1. By capturing this city and thus blocking the primary route to Da Nang, the Second NVA Division could let slip the wrath of its three reinforced regiments on the core of the Second ARVN Division, defending the garrison at Chu Lai, only a dozen kilometers to the south, and cut them off from Da Nang.

Orders received this afternoon from Lieutenant General Hoang Minh Thoa, vice commander of the North Vietnamese Army and commanding general of the 968th Corps, had mobilized the North Vietnamese and Viet Cong regiments throughout the regions north and west of Hue and south and west of Da Nang and Chu Lai to position themselves to launch coordinated attacks, isolating Hue and cutting off Da Nang. The NVA strategy sought to seize these objectives before scattered ARVN and South Vietnamese Marine forces could consolidate and reinforce the defenses of Da Nang. The Second NVA Division now stood poised to overrun Tam Ky before dawn and then take Chu Lai.

Nearly thirty kilometers north of where Colonel The held his Thirty-eighth NVA Regiment, ready to assault Tam Ky, Colonel Le Cong Than casually inspected a company of black-clad guerrillas from his brigade of more than three thousand Viet Cong, the Forty-fourth Line Front. Colonel Than's forces now controlled most of the villages and countryside south and west of the big iron bridge that carried Highway 1 across the Cau Do River near the southwestern outskirts of Da Nang.

As the colonel slowly strolled among the ranks of this unit of nearly four hundred soldiers, he spoke in a quiet voice to men he chose at random and wished them good fortune. Tonight, divided into small squads, they would begin their infiltration of Da Nang itself. Just as their colleagues had done in Ban Me Thuot, these guerrillas, smuggling explosives and weapons in carts and on bicycles, would position themselves at key points in the city. When the invasion of Da Nang commenced, they would attack from within the city.

For the past two weeks, along with the Forty-seventh and Ninety-sixth NVA regiments, and the 304th NVA Military Police Regiment, Colonel Than's guerrillas had purposefully raised havoc throughout the western mountains and the more immediate farmlands surrounding Da Nang, Hue, and Chu Lai, loading the cities and all of their connecting roadways with refugees. The tactic virtually halted any of the enemy's overland movement, leaving the scattered South Vietnamese forces choked in place. The action also had a surprising psychological effect on both sides. For the South Vietnamese, it caused panic and prompted widespread and massive desertions among the defending forces. At the same time, this motivated the Viet Cong and North Vietnamese soldiers to a nearly euphoric state. Their confidence and morale soared.

With the coming morning's predawn attacks set at Hue, Tam Ky, and Chu Lai, the Forty-fourth Line Front also had the task of guarding and blocking any traffic attempting to depart Da Nang.

Their noose now in place, ready to snap the enemy's neck, Colonel Le Cong Than and his three thousand guerrillas waited for morning.

Chapter 10

THE LOST BRIGADE

HUE, RVN—SATURDAY, MARCH 22, 1975

EXPLOSIONS JOLTED AWAKE South Vietnamese Marine Corps Lieutenant
Colonel Tran Ngoc Toan, who sat in a chair catnapping at his Fourth
Battalion command post, and sent him tripping to his feet. The colonel
rubbed his eyes and yawned, listening to the salvo's thunder, and
waited for the action's first situation reports to come across the 147th
Brigade's radio network.

Even at 4:00 a.m., Toan could not allow himself to relax into any
deep slumber, despite the infantry commander's not sleeping in his bed
now for several days. For rest, the Marine sometimes caught an hour
or two nap on the nearby duty watch's cot, but mostly he got his shut-
eye from dozing in a chair, among the hum and bustle of his battalion's
operations and communications center. Command decisions these days
required immediate action because combat respected no clock, especially now that the NVA's shelling of South Vietnam's imperial city had
begun to intensify.

The sun not yet risen, the volume and frequency of the bursting artillery rounds, walking closer to his unit's position, told him that per-

haps this finally represented that ill-awaited, fateful knock that proclaimed the tiger now clawed at their door. This morning, the Communists attacked Hue in earnest. From here on, they would launch no more probes, no more harassment fire, no more withdrawals. Their great engine of doom had begun to roll.

A few days earlier, Toan's 147th Brigade had retreated from the northern reaches of I Corps, along with the 258th and the 369th brigades which, with the newly formed 468th Brigade, represented the entirety of infantry of the South Vietnamese Marine Corps (an armed force comprised of a single infantry division with associated supporting arms and elements, originally designed, outfitted, organized, and trained by the United States Marine Corps). Since 1973 the three Viet Marine brigades had operated from outposts spread along Highway 9, which extended across the northern badlands from Dong Ha at the coast to Khe Sanh in the far western mountains, overlooking the Laos border. From the old American firebases with haunting names like Con Thien, Camp J. J. Carroll, and the Rockpile, they patrolled the southern flank of the DMZ. Simultaneously, the Viet Marines had manned the defense garrisons at Quang Tri City and the key coastal enclaves of Quang Tri Province. When President Thieu transferred the ARVN Airborne Division from Da Nang and Hue to bolster the defenses of Saigon, Lieutenant General Ngo Quang Truong, the MR 1 commander, ordered the Vietnamese Marine Corps redeployed from Quang Tri to the regions around Hue and Da Nang to fill the defense voids left by the departed airborne units.

With the departure of the Marines from Quang Tri, the ARVN soldiers who had remained behind, manning the outposts and garrisons, on March 19 threw down their arms, discarded thousands of tons of weaponry, equipment, munitions, and stores, shed their uniforms, and fled their posts. Without receiving a shot of enemy fire, they abandoned the entire province and its capital, along with a war chest of arms and supplies, to the advancing Vietnamese Communists.

Three days later, Lieutenant Colonel Toan sat on a metal folding chair, catnapping in the sleepy morning hours before dawn outside Hue. From here his Fourth Battalion and three others of the 147th Marine Brigade, the Third (on loan from the 258th Brigade), the Fifth and the Seventh, along with an artillery battalion and a handful of support detachments, stood as the primary defenders of the ancient Vietnamese capital and its heralded Imperial Palace and Citadel.

With the onslaught of North Vietnamese and Viet Cong forces pouring at them from three sides, Brigadier General Bui The Lan, Commandant of the South Vietnamese Marine Corps, responding to General Truong's directives, sent the 369th Marine Brigade, comprised of the Second, Sixth, and Ninth battalions, to fill the vacated airborne defense positions north and west of Da Nang and deployed the 258th Marine Brigade, with its two remaining battalions, the First and Eighth, to assume defenses at the abandoned airborne positions south of Da Nang. The 468th Brigade, comprised of the Fourteenth, Sixteenth, and Eighteenth battalions, took up positions north of Da Nang along Highway 1, extending a defense line from the Hai Van Pass northward to the coastal enclave of Phuoc Tuong and its heliport thirty-seven kilometers southeast of Hue. Commandant General Bui The Lan simultaneously relocated his South Vietnamese Marine Corps headquarters from Huong Dien, located in Thua Thien Province, twenty kilometers northwest of Hue, to the airfield compound at Marble Mountain, located on the China Beach peninsula, stretching seaward along Da Nang's southeast side, just a stone's throw from General Truong's MR 1 headquarters, located across the Han River at Da Nang Air Base.

Colonel Toan listened to the anxiety-punctuated radio chatter from excited operators transmitting messages from the front-line positions engaged under heavy attack. Words, such as *fire mission*, *danger close*, *snake eyes*, and *echo-zulu*, crackled among the choppy Vietnamese slurry. At a long table stacked with receivers, radiomen hurriedly wrote notes on flimsy pages from yellow pads and quickly handed them to runners who took the slips to operations specialists standing over a map spread on a another table in the center of the sandbag-reinforced command bunker. Above them a string of forty-watt incandescent lightbulbs blinked off and on as a 120-millimeter mortar round burst outside.

While the Vietnamese Marine lieutenant colonel waited to see a first appraisal of the morning attack, he thought of the old woman who no doubt sat at her bedchamber window in the Imperial Palace, looking at the fireworks' reflections rippling across the water of the Perfume River. At 86 years old, Tu Cuong, the mother of Vietnam's last Nguyen emperor, Bao Dai, stubbornly clung to her dynasty as well as her lifelong home. Conversely, her son, the emperor, stubbornly clung to his wealth and luxurious countryside villa in France, where he had lived in exile since 1954.

General Truong had fumed that he would send armed soldiers and a helicopter to wrestle the old woman from the palace, if push came to shove. The Marine lieutenant colonel smiled, considering the idea. He would like to see a gang of young soldiers try to wrestle the old queen mother from her lair. He seriously doubted that even a full platoon could succeed in removing her from Hue. She would surely die there. He hoped that the Communists would show the old woman mercy, if nothing else, simply from respect for her age.

Yesterday afternoon, he had watched and smiled as the American consul general from Da Nang had flown an entourage of reporters and photographers to the various Viet Marine positions, including his own Fourth Battalion headquarters. Albert Francis had told the journalists that Hue stood secure. Less than twelve hours later, Lieutenant Colonel Toan crouched inside the command bunker while impacting 130-millimeter, NVA artillery shells exploded overhead, sending cascades of dirt from the stronghold roof onto the line of chattering radios, onto the operations map and table, and onto the duty cot.

He considered that Hue might stand one or two more days, at the current state of conditions, but without higher headquarters executing some sort of reinforcing strike that would push the enemy off balance, the city would soon surely fall. Toan's final orders called for the brigade to defend Hue to the last man. He considered the grim possibilities that the prospect held in store and then tried hard not to think again about such realities. For now, he lived for the moment.

"The Communists have cut Highway 1 at Phu Loc!" a radioman shouted to anyone who might hear the news.

While a place called Phu Loc enclave, a cluster of three tiny villages, lay to the south near Chu Lai, this Phu Loc was a district capital located forty kilometers south of Hue, straddling Highway 1 on the northern approach to Hai Van Pass. The 468th Viet Marine Brigade held responsibility for those defenses, Lieutenant Colonel Toan thought to himself.

"Any word from Fourteenth Battalion or from the 468th Brigade CP?" Toan asked the operator, now standing over the young Marine's shoulder and listening as the radio chattered. His operations officer, a major, and two captains, the S-3 alpha (assistant operations officer) and the S-2 (intelligence officer) also stepped closer to hear. Worried looks crept across every man's face who had heard this disturbing news.

"No word, sir," the operator said.

"I think the Fourteenth Battalion had that area of responsibility," Toan said to the operations officer.

"Might have been the Eighteenth Battalion, sir," the intelligence officer said.

"If the enemy has blocked Highway 1 at Phu Loc, then whichever battalion, be it the Fourteenth, Sixteenth, or Eighteenth, has likely perished, or hopefully fallen back to secondary positions southward," the operations officer said absentmindedly.

He had said what they all had thought, but Lieutenant Colonel Toan wished that he had kept the words to himself. They only underscored what he already felt gnawing at his gut. His Fourth Battalion, along with the 147th Brigade and their supporting arms from the First ARVN Division, had no place to retreat. Surrendering, much less dying, did not sit well with the Marine.

"Sir," the radio operator said, "the 468th Brigade reports heavy casualties, and all battalions have fallen back to Hai Van. They also report that tens of thousands of civilians are running from the fight both toward them and to the north, toward us."

Toan knew that this panic would only grow worse as the artillery intensified into Hue. Trying to escape the slaughter, the people would run the only direction available to them, toward the sea.

"BRIGADIER GENERAL BUI," Lieutenant General Ngo Quang Truong said on the telephone to the Commandant of the Vietnamese Marine Corps, "how many of your men remain in Hue?"

"Sir," the Marine commandant responded, "slightly more than three thousand troops, the 147th Brigade reinforced with the 3rd Battalion, 258th Brigade. I do not have the exact numbers of First ARVN Division soldiers who still remain there in support elements."

"Get these men out of Hue," Truong said with quick words to emphasize the urgency of his order.

"Sir," Brigadier General Bui The Lan said, "the President ordered us to defend Hue to our deaths. The four battalions holding that ground will stand to the man if needed."

"We need them here. Without those forces, Da Nang will surely fall," General Truong said. "Tam Ky and Quang Ngai City are only hours from demise. Chu Lai will then fall soon afterward. With the enemy now threatening the northern slopes of the Hai Van Pass, Hue is cut off and will surely fall too. Therefore, you must redeploy those units to Da Nang. Since Highway 1 north now belongs to the enemy, your only egress from Hue is by sea."

"Yes, I know that," the Marine general said firmly. "We have a number of navy vessels augmented with landing craft just returned from there. Already today, when several of these ships tried to evacuate some elements of the First ARVN Division at the docks at Tan My, panicked civilians overran the ships, and they had to pull out. I am told that these same vessels, using their LCM landing crafts, can rendezvous with the 147th Brigade on the beaches away from the piers and the crowds and can evacuate our men and equipment."

"Then by all means, General, see to it immediately. We need those forces here as soon as possible," Truong snapped and hung up the telephone without another word.

The Viet Marine commandant looked at a colonel who stood wide eyed at the office door. "Send a flash message to the 147th Brigade," the general began. "They should prepare to move from their positions no later than dawn and maneuver to Tan My, where navy ships will await their arrival offshore. Upon contact, the ships will deploy landing crafts that will move inland and extract the brigade from the beaches. They must signal their positions to the vessels with red smoke grenades and green star clusters."

BY THE TIME the 147th Marine Brigade received its bug-out orders, the sun had already begun to set in Hue. The unit's three thousand Marines spent nearly the entire night packing their gear, loading their munitions, and hitching their mobile artillery to trucks for movement. They began their rearguard maneuver, southeastward to Tan My and the strand of beaches east of the city, shortly before dawn on Sunday, March 23.

Lieutenant Colonel Nguyen Ngoc Toan stood on the hood of his jeep, straining his eyes through forty-power binoculars, searching for ships along the horizon or the sign of an LCM dancing among the eight-foot waves beyond where the surf crashed across submerged sandbars lurking like whales in the low-tide shallows several hundred yards from shore. Toan shook his head at the major, his operations officer, who stood by the jeep, and then looked up the beach at the brigade commander, who also stood on the hood of his jeep, binoculars held to his eyes, searching the skyline for ships.

Finally, the radio operator seated in the back of Toan's jeep shouted over the loud roar of the crashing surf. "Sir," the Marine said, "ships will close on our position in three hours."

"What?" Toan responded, the sudden sense of panic coloring his voice. "It takes no more time than that to cruise by sea from Da Nang to Hue. They must just now be leaving port in Da Nang!"

While the Commandant of the Vietnamese Marine Corps had issued clear orders, in the fractious confusion of the ongoing battles not only at Hue, but overwhelming his other three brigades surrounding Da Nang, the general's staff had neglected to inform the Vietnamese navy of the planned extraction of the 147th Brigade from the beaches at Tan My until the brigade had already mounted out for their rendezvous. By the time the ships left Da Nang, the Marines already had arrived at the beachhead. Furthermore, the order for ships and landing crafts had failed to explain that the heavily reinforced 147th Brigade contained double the numbers of men and equipment common to a typical Marine brigade. Therefore, the navy sent too few vessels as well.

"Major," Lieutenant Colonel Toan said, now in a voice driven by command resolve, "prepare the battalion to establish a hasty defense. The enemy has already mobilized its forces toward our positions as we speak. In three hours, we will be under heavy fire."

Already, the other three battalions had also begun deploying their forces in hasty defenses. They laid in their field artillery, mortars, and TOW missile batteries in a rear-facing arch behind the brigade, that now sat like a duck in the wrong end of a shooting gallery, stranded on the bare beaches at Tan My with their backs to the sea.

Slightly less than two hours later, the first NVA rounds from 130-millimeter field guns exploded into the center of the brigade's line. The Marines pounded back with their string of 105-millimeter howitzers and rapidly spent the brigade's supply of TOW missiles, trying to take out the advancing NVA armor that now rained direct fire on the Marines from their main weapons and heavy machine guns.

"Ships!" cried a young Marine keeping watch, crouched in front of Lieutenant Colonel Toan's jeep. "I see two ships, and I see six LCMs circling in the water."

"Pop the smoke and the star clusters," the operations officer shouted to a handful of Marines crouched near him.

All along the beach, amid the explosions of incoming enemy fire, red smoke poured from grenades tossed along the shore to signal the landing positions, while an array of green flares popped in the air above them. Aboard the ships, green star clusters rocketed skyward, signaling back to the Marines that the Navy had a fix on their positions.

"They cannot land here," Toan quickly surmised, taking note of the shallow water and surf crashing over the submerged sandbars far from shore. "We will have to swim to the boats."

The words had no more than cleared his lips when he saw the brigade commander and a score of Marines dash into the surf and start wading and swimming toward the sandbars.

Seeing their senior commander's sudden departure, hundreds of other Marines now dashed toward the surf, hoping to also swim to freedom. Tran Ngoc Toan, however, fought the urge to panic and held his ground. With bullets snapping through the air, he climbed to the hood of his jeep where he stood for his men to see.

By now, the North Vietnamese Army had closed on the beach and sent infantry running and shooting at the stranded and panicked Marine brigade.

"Destroy all the crew-served weapons, and gather what firepower you can carry," the lieutenant colonel shouted to his men while still standing on the jeep. Bullets from the rifles of the closing enemy infantry thudded into the sand, pinged off the jeep, and zipped past Toan's ears. Yet he kept his perch, holding his Marines' faith with his courage.

From his high mount, the Fourth Battalion commander could see the slaughter already taking place on the beaches near the advancing enemy soldiers. Dead bodies quickly began to litter the ground and bobbed and washed in the surf. Out at the breakers, he could see the brigade commander and the smattering of men that remained from the crowd of Marines who had fled with him scrambling up the sides of the few landing crafts that had even bothered to brave running aground on the sandbars to rescue the men.

Artillery shells from the North Vietnamese 130-millimeter fieldpieces exploded in the water, turning back the majority of other LCMs that had faintly attempted the rescue, and now targeted the three boats that sat grounded on the sandbars as Marines scurried up their sides. With each explosion in the crashing surf, bodies and body parts of fleeing Marines tumbled in the air and disappeared into the surging foam.

"Sir," shouted a young captain, standing by the jeep, "what shall we do?"

"Follow me!" cried Lieutenant Colonel Toan as he leaped from the jeep and dashed southward along the sandy Tan My Peninsula.

Waiting for the navy to arrive, Toan had already realized the worst-case possibility and now counted on it. Even at high tide the landing crafts would have had difficulty getting past the sandbars. At low tide, as it was now, the trek was impossible for them.

To make their escape, Toan concluded, would require his Marines scuttling their vehicles and heavy arms, abandoning nearly everything on the beach. Then they would have to wade and swim the several hundred yards to the boats.

In the best case, with no enemy fire, many men would no doubt drown. Under heavy enemy fire, he knew that the attempt would net an unfathomable death toll, and few could actually make the escape. Witnessing the brigade commander and the unfortunate Marines who followed him, and who now died in the surf by the hundreds, proved his estimation correct.

Toan knew that a small fishing village lay far to the south and that he and his men could possibly find boats there too. In boats, they could sail under darkness to Da Nang.

"Follow me!" Toan again shouted to his men. "Hurry, and keep together!"

The North Vietnamese forces saw the string of 450 Viet Marines running southward and then shift their flight on an angle that led away from the beach, obviously seeking cover behind the tree line on the strand's western side, well south of the approaching North Vietnamese Army's lower flank. With more than two thousand other Vietnamese Marines still before them, some fighting from small dunes while others ran hopelessly into the surf to drown, the string of a few hundred Marines seemed insignificant in comparison, and thus the Communists let them go. Their nets already sagged full with the catch they had before them.

UNITED STATES CONSULATE, DA NANG

"SERGEANT ARRIOLA!" Staff Sergeant Walter Sparks barked, entering the door to the security detachment office. "Get ready to initiate the evacuation plans. We've got to get our shit together. Charlie is on the front porch. Time to get out of Dodge."

Lazaro Arriola sat at the sergeant-of-the-guard desk, pecking at the keys of a pale green electric typewriter, when Sparks bounded through the doorway. "No big surprise," he said, pulling the fresh duty roster for April from the machine and handing it to the staff sergeant.

"Forget this," Sparks said and handed the paper back to the sergeant. "The balloon just went up. Everyone is now on duty until I say otherwise."

"I guess you saw the messages then, about Tam Ky and Quang Ngai, and it looks like Chu Lai too," Arriola said.

"I just got out of a hot meeting with Mr. Francis, and that ain't the half of it, pal," Sparks said, pulling open the drawer of the file cabinet and yanking out a two-page operations order, which the CIA logistician had condensed from the thirty-six-page original evacuation plan drafted by the consulate security boss.

"How can it be any worse?" the sergeant said, allowing Sparks to take the seat behind the desk.

"Add Hue to that list," Sparks said. "The whole fucking Vietnamese Marine Corps up there got wiped out on the beach this morning, and the rest of the ARVN has either turned tail or turned cowboy and gone on the rampage."

"Hue fell?" the sergeant asked.

"Not quite yet, but with what little they have left to fight with up there," Sparks said in a sad tone, "it might as well be over. The NVA have the highway south of us cut, and now north of us too. It will take a few days to mop up Hue, Tam Ky, Quang Ngai, and Chu Lai, but rest assured, when that gets done, they're a coming to our door."

"How are we supposed to get out then?" Arriola said.

"The skipper has got a line on a fleet of Air America planes and helicopters," Sparks said. "We're going to fly out. The rest of the folks here, well, that's another story."

"What do we have, ten thousand Americans here?" the sergeant said.

"That's just the legal ones," Sparks replied. "Then you have to consider the deserters and other American shit-birds gone native in Dog-patch who want to go home with us now too. Also, we have the Brits, the Aussies, the Koreans, and who knows what other brand of Luke the gook from Europe, here legal and illegal, but needs to get out. So according to Mr. Francis, he and our *I Spy* boss have laid on a fleet of barges that will ferry all these people, and whatever South Vietnamese friendlies we decide to take, out to a convoy of United States Maritime Service merchant ships, headed our way as we speak."

"When do we leave?" the sergeant asked. "Not that I am afraid or anything, but just wondering how much time we have to get this all done."

"That's up to Charlie," Sparks said, now pulling out a lined tablet and beginning to write. "I suppose that we may have a few days, maybe a week, but once the NVA have Hue and Chu Lai under wraps, they are coming for us here, and in a hurry."

The staff sergeant studied the short list of names he had just written, listing himself at the top, then Sergeant Venoy L. Rogers, and Sergeant Arriola, and Sergeant William S. Spruce next, and then two corporals, Leonard A. Forseth and Ronald W. Anderson last. Below that, based on a priority-driven agenda of slug lines from the two-page operations order, he began to write a more elaborate and detailed series of tasks that he and his five subordinate Marines must perform before the Communists came to town.

FARMLANDS SOUTH OF TAN MY

LIEUTENANT COLONEL TRAN Ngoc Toan lay behind a manure pile in the gray evening light, waiting for full darkness. Near him, all in similar hiding places, his 450 survivors of today's disaster waited and silently watched with their commander. They could still smell the smoke from the day's battle and thought of their comrades that they had left lying dead on the beach or captured by the enemy.

Toan had stopped at the tree line when his Marines first entered it from the angry, fire-swept beach, watching his men dash past him, counting souls, and ensuring that the last man made it safely to the cover. As his men scurried by him, the lieutenant colonel could see the other battalions still on the beach, fighting and fleeing to their deaths in the sea. Their commanders, his friends, valiantly stood their ground, right to the bitter end. He felt heartsick as he saw them throw down their rifles and put up their hands.

The green-clad NVA soldiers, with their helmets shaped like turtle shells, seemed to swarm the surrendered leaders like a gang of hungry dogs after a meaty bone. His soul ached for those men, his friends. However, these 450 Marines who had followed him from the beach were also his friends and comrades. While he grieved for the loss of so many and ached at the capture of his colleagues, he knew that these Marines now with him had entrusted their lives to his leadership. He owed them his best, not his regrets.

Lying on the manure heap, the lieutenant colonel closed his eyes and finally allowed himself to doze. The thunder of battle still raged close enough to shake the ground, but his years of experience told him that the fire pointed well away from this small Vietnamese fishing village on the southern tip of the Tan My Peninsula. He finally felt safe from the shelling and slept quietly.

"Sir," a whisper came to the lieutenant colonel's ear, and a hand gently nudged his shoulder. "Night has long since come."

Toan opened his eyes and looked to see his operations officer lying next to him. Without a word, the battalion commander gave the major a pat on the shoulder and then stood, dusting the manure from his tiger-stripe camouflage uniform. He took his black beret from the cargo pocket on the side of his trousers and tucked it on his head. Then quietly, he walked alone to the house at the edge of the village, upon whose manure he had slept.

A dim light shown from the open doorway, coming from a kerosene lamp set on a small table in the center of the room and a cooking fire burning inside the open hearth of an old cast-iron stove. Flames licked through small cracks surrounding the cook plate on top and lapped at the sides of a clay crock filled with boiling water, rice, a few vegetables, and fish. The aroma of the food drifted out the door and tied Tran Ngoc Toan's stomach into a hungry knot.

The Marine commander stepped quietly in the darkness, hoping that the family dog, who lay just inside the doorway, did not notice him. In the nighttime shadows, Toan looked inside the house and saw an old man and a young woman with two small girls seated on stools by the table. The family spoke to each other in low voices. On the wall, above a small side table with two unlit candles and a photograph of a younger man, a wooden crucifix hung.

"Catholics," Toan said to himself. "There must be others here too. They will surely help us."

The dog never barked, but raised his head with his ears perked when the Marine approached the open door. As the old man came to him, Tran Ngoc Toan politely took off his beret and bowed his head.

"Sir, Colonel, sir," the old man said, smiling at the sight of the Marine officer, "please come inside, quickly."

Just as the Marine stepped through the door, the old man pulled down a black drape, closing the entry.

"No one saw you come here?" the old man said hopefully. "VC roam everywhere these days."

"No one, except my battalion, who hides in the woods near here," Toan said.

"Your battalion?" the old man said, fully surprised. "I thought everyone died up there today, or were captured. A full battalion escaped?"

"There are perhaps 450 of us, not my full battalion," Toan said. "Many of the men are from my battalion, but others come from our sister battalions too, all of whom were decimated today."

"Such a horror," the old man said. "My son died last year, not far from here, killed by the VC. They murdered him as he pushed his bicycle home from Hue. They took everything and left him dead on the roadside. These are his daughters and his widow. You are the enemy of his killers, so you are our friend."

"We need boats," Toan said as the old man ushered him to the table and offered him the seat facing toward the door.

"We have no boats here today, nor tomorrow," the old man said. "Not nearly enough of them at any rate to accommodate 450 men. Such a resource, sir, will take much time and effort to acquire."

"Can you help us find these boats?" Toan asked. "Will others in this village help us?"

"Yes, sir," the old man said and smiled, "without question. However, this will take great care, and small steps, so that we do not draw attention. Perhaps a week, or more."

"We must get to Da Nang," Toan said.

"I know this, but we have the VC very near us daily, and they always inspect this village because we are Catholics and have our loyalties to God, not Ho Chi Minh," the old man said. "We must gather the boats and spirit you and your battalion away, all under the watchful eye of our tormentors."

"Of course, we can understand if this presents too much risk for your village," Toan offered. "We can very likely slip through the forests along the coastline and get to Da Nang that way."

"I think not," the old man said. "We take our boats along the coast each day, fishing and such, and we see the massive numbers of VC and NVA moving about there. You must hide in the forest, far away from the trails. I will show you a place tonight. You cannot make a fire or talk. You and your men must wait there until I come for you. I am the village elder, here, and my word has power. I must organize this on my own, quietly. In one week, perhaps a day or two more, we can perhaps gather enough boats and reliable friends so that we can smuggle you past our enemy to Da Nang."

The lieutenant colonel bowed his head and held his hands to his forehead in a prayerlike gesture, paying homage to the old man.

"Now, sir," the old man said, "please eat."

The woman, who had stood quietly with her two daughters, walked to the stove and took a bowl from a shelf on the wall behind it. She began to dip the stew from the pot, and the Marine's stomach growled in hungry response.

Then Tran Ngoc Toan stood and bowed politely to the old man.

"Sir, I cannot take your food," he said. "I cannot eat what little you have, nor can I eat while my men do not."

The old man started to argue with the obviously hungry Marine, but then nodded his head. As the village elder, he understood the importance of leadership and living the example.

"Then, we should go now," the old man said, taking a conical straw hat from a mat on the floor, where he made his bed, and tying it to his head. "This place to hide has water, and you may find things to eat there too. In the morning, I will return there with one or two trusted friends, and we will bring you what food that we can gather. It will not be much, so you must hunt and gather most of what you eat. However, you must not build any fires nor make any sounds. The VC here will surely find you otherwise."

As the two men slipped out of the small house, disappearing into the pitch darkness, the dog remained behind, quietly guarding the doorway.

"My men are well trained," Toan assured the old man. "We can forage for ourselves and live without fires. We will be fine, I promise you."

HQ, FOURTH MARINE REGIMENT, CAMP HANSON, OKINAWA

"SKIPPER," a young lance corporal called into the Quonset hut headquarters of Company D, First Battalion, Fourth Marine Regiment, located at Camp Hanson, Okinawa. "Colonel Gray issued a commander's call, ASAP."

Captain Walter Wood stood from behind his desk, tucked on his utility cap, and jogged out the doorway to the Fourth Marine Regiment's headquarters where Alfred M. Gray, a future Commandant of the Marine Corps waited.

The Company D commander joined the flow of other Marines entering the room where Lieutenant Colonel Charles E. Hester, the young captain's battalion commander, sat to the left of Colonel Gray at the head of a long table. Quickly the First Battalion's staff officers, company commanders, platoon leaders, and a score of senior staff noncommissioned officers also took their seats.

"Gentlemen," Al Gray began, "as we speak, Hue City has surrendered to the Communists. Nearly four thousand South Vietnamese warriors, most of whom were Viet Marines, have fallen in that battle."

A no-shit mumble rose like a tidal wave and crashed against the walls of the small room as the shocked Marines heard the report. Rumors had told that the NVA had launched a surprise offensive and had taken a few small "villes," but the news of Hue stung these Vietnam War veterans deeply.

"Chu Lai won't last another day," Gray added, and more mumbles greeted his words. "We have a warning order issued today. We're heading for Da Nang."

Gunnery Sergeant Russ Thurman sat among the group of staff NCOs with Staff Sergeant Sonny Bice, the Fourth Marine Regiment's correspondent. His junior assistant, Lance Corporal Eric Carlson, had already deployed several weeks ago with Colonel John F. Roche III and the Thirty-first Marine Amphibious Unit, with the Second Battalion, Fourth Marines "Magnificent Bastards" as its battalion landing team. Carlson relished the idea of being a Magnificent Bastard.

Colonel Roche and the Bastards had deployed to the Gulf of Thailand, anticipating the second shoe to drop in the long-awaited fall of Phnom Penh and the 31st MAU's execution of the op plan, Operation Eagle Pull, the evacuation of the Cambodian capital.

"Joe Carr will throw more furniture," Gunnery Sergeant Thurman told Sonny Bice as he listened to the Fourth Marines's operations officer describe the latest intelligence reports from Da Nang.

At this point all the Marines had in hand was a warning order from Major General Carl W. Hoffman, the III Marine Amphibious Force commanding general, issued via Major General Kenneth J. Houghton, the Third Marine Division's commander. Because Second Battalion, Fourth Marines now sailed off Cambodia and First Battalion had just completed its deployment training in preparation for pulling the next pump, they picked up the ticket for the immediate departure to Da Nang.

Russ Thurman barely had time to report news of the emergency deployment to his boss, Captain Jerry Shelton, and then hurriedly stuffed a seabag. After drawing 782 gear from supply and a pistol from the armory, he raced by speeding jeep, with Lance Corporal Don Tompkins at the wheel, across Okinawa to White Beach, where Colonel Gray, Captain Wood, and Company D from the First Battalion had already begun embarking their weaponry and boarding Rear Admiral Donald E. Whitmire's Task Force 76 flagship, the amphibious command vessel USS *Blue Ridge* (LCC 19).

While Gunny Thurman, Colonel Gray, Captain Wood, and the Delta Company Marines boarded their ship, the remaining three companies of First Battalion, Fourth Marines waited for their transport to arrive, the amphibious transport dock ship, USS *Dubuque* (LPD 8), which now steamed full tilt boogie from Subic Bay, Philippines, where it and two other ships from Amphibious Ready Group Bravo had put in for repairs. Once they had reached the Vietnam coastal waters, they would rendezvous with the USS *Frederick* (LST 1184) and the USS *Durham* (LKA 114), still preparing to get underway at Subic.

No one had truly expected the calamity that now took place in the I Corps region of South Vietnam. Losing the heart of the Central Highlands had been bad enough. The collapse had literally taken the Americans by surprise and left them with their ships and forces out of place.

Two days after Colonel Gray and his first element Marines had embarked the *Blue Ridge*, Major General Hoffman formally activated the

Thirty-third Marine Amphibious Unit, placing it under Gray's command. He attached the aviation element, Marine Medium Helicopter Squadron 165 as the MAU's air element. However, that presented a new set of problems, adding more frustration to the delays.

While HMM-165 had some aircraft at Marine Corps Air Station, Futima, Okinawa, several of its CH-46 Sea Knight helicopters sat on the tarmac at Cubi Point, Philippines. Furthermore, the ARG-Bravo vessels hosting the 33rd MAU had no amphibious landing platform ship, typically used to support the air arm of the MAU. Not to be deterred, Al Gray and HMM-165 commander Lieutenant Colonel James P. Kizer put their heads together and spread the helicopters among the ships, according to the size of their chopper decks.

The *Frederick* and the *Durham* took a single CH-46 aircraft and support detachment each, while the *Blue Ridge* hosted two detachments of UH-1E Hueys, and the *Dubuque* carried seven CH-46 helicopters, crews, and ground support, plus jammed her bowels with the remaining three companies of First Battalion Marines, their supporting amphibious assault vehicles (amtracks), artillery, tanks, and other heavy movers. For the Marines assigned to the *Dubuque*, it would be a very tight and uncomfortable voyage to South Vietnam.

Although they had solved the logistics problems and now had the unit's task organization filled, the Marines still sat far from Da Nang, hurriedly trying to mount out for the rescue. The day pages for that final week of March 1975 seemed to fly off the calendar while the majority of the newly activated Thirty-third Marine Amphibious Unit, most of their air assets, and all of their heavy gear still waited on Okinawa for their ride to arrive.

While the northern provinces of South Vietnam fell like a house of cards, the rapid pace of events pressing toward Da Nang outstripped Marine Corps planners' ability to adjust ongoing preparations in Okinawa, changing from green side out to brown side out by the hour. Every plan put to paper seemed destined to be overtaken by events.

In the coming days, before the bulk of the 33rd MAU could depart Okinawa, General Hoffman ceded to a plan organized by Third Marine Division commander, Major General Houghton. It virtually deactivated the 33rd MAU, sending Colonel Gray elsewhere, and then designated the unit as the Amphibious Evacuation RVN Support

Group, with the Ninth Marine Amphibious Brigade's chief of staff, Colonel Dan C. Alexander, in command. Their mission changed from that of a Marine Corps combat landing force, bristling with tanks and artillery, to that of shipboard security forces, now prepared to take aboard evacuees and refugees, rescuing them at sea.

Chapter 11

COLLAPSE OF DA NANG

DA NANG, RVN—THURSDAY, MARCH 27

WHITE SMOKE DRIFTED from the hibachi wagon parked on the sidewalk in front of where Le Cong Than and a young pair of his Viet Cong soldiers had perched on the seawall above the Han River, across the street from the American consulate. The three guerrillas slowly nibbled and savored the braised beef skewered on sticks that the Forty-fourth Line Front commander had bought and shared with his two comrades.

As they sat in the warm sunshine and happily chewed the tasty, thin strips of spicily marinated, flame-roasted flank meat, the guerrillas eyed every person entering or leaving the consulate, paying particular attention to the numbers of soldiers that they saw on post outside and meandering inside when the big gates swung open. While the men made mental notes of their sightings, three United States Marines dressed in stiffly starched, drab green uniforms with their trousers bloused above spit-polished boots, each man carrying a rifle and wearing a pistol, walked across the street and bought barbecue from the middle-aged man with the hibachi wagon. During the brief wait for their purchases, the Americans said hello to the Viet Cong trio, who in return nodded and bowed respectfully to the men, flashing their most innocent smiles.

It seemed ironic to Le Cong Than that at another time and another place these very Americans could have just as easily died by his bullets, or he by theirs. In another place and time, likewise, they could have embraced each other as comrades. Their friendly smiles and casual exchanges of greetings felt strange and somehow sad to him. Like himself, these men filled the billets of pawns in a great political exchange bartered with blood, driven by men who rarely feared for their own safety, dwelled in relative splendor, and too often held little value for the lives of the men who died for their purposes.

"These orange sodas that you have in your tub of ice, may we have three please," Than said to the hibachi man.

The man leaned down and took out three bottles and snapped off the tops with an opener tied to his wagon's push handle with a cotton string, turned nearly black from oil and grime from the man's hands.

"Also, I think that my sons and I would like to try the roast chicken too," Than said, pointing at a row of breasts turned dark golden as hot grease sizzled through their crispy skins.

"These are my favorites," the hibachi man said, skewering three large breasts on sticks and handing them to the trio who wore straw, conical hats and black muslin shirts and pants.

Than unfolded a stack of pink and orange Republic of Vietnam five-hundred-piaster bills and peeled off three. The man lifted the lid on a finger-smudged and well-worn Roi Tan cigar box to extract change.

"Keep it as a tip, my friend," Than said, imitating the occidental custom, as his two so-called sons smiled.

"Thank you, sir," the hibachi man said, closing the box lid quickly and returning to his mundane chores, tending the roasting chicken and beef and wiping away grease spatters with a badly oil-and-soot-stained cup towel.

"What news of the war do you hear?" Than asked casually, tossing his empty beef stick into a nearby trash barrel that the city had stationed at the curb and then taking a drippy bite of the tangy braised chicken.

"Even though the Communists have begun firing some rockets and artillery on the city this morning, I still believe that the Americans will finally come. They will land here any day," the man said hopefully. Then the man looked Than in the eye. "I am friends with the people in the consulate, and they assure me that the Marines from Okinawa, Hawaii, and from Camp Pendleton in California, USA, have boarded a great fleet of ships and now steam our way to turn back the Communists."

"This is true?" Than said.

"They have many CIA working here," the hibachi man told Than in an almost whispering voice, casting a pall of apparent secrecy over what he disclosed. "I am their friend, and they tell me many things when they come here to buy lunches."

"Ah," Than said in a praising tone, supporting the man's ego. "How do they come to trust you with such information? You might very easily be a Viet Cong spy."

The man untied his apron, pushed it aside, and then lifted his white shirt, exposing a spiderweb of scars punctuated by large, round pocks covered with thin, slick tissue.

"They trust me because of these," the man said proudly. "I served for nearly three years as a patrol scout for the Marines here, the Seventh Regiment, based just south of Da Nang. I was a Vietnamese Marine Corps sergeant, assigned to them. I got these scars on Charlie Ridge, in the mountains southwest of here."

"You do not blame the Americans for your wounds?" Than asked.

"The Communists shot me!" the hibachi man said. "The American Marines saved me. They flew me by helicopter to Charlie Med, where the American doctors gave me American blood and took out the Communist bullets and shrapnel."

"Many have suffered such as you," Than said, considering his own men who carried similar scars from combat.

"Too many, I think," the hibachi man said.

"Yes," Than said, honestly agreeing with the vendor. "Did you return to service after that?"

"No, sir," the hibachi man said. "I lost one of my lungs, part of my stomach, and some other things, so I am medically retired. I get a small pension each month, and I sell food and drinks from my cart."

"I can see now why you are such a trusted friend of these Americans here," Than said.

The hibachi man smiled proudly, retied his apron, and began again adjusting the chicken and beef as it cooked over the bed of grease-flaming charcoal.

"I gather that you have come to Da Nang to escape the NVA attacks," the barbecue vendor said, turning his head over his shoulder to speak to his three new friends. "I see so many people from Hue, Tam Ky, Quang Ngai, and Chu Lai now filling the city. They crowd all the streets, so we can hardly get around. Everyone seeking refuge."

"Certainly, yes," Than said, trying to sound excited, and his two comrades nodded emphatically with him. "We have a farm just northwest of Tam Ky, and the North Vietnamese raided our home three days ago. They took nearly everything from us and set us on the road. Lucky for me, I had my money hidden, and I managed to sneak back and retrieve it so that while we have no home at the moment, we do have resources.

"These are my sons, Ty and Giap. Their mother, and their wives and children, all fled with us to Da Nang. We have our camp just up the roadway beyond the guard station, by the riverbank, on the concrete walkway below the seawall. Many people have also camped there.

"My sons and I decided to try and hear some news from the Americans, so we came. Then we smelled the smoke of your fire. It smelled so good that we decided to eat before we ventured across the street."

"Oh," the hibachi man said, "I do not believe that the Americans will tell you anything, nor even allow you through their gates. With so many refugees flooding Da Nang, they have this street blocked from most traffic, except for people such as myself and those with official business at the consulate. This is one of the few places that one can come where there is not yet utter chaos."

"Yes, and that is why my family camped on the river, just beyond the blockade," Than said, elaborating his lie to a more convincing truth. "We feel safe knowing that just above our heads we have armed soldiers guarding the street."

The hibachi man looked a half block up the street where two armored personnel carriers sat in the middle of the thoroughfare with their machine guns trained on the foot traffic, bicycles, and handcarts that ventured past the soldiers standing guard. They allowed no motorized vehicles beyond them. The crew of ARVN military police searched every bag and package, bicycle and cart, and examined the push cart vendors' licenses too. Pedestrians who carried no packages passed easily with only random questions asked them by the guards.

Than and his two subordinates, who accompanied the colonel as bodyguards among other duties, had quietly studied the blockade, watching the security processes and evaluating their risks in passing the checkpoint. Satisfied, the three Viet Cong passed off their pistols and bicycles laden with weapons and explosives, hidden in packages tied in high stacks on the racks behind the seats, to comrades who now awaited the guerrilla trio's return.

Before dawn, Than and the Forty-fourth Line Front had begun infiltrating Da Nang, moving easily with the vast throngs of refugees that now crowded every street and alley and choked Highway 1 to a standstill. Every hotel in and around Da Nang overflowed, and temporary shanties sprang up in every open spot along the thoroughfares and between the buildings.

Da Nang's police force had days ago found itself overwhelmed and badly losing control. Chaos seemed to grow by the second. General Truong ordered his military police, along with as many support soldiers as he could spare from the defense lines, to bolster the city's law enforcement efforts. As the pressure mounted with each passing hour, it seemed that only the stretches of a few hundred feet running before government buildings and friendly foreign consulates represented the only real order that the police and military could now manage, and the current tide of humanity, shocked this morning with sporadic Communist shelling, threatened those checks.

"When the Americans come and the Marines land," the hibachi man said, "Da Nang can then begin to relax. They will turn back the Communists, and people can return home."

"I wish that they were here now," Than said. "I am very frightened for my family."

"Yes, I have heard about scores of cowards who have chosen to desert rather than fight. They shed their uniforms, but kept their weapons, and in rogue bands roam the backstreets. These traitors have begun looting homes and businesses and robbing defenseless people," the hibachi man said and spat on the ground to illustrate his disgust. "We have always had the cowboys, renegade gangs of criminals, but we managed their few numbers. Now, these deserters have gone cowboy too and present a very big danger to everyone. We all fear for our families, not only from the VC, but more so from these new cowboys."

"That will stop soon, I am certain," Than said confidently. "Even if the Communists come here, they will put an end to such evil."

"What are these?" the soldier that Than had introduced as Giap said, pointing to a basket of odd-looking oblong objects, fried golden with flat sticks jutting from them.

The vendor picked one up, squirted mustard on one side of it and ketchup on the other side, and handed the hot corn dog to the young man.

"Take a bite," the hibachi man said. "An American hot dog, covered with a cornmeal batter and deep fried. They call it a corn dog. I thought they were common everywhere, even in Tam Ky."

"Oh, I have seen these quite often, from vending carts in Tam Ky," Giap said, blushing as he bit off the top of the corn dog. "I have never taken the time to eat one, until now. After seeing them for so long, my curiosity about how they tasted could wait no longer."

"Do you like it?" the hibachi man said.

"Quite good!" Giap said, eating more.

"Here," Than said, handing the man four more five-hundred-piaster notes, "put however many this will buy into a bag, and we will take them back to our family. They might enjoy a new treat."

Filling a sack with eight corn dogs, the hibachi man tucked the bills in his cigar box and watched as the Viet Cong trio walked back toward the guards at the blockade. He kept watching them as they calmly stood and spoke to the sentries, bowing and nodding, opening the sack of corn dogs. Then the three men casually walked past the checkpoint and disappeared into the crush of refugees.

INSIDE THE UNITED STATES CONSULATE, DA NANG

"WHERE'S MINE?" Walter Sparks said to the trio of Marines he met as they jogged up the concrete stairs at the edge of the courtyard inside the American consulate.

"I didn't see you around when we left, Staff Sergeant, or I would have asked," Sergeant Bill Spruce said, with corporals Leonard Forseth and Ronald Anderson flanking him, their hands filled with beef on sticks, chips, and sodas.

"Just kidding. In meetings before daylight this morning. You couldn't have known if I even wanted anything," Sparks said, putting the Marines at ease. "Anybody wants me, I will be right back. I'm just going to run across the street, grab a snack, and see what news old Nguyen knows."

"He was talking to three VC when we left him," Spruce said with a laugh.

Staff Sergeant Sparks sprang down the remaining steps and trotted across the corner of the consulate courtyard and past the sentries who opened the vehicle gate to let him out since two days ago they had permanently blocked the pedestrian gate. As he stepped down the driveway, first looking for trouble both ways, he saw the familiar face of his old friend Nguyen, the hibachi man, smiling at him, holding up a dripping cold can of Coca-Cola and a corn dog.

"I talked to three VC, just now," Nguyen said. "They spent thirty-five-hundred piasters on beef and chicken and corn dogs, and orange sodas."

"Hungry crew, weren't they," Sparks said. "Sergeant Bill already told me that you had three VC here."

"He did?" Nguyen said, wide eyed and excited.

"He was joking, relax," Sparks returned. "He didn't know."

"They were VC though," Nguyen said. "Truly!"

"How do you know?" Sparks asked.

"They know nothing about corn dogs," Nguyen said. "They also don't smoke any cigarettes or even ask about tobacco."

"That makes them VC?" Sparks said.

"Maybe," the vendor said. "Maybe not."

"What else they do?" Sparks asked.

"They sit here, eat, watch the gate," Nguyen said, pointing at the whitewashed walls and front portal of the American consulate.

"Probably VC then," Sparks said, pouring ketchup and mustard on his corn dog and then reaching for a bag of Fritos corn chips. He handed the vendor five hundred piasters and took the Coke and chips in his free hand. "I'll let the spooks know about it. They might come over and talk to you later."

Nguyen the hibachi man smiled at his friend and wiped his hands on his apron as he watched the Marine walk back across the street and disappear through the consulate gates.

NEAR THE SOUTHERN OUTSKIRTS OF DA NANG

TRACERS FILLED THE night sky above Colonel Hoang Duc The's head, arching and crossing each other by the thousands of rounds fired. The Thirty-eighth NVA Regiment's commander watched as bursts of 130-millimeter artillery punctuated the light show that rained a hail of steel and lead. The furious downpour quickly decimated the defenses of the Fifth ARVN Regiment, dug in at the big iron bridge that crossed the Cau Do River, on the southern outskirts of Da Nang.

The Second NVA Division, comprised of the First, Thirty-first, and Thirty-eighth regiments, and now reinforced with the Fifty-second NVA Brigade, had routed at much of the Second ARVN Division's forces that defended Tam Ky and Quang Ngai on March 24 and then, two days later, took Chu Lai. With those southern enclaves over-whelmed, the NVA left behind elements of the First and Thirty-first regiments, which had led those attacks, to take a respite from battle and mop up. Meanwhile, Colonel The and his Thirty-eighth Regiment, now leading the charge, pointed the Communist army's spears toward Da Nang. Taking point on the attack, they quickly leveled the few dug-in remnants of the Fifth ARVN Regiment and now adjusted the brunt of their firepower on what remained of the First and Eighth regiments of the 258th South Vietnamese Marine Brigade, who along with the 369th Marine Brigade now represented the only tactically sound units left defending Da Nang. Together their warriors numbered something fewer than six thousand strong.

Colonel The's men first engaged the Fifth Regiment north of Tam Ky and quite literally had to run after their prey to keep them in range, once they had broken the defenders from their strongholds. The ARVN hardly returned any fire before beating their hasty retreat. At one point, the colonel had to order his men to drop their packs and sprint after the fleeing soldiers.

Seeing the tens of thousands of refugees jamming the roadways, leaders of the advancing North Vietnamese Army quickly realized the great advantage that the traffic-packed highways gave them. They soon adopted the tactic of firing rockets and artillery into communities, de-spite no military forces holding those grounds, so that the inhabitants would flee and fill every thoroughfare. This caused grave concern among the ARVN soldiers, most of whom had families in the local areas, and scores of them deserted their ranks, seeking to look after their loved ones instead of fighting. The jam of people on the roadways also virtually stopped the South Vietnamese from moving any crew-served weaponry, munitions, equipment, or stores. It left their remaining ranks afoot and ferrying any supplies and ammunition on their backs. This prospect sent even more of their faltering ranks over the side.

As The's regiment edged closer to Da Nang, moving one by one past the small farming hamlets scattered among the rice fields south and west of the city, peasants ran out to greet his soldiers and brought them bowls of rice and cups of water. Old women sat stoically in the doorways of their grass-topped huts and watched the hordes march by.

ON HIGHWAY 1 AT DA NANG'S SOUTHERN EDGE

"DIRCK, LOOK OUT where you're going," Alan Dawson, United Press International's bureau chief for both Vietnam and Cambodia, called to his friend, Dirck Halstead, a photojournalist for *Time* magazine, who clumsily tripped along the roadside, looking at the misty, early morning world through his Canon F-1 camera's viewfinder rather than watching where he stepped. The pair had hitched a ride on an Air America helicopter from Saigon, March 22, taking part in Consul General Francis's press show in Hue only three days before the besieged city surrendered to the Communists.

Dawson had fired a quick cable to his Saigon bureau, posting a one-paragraph blurb citing Al Francis's optimism in stark contrast to the visibly crumbling reality that surrounded the city. It went nowhere because Hue fell before he could use it as a part of any real story. Besides, the comments would have served little more purpose than to make one of the better American representatives in South Vietnam look nearly as foolish as the ambassador appeared of late. In the face of all the disaster, with the northern provinces crumbling by the second, Graham Anderson Martin kept his harangue loud and rhetoric clear that South Vietnam would stand despite current appearances and finally turn back the raging tiger.

"Dirck, you have to keep up with me, or we'll get separated in this mess," Dawson called a hundred yards behind, where a camera-bedangled Halstead crouched, snapping pictures of the face of a crying child, apparently lost in the throng of people jammed on Highway 1 on the southern outskirts of Da Nang. Behind the child, in the scene that the 24-millimeter lens had framed, dozens of frantic peasants crowded each other, pushing by inches toward the overspilling city. In the distance beyond them, columns of black smoke rose from the burning villages left by the Communists' artillery and rocket fire that had for the moment ceased with dawn.

"Coming," Dirck whined and sadly patted the tyke.

"Leave her there, Dirck," Al Dawson shouted, seeing the look on the face of his friend. Dirck Halstead had a heart too big to leave a crying child behind. "Her parents will find her right there. She has a better chance sitting it out here than you hauling her to Da Nang with you. Besides, what on earth could you do with her? Take her back to Washington, DC?"

"Right, of course, you're right," Dirck said and patted the child once more. Then he turned and pushed his way toward Dawson, who now stood at the side of Highway 1, waiting.

"We want to turn right, just up here," Dawson said, pointing to a branch in the highway. "Then we walk three or four miles out China Beach to the Marble Mountain. We can probably catch an Air America chopper ride back to Saigon there. First helicopter we see, we're getting on. We need to get out of here, fast."

"Bloody nightmare!" Dirck said, walking at his friend's side, holding one of his three cameras high in his hand, snapping random overhead shots of the crowded roadways. "Even in the worst case, I could not have imagined seeing anything like this."

"It will only get worse tomorrow," Dawson said, plodding forward through the mill of people crowding even this side road that led only to the military helicopter base and naval pier and the China Beach resort on the opposite side of the peninsula.

"Right," Halstead said, searching the sky and catching the flashing red beacon on a gray Huey descending toward the landing site ahead of them. "If we hurry, maybe that guy can hitch us a ride home."

VIET MARINE HQ, MARBLE MOUNTAIN

"SIR," the captain who served as Brigadier General Bui The Lan's aide anxiously called to the South Vietnamese Marine Corps Commandant, "I can raise no one at General Truong's headquarters. No one answers their telephones!"

"Let me try," the general said, suspiciously. He dialed one number, then another, and then another. No one answered.

"Sir," the captain then added, "our OP on the hill reports that the MR 1 command has taken every air transport asset out. We have no helicopters or any other utility aircraft. General Truong and his staff have apparently fled south. They have also fully closed Da Nang Air Base, and what few flights still leave from Marble Mountain landing field are strictly controlled by the Americans and limited to their people."

"Send the chief of staff here immediately," the general fumed. After General Bui gave the captain a few additional instructions, the aide left.

In a moment, a disheveled colonel stepped through the doorway and looked anxiously at the general.

"MR 1 command has abandoned us here," the Marine commandant said bluntly. "They have apparently taken all air transports, and evacuated what numbers of their own people that they can carry. With Da Nang Air Base closed and no lift capabilities at Marble Mountain able to handle our numbers, we have few options."

"I gathered that," the colonel said.

"We have two brigades on the fringes of the city, and they cannot hold those defenses on their own," the general said. "Send orders for them to abandon their equipment, scuttle the heavy arms, and deploy their forces, as best they can, to this headquarters, immediately.

"We have navy ships landing at our docks tonight, and I will hold them here until morning. These boats can carry fifteen hundred men. That means we will have to make at least three trips to evacuate all of our remaining Marines, if they can get here in time."

"I will send the order immediately," the colonel said and turned to leave the general's office, but the general's voice stopped him.

"The captain has the information," the general said. "Come and sit for a moment while we consider the finality of the situation here."

The colonel sank slowly into a chair near a coffee table and let out a long sigh as he stretched his legs. He had not relaxed in days, and the stress had taken a heavy toll on him.

"I do not blame General Truong," Bui The Lan said sadly. "Our problems began with the president's redeployment of MR 1 forces to Saigon. He robbed us of any ability to maneuver a reserve force that could reinforce the units where the enemy struck. Without that ability to maneuver reserves where needed, our forces could only sit and be overrun. Then, we had to fill the gaps in our defenses here and at Hue left by the Airborne Division, giving up our strongholds in Quang Tri without so much as a fight.

"This perceived loss alone had an untold impact on the morale of our soldiers and our Marines. It shook their very confidence.

"With so many of the First and Second ARVN divisions' soldiers having come from homes in these provinces, I am not surprised at their massive desertions. They are understandably torn between their families and their duties to their country. Witnessing poor leadership, they chose to run with their loved ones. The civilian panic itself left our own forces unsettled, and most of them come from homes in the south, near Saigon.

"Losing the 147th Brigade hurt us badly and I think destroyed the confidence of General Truong. I believe he had tied all of his hopes on their coming here to bolster our defenses. With news of their loss, Truong went silent."

"What shall we do, General?" the colonel said in a tired voice, truly at a loss of ideas.

"We will regroup our Marines at Vung Tao," the general answered. "With the men we have here from the 468th Brigade and the six thousand or so from the 369th and 258th brigades, if they can retreat here by tomorrow, and if we can evacuate them successfully, then we can reconstitute a respectable force. However, we will need equipment."

Brigadier General Bui, however, lost both equipment and troops to his plan. When the two remaining South Vietnamese Marine brigades received the retreat orders, the discouraging news fractured their battalions into roaming armed bands. They took what combat equipment they could carry and abandoned their crew served weapons without destroying them. Scuttling the artillery pieces, tanks, and heavy guns took time—time they now realized they did not have.

Running from their defensive strongholds, the Viet Marines fled toward the city in roving groups of two, three, and four men, as well as in more organized squads of a dozen and more. While many of the Marines fought through increasing numbers of NVA and Viet Cong forces, cowboys, and frantic civilians, struggling to continue to carry out orders and rendezvous at Marble Mountain for evacuation, others simply went on a rampage.

NAVY PIER, MARBLE MOUNTAIN

"YOU MUST LET us on the boat!" the frantic man in a white shirt and slacks screamed at the Viet Marine standing guard at the gangway of the South Vietnamese Navy boat while scores of his comrades scrambled aboard, behind their commandant, Major General Bui The Lan. The civilian clung to the chain-link fence that bordered the docks, and he stood, slammed into the steel mesh, pushed by hundreds of other civilians who had heard news of a seaborne evacuation at the Marble Mountain boat basin and desperately sought to make this last-ditch passage from Da Nang.

"Only Marine Corps personnel," the guard shouted coldly.

Viet Marines had begun boarding the vessels at 6:00 a.m., March 29, while their cohorts from the 369th and 258th brigades straggled through the gates at Marble Mountain in groups of three and four and hurried to join their brothers already aboard the ships. With the retreating bands of Marines came hundreds of other South Vietnamese soldiers they had met along the way. Seeing the soldiers heading toward apparent safety, scores of frantic civilians followed them.

When the first group of ships carrying the Viet Marine commandant and fifteen hundred of his men pushed away from the pier, the lucky few aboard the vessels watched as the panic-stricken crowds tore down the chain-link fence and toppled the guardhouse at the entrance to the docks.

Dozens of fellow Viet Marines waved hopefully at their departing brothers and then began dealing with the advancing crush of people by shooting their rifles directly into the clamoring throngs.

When the South Vietnamese Navy ships returned to the pier that afternoon for their next evacuation loads, they approached a disastrous sight. Vying for space in the next boats out, Viet Marines had engaged in a heavy firefight with ARVN soldiers, slaughtering untold numbers of them and civilians caught in their cross fire. Rather than tying up and taking aboard the embattled Marines, the ships turned and headed back southward to Nha Trang and Vung Tao.

Chapter 12
ESCAPE FROM DA NANG

"GUNNY," Al Francis called to Staff Sergeant Walter Sparks, who jogged along the upstairs walkway at the American consulate. "Give me a quick status report."

"Sir, the street blockades went defunct yesterday evening while you were out at Marble Mountain," Sparks replied. "All nonessential consulate staff, both military and civilian, have successfully departed to Saigon. That handful of Vietnamese who mans the outside gates and the five interior guard Marines I kept here with me represent our full combat complement. Only reason these ARVN have not deserted like all the others, I made a command decision and promised them safe passage out with us. We needed their firepower, so I struck a deal with them.

"We've got bedlam in the city, getting worse by the minute: nonstop traffic jams at the gates, cowboys and renegade ARVN shooting up the streets, and everybody and their cousins still wanting evacuation tickets. So far we've kept things pretty tight inside the consulate, except for a few South Vietnamese Army officers who straggled up with their fam-

ilies. Maybe we can still get them out on one of the Air America flights
from Marble Mountain."

Francis looked toward the front gate and then gazed over the portal's red tile roof, looking blankly at the tops of the trees that grew in
a line along the street outside. Exhaustion showed on his face as he
shifted his eyes back to the staff sergeant and spoke in a dry voice,
"Not likely, Gunny."

"Marble Mountain out?" Sparks asked sadly.

"Situation there has become untenable," Francis said. "Security
started falling apart this morning, putting the flights in serious jeopardy, so Saigon shut them down. The Viet Marines billeted there will
depart by boat in the morning, so forget any help from them. Meanwhile, with the Vietnamese seeing the evacuation flights running hot
and heavy, they've started crashing the airfield fences. So Marble
Mountain has begun to run amok. The Marines have the dock still secured for their departure, but that's it."

"I thought something like that had gone on," Sparks said. "I was
on the radio with the Air America guy at the terminal, and he told me
that it was all over. The planes wouldn't land."

"Saigon suspended all Da Nang flights at about 10:30 this morning," Francis said. "It has been an absolute nightmare.

"Yesterday, after first diverting the lighter aircraft missions to Marble Mountain because they were so easily overrun by the mobs, I finally
had to shut down all operations at the Da Nang terminal at eight o'clock
last night. By then, the crowds had begun overrunning everything.

"Luckily, Air America had dropped in with a CH-47 helicopter, so
I took that aircraft, put the last outbound load of evacuees on it, along
with the Da Nang terminal crew and myself, and we went to Marble
Mountain. The evacuees, mostly a bunch of American contractors who
should have left here days ago, and for one reason or another stalled
until the last minute, caught an Air America C-47 to Saigon. I had the
remaining Americans that we had working in the terminal brought to
the consulate compound last night. We'll all ride out together, late
tonight, when we shut things down here. I've arranged for a helicopter
lift with Air America to take us out."

WHEN EVACUATION OPERATIONS at Da Nang Air Base began, they flowed
smoothly, and the Americans and Vietnamese awaiting their turns for

departure remained orderly. People came to the consulate, verified their identities, established that they met the criteria for space on the flights, and got a ticket.

As flight after flight lifted from Da Nang Air Base, the North Vietnamese closed on the city. During early morning on March 27, the Communists sent a barrage of 120-millimeter artillery rounds crashing into Da Nang's heart, killing eleven people with the first impacts. Terror immediately radiated outward from that opening salvo, like a circle of waves from a rock crashing into a pond. At once frantic people let go of what little control they had maintained, and now they fled blindly though the streets. Soon boats crowded the Han River, overloaded with people running to the sea, desperately tempting their fate against the treacherous currents, rocks, and tides, hoping to escape down the coastline. Simultaneously, crowds of other panic-stricken Vietnamese led by deserted soldiers converged on Da Nang Air Base, hoping to bargain passage or even force their way aboard the departing flights.

Moments after the Communist rockets and artillery began striking throughout the city in sporadic clusters, gunfire erupted in the streets. The cowboys, joined by renegade deserters, began shooting and looting as rumor spread of the NVA now lurking within Da Nang's outskirts, poised for the kill.

ARVN rangers, some of South Vietnam's most disciplined and best trained soldiers, deserted their posts by scores and joined the chaos, roaming the streets in armed bands, shooting anyone who crossed them. They too advanced on the airport, hoping to commandeer flights.

That same morning, Al Francis had gone by jeep to Da Nang Air Base to observe the evacuation operations there. The short drive that during calmer days usually lasted only fifteen minutes now took nearly two hours to negotiate. The consul general's nerves had already spent themselves by the time he arrived at the airport shortly before nine o'clock.

Inside the terminal, people jammed and shoved each other. An individual could not simply walk from one place to the next, but had to find the direction of flow that went the desired way and jump in it. Security and order rapidly fell out of control.

Al Francis's temper bubbled tight against his temples as he held a black, foot-long two-way radio with its flat tape antenna in his right hand and slapped it repeatedly into the palm of his left hand. He watched two of the CIA operations crew helping a group of Vietnamese families with a chorus of crying children across the crowded terminal, pushing hard to plow through an opposing current of frantic people. A plane waited for them at the gate, and they were the last passengers scheduled to board it.

Before the escorted group had reached their departure point, a white with red trim World Airways Boeing 727 taxied into the chocks at the next gate. Seeing the fresh flight rolling to a stop, a swarm of unticketed Vietnamese suddenly bolted for the plane. They overran Al Francis, the CIA escorts, and the authorized passengers, attempting to commandeer seats aboard the newly arrived aircraft.

As other unticketed Vietnamese saw the group pushing their way through the gate, they too joined the mayhem. Rapidly, the entire terminal started to boil over.

The normally well-composed consul general suddenly bellowed a war cry and began swinging at the unruly mob with his left fist and lashing at people with the foot-long radio that he clutched in his right hand. As if he wielded a leather-covered brick, he slammed the walkie-talkie against the forehead of one man, who tumbled backward, dazed. Then Francis spun in a circle with his arms whirling to clip his next victims, and the radio's flat tape antenna, following the spin, snapped with a harsh sting across several offending people's faces and necks.

"Where is the mayor of Da Nang? Get me the mayor," Francis shouted, his anger bulging the veins in his neck like fire hoses and turning his face dark red. "Why isn't he here, managing this?"

One of the consul general's bodyguards then saw the mayor, standing out of the way, horrified at the outburst from the American diplomat. Francis's security agent grabbed the trembling politician by the arm and dragged him to his boss.

"Goddamn it, man," Francis scolded the mayor, "why aren't you in control here? At least give us a hand. After all, these are your people!"

Colonel Garvin McCurdy, an army officer from the Defense Attaché's Office in Saigon, had flown to Da Nang to help Al Francis with the overwhelming logistics problems of controlling the flow of the air evacuation process. He had just arrived on the World Airways 727 that had moments earlier taxied to the gate. The soldier never got off the tarmac when Francis stepped out the terminal door, spun the man in his tracks, and put him back on the same aircraft, sending him immediately to Saigon to plead for more planes.

The jet engine roar of one after another flight of World Airways Boeing 727 and McDonnell Douglas DC-8 jets had kept rolling day and night, launching and landing around the clock, ferrying out approximately 250 people at a time. Among the jets, carrying smaller loads of a dozen to fifty passengers, buzzed a swarm of propeller-driven, lighter aircraft, mostly Air America Convair 580s, Douglas DC-3s and C-47s, a scattering of oddball bush crafts and puddle jumpers, and a nonstop flock of helicopters.

As the city crumbled by the second, overflowing into the terminal at Da Nang Air Base, virtually bringing operations there to a standstill by midmorning on March 27, Air America CH-47 helicopters began ferrying groups of outbound citizens to Marble Mountain's airfield. The runway there was shorter, primarily used as a helicopter and light-aircraft base, but security seemed much better because of its relatively isolated location. Controllers hoped that from Marble Mountain the airlift could buy time to make a few more hops.

When MR 1's commander, General Truong, and his staff fled their headquarters that same day, flight operations at Da Nang Air Base rapidly deteriorated. The ARVN soldiers and police squads who had stood the sentry watch there quickly evaporated. With no reliable military presence or police holding in check the airfield's badly strained security, the frantic crowds immediately took over the terminal and flight line, destroying everything in sight. A number of panic-stricken soldiers had even tried to fly out some of the several dozen F-5 fighter jets that the South Vietnamese Air Force had abandoned. Anything that anyone could throttle up and steer skyward had either flown south or crashed.

When the Viet Marine Corps command saw the tents folding and wanted to bug out too, Saigon controllers quickly deemed Marble Mountain no longer safe and cancelled all further flights there as well. Now, for the frantic nearly two million residents and refugees who jammed Da Nang's streets and byways, embarking on the South China Sea or joining the long slog of humanity packed on Highway 1 snaling southward represented their only routes of escape.

From March 25 until the morning of March 28, the airspace above Da Nang had swarmed with aircraft like flies around a filthy outhouse on a hot day. When the sun set that final day, the sky lay empty and quiet. The American consulate also stood nearly vacant except for Walter Sparks, his crew of five Marines, Al Francis, and a handful of his staff.

As the evacuation rolled into high gear the first day, American and South Vietnamese staff at the consulate had issued more than four thousand air tickets when they lost count. On the first planes to depart, Al Francis had packed aboard every consulate staff member, dependent, and other American civilian stationed there that he deemed nonessential. If the consulate were to get overrun, he wanted the minimum number of Americans to fall victim to the situation.

On the second day, the skeleton crew played things by ear. One staff officer had asked Consul General Francis about some provisions outlined in their revamped evacuation plan, to which the diplomat simply replied, "Improvise." As the second day of the evacuation wore into the third, events ran pretty much by the seat of the pants of the person in charge of the operation at the time. "Make a command decision" became a common phrase quipped among the staff when anyone raised a question.

Staff Sergeant Walter Sparks and his Marines excelled at seat-of-the-pants operations. Life in the corps had taught them one thing: Operation plans often make good toilet paper when the soft stuff runs out. They had learned not to fret when events did not develop quite as the planners had envisioned them. From their first days in boot camp, Marines learned profound lessons from harsh teachers on how to improvise. Thus when everything seemed bound for hell in a handbasket, Sparks and his men calmly shifted gears without losing step.

While the Saigon embassy staff had wrangled every available plane for the massive aerial evacuation from Da Nang, Major General Homer D. Smith, Jr., the defense attaché, had realized early on that despite Ambassador Graham A. Martin's unflagging optimism, the airlift could not continue if the city's defenders ran out. Smith and his pragmatic crew reckoned that once the enemy stood at Da Nang's gates, the ARVN units manning the ramparts would most likely disappear, as others had done since the collapse began in Quang Tri.

Based on that consideration, as well as others to include expedience and load capabilities, the defense attaché and his staff, even before Hue had fallen, began rounding up scores of merchant ships and seagoing barges and mustered them into an evacuation flotilla, a day's passage away, should Da Nang need them in a hurry.

On March 27, as controllers in Saigon realized that the air evacuation from Da Nang would soon fail, the embassy staff sent a flash message to Washington, DC, advising Secretary of State Henry Kissinger of the situation. With conditions on the brink in Phnom Penh, the navy had most of its otherwise available shipping and helicopter assets committed to Operation Eagle Pull, providing evacuation support of the Cambodian capital. Therefore, Kissinger sought assistance from the Military Sealift Command, requesting merchant vessels to carry evacuees from Da Nang. However, the soonest any of their vessels could arrive at Da Nang would be late in the afternoon of March 28. Until then, Al Francis and his crew had to deal with life as best they could.

DA NANG CONSULATE COURTYARD—6:00 P.M., MARCH 28

"FUCK IT," Walter Sparks said under his breath, throwing the last of a pile of papers into the burn barrel and watching the flames destroy them. His Marines had spent the past three days shredding and burning the consulate's mountains of files and classified materials. Today they finished the last of that chore.

"What's wrong, Staff Sergeant?" Corporal Leonard Forseth said, tossing in the final batch of papers from the consul general's desk and hearing Sparks grumble.

"I guess in the back of my mind I never wanted to admit that it would come to this," Sparks said. "We destroyed a lot of history these past few days, a lot of stuff. We're walking out after all these years and all those Marines who got killed and wounded right out there in those hills. Just walking out and burning everything."

"Oh," the corporal said, looking up at the distant mountains. "I thought you were pissed about leaving your own gear behind. You know, your apartment, your clothes and stuff, and all that terrific stereo equipment."

"Hell, yeah, that pissed me off too," Sparks said and laughed. "That's just junk, though, Corporal Forseth. What really hurts me, and I mean cuts right into my heart, is the thought of all that our corps spent in lives and sacrifice out here, and we finally end up walking out on it."

"I guess that bothers me most too," the corporal said. "I mean, I hated like hell leaving my stuff at the Marine House and getting locked down in here for the past three days. I would have liked to have gone and gotten my gear too. Then I think about what you said, all the lives we spent for this country."

Walter Sparks picked up a broom handle with one end charred and jammed it into the flaming barrel, stirring the ashes to ensure that all the documents had completely burned. Then he put his hand on the shoulder of the young corporal.

"Let's go make muster with the boss," he said. "It's getting about that time."

Al Francis had already gathered with the remaining Marines and his staff when Walter Sparks and Leonard Forseth walked into the courtyard from the rear of the consulate. A string of vans and the consul general's staff car sat waiting for them, pointed toward the compound's front gates.

"Here's the consulate flag," Sparks said to his boss, taking the official colors, folded in an appropriate triangle, and handing them to Francis.

At 6:30 that evening, March 28, the consul general, his remaining staff, including the Da Nang air terminal crew, Walter Sparks and his five Marines, and the squad of ARVN soldiers who had remained to guard the consulate left the American compound for good. One by one the vehicles crept onto the corniche that fronted the Han River and led along Da Nang Bay. When the last van dipped down the driveway, it stopped for a moment so that the four ARVN soldiers standing sentry outside the gate could pile aboard. As it pushed forward, pressing its way through the mob that filled the street, hundreds of screaming people flooded inside the now-abandoned American consulate.

Staff Sergeant Sparks looked out the front window of the last van as it stopped to take on the exterior guard. His friend Nguyen's hibachi cart lay cold on its side. Scavengers had already picked the carcass clean, leaving only the metal box of the cart. They had even taken the wheels.

"Poor old Nguyen," Sparks said from the front passenger seat.

Within an hour of their departure, the maddened crowd had ransacked the American consulate. Angry deserters then set the entire compound ablaze.

Le Cong Than and several of his Viet Cong guerrillas from the Forty-fourth Line Front watched as the caravan left and then stood nearly speechless observing the spectacle of the consulate's immediate destruction. He had hoped to use the beautiful French citadel for his headquarters once the Americans had departed.

The American diplomatic caravan drove to the International Commission of Control and Supervision's landing zone, where Al Francis had arranged for Air America helicopters to evacuate them. At the ICCS compound, away from the bustling traffic that had surrounded the American consulate and jammed the street that ran along the Han River, life relaxed to a remarkable quietness as the sun set.

In the darkness the small group sat beneath a silent sky. No helicopters, only the distant noise from the traffic-filled streets of Da Nang broke through the quietness.

"Gentlemen," a voice announced from the darkness of the open back door of the consul general's car. "I've got good news and bad news."

"Bad news first, sir," Sergeant Venoy Rogers spoke in return.

"We have no helicopters," Al Francis then said, stepping into a dim circle of light cast from a nearby security lamp attached to a utility pole. "It seems that Air America cannot get fuel from the Vietnamese, probably due to the chaos at Marble Mountain. So they cannot come and get us. That's the bad news."

"The good news, sir?" Walter Sparks then asked.

"We're going next door to my house, have a cocktail, and plan what to do next," Francis said.

The consul general lived a little more than a half mile from the American consulate. His villa with high security walls, however, stood in a relatively quiet neighborhood, off the track of the roaming cowboys, bands of renegades, and unruly mobs that now seemed bent on destroying everything in the city, taking special vengeance against anything or anyone that even looked American.

Once inside the protection of his home's gates, the bulk of the group sat down and waited. Meanwhile, Walter Sparks and the others who comprised Al Francis's Black Box team sat with him at the dining table and considered what options now existed for them.

"What about getting a small frigate or destroyer in here?" the CIA logistician asked.

"What if we did?" Francis asked back. "First of all, the ship would immediately get targeted by the NVA. It would have a better chance at Marble Mountain, but not on the Han River, so deep in the city."

"How about those barges that what's his name at the DAO mentioned," the security boss said. "Alaska Barge and Transport Company. That's the name of them."

"Go on, you've got my attention," Francis said.

"Have them push a couple of barges into the river, distract the Vietnamese, and then put a little boat at the dock across from the consulate for us to get on," the consulate security chief said. "There's a guy I can call."

"Let's do this," Francis said. "There is an entire ARVN company squatted up the street from the consulate. The minute they see the barges, they will want on the first one and will probably start shooting their way aboard if we don't let them. So we put a big barge in the wide open water, up the street, where they've bivouacked along the seawall. Get their attention by setting it way out in the open water where they can see it and have it start working toward them. That will keep them busy, guarding the docks and keeping a lot of people out of our way too. Meanwhile, we have a smaller, less attractive barge pushed to the dock across from the consulate. We jump aboard and shove off immediately."

"Better than sitting here, waiting for the Viet Cong to knock on the door," Walter Sparks said with a smile.

One of the CIA operations agents tapped Al Francis on his shoulder and whispered in his ear.

"Where are they now?" Francis said.

The agent shrugged. "Probably still out around Marble Mountain someplace. Somewhere they came up with a couple of choppers and some planes with fuel to do a round-trip from Nha Trang, so they're getting the people out on them."

"We couldn't use them?" Francis asked.

"Not a chance," the agent said. "These are deep-cover people that if we don't get them out, the NVA will kill on the spot. You know these guys. They'd tell you to piss up a rope quick as look at you."

"The NVA would just as quickly kill these guys too," Francis said. Then he turned to the six men seated at the dining table.

"Gunny," Francis said, looking squarely at Walter Sparks, "you will take charge of getting this motley crew aboard the barge."

Then he looked at the others. "These vessels are really not much more than big, long Dumpsters. They normally use them to haul stuff like pipe, lumber, dirt, and rocks, not a very hospitable place for people to ride. However, they have fairly high steel gunwales that will offer some protection against shoreline gunfire. Everyone going aboard must bring ample water and whatever material they can use for shade. There is no telling how long you will be on the water. With the afternoon sun, those cans will get awfully hot."

The consul general then tossed a one-page teletype message on the table and said, "State Department has dispatched a couple of MSC ships our way, big deep-draft cargo vessels, the *Pioneer Contender* and the *Greenville Victory*. They should arrive on station at 0800. Instead of those barges trying to work down the coastline, they will navigate straight out to sea and rendezvous with these two.

"Questions?"

"Sir, by you putting me in charge of getting this motley crew aboard the barge, do I gather you have other commitments?" Walter Sparks asked.

"I have a couple of operators out of pocket at the moment, and myself and Bwana Jim over there will have to go tend to that bit of business," Francis said. "All hush-hush and shush-shush, you know."

"You know, sir," Sparks said in a low voice, looking straight at Francis, "I am charged with your personal safety as my primary mission."

"Gunny," Al Francis said and put his hand on Sparks's shoulder, "I very deeply appreciate your concern for me. Placing your life on the line for me means a great deal. I don't forget things like that, or people like you. There is a living room and front yard full of people out there who need your leadership now. So I am making this an order. You will see to it that these fine men get to the barge, out to sea, and aboard one of the MSC ships safely. You got that?"

"Yes, sir," Sparks said and smiled. "Understood."

"Besides, Gunny," Francis said, now standing and putting his arm over Walter Sparks's shoulder, leading the Marine toward the living room, "it's not like I will be alone. I do have my sidekick with the thick neck standing over there and our two wayward pals in the bush for company. Don't worry. I intend to see you in Saigon in a day or two."

"IT'S LIKE WE'RE the Dirty Dozen, except dirtier," Corporal Ronald Anderson whispered to Staff Sergeant Walter Sparks and the other four Marines. "Hiding in the back of a trash truck, sneaking out in the middle of the night, all pretty damned theatrical if you ask me."

"Nobody asked you," Sparks grumbled from beneath the canvas that covered the vehicle's staked bed, hiding the consulate's last batch of evacuees from Da Nang.

Two of the ARVN soldiers had stripped off their uniforms, borrowed clothes from an unsuspecting neighbor of the consul general, and ventured off into the night in search of a vehicle that could carry the company of people to the consulate dock unnoticed. At 3:00 a.m., the two thieves returned with a long, flatbed truck topped by a heavy green canvas, under which rode a load of garbage.

Although they dumped the thirty-foot long pile of trash on the consul general's lawn, they could not dump the dankness of the truck bed's interior, nor its smell.

"Didn't they clean up roadkill with this truck?" Sergeant Bill Spruce groaned. "I know some of it is still sticking to the sides."

"I think that's hog guts you're smelling," Sergeant Lazaro Arriola responded sarcastically. "I saw this truck parked at the slaughterhouse yesterday, hauling off their shit."

At 4:30 a.m., the two ARVN soldiers seated in the front of the truck pulled it to a stop at the docks across the street from the consulate. Walter Sparks and the others hiding in the back could hear the people outside, talking and slapping the door of the truck. The Vietnamese sentry who rode on the passenger side got out and said something harsh to whoever had banged on the truck and then walked to the back and put his head under the canvas.

"No ships yet," he said.

"They were supposed to be here at 3:30 this morning," Sparks whispered.

The soldier just shook his head, "No ships yet. I will tell you when I see them."

Dawn's gray light began to leak through the gaps in the corners of the canvas, and Walter Sparks peeked out when he heard the deep rumble of a tugboat's twin diesels as it pushed a three-hundred-foot-long barge tied ahead of a second barge half its length. Then a crewman disengaged the lines that coupled the larger barge to the smaller one and the tug.

Just as the big barge uncoupled, the tug heaved its engines hard forward and sent the hulking open ore hauler sliding toward the shore where thousands of Vietnamese and renegade soldiers gathered. Quickly, the ARVN soldiers bivouacked there, just as Al Francis had predicted, opened fire, and established a barrier that kept the people at that end of the street at bay. This was their barge, and they would board it first.

Sparks immediately bailed from under the canvas when he heard the tugboat's diesels roar in reverse, slowing the smaller barge as it skidded along the small docks across the street from the consulate.

"Everybody jump aboard now!" Sparks commanded.

In a matter of seconds, the Americans had all scrambled aboard the bouncing nose of the great vessel. Then to their shock came a tidal wave of people running at the ship. The ARVN soldiers had turned automatic weapons on the crowd, but still they came. The slaughter became intense.

"Get it out of here!" Sparks shouted, pumping his fist up and down for the tugboat's skipper to see.

Despite the boat grinding into reverse, pulling back, hundreds of Vietnamese began leaping and diving aboard the vessel. Walter Sparks and the Americans could only hurry to the stern of the barge, wait in a point of safety, and watch the horror unfold.

Hundreds of boats now crowded the river, and thousands of people scurried aboard the three-hundred-foot-long barge set adrift. They futilely waved their arms at the tugboat captain to hook on and pull them too. However, the load now crammed aboard the 150-foot barge that the tug struggled to push strained the boat's full worth as it shuddered to get underway.

As the tug pushed and pulled the barge to get it to turn against the river's current, its great steel nose crashed and ground into the rocks and concrete of the seawall. While the operator tried to maneuver the barge out and push it down the river, people tried to leap aboard and fell into the water. Others, desperate to at least save their children, threw toddling and infant babies at the barge. Their small bodies crashed against the steel sides of the great hauling vessel. Most of them dropped into the water too. Before the babies disappeared beneath the surface, their screams echoed above the drone of the tugboat's engines.

Each time the tug surged the barge forward, in its attempts to turn and get underway, it rode into the seawall and rocks, crushing the old people who had fallen into the water, trying to board, and the fallen children.

Walter Sparks watched the carnage, horrified at what he saw and heard. Each surge brought death screams from men and women and small children, smashed between the stone and steel.

Despite the river of death flowing red at the consulate docks, parents kept throwing their babies at the departing barge. Insanely they hoped that people who now overflowed the space on the vessel might reach over the side and save the child. The few who did rescue a baby only brought a shower of more children.

As the overcast dawn shone its first light across the water, the tug pushed the badly overloaded barge toward the sea and its rendezvous with the *Pioneer Contender*. Walter Sparks looked back at the tragic scene, watching it shrink in the growing distance as fog began to shroud the river. Even in combat he had never seen such carnage.

Seeing the tugboat depart, the ARVN soldiers guarding the docks opened fire on the barge. Bullets ricocheted off the ship's steel sides and dinged into the tug's woodwork. Boats crowded with panicked passengers sped after the barge, some also opening fire on the vessel since they could not catch it.

Later, these same soldiers commandeered a smaller tugboat, threw its passengers off, and used it to push the bigger barge out to sea.

At eight o'clock on the morning of March 29, the Alaska Barge and Transport Company tugboat, with Walter Sparks now riding in the wheelhouse, entered the open sea outside Da Nang Bay. There, in the distance, came the *Pioneer Contender*, exactly on time.

Once the MSC cargo vessel had stopped on station, it sent a whaleboat to the barge and took aboard Staff Sergeant Sparks and his Marines, along with the other Americans from the consulate. The *Pioneer Contender's* master stood at the top of the gangway as the Americans climbed aboard.

"What's all this?" the captain said, pointing at the barge swarmed with its Vietnamese passengers. As the ship sat waiting for instructions, more and more small boats began gathering at its sides, unloading their passengers on the already overcrowded vessel.

"What's all what?" Sparks said, caught off guard.

"My instructions are to put into Da Nang and pick up vehicles, American cars and trucks," the captain said. "What's all this? All these people?"

Walter Sparks laughed and said, "You got some bad scoop, skipper. There's about a million people wanting out of Da Nang right now. We brought a good bunch of them with us."

"Judging from the boats in the distance," the captain added, "it looks as if the rest are coming close behind you."

"We better get things underway then," Sparks said.

"We will pull the barge alongside and load the people straight up on the cargo nets," the captain said. "Sergeant, you and your men must disarm all evacuees before they get off that barge. I will have no gun-fire aboard my ship."

"We'll just have to do that as they come up the side," Sparks said. "If it's alright with you, we can just toss the guns into the ocean."

"Fine," the captain said.

For the next ten hours, Walter Sparks and his five Marines unloaded the barge, taking every weapon from the passengers in the process.

The horror that they saw on the docks played again as the barge rode along the side of the big ship. The two vessels' hulls slammed and ground as the waves and currents washed them back and forth.

Men pushed women and children out of their way, trying to scramble aboard the cargo ship. They could not wait their turns to board. Children and old people fell into the water, and the ships crushed them.

Panic soon overtook the passengers still aboard the barge as more and more heavily laden small boats pulled alongside and unloaded people onto it. Sporadic gunshots echoed among the chaotic throng, randomly killing and driving the people into a maddened crush trying to board the ship.

At sunset, Walter Sparks helped the final old woman onto the deck of the *Pioneer Contender*. He then gathered his five Marines for the grizzly duty of searching the barge for anyone still living among the deck strewn with corpses.

A dozen dead bodies lay pushed in a heap, and among them Sparks heard a groan. There he found an old man lying, exhausted, suffering from shock and a broken leg.

Near him, an old woman lay in a heap. At first the Marine thought that she was dead. Then she moved.

In the last light of March 29, Sparks, Sergeant Arriola, Sergeant Rogers, and Corporal Anderson finished their search for the living and carried the two survivors aboard the waiting ship.

Pushing slowly underway for Nha Trang, the *Pioneer Contender*'s crew cut the lines from the barge and set it adrift. With the ship free from its drag, the skipper then rang the engine room for flank speed.

Throughout the long day, Walter Sparks kept asking members of the consulate staff, now communicating with the ship's radios to Saigon, to let him know if they heard any word regarding the fate of Al Francis and the other Americans with him. Late that afternoon they made contact with the CIA team by radio. They needed extraction.

Sparks had already informed the ship's captain that when they had off-loaded the evacuees, he intended to return to Da Nang with him to rescue Al Francis and the American crew that remained with him.

"Let me have that phone a minute, sir," Sparks told the shipmaster, standing in the vessel's wheelhouse, watching the lights of Nha Trang grow larger in the distance ahead of them.

The shipmaster had already tried to plead the Marine's case, yet the party on the other end of the call flatly said no dice to him.

"Sir," Sparks began, "I am the staff NCO in charge, and my duty is the safety of the consul general, and he is sitting on a barge, as we speak, waiting to be picked up."

Again, the answer came a hard negative.

"Consulate communications people have made contact with those Americans," Sparks argued. "They got back to the docks and managed to get on a barge and need to get picked up. Right now renegade ARVN have commandeered most of the barges and tugs and have opened fire on anyone who approaches them. The consul general is in danger!"

Again, without explanation, the voice on the telephone told Walter Sparks that he and his Marines had finished their jobs, the consul general currently sought other evacuation options, and that the Marines returning with the ship would present far greater risks.

AL FRANCIS SPENT much of the morning struggling his way to Marble Mountain, where the ad hoc airlift of deep-cover intelligence operators had finally wrapped up.

Because returning to Da Nang presented significant risk for the American diplomat, Francis remained at Marble Mountain while his American cohorts hiked back to the consulate and found it ablaze. They also found that the ARVN who had once guarded the docks there had gone on a rampage. They had begun shooting indiscriminately, killing anyone they pleased, had raped scores of women, and were looting homes and shops, stealing gold, jewels, and other valuable barter goods. The Americans had used a handheld radio to make contact with one of the Alaska B & T tugboats, *Oseola*, whose New Zealander skipper braved the ARVN gunfire and rescued most of the remaining Americans, except for Al Francis.

While several of his cohorts had sailed a boat back across the river to Da Nang, looking for other Americans, the consul general remained at the Marble Mountain landing zone, helping to get the unauthorized airlift finished. Then as advancing NVA forces closed on the airfield, he and two British social workers fled to the swift boat basin and navy pier at Monkey Mountain, where he had hoped to find more evacuation barges, but found himself stranded instead.

As he hiked to Monkey Mountain, Al Francis looked at the sky and to his surprise saw a World Airways 727 climbing steeply, black exhaust smoke pouring from its three screaming engines, running full thrust from a hail of tracers, followed by the arcing white contrails of several futilely shot, surface-to-air rockets. He watched, amazed, as the passenger jet banked steeply away and roared toward the sea. Then, to his astonishment, he heard the thundering rumble of a second set of engines, echoing from the ground at Da Nang Air Base.

ALMOST FROM THE war's beginning, World Airways, with its flamboyant gunslinger boss, Ed Daly, had ferried thousands of American soldiers, sailors, airmen, and Marines, along with a host of government civilian employees, officials, and contractors in and out of South Vietnam. He hired the toughest, bravest pilots and crews and paid them well for their hazardous work. Daly also led his company by example, not putting an aircrew in a situation where he would not willingly stick his own neck.

In 1950, Daly had to borrow the fifty thousand dollars that it took him to buy World Airways, founded in 1948 by Benjamin Pepper with a fleet of three Boeing 314 Clippers. At the time Daly purchased the struggling firm, the Beroviche Steamship Company held title to the airline, acquiring it from Pepper a year earlier, and had added a pair of war-surplus Curtiss C-46 Commandos to the fleet, operating one to and from San Juan and using the second C-46 as a source for spare parts. With five well-worn airplanes representing the sum of the airline's principal assets when Daly bought the ailing firm, he also assumed the company's debt of more than a quarter of a million dollars. A year after Daly closed the deal that gave him World Airways, he leased a more modern Douglas DC-4 from Braniff Air Lines and began flying passengers under government contract.

After Ed Daly struggled for nearly five years, the Hungarian Revolution of 1956 finally dealt him a meaningful hand. He leased a second DC-4 and contracted World Airways to fly Hungarian refugees to

America. During the refugee airlifts, his two aircraft made fourteen trans-Atlantic crossings, and Daly found his way to the news pages and picture magazines by personally flying on several of the missions and visiting many of the refugee camps.

The good PR paid off, and Daly landed World Airways its bread-and-butter contract with the Military Air Transport Service, ferrying American soldiers on daily routes between Tokyo, Okinawa, Taiwan, and Manila. In 1959 the Civil Aeronautics Board upgraded World Airways's certification, broadening its operations to carrying military personnel and equipment on transcontinental flights, and then beyond. The move enabled Daly to equip his company with the big iron, the Lockheed Super Constellation and Starliner flagships.

As America pumped more and more of its military forces into the Vietnam War, Daly's World Airways became known as the Freedom Bird, flying military replacements and outbound veterans on daily hops between Okinawa and the conflict's entry and departure points at Saigon and Da Nang. In those days, World Airways flew a grand fleet of stretched Boeing 727 and 707 aircraft, with Daly frequently riding in and out of the combat zone. Always looking to do a good turn for his best customer, at Christmas time he personally delivered tons of holiday treats and decorations, including planeloads of trees, hams, and turkeys to the GIs on the front lines.

While NVA forces positioned themselves for the kill in Vietnam, the Khmer Rouge closed on Cambodia's capital, blockading it except from the air. From February 15 to 26, Daly unflinchingly had two of his World Airways DC-8 jets making six runs a day from Tan Son Nhut to Phnom Penh, flying relief supplies to the beleaguered city.

Thus, when the call for evacuation aircraft for Da Nang ran up its red flag, Ed Daly patriotically grabbed it and ran. Refugee flights had, after all, opened the door to success for his airline.

Almost from the onset of his involvement with the Vietnam War effort, Daly had developed a deep sense of concern for the people of Vietnam. He felt a genuine duty to keep a promise made by America to not abandon the South Vietnamese people. Therefore he felt that flying Da Nang's refugees from the onslaught of the enemy was the least he could do for them. He was a man of his word.

Before chaos had shut down Da Nang Air Base, flight mission controllers in Saigon had contracted Daly to fly two of his stretched Boeing 727 passenger jets into Da Nang to ferry out more people on March

29. Despite Saigon's repeated messages to him, advising that Da Nang no longer provided any form of security or safety for his aircraft and that they had cancelled all further evacuation flights there, Ed Daly, nonetheless, launched the two 727s from Tan Son Nhut bound for Da Nang with the pistol-toting World Airways president riding shotgun in the lead aircraft.

"Bring her down steep," Ed Daly reminded his pilot, Ken Healy, from the 727's jump seat. "Keep her at four thousand feet, and then dump it like a rock onto the runway."

The two crews and the World Airways boss had finalized their strategy before leaving the tarmac at Tan Son Nhut for the forty-minute hop to Da Nang. Coming in high and steep was nothing new to the veteran pilots, nor to Daly. That's the way he ran his life. Run hard, come in hot, high, and steep, drop like a rock, and then flare for all you're worth. Otherwise you crash and burn. Not only a tactic practiced by combat pilots, but a philosophy for living.

"Da Nang tower, World Airways oh-one, lifeguard," Ken Healy called to the unmanned control tower. No answer.

"We're on our own, boss," he then called to Daly who sat on the jump seat, wearing a headset with boom microphone suspended below his lip.

"Steep angle, and stay hot down the off-ramp and on the taxiway," Daly replied to him. "Oh-two is right on our six, so get off the runway fast."

"Roger that," the pilot responded, taking the 727 into a dirty dive, flaps and wheels dragging all the air they could grab.

The first plane hit the runway hard, had its speed brakes deployed, reverse thrusters kicked full, and wheels smoking as Healy leaned the aircraft hard on its struts, taking the first high-speed ramp off the main landing strip.

"Keep her hot, right up to the terminal," Daly growled on the intercom. "Don't slow down. If people get in front of you, just run them down."

As the first plane touched down, thousands of deserting Vietnamese soldiers, along with cowboys, other civilians, and their families ran toward the Freedom Bird. Seeing that many had rifles, Daly made a quick decision.

The second 727 had just begun its flare, nose high and reaching for earth with its main struts, when Daly barked at its pilot on the radio,

"Slim, don't stop. Touch and go! Touch and go! If you splatter a few on the runway, so be it, but get back in the air."

Just as the wheels smoked onto the runway, the 727's engines roared full thrust. In a few hundred feet, the aircraft lifted and banked hard right, retracting its landing gear and pulling up its flaps. Climbing hard and fast, it turned toward the sea and made its way with empty seats to Saigon.

"Turn it around right here, Ken," Daly then said to his pilot. "We'll just kick open the hatch and keep the engines turning. Once we get a load, hotfoot this baby back to the main and let's get airborne."

A Golden Gloves boxer as a youngster, Ed Daly unplugged his headset and hustled to the aircraft rear ventral door, ready for the hand-to-hand combat that he knew awaited him when he popped the hatch and dropped the air stairs. He had hoped to ferry out women and children, but when the hatch opened, automatically releasing its internal stairs, a crowd of angry men, scores of them soldiers, clambered aboard as the steps slid down.

Looking outside, Daly saw frantic men pop open the 727's door to the cargo hold, and people began flooding inside that space too. In seconds, the aircraft jammed with passengers crushed shoulder to shoulder, pushing themselves into every corner and gap that they could find.

"Forget the welcome-aboard speech," Daly cracked to Ken Healy over the crew phone intercom. "Throttle this mother up and roll."

"Skipper, the runway is jammed with people," Healy called back.

"Then just build a fire in it here, and launch from this taxiway!" Daly shouted back, at the same time kicking a Vietnamese man in the chest, rolling him backwards off the air stairs as the plane began to move out.

As Daly struck one man, two more running behind him took his place. He slugged and kicked one man after another off the stairs, trying to close the hatch so that the plane could take off. Finally, Ed Daly drew his pistol and began slapping the onrushing men with the gun's butt. All the while, Ken Healy had pushed forward the throttles, and the big plane picked up speed down the five-thousand-foot-long taxiway.

As the jet lumbered forward and gained speed, people ran from its path. One frustrated soldier hurled a hand grenade at the departing aircraft. It exploded on the wing, damaging the flaps.

Under the plane, legs and bodies dangled from the three wheel wells. Other frantic souls clung to the landing gear struts and tried to stand between the spinning tires. Quickly, many of them fell. Body after body tumbled from beneath the airplane, broken and crushed, and littered the taxiway.

As the jet developed lift, stretching out its gear, the unlatched cargo doors rattled in the hundred-mile-per-hour wind, and Ed Daly pulled with all his might on the air-stair and hatch cables. He finally managed to secure the ventral door when the last man trying to climb the retractable ladder fell off. At that same second, the 727 picked up its nose, its airspeed finally high enough to lift it off the ground, and began its rotation and climb.

The normal 525-mile-per-hour, forty-minute flight covering the 350 miles from Da Nang to Saigon took Daly's badly overloaded plane two hours to journey. An unknown number of people clung on spars and braces inside the wheel wells, so Ken Healy had to leave the gear down. Dozens more had jammed themselves in the cargo holds. With the outer doors ajar and therefore no pressurization, Healy had to keep the plane's altitude low and airspeed at minimum, flying below ten thousand feet and averaging only 175 miles per hour.

When Daly's plane landed at Tan Son Nhut, he had counted 338 people inside the passenger cabin. He had no idea of the numbers who had ridden in the wheel wells and cargo hold.

A day after the heroic flight, the World Airways boss expressed his disappointment about the mission. He had intended to carry out families, and mostly women and children. In the end, of the 338 accounted passengers, only eleven women and children had managed to get aboard the heroic flight.

Photographs of a gun-wielding Ed Daly and news of Da Nang's last flight flashed across the media wires throughout the free world and bannered most newspapers under headlines, "Da Nang Falls."

EASTERN BEACHES BELOW MONKEY MOUNTAIN

"AHOY!" Al Francis shouted happily, keying the microphone on his handheld walkie-talkie. "Ahoy!"

"Blink your light three times," a voice on the radio responded.

Al Francis took the small, pocket-sized penlight that one of the CIA agents had left with him, along with a handheld tactical radio, and flashed it three times at the green, red, and white position lights from the South Vietnamese Navy patrol boat that motored toward him and two British companions.

"We cannot risk running aground," the voice came back on the radio. "You'll have to swim to us."

At just past midnight on the morning of March 30, the water washed cold on the consul general's bare feet as he and two other stranded souls waded into the surf that washed along the beach at Monkey Mountain. As he swam the half mile to the waiting patrol boat, he thought of sharks and other frightening sea predators lurking in the black water. Hammerheads, tigers, white tips, and reefers—they all prowled this tropical sea, and sharks seemed to bite best at night. Although his joy of finally making contact with his rescuers eliminated the feelings of fatigue from his long day's journey and desperate wait on Monkey Mountain, listening to a walkie-talkie that made no sounds until midnight, the idea of a man-eater careening from the depths and clamping him between its razor teeth helped Al Francis kick the distance with Olympic speed.

One toss of a life ring tied to a line pulled the American diplomat the final few feet to the waiting boat, where several hands pulled him aboard.

Walter Sparks learned of Al Francis's rescue when he arrived at the American embassy in Saigon the next morning. He also learned that several other Americans had managed to drive motorboats from Da Nang to the rendezvous area and had gotten aboard the *Pioneer Contender* when it returned. Other Americans had also managed to escape aboard the tugboats that rode alongside the *Pioneer Contender* that night.

For the next few days, Sparks and his Marines pitched in and lent a hand at the embassy. Soon, along with other nonessential Americans, they caught planes to the Philippines and then on to Okinawa.

All that they had were the clothes on their backs. They had lost all their personal possessions, including their uniforms. Although Sparks issued protests, citing that their losses were due to their duties, Uncle Sam felt no sympathy for them and offered no form of reimbursement.

During the two days following Sparks and his Marines' escape from Da Nang, other Military Sealift Command ships returned to Da Nang, rescuing more than seventy thousand Vietnamese from the coastal waters. Even one day after Da Nang's fall, on April 1, the *Con-*

tender's sister ship, the *Pioneer Challenger*, sat just beyond the city's bay taking aboard more evacuees.

An untold number of South Vietnamese people, ranging well into the thousands, also died trying to escape. Many were killed by their country's own soldiers.

When the MSC ship, *Greenville Victory*, arrived on station behind the *Pioneer Contender*, the renegade ARVN soldiers who had commandeered a tugboat seized control of the ship when they boarded. The ship's hijackers forced the captain to sail the vessel to Vung Tao, well away from its ordered destination of Phu Quoc Island, the port that the Saigon government had designated to receive all refugees evacuated by sea from Military Region 1.

Vice Admiral George P. Steele, commander of the Seventh Fleet, sent a United States Navy cruiser to ride alongside the *Greenville Victory's* port side and a United States Navy destroyer to ride at the starboard side. Both warships trained their deck guns on the bridge of the captured ship.

Near the coastline of Vung Tao, the *Greenville Victory* dropped its anchor, and the South Vietnamese deserters scampered down the chain and swam for shore.

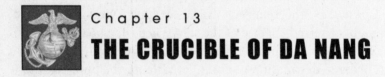

Chapter 13

THE CRUCIBLE OF DA NANG

DA NANG, RVN—SATURDAY, MARCH 29

PLUMES OF SMOKE rose from Da Nang, merging into an overcast sky as Colonel Hoang Duc The sat on a stack of ammunition boxes, overlooking the Han River, perched atop the concrete building that had once housed the III Marine Amphibious Force headquarters. The former United States Marine Corps command post sat midway on the Tien Sha Peninsula, north of Marble Mountain, on the riverfront side of the long strand of sand and rock, directly across the water from the American consulate and behind the China Beach Sea Load Lines jetty and pier. The commander watched the ongoing destruction through powerful binoculars and listened as a team of his Thirty-eighth Regiment's forward observers called targets for the Second NVA Division's artillery and rocket batteries that now held the southern neighborhoods of South Vietnam's second-largest city in an ever-tightening noose.

The Communist forces, now advancing behind a full artillery assault, had augmented their firepower with a multitude of 155- and 105-millimeter howitzers that they had captured with massive caches of ammunition and other arms, abandoned by the fleeing First, Second, and Third ARVN divisions and the South Vietnamese Marine brigades. The Americans had brought the great stockpiles of weaponry and munitions and then discarded them to the ARVN when the last United States Army and Marine Corps units exited South Vietnam in 1973. Rather than hauling the war supplies home with them, the departing American forces had cleverly labeled nearly all their still serviceable arms and materiel as "junk" and left it behind. According to the provisions established by the Paris Accords, with the arms stockpile regarded as scrap, the weaponry, munitions, equipment, and vehicles technically did not count as military supply or support.

As cold mist and fog swirled around Da Nang, that same so-called junk today turned its shock and horror full force against its former owners. Its firepower greatly augmented its new owners, the North Vietnamese forces encircling the city; an army of more than thirty thousand uniformed infantry troops plus their supporting elements, comprised of the Third NVA Division, moving from the north, the 304th NVA Division, closing from the west, and the Second NVA Division and Fifty-second NVA Brigade, advancing from the south. Meanwhile another ten thousand Viet Cong from the Forty-seventh and Ninty-sixth regiments, and the Forty-fourth Line Front brigade had infiltrated Da Nang and now moved through the streets from the eastern waterfronts toward its heart.

Directly across the river from the United States Consulate, the NVA colonel watched flames and smoke boiling from the American compound. Despite the blaze, that morning a lieutenant had reported to him that a company of Viet Cong from the Forty-fourth Line Front had entered the consulate and had found one of the radios intact and still operating. They had used the system to signal Saigon.

An unsuspecting voice asked, "How are things going in Da Nang?"

The gleeful Viet Cong then passed to him a message for Nguyen Van Thieu: "Tell your president that Da Nang now resides securely in the hands of liberation soldiers."

All along the river, Colonel The could see hundreds of thousands of people crowded on the street above the seawall and along the Han River's edge. Barges, tugs, fishing launches, sailboats, and even outboard motor skiffs maneuvered under a hail of gunfire. Dead bodies littered the water and floated in reefs like drifting trash among the ten thousand large and small vessels crammed with standing passengers.

The commander of the Thirty-eighth NVA Regiment did not like looking at the human tragedy unfolding on the river and turned his field glasses away from that scene and panned his view across the bay. He brought the binocular lenses in focus on the deepwater docks at the peninsula's end, below Mong Ky Mountain, which the Americans had come to term Monkey Mountain.

South Vietnamese Navy swift boats and patrol cutters still ran in and out of the long concrete docks at Monkey Mountain's Thong Nhat Allied Piers and Market Time Swift Boat Base. As Colonel The looked more closely, he could see dozens of tiny silhouettes of men darting among the buildings and along the roadway that serviced the various docks.

"ARVN soldiers," he told himself, watching the men scurry from place to place. "They have retreated to this bitter end and have no place else to run."

The NVA colonel told his forward observers to instruct the artillery batteries to immediately engage the docks as primary targets. In a moment, a shower of American-made 105-millimeter artillery rounds, descending through a chilly drizzle that had now begun to fall, rained on the new impact area. Spotter rounds found the distance, and hastily the observers called their gunners to fire for effect. Quickly, the salvos began turning the naval facility to rubble.

THONG NHAT ALLIED PIERS AT MONKEY MOUNTAIN

"GENERAL TRUONG!" the major cried to his commander. "We cannot stay here any longer. Their artillery has found its range and has us bracketed. They will soon fire for effect."

Lieutenant General Ngo Quang Truong rose from the deck chair where he had sat, watching the smoke rising from Da Nang. His heart had sunk as he saw the explosions of direct hits on what he estimated was his former headquarters compound, beyond Da Nang Bay, across the city, near the airport. He had heard far too many reports about how his command had run amuck and how hundreds of his soldiers roved in armed bands, raping and murdering Da Nang's own citizens and callously looting anything of value. The shame of it burned deeply in his heart.

American Consul General Al Francis had seen the general a few minutes earlier, just as the first artillery rounds began to strike near the fences and in the water, sending the South Vietnamese Navy swift boats and patrol cutters hastily to sea. Two British social workers had accompanied him here from Marble Mountain.

The pair of Brits and a German missionary had come to Francis's aid when a group of South Vietnamese soldiers had attacked him. The angry and exhausted American told General Truong how the soldiers appeared from nowhere, attempting to commandeer an airplane he had just loaded with evacuees. He had single-handedly fought the renegade band away from the aircraft, allowing it to taxi beyond their reach and then take off. The soldiers then retaliated on Francis, beating the consul general and leaving him lying limp on the Marble Mountain air facility taxiway.

His face now badly swollen and bruised, Francis and his two British companions asked the general if he had any barges or boats they could use. The American pled his case, explaining that many more people, among them several American and British citizens, desperately needed to escape.

A CIA logistician whom some of the Marines had jokingly come to call Oppie at last report sat trapped in the office at the American commissary supply warehouse compound with a mob of more than three thousand angry Vietnamese outside his window. He had radio contact with other agents, but had no way out except by his own wit.

In another incident, rioting Chinese Nung guards whom the CIA had employed to provide security for their residential compound, at the corner of Gia Dinh and Le Loi streets, had opened fire on two American agents who had sneaked over the facility's back wall in an attempt to retrieve some of their personal belongings. The two men managed to dodge the hail of automatic-rifle fire and escaped in a mad, broken-field dash through the front gates with only their lives. Their whereabouts in the city also remained unknown.

Then, at last count, Francis said that he knew of approximately one dozen USAID employees, along with some British and German social workers and several South Korean diplomatic visitors, stranded near the ferry landing on the Han River across the street from the blazing consulate. Now with the intensive NVA shelling that had commenced, they faced great peril in their location.

Dejectedly, General Truong expressed his regrets to Al Francis. He had nothing to offer, not a barge nor even a small boat. He no longer even had an army.

The American diplomat had seemed surprised when he first saw General Truong. He had thought that the MR 1 commander had fled to Saigon with his staff a day ago. Truong had then told Francis that he had only gone to the Monkey Mountain seaport to try and regroup his forces. He had not given up after all, at least not until he finally realized that he no longer had any forces.

"This handful of soldiers, my loyal friends, this is all that now remains of my command," Truong said sadly, pointing to a haggard partial company of ARVN troops armed only with a few rifles and hardly any ammunition.

Francis and his companions bid farewell to the general and his command and then jogged up the concrete roadway that fronted the piers and crossed through the fence at a small pedestrian gate that opened to the beach. The trio ran along the outwardly curving sand and then disappeared around a rocky point.

Through the cold rain, while artillery rounds fired from his own guns began to focus on their target and increase in intensity, General Truong and his aide, followed by his loyal troop of fewer than a hundred soldiers, ran along the beach, northward from the concrete piers. The men followed the tracks left by Al Francis and his British friends, around the rocky point, and soon put the extended fingers of Monkey Mountain between them and the artillery that now fired for effect into the heart of the Tien Sha Ramp, the Market Time Swift Boat Base, and the Thong Nhat Allied Piers.

"I cannot swim," General Truong said, embarrassment sweeping over him as he watched his aide stripping off his boots.

"I will help you, sir," the aide said. "Hold to my back, and I will swim for both of us."

A small South Vietnamese Navy patrol boat bobbed in the waves just beyond the surf line, waiting on the two officers and a randomly chosen dozen of his loyal men to swim to it. The skipper of the vessel had recognized the general jogging on the beach and knew well that he could not allow the man to fall prisoner to the North Vietnamese or Viet Cong. He had his crewmen wave their hats and T-shirts at the string of men on the beach and beckoned them to swim to the boat.

General Truong at first tried to order as many of his men as he estimated that the boat could carry to leave ahead of him. They could then send for other boats to rescue those who remained on the beach with him. None of the soldiers would hear of it, however, and they urged the general to forget his compassion for them and to get aboard first. They would wait for him to send another boat for them.

"I should have died defending my command," General Truong said to his aide as the two men waded together through the surf.

"We both would have died then," the major said. "I am glad that you chose to live and fight another day."

ROOFTOP ABOVE FORMER III MAF HQ, DA NANG

HOANG DUC THE smiled as he saw the rounds striking the swift boat base and the long concrete piers. He could see the people scattering and the boats trying to depart through the barrage. He looked forward to mopping up the peninsula once the shelling had done its job.

Hopefully, most of the two million refugees who had flooded into Da Nang would now leave because of the city's heavy bombardment, making the job of returning order and discipline to South Vietnam's second largest metropolis much easier. The gigantic cascade of refugees fleeing southward along Highway 1, and now by sea, also added great momentum to the Communists' initiative. The people would descend upon Phu Cat and Nha Trang like a great tsunami, overwhelming the defenders long before his army attacked.

NVA FIELD HQ, NEAR BAN ME THUOT

"GENERAL TRAN, MY friend, join me for another smoke," General Van Tien Dung said to Tran Van Tra.

"We must have won another battle," General Tran said, drawing out a cigarette, placing it between his lips, and allowing the North Vietnamese Army's supreme commander to put the flame of a freshly struck match under its exposed tip.

"For a man who does not smoke, I find myself indulging in tobacco more and more," General Dung said, now igniting his own cigarette. "Each time I hear good news from the front lines, I feel like lighting up one of these things and celebrating."

"I also have good news, from the Ninety-sixth and Forty-seventh regiments and the Forty-fourth Line Front," Tran Van Tra said, blowing smoke and smiling. "They have surrounded the civic center and now occupy the American consulate. Fires gutted most of the buildings, but they managed to put many of them out by carrying the burning furniture into the courtyard. They also captured the CIA logistics base with many good trucks and warehouse goods. When they opened fire on the ARVN soldiers who were there looting, rather than standing for a fight, the enemy fled like children."

"They have run like cowards," Dung said, laughing loudly. "It is wonderful! I have reports from the 304th Division that tell of our army having to drop their packs and chase after the enemy, quite literally running as fast as their feet could carry them!"

"Our commandos have now begun to take charge of the northern sectors of Da Nang and have restored order there," General Tran said. "We encounter some resistance from time to time, but mostly the shooting comes from the ARVN deserters killing their own people."

"General Le Trong Tan (North Vietnamese Army vice chairman of the Joint General Staff) arrived in the Da Nang sector's Fifth Region on Thursday and reports that possibly by tomorrow morning we will hold the entire city secure," General Dung said, beaming. "He is allowing the refugees to freely go southward along the highway since they provide such an excellent blocking force to move ahead of us. However, he has ordered his forces to stop the people from attempting to leave by sea. Thousands have died in the water trying to escape, and for their sake he said it must end."

Then General Dung smiled wryly and chuckled as he spoke, "Our good friend Colonel Vo Dong Giang reported to me this morning that the foreign minister has lodged a formal protest to the Joint Military Council for the American government's intrusion with their fleet of ships in bay of Da Nang and their shipments of relief goods to Saigon. He has cited that these actions gravely violate the Paris Accords."

"Of course," Tran Van Tra said smiling, "while the foreign minister protests, our tank brigades and artillery have fully engaged what little remains of Da Nang's defenses. Most resistance now comes from isolated pockets of a few stubborn South Vietnamese Marine battalions."

CENTRAL DA NANG, NEAR THE AIRPORT

UNTIL THIS MORNING, the North Vietnamese and Viet Cong forces had attacked only at night, trying to catch the ARVN defenders asleep. Now they launched their assaults in the daylight, advancing openly in the cool rain.

Le Cong Than had sent a company of Viet Cong from his Forty-fourth Line Front brigade to occupy the American consulate and try to extinguish the fires there. He had hoped that they could minimize the damage done to the city, but no one throughout the Communist chain of command had imagined that the enemy's armed forces would fracture and turn on their own people and the city they had fought to defend.

Now, fully armed with rifles at the ready and bandoleers of ammunition draped across their backs, the Viet Cong commander and his black-clad guerrillas moved on to Da Nang Air Base to put down the renegade violence going on there. Ahead of them a company of Soviet built T-55 tanks and infantry from the 304th NVA Division, which had attacked Da Nang from the west, pushed down the high fences, clearing a path for Le Cong Than's assault troops to follow them.

Inside the airport terminal, frantic civilians hopelessly waited for flights that would never come. Upon seeing the NVA tanks followed by a horde of Viet Cong and North Vietnamese uniformed soldiers breaching the airport fences, the panic-stricken civilians suddenly erupted out every door, running madly for their lives. They scattered across the tarmac and onto the runways, fleeing to nowhere.

Beyond the terminal, a company-sized congregation of South Vietnamese Marines had sandbagged themselves into a line of fighting emplacements near a hangar. Their defensive positions butted into the ten-foot high, barbed wire–topped chain-link fence that secured the airport from the outside community.

When the tanks first crashed the fence, the Viet Marines had opened fire with their 60-millimeter mortars and machine guns. Even though more than three thousand unarmed civilians now scattered across the tarmac and taxiways, the Marines never let up their fire. It cut down men, women, and children with the grazing hail of bullets and barrage of exploding mortars.

While three tanks pressed forward, sending high-velocity rounds exploding from their main guns and interlacing automatic fire from their machine guns, two tanks veered to the Marines' right and left flanks. With the tanks shielding two platoons of infantry soldiers who followed them, the Communists then cut the high fence at both flanks and tied the two loose ends of the center span of chain-link to the rear of each of the outside tanks.

Amazed at the creative genius of the spur of the moment plan, Le Cong Than watched as the ground troops ran for cover and the pair of tanks pulled the fence around the embattled Viet Marines. As the tanks sped forward, dragging each end of the fence toward the three center tanks, the men who fought in its center quickly realized the Communists had ensnared them.

Crowded together, like a Spartan circle, the Marines kept firing at their armored enemy.

Slowly the tanks pressed forward, squeezing the trapped men into a tighter circle. Then the infantrymen who had moved into positions behind the tanks dashed forward and hurled grenades into the circle. One after another, dozens of NVA soldiers tossed the deadly explosives among the trapped Marines. In a matter of minutes the several hundred South Vietnamese warriors who made their last stand lay dead on the tarmac.

With hardly a glance back at the carnage, the tank crews quickly cut the fence loose from their vehicles and focused their work on the terminal and surrounding buildings, which had now gone nearly vacant. Any civilians and ARVN soldiers who now remained stood quietly on the airfield's tarmac with their hands raised clearly above their heads. At the far end of the field, hundreds of other South Vietnamese clambered over the tall fence.

HAN RIVER BY III MAF HQ, DA NANG

"HERE, GATHER WHAT boats you can take from these people," Colonel The shouted to a captain who commanded one of his regiment's companies.

The NVA soldiers fired warning shots over the boats that tried to flee along the river and began turning the dozens of small crafts toward the near shore. Artillery from the captured 105-millimeter howitzers and the Thirty-eighth Regiment's own battery of 130-millimeter artillery, platoons of T-55 and T-57 tanks, and multiple arrays of 122-millimeter Katusha rockets, each system firing forty missiles at a time, pummeled the opposite shore, leaving the fleeing people the option of either dying in the hellish barrage or landing on the docks below the seawall where Hoang Duc The stood.

"Take those boats and move two companies across to the opposite ferry landings and secure them," he commanded.

Within thirty minutes, more than one thousand North Vietnamese soldiers worked their way across the Han River. From the opposite shore, a company of Viet Marines ambushed the waterborne soldiers.

Colonel The screamed to his artillery liaison, "Open fire across the river. Do not let up."

As he waited for the barrage, the colonel saw his reconnaissance commander fall backwards as a bullet struck him in the chest, killing him almost instantly. A second shot then took down the boatman standing at the tiller.

Then suddenly, identical immense shotgun blasts striking the ground on the opposite shore, one after another forty-round salvos of 122-millimeter Katusha rockets pounded the Thirty-eighth Regiment's newfound enemy. The explosions immediately suppressed the machine gun and rifle fire coming from behind a stone wall a few hundred yards downriver.

"I want a constant barrage laid on those positions until I say stop," Colonel The shouted to his artillery liaison.

Apparently, when he had ceased his artillery and rocket fire, once he had captured the boats, the Viet Marines had moved into position, seeing the opportunity for their ambush. Colonel The had allowed complacency to influence his decision to save ammunition, rather than maintaining a suppression fire while his men crossed the river's dangerous open water. The wounded men and the bodies of his dead would remind him to not repeat such a mistake.

Late that afternoon the sun finally emerged, and a sweltering heat struck the beleaguered city. All three NVA divisions and the two regiments and brigade of Viet Cong finally linked their forces, finishing off what little resistance now remained. Much of the North Vietnamese Second Corps had also now moved from Hue to Da Nang, operating as a massive reserve, enabling the attacking divisions to achieve maximum maneuverability.

By dawn, on Easter Sunday, March 30, 1975, Da Nang belonged completely to the Communist forces.

DA NANG, NEAR THE UNITED STATES CONSULATE

WHILE MANY OF his Viet Cong guerrillas celebrated their victory, Le Cong Than sat with several of his officers at the edge of the Han River, watching as scores of South Vietnamese people continued to crowd on boats farther downstream. On the horizon, beyond the outer bay, he could see the silhouette of the *Pioneer Challenger* drifting in the haze as it continued to pick up refugees.

Even though General Le Trong Tan had ordered his army to not allow further evacuations by sea, thousands of people still fled on the water. Thus NVA patrols now worked along the river's edge, turning people back. Le Cong Than and a battalion from his Forty-fourth Line Front joined the police duty.

"There, look," the Viet Cong commander said, pointing to a small tugboat that began drifting away from the opposite shore, several hundred yards downstream, more than fifty people jammed on the deck of the small craft.

"The current is taking them out," a soldier in a watchtower above the colonel called down.

"Fire the mortars across their bow," Than said.

Just as the first round exploded in the water, someone on the bridge of the small ship hoisted the yellow and red banner of the Republic of Vietnam above the wheelhouse's roof.

"They must have ARVN aboard the ship," the colonel said. "Keep your mortars ahead of the boat, and call for artillery to open fire on them as well."

Although the 60-millimeter mortars that exploded ahead of the tugboat did little to dissuade its pilot, the sudden burst of 155-millimeter rounds erupting only fifty feet away from the vessel quickly sent the craft's screws into full throttle reverse. Huge geysers of water shot up from the river with each artillery strike, gushing water over the vessel and its passengers.

"Now, adjust your mortars toward the opposite shore, so that they can only bring that boat to me," Le Cong Than called to his men.

Slowly the craft came to a stop at the ferry landing where the Viet Cong soldiers took the passengers prisoner and brought the boat's skipper to their commander.

"I can lock you in prison right now," Than told the boat's captain, "or you can swear your allegiance to me and act as my pilot. I intend to take command of your ship. We can wait here for my men to bring me a qualified pilot or you can volunteer."

In less than an hour, Le Cong Than and a squad of his men, armed with mortars, machine guns, rifles, and grenades, motored downriver in the tugboat, the flag of the Provisional Revolutionary Government fluttering on the mast above the wheelhouse. As they cruised toward the open bay, the colonel spotted a long, dark silhouette drifting through the distant haze.

"Do you see it?" he said, pointing out the object for the pilot. "Steer toward it, cautiously."

Slowly the tugboat approached the dark object, and soon Le Cong Than realized that the derelict was a barge. A few people squatted on its deck; most of its passengers lay down.

"Throw any arms overboard and raise your hands," the Viet Cong commander shouted over the tugboat's loudspeakers.

Few people moved, but one man stripped off his white shirt, and waved it as a flag of truce, and beckoned the tug to draw alongside.

With his machine guns trained squarely on the barge's passengers, Le Cong Than had the tugboat's pilot maneuver the small ship to the rear of the barge. Once they had pushed the barge snugly in place, he sent four of his soldiers to immediately begin lashing the two vessels together with several of the two-inch-thick hauling lines stacked on the tug's deck.

Slowly the pilot turned the long barge toward the mouth of the Han River and began pushing it toward Da Nang. As the tug's twin diesels groaned forward, Than deployed his squad of soldiers across the stern of the barge and called for a representative to come forward.

As the barge and tug cruised toward the city and the docks by the still smouldering American consulate, two men came forward and talked to the colonel.

More than four thousand people, mostly ARVN soldiers and their families, had crowded on the barge at Hue, just as the city had begun to fall. The tug that had pushed them out the Perfume River and beyond the barrier islands, into the open sea, had abandoned them. The skipper had feared he had too little fuel and moved too slowly, making them an easy target for NVA artillery. So he cut them adrift and proceeded south with a deck full of well-paying and well-armed passengers.

For five days the people had drifted, riding with the prevailing currents, too far from shore to even consider attempting to swim for land. They had no food and very little water when they began and, after the third day, had no water at all.

Several hundred of the people had already died from dehydration and exposure. Many more had little hope, even with food and water.

While Le Cong Than and his Viet Cong soldiers rescued the hapless refugees from Hue, the American merchant ships continued to ferry out thousands of South Vietnamese refugees who still managed to escape Da Nang. The *Pioneer Challenger* made her last evacuee run on April 2.

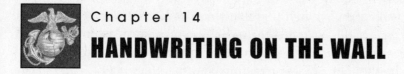

Chapter 14
HANDWRITING ON THE WALL

ORA WAN BAY, OKINAWA—EASTER SUNDAY, MARCH 30

SUNLIGHT GLARED OFF the white-capped waves as the distant amphibious assault vehicles danced through them, causing Corporal Steve Tingley to squint as he searched for a decent picture to snap. Staff Sergeant Don Gilbert, the III MAF command newspaper's senior editor, had sent him to the landing at Camp Hanson to grab a breaking-news photograph for the front page of the *Okinawa Marine*.

"Nothing more boring than some specks on the water and a big ship sitting still," Tingley said under his breath, as he released the shutter on his Nikon F2 camera with its 80-210-millimeter zoom lens pulled fully out to its maximum telescopic power. He exposed several frames of the monotonous seascape, making sure that he had his all-important fail-safe shot in case nothing more attractive appeared. Sergeant Gilbert would at least have a usable, albeit boring, graphic to illustrate the weekly tabloid's headline, "1st Battalion, 4th Marines Returns to Vietnam."

Offshore, the USS *Dubuque* (LPD 8) lay almost motionless on Ora Wan Bay, taking aboard the heavy equipment of Battalion Landing

Team One-Four. An amphibious transport dock and landing platform ship, the *Dubuque*, and other LPDs like her, featured a large helicopter landing platform designed on her stern and below that deck a set of gigantic sea doors at her waterline, built to allow the Marine Corps's tracked amphibious assault vehicles to swim in and out of the ship's massive cargo hauling belly. Inside this great naval vessel, the Marines could transport almost anything that they needed for war.

As Steve Tingley watched the LVTP-7 amtracks splashing through the whitecaps, shooting rooster tails behind them as they drove toward the ship, he thought of Christmastime and the *Nutcracker Ballet*. The behemoth ship, sitting in the water as the amtracks disappeared inside her gaping doors, reminded the corporal of the *Nutcracker*'s Mother Buffoon, lifting her skirts while children skittered beneath them.

Lance Corporal Donald Tompkins honked the horn of the olive drab green Ford Econoline van.

"Hurry the fuck up!" he shouted to Tingley. "It's Easter Sunday, for crying out loud!"

"What are you going to do?" Tingley called back, looping the camera across his shoulder and walking back to the vehicle. "Go to church?"

"I might!" Tompkins crowed and then laughed hard. Neither Marine had darkened the chapel door in the entire year they had called Okinawa their duty station and home away from home.

"Tommy-Guns, they would close the church before they let the likes of you inside," Tingley said with a cackle.

"I want to catch Sunday brunch before they close the chow hall," Tompkins said, dropping the van in gear and sending a shower of rocks spewing from the back tires as he rolled onto the highway. "Holiday menu, you know."

"Let's stop at Camp Courtney and see if I can get a better angle on the ship," Tingley said, still thinking of trying to pull a dramatic shot from the photographically boring event.

"Fuck you and the horse you rode in on," Tompkins growled as he careened through the narrow streets and bustling traffic in Ishikawa, following the road around the crescent shore of Ora Wan Bay. "You got a shitload of pictures back there. What's wrong with one of them?"

"You'll do what I tell you to do, or I'll write your puke ass up," Tingley snapped.

"Fuck you, ass wipe," Tompkins popped back and smiled. "You taking prick lessons from Sergeant Teeling nowadays?"

"Tompkins," Tingley said in a more friendly tone, "I need to get the shot from Camp Courtney. It gives me a better angle with the sunlight. Come on. I'll spring for *yaki soba* in terrible Taragawa, at Suzi's café."

"Okay," Tompkins said, smiling. "Shoot your shit at Camp Courtney, and then we go to eat."

"Right," Tingley said. "After chow, we can go to White Beach and get some pictures of the battalion landing team Marines assembling on the pier and marching onto the *Dubuque*, when it gets there."

"Oh, the fuck you say!" Tompkins howled. "It's Easter Sunday! Skipper's going to have to give me tomorrow off then, or better yet, Friday."

"I'll talk to Captain Shelton," Tingley said. "I am sure he will do what's fair. This is important."

The corporal then turned up the portable radio that Tompkins carried on the van's console. Elton John played piano and sang "Crocodile Rock" on the American Forces Radio and Television Service's Far East Network, broadcasting from Kadina Air Force Base in the heart of Okinawa.

"Here, donate me one of those Winstons. I'm out of my Kools," Tompkins said to Tingley as the corporal pulled a cigarette for himself from the red-and-white pack that he had carried inside the blouse of his utility trouser leg, tucked above his spit-shined boot. Although the Marine Corps utility uniform's olive green sateen shirt sported two ample breast pockets, one carried nothing inside either of them, keeping the two pouches buttoned shut and starched flat, especially the left one which had the Corps emblem and *USMC* stenciled on it.

"I suppose you want a light too," Tingley said, handing his driver a smoke.

"Yeah," Tompkins snarled, "and you can kick me in the chest to get it started too." Then he laughed at himself, having cut off the corporal from the tired old joke.

"Shut the fuck up and listen to this shit," Tingley said, suddenly drawn to a news report on the radio.

"This morning at a news conference in Saigon, South Vietnamese Vice Premier Phan Quang Dan had these few words for reporters," the radio announcer said.

"It is lost!" Vice Premier Phan said in the recorded sound bite. "The Communists have taken Da Nang."

The announcer then continued, "Following the formal recognition of Da Nang's surrender by the South Vietnamese government, North Vietnamese and PRG spokesman Colonel Vo Dong Giang told reporters today at the Joint Military Commission press center at Saigon's Tan Son Nhut Airport that the Provisional Revolutionary Government had already claimed victory and had raised its flag over the Da Nang Community Center and Town Hall Saturday afternoon.

"Press Secretary Ron Nessen today told reporters at an impromptu press conference at Palm Springs, California, where President Gerald Ford has gone to play golf and vacation during the Easter weekend, that the President has reacted to the news with great sadness and has called the loss of Da Nang an immense human tragedy."

"Well, no shit! Ford probably missed his putt when he heard about that one," Tompkins said as he slammed the van to a stop, sliding it across a gravel parking lot overlooking the beach near the Camp Courtney and III MAF Headquarters entrance. "Like it's a big surprise. So what the fuck are these guys doing out here then?"

Steve Tingley said nothing to the surly lance corporal, but walked to the rocky ledge overlooking the beach and southern shore of Ora Wan Bay and began snapping pictures of the ship and the amtracks from the new angle. As he released the shutter and listened to the camera's motor drive advance the film, he noticed something curious about the scene. It did look much the same, yet something odd about it struck him. Amtracks swam in the water, the ship sat in the bay, and now and then a puff of black smoke rose from its exhaust stack behind the bridge. Then suddenly the corporal realized what made the picture look strange. The direction the amtracks now migrated. Instead of the amphibious assault vehicles swimming one after another toward the ship, they now maneuvered in a long procession back to shore.

"Goddamn it, Tompkins!" Tingley shouted, running to the van and jumping through the open passenger door. "We've got to get back to Camp Hanson. Something's gone wrong. All the amtracks have turned around. They're all headed back to the base! We've gotta get over there fast so I can get some pictures and find out what's going on."

AS NEWS OF Da Nang's loss reached the III MAF command center in Okinawa, the Marine amphibious force's boss, Major General Carl Hoffman and Third Marine Division's commander, Major General Kenneth Houghton, halted all embarkation operations and again revised their planning.

Realizing that now the mission had changed to one of seaborne security rather than a combat landing, they pulled all the heavy equipment from the ships and sent support elements such as the amtracks, artillery, and heavy mortars back to their respective garrisons. They would now only mount out the First Battalion, Fourth Marine Regiment's generic infantry as shipboard security for the now more than twenty merchant and Military Sealift Command vessels that had gathered in the waters off Qui Nhon, south of Chu Lai, still rescuing Da Nang's refugees from the sea.

By dusk Easter Sunday, the Marines had off-loaded their heavy combat gear, along with the battalion's headquarters and service company, but kept the HMM-165 helicopter squadron aboard and embarked the remaining rifle companies of the First Battalion, Fourth Marines. Steering toward the setting sun, LPD 8 USS *Dubuque* made way for her rendezvous with MSC ships, *Pioneer Commander, Transcolorado,* USS *Miller, Greenville Victory, Pioneer Challenger, Pioneer Contender,* and fourteen other merchant vessels of various flags that swarmed with an ever increasing number of refugees.

Throughout the day and night, South Vietnamese swift boats and patrol cutters heroically braved heavy Communist artillery fire, venturing back to enemy territory to rescue more people. While the Republic of Vietnam's army may have run from the enemy, and the South Vietnamese Marine Corps may have disintegrated in Da Nang's defense, the country's navy continued to operate with great valor. With quickness and maneuverability their only defenses, the small, speedy vessels returned to Da Nang again and again, plucking people off the shores at Tien Sha, China Beach, and Monkey Mountain.

SAIGON, ROOFTOP BAR AT THE CARAVEL HOTEL

"HELLO, BOYS," White House photographer David Hume Kennerly said as he stepped through the doorway of the rooftop cocktail lounge of the Caravel Hotel and encountered a host of Saigon's established international press corps seated at several tables shoved together, covered with glasses and pitchers of beer.

"David, come join us for dinner," Time-Life photographer Dirck Halstead called loudly, waving his hand to the fellow photographer.

Kennerly smiled and pushed a chair between Halstead and NBC News contract motion picture photographer Neil Davis.

"Hey, hey, mate, take it easy on the elbows," Davis said in his Australian brogue as Kennerly shoved in his seat, jamming Davis into the chair occupied by CBS News sound technician Derek Williams.

Vietnamese journalist Ha Thuc Can, under contract with CBS News as a motion picture photographer, sat to the right of his colleague, Williams, and Ky Wahn, a Vietnamese still photographer under contract with the Associated Press, sat on Can's other side.

The United Press International bureau chief for both Vietnam and Cambodia, Alan Dawson, held the spot at the table across from Halstead, while Associated Press correspondent from the Saigon bureau, Peter Arnett, occupied the chair to the left of Halstead, at the head of the table.

Dutch still photographer Hubert "Hugh" Van Es sat by Dawson, in the corner by a troublesome, thickly foliated potted palm whose prickly fronds kept drooping over his head.

"I think you know just about everyone here," Halstead said to Kennerly, pouring him a glass of beer from the nearest pitcher.

"Nearly everyone," Kennerly said, "Neil there, and Peter, of course, Hugh Van Es, and Alan."

"Well, this is Derek Williams, sound man for Ed Bradley, or is it Morley Safer this week?" Halstead said.

"Whoever holds the microphone," Williams said, smiling.

"I did meet the gentleman at the end of the table, I believe, in the darkroom at the AP," Kennerly said, smiling at Ky Wahn but not remembering his name.

"The man next to him is one of Derek's counterparts with a camera at CBS, Ha Thuc Can," Halstead said. "Ha Thuc Can can get it done when others can't."

"I think he has special connections with the other side," Williams quipped and nudged Can on the shoulder.

"Special relations with the devil, you mean," Davis said and laughed.

"Can has covered this war since the beginning," Peter Arnett said in his crisp New Zealand eloquence. "All kidding aside, this man, Can, is one tough cookie. He is one of the best and most effective Vietnamese journalists that we have over here."

"That's why we buy him dinner and beer every night," Hugh Van Es said, swatting the palm leaf off the top of his head. "We bribe him so that he will take us with him when the shit hits the proverbial fan."

"I am hardly more than an overindulged office boy," Ha Thuc Can finally said, humiliated from the abundant praise by his friends.

Ky Wahn looked at Can and smiled at the man's simplistic identity of himself for the overindulgent Americans and Western newsmen. He sipped his beer quietly and considered the many things that these haughty and often boisterous fellows did not know about himself and his cohort, Ha Thuc Can.

"So David," Peter Arnett began, "what can you tell us about this fact-finding mission, of which you are party, for President Ford?"

"If I tell you, then I have to kill you," Kennerly joked. "Honestly, I am hardly more than an overly indulged office boy."

Kennerly then raised his glass of beer toward Ha Thuc Can, saluting the man while the others at the table chuckled politely at the photographer's play on Can's words.

"Seriously, David," Arnett insisted, "what is going on with these guys? What do they expect to accomplish?"

"Political hand-wringing for the President, mostly," Alan Dawson interjected. "Gives Ford an out with the veterans. He can say, 'At least I tried, boys.' "

"I don't think President Ford is looking for a political flag to wave at the vets," Kennerly said, defending his boss. "I honestly believe he wants to see if there is anything he can do to save what is left of South Vietnam."

"Well, I am pissed at you guys, arriving at three o'clock the other morning," Van Es said. "I got nothing of it, just some very dark frames of Air Force One as it parked in the floodlights at the Tan Son Nhut Air Base terminal and some shadows of people coming down the ladder."

"I think our in-the-dark arrival is probably pretty indicative of nearly everything about this visit," Kennerly said apologetically to Van Es. "I see lots of track covering, and Graham Martin certainly does not want to go down with the legacy as the ambassador who lost Saigon."

"This all about appearances?" Halstead said.

"Smoke and mirrors," Dawson said. "Ford has his hands tied, double knotted. Case-Church Amendment says that America must do nothing. No military equipment, no American forces, nada, zip. You have the United States Army chief of staff, General Frederick Weyand, holding Ambassador Graham Martin's hand back to Saigon, with a raft of bureaucrats from the State Department, Defense Department, NSA, and CIA too, I imagine, all coming here to do what? Spend a week touring the bases and then dream up a grand scheme to save the country? No. I call it C-Y-A. Cover Your Ass."

Kennerly smiled at his colleague and said nothing. He knew that Al Dawson had tapped the Ford administration's political pulse, whether or not the President fully realized what throbbed in the heart of that inner sanctum. Secretary of State Henry Kissinger and Assistant Secretary of State Phillip Habib, who oversaw America's delegation in Saigon, certainly had a lot of C-Y-A going on.

ONE OF THEIR more important C-Y-A maneuvers brought a sore and groggy Graham Martin off sick leave to Washington, DC, to attend the skull session on the Weyand trip. Martin had gone home to North Carolina after he underwent significant dental surgery at Walter Reed Hospital and had hoped to recuperate there for several days before returning to South Vietnam. Kissinger and Habib wanted Martin back on the job in Saigon so that he could absorb the blame, in case the worst did happen.

For the Ford administration, the fate of South Vietnam did not rank nearly as high on the scale of importance as did the world's opinion of America and how it regarded whether the nation did or did not keep its commitments, especially those made to smaller, struggling countries fending off the dogs of Communism.

Long ago, under the watch of President Richard M. Nixon, American political interests had already written off South Vietnam. The Paris Peace Accords stood testimony to that fact, virtually selling the highly United States–dependent nation down the proverbial river. The Case-Church Amendment of 1973, specifically banning all bombing in Cambodia and further banning all American military intervention by land, sea, or air anywhere in Southeast Asia, underscored that write-off. Kissinger had simply engineered a so-called decent interval to distance America from its South Vietnam commitment. Given an adequate passage of time, the world would not hold America accountable. Unfortunately, Kissinger's decent interval had not nearly run its course.

High on the agenda of foreign policies that rested in the balance came Kissinger's Middle East peace. He had spent the previous ten days there, hammering out a new plan between Israel and its warring Moslem neighbors. Ruins still smoldered in Egypt and on the Gaza

Strip. The day after he had returned from his Middle East mission, March 25, Kissinger and President Ford held a meeting to finalize their plans for the Weyand fact-finding mission.

Their meeting included attendance of national security expert General Brent Scowcroft, General Weyand, and Ambassador Martin. It did not include attendance or even notification of Secretary of Defense James Schlesinger, even though their discussions and planning heavily involved Department of Defense assets, personnel, and one of its most high-ranking military officers, General Weyand.

Secretary of Defense Schlesinger and Secretary of State Kissinger stood at direct odds when it came to handling the latest events in South Vietnam. Schlesinger had told President Ford when President Thieu had begun to panic and the Central Highlands fell that he believed this represented the final Communist offensive and that South Vietnam had little hope of surviving it. He told President Ford, "The handwriting is on the wall."

While Secretary of State Kissinger and Ambassador Martin spoke with great optimism for South Vietnam rallying and even toyed with the notion of using detente with the Soviet Union as a hole card to encourage Moscow to stop the North Vietnamese short of Saigon, Schlesinger voiced caution. Kissinger had urged the President to empty the warehouses of South Vietnam's allocations of war supplies and to expedite those shipments, while Schlesinger wanted them held back. Pragmatically, he reasoned that with South Vietnam now a lost cause, anything America sent to the country would wind up in the hands of the Communists.

Schlesinger's pragmatism stood in direct contradiction to Kissinger's foreign policy strategy, America's not losing face with the rest of the world should South Vietnam fall. As it stood, the secretary of defense found himself standing on the outside of the President's inner circle.

During their March 25 meeting, President Ford and Secretary of State Kissinger mulled over an inventory of more than $300 million worth of war goods sitting in James Schlesinger's warehouses, earmarked for South Vietnam. They could send them now, tagged as emergency relief, or they could hold off until after General Weyand had made his assessment of the situation. With the Weyand report in hand, they could then ask Congress for much more than the current Saigon-destined stockpile and the nearly $700 million in not-yet-spent South Vietnam aid budget authorizations still sitting on the books.

Based on those budget authorizations, Major General Homer D.

Smith, Jr., the defense attaché in Saigon, had already put together a sizable shopping list on behalf of the South Vietnamese. Kissinger and President Ford agreed that Schlesinger's top logistical genius, Eric Von Marbod, could tweak that shopping list and give them even more ammunition to lay at the feet of Congress.

If the House and Senate would approve a massive emergency infusion of war goods to South Vietnam, based on the Weyand assessment, then in the worst case, if Saigon fell, the world could not blame America for it. The United States had the goods on the way. The failure of South Vietnam's resolve would then have to shoulder the blame. America had not, after all, run out on a friend.

It was a very neat C-Y-A strategy. It would allow America to retain the respect of those other nations who also looked to the United States for a commitment to their protection.

While Freddy Weyand, Graham Martin, David Kennerly, and a cast of State Department, Defense Department, NSA, and CIA bureaucrats winged their way to Saigon, Secretary of State Kissinger publically laid the foundation for their strategy with Congress and the people of the United States at a press conference.

While leading off with a bit of hand-wringing about failed Middle East peace initiatives, he led the unaware reporters into the sales pitch of his appearance before their cameras and microphones: America's credibility's hanging in the balance of South Vietnam.

"The United States cannot pursue a policy of selective reliability," Kissinger told the reporters. "We cannot abandon our friends in one part of the world and not jeopardize the security of friends elsewhere.

"The problems that we face in Indochina are an elementary question of what kind of people we are. For fifteen years we have been encouraging the people of South Vietnam to defend themselves against what we conceive to be an external danger. Now we stand on the brink of betraying that trust.

"In the past four years, Congress has dramatically cut aid to South Vietnam, going against a long-standing commitment. As a result, that nation now falters because of a grievous lack of spare parts and replacement equipment."

AL DAWSON TOOK a long sip of his beer and then looked at Kennerly.

"You have your loyalties to the president, granted, and I'll allow him the benefit of the doubt," he said. "Gerald Ford is a very nice guy. I have no doubt about the honor of his intentions. He means well. Kissinger, on the other hand, has a few cards up his sleeve. He reminds me of Benjamin Disraeli, Queen Victoria's prime minister. Smart to a T."

"I read what we carried on the AP wire about Kissinger's press conference," Peter Arnett said. "I think that he challenged and chided Congress with his statement that America cannot betray this sacred trust with South Vietnam. However, we had a number of follow-up stories to his press conference, and they contained some very good information from highly placed Pentagon sources. The facts our reporters uncovered literally shatter Kissinger's spare-parts and grievous-short-supply argument.

"Most of this year's allocation, something to the tune of $700 million, has not even left the proverbial barn. The money has yet to be spent! Furthermore, our Pentagon sources report that South Vietnam has ample supply of not only spare parts and equipment, but arms and ammunition. Or I should say, had, considering this morning's announcement of the loss of Da Nang."

"I was leading up to that very point," Al Dawson said. "Kissinger cares nothing for Vietnam, north or south. This is all about his Middle East peace and what the rest of the world thinks of America after this toilet gets flushed."

"So, welcome to Saigon, David," Dirck Halstead interjected to lighten the moment.

"Look," Kennerly said, "I just work for the guy, and I just take pictures. However, I believe that Gerald Ford will do everything he can for these people."

"Well," Derek Williams said, "if that's the case, where are the Marines?"

"Sitting off Cambodia," Neil Davis said. "They've been there all month."

"The correspondent for *Stars and Stripes* in Okinawa tells us that the Marines can't seem to get their act together," Arnett said. "His last word this morning reported them still trying to load a ship and the Fourth Marine Regiment still sitting on their packs at the navy pier."

"Purely an evacuation force," Dawson added. "Don't get your hopes up that the war will start all over again."

"So, what about tomorrow?" Dirck Halstead said.

"With all of I Corps now in their hands, who knows what's next?" Dawson said. "My bet, Nha Trang."

"I'm heading up there tomorrow," Kennerly said. "I wanted to get some shots of the people on Highway 1, and I heard that it is getting very messy just north of Nha Trang."

"Phu Cat and Qui Nhon are between there and Chu Lai," Dawson said. "The evacuation boats have dumped a lot of people at those ports, so I am sure they have already flooded Highway 1 from those points south. Nha Trang might be a good bet for some really nasty crowd shots."

Chapter 15

PANIC SPREADS SOUTH

**DA NANG, DEMOCRATIC REPUBLIC OF VIETNAM—
TUESDAY, APRIL 1**

A UNIFORMED NORTH Vietnamese captain led the procession of nine men to their final stop. Divided into groups of four and five individuals, the captain's troop had lashed the men by their wrists to a pair of bamboo poles. The soldiers had used American communications wire from a captured spool to bind their prisoners' hands, pulling it so tightly that the men's fingers immediately turned purple. In the blistering midday sun, the nine stood with their heads down, waiting as flies and gnats swarmed them, tracking through the sweat that ran down their faces.

Three of the men had served as district police chiefs in Da Nang, and the remaining six had spent careers in the city as public administrators for the region. After two days of sometimes brutal interrogation, followed by a rubber-stamp trial, they had ridden in the back of a truck, traveling west from the city to the mountain that the Americans had numbered 327 and had called Freedom Hill.

The truck had rolled by the communications and radar facility on the mountain's summit and had then turned down a gravel road that led to the former United States military prison there. The ARVN had converted the old Freedom Hill Brig to a prisoner of war camp and had kept it filled tight with captured Viet Cong and North Vietnamese until the NVA liberated the place on March 28.

As the truck passed by the tall, ironclad gates and drove along the edge of the high fence, topped with several coils of razor wire, thousands of shoeless men stared out through the confines at the dusty vehicle rumbling by with its one-way human cargo. Some of them wore uniforms, but most did not. All had served as ARVN soldiers or South Vietnamese Marines. They watched stoically, knowing full well where the dirty green Russian-built transport with the red star painted on its door was headed.

The truck jerked to a stop a few yards from a six-foot-wide, twenty-foot-long, eight-foot-deep trench that crews of prisoners had dug a few hours earlier in the red clay soil on the north slope of Freedom Hill, beyond the stockade perimeter. Near this filthy gash, a series of half a dozen long mounds of recently turned earth marked other similar digs, filled to capacity only this mornings and then covered with soil. Upslope from this site, a dozen prisoners hacked with picks and shovels, making ready a fresh trench. The haggard bunch kept their heads down as they toiled at the hole. None of the men dared to even raise an eye as the truck pulled past them and halted.

A growing pile of bloating corpses sprinkled with hydrated lime lay at the bottom of this currently filling human refuse pit. Some of the people dumped there had finally lost their struggles with wounds they had received days earlier, at last succumbing from blood loss and infection in the Freedom Hill prison. Most, however, had died from the telltale single gunshots to the backs of their heads, administered after the Provisional Revolutionary Government and Democratic Republic of Vietnam coalition authority in Da Nang had ordered them executed.

"Forward!" the captain shouted to the nine men. Soldiers yanked hard at the bamboo, pulling the two lines of prisoners off balance as they stumbled awkwardly toward the edge of the trench, shuffling in a sidestep with their wrists tied to the pole at their backs. By now, all feeling had left their hands, and their heads rang from the boiling heat.

"For your crimes against the people," the captain recited ceremoniously, "the council of the people has decreed that you shall be put to death."

Then, one at a time, starting from the center, the captain shot each prisoner in the back of the head with his pistol, just as he snipped the bonds that lashed the man to the rail. The officer had developed his timing precisely, shooting each victim at the same instant that he severed the bindings so that the dying, often writhing person fell neatly onto the pile of other dead at the bottom of the pit. In the past two days, the NVA officer and several others like him had practiced and honed sharp their death-rendering skills on scores of prostitutes, gangland cowboys, criminals, and other incorrigibles and crazies that the newly seated coalition government had deemed detrimental to Da Nang's liberated society and rubber-stamped their condemnation.

The three chiefs of police and six city administrators died quietly, keeping their dignity and honor intact, even as each of them fell headlong into the mass grave. None of the men whimpered or pled.

Four South Vietnamese Marines lay still in the tree line a few hundred yards away at the base of Freedom Hill and had watched the truck arrive. They saw the nine men march to the pit and die. Gunshots earlier that morning had drawn them here to investigate. Now they hurried to report what they had witnessed to their leader, who waited in the jungle.

147ᵀᴴ VIET MARINE BRIGADE SURVIVORS NEAR DA NANG

LONG BEFORE DAWN, several boats had made their way down the shore toward Da Nang. Embarking on their journey at sunset, they had oared silently past the rocky promontory where the Hai Van Pass juts into sea at the northern end of Da Nang Bay. In the night, they quietly slid by the Esso depot on Lien Chieu point and then slipped inland at the Nam O Bridge, paddling upstream on the Cu De River.

Protected by the cover of the early morning's darkness, Lieutenant Colonel Tran Ngoc Toan bid farewell to the Catholic fishermen who had saved him and his 450 Viet Marines who had escaped the decimation of their 147ᵗʰ Brigade on the beach at Tan My ten days ago. Silently, the gaunt yet still disciplined company followed its leaders southward through the forests.

As the sun rose, they skirted along the western fingers of Hills 282 and 364. Then they began to edge eastward around the base of Hill 268 and moved toward Da Nang along the northern slopes of Hill 327. Their kindred American Marines had built the compounds on most of this place and had trained many of the Viet Marines in patrolling and ambush tactics in these same grounds and surrounding forests. The lieutenant colonel and his troop of 450 survivors knew this land well and traveled easily through it despite the ever present North Vietnamese troops patrolling the roadways and fringes of the compounds.

As the Viet Marines pushed forward, Lieutenant Colonel Toan sent scouts ahead of the main body to guide them away from any enemy units. Most of the men still carried their individual light arms, but Tran Ngoc Toan knew well that without heavier firepower and ammunition they stood little chance if they engaged any North Vietnamese units. Their best defense rested with their stealth in movement.

"Colonel, sir," the four reconnaissance scouts whispered to Toan, hidden at their rendezvous point. "North Vietnamese occupy Hill 327. Their trucks also move freely to and from Da Nang. Many patrols scout the perimeter. Dead bodies litter the sides of all the roadways in every direction."

"As I feared," Toan said, "Da Nang may well be lost. Rather than risk encounter by trying to get into the city, or back to the sea, I propose that we continue to travel southeast. I know some villages west of Cam Ne. I think that the people there may help us."

None of the soldiers argued the colonel's decision. They knew no one in Da Nang, nor did any of the men have family there. Most of them called Saigon or one of its many surrounding communities home. Moving southward brought them closer to their loved ones.

UNITED STATES EMBASSY, SAIGON

"SIR, AMBASSADOR MARTIN and I met with President Thieu this morning, and he has again pled for help," General Frederick Weyand said to President Gerald Ford and Secretary of State Henry Kissinger in a conference telephone call to Palm Springs from the United States Embassy in Saigon. "Given what they have lost in Da Nang, it will require at the very least another $700 million in equipment and supplies on top of what we have already committed to them."

"Congress will never agree to more than $1.5 billion after they cut the authorization by half that much last year alone," President Ford said.

"Mr. President, Graham Martin here," the ambassador to South

Vietnam interjected. "If we can only reassure President Thieu that America has not abandoned South Vietnam, I am certain he can lead their forces to rally. All of this doomsday reporting by the media has set the South Vietnamese armed forces on their ears. We need to demonstrate some resolve and reassure them."

"Shipments of equipment and supplies will go a long way in doing that," General Weyand said. "When I return in a few days, I will give you a formal report, but for now it looks like they will need at least double what Congress has already allowed them in the current budget."

"I still believe that we can negotiate a settlement," Ambassador Martin said. "With Da Nang now theirs, and the occupation of the northern provinces and Central Highlands taxing their manpower, I think we have a strong hand with the defenses around Saigon. Also, do not give up on the Soviet Union factoring in this deal. They want detente; they need to play ball with us."

As always, Henry Kissinger mostly listened and spoke little. He too supported the notion that perhaps the United States, with some pressure brought to bear by the Russians, could reason with North Vietnam to settle on keeping what they had gained in the northern provinces and Central Highlands, and to leave Saigon alone. President Ford shared those hopes as well, but not nearly the optimism of Martin.

Kissinger and President Ford both knew in their hearts that the odds of their hopes finding fruition dwindled more and more with each day's events. It seemed that when one thought matters could not get any worse, they invariably did.

President Ford and Kissinger also knew well that President Nguyen Van Thieu had lost a great deal of credibility as his nation's leader, not only with his own people and their armed forces, but with the international political world as well. Backing a loser did not sit well with either man.

"Mr. President," Graham Martin said, "one way we can persuade Congress to approve these emergency appropriations would be to gain massive public sympathy."

"Are we talking about Ed Daly's orphan refugee initiative?" President Ford asked.

"This may have merit," Kissinger interjected. "Ambassador Martin has already received approval from South Vietnam's minister for refugee affairs and the backing from President Thieu."

"I don't want Ed Daly out grandstanding World Airways with a bunch of orphan children," President Ford snapped back.

"This would be our program, sir, " Kissinger offered. "Operation Babylift. We will have the USAID spokesman at the State Department announce it to the press in the morning. The public will show great sympathy for our efforts to reduce the suffering of the children in Vietnam with the relocation of more than two thousand orphans to the United States."

"This will sway public opinion," Graham Martin said, underscoring his boss's comments.

Within hours of the Operation Babylift announcement, Major General Homer Smith had alerted the DAO staff's Vietnamese female employees to prepare to depart Saigon as nurses and escorts for the children. The volunteerism served two purposes: It did provide chaperones for the two thousand orphans, but it also provided Smith the means of evacuating several hundred loyal female workers who would otherwise not get out of Vietnam.

Not only did Smith see the writing on the wall, taking the opportunity to help his own staff evacuate, so did many of Saigon's formerly complacent citizens. As each day rolled forward in April, more people booked flights out of Saigon. Pan American Airways had all its seats booked on its two flights per week through the middle of April. Likewise China Airlines found its flights similarly packed. However, the most telling message came from the six hundred eastern-bloc members of the International Commission of Control and Supervision. Suddenly, they too boarded early April flights out of Saigon.

OUTSIDE THE AMERICAN EMBASSY, SAIGON

"AMBASSADOR MARTIN, WHAT is going on here?" Peter Arnett asked as Graham Martin approached him on the front walk at the embassy. "We have had reports this morning that an NVA division now sits only forty-five miles north of Saigon. We also have heard from intelligence sources that as many as five North Vietnamese divisions have mobilized from the northern provinces and the Central Highlands, also headed this way. Reporters returning from Nha Trang say it is under siege and that the ARVN have fled there. They say the NVA are now heading to Saigon."

"Rumors, Peter," Martin said. "There is no danger to Saigon. At this time we have the greatest concentration of military forces in this nation's history surrounding the city, heavily equipped and well dug in. The Republic of Vietnam enjoys absolute air superiority. So I assure you that there is no danger to Saigon."

Arnett had already met with his "undisclosed sources" within the Defense Attaché's Office and had heard their spin on the facts. They did not express nearly the optimism that Martin kept trying to peddle. Yes, Saigon had significant ground and air defense forces. However, neither Graham Martin nor the White House had fully applied the refugee factor to the equation. They told Arnett that given the great tide of humanity currently rolling southward on Highway 1, now engulfing besieged Nha Trang, with Vung Tao, Xuan Loc, and Bien Hoa still standing along its route, and with it exponentially increasing in numbers with each city that it swept across, when this refugee flood finally struck Saigon, it would without doubt overwhelm the city.

When he returned to the Associated Press's Saigon bureau, he put his story on the wire, with a message to the Washington, DC, bureau. He wanted to hear Secretary of Defense James Schlesinger's take on Saigon's situation.

The following morning, the AP wire carried that interview, and Peter Arnett ripped the canary yellow paper off the teletype machine when the story ran. Schlesinger not only voiced strong reservations about South Vietnam's future, but bluntly voiced his pessimism. Not only did his lack of faith in Saigon's future elevate Graham Martin's and Henry Kissinger's ire for him, but it raised President Ford's hackles as well. In the story the pragmatic defense secretary said, "The next thirty days will tell us if South Vietnam in any form will live or die."

NEAR THE ARVN TWENTY-FIFTH DIVISION AT CU CHI

IN THE PITCH darkness of the forest, Le Van Reung stared at the radium dial of his Timex wristwatch. In the moonless night its face glowed so brightly that he had to squint to look at it. At one o'clock in the morning, he and his squad had made good time from the camp where his brigade commander awaited their return. His unit, with a regiment from the 320th Division, had traveled on foot for twelve hours a day during the past week, moving secretly from Ban Me Thuot southward

along the Cambodian border. Now Reung and his twelve guerrillas
slipped through the night to take reconnaissance positions outside Cu
Chi at the ARVN Twenty-fifth Division's Dong Zu Base.

The remainder of the 320th NVA Division had joined with elements
of the 316th and 10th NVA divisions and then moved openly down Highways 14 and 21 toward their next series of objectives that culminated
at Nha Trang. Above them, Colonel Huang Duc The had led his Thirty-
eighth NVA Regiment as the spearhead unit for the Second NVA Division and raced down Highway 1, consuming Binh Dinh, Phu Cat, and
the port cities of Qui Nhon and Tuy Hoa. They had encountered the
Twenty-second ARVN Division at Binh Dinh and had chased them to
Qui Nhon, where the South Vietnamese soldiers had finally fled and
evacuated by sea.

Converging at Nha Trang, Colonel The and the Second NVA Division would join sixteen other North Vietnamese divisions along a line
that extended westward from Cam Ranh Bay to Cambodia. Meanwhile, far to the south, six more NVA divisions converged along the
southern flank. From these new lines of departure, they would ultimately close on Saigon from five fronts.

As the northern units hastened to Nha Trang, tens of thousands of
peasants streamed along both sides of the roadways where the North
Vietnamese divisions traveled. Their trucks festooned with flags and
victory banners, and honking their horns incessantly, the Communist
units pushed past the crowds of refugees, rarely stopping to even question the people. Riding in the vehicles' beds, North Vietnamese Army
and Viet Cong soldiers waved at the crowds and cheered. The peasants
smiled politely and returned the gestures, but still plodded southward
toward Saigon.

"How many of the big guns do you see," Reung whispered to a
comrade who peered through a captured American starlight scope as-
sessing several batteries of ARVN 175-millimeter artillery laid across
the camp.

"So many I cannot count them," the guerrilla answered.

"Count the tubes," Reung said. "How many tubes do you see?"

"Seven tubes, but it looks like much more than only seven," the
Viet Cong looking through the night-vision device said.

"Here, let me see," Reung told his comrade and took the starlight
scope and put it to his eye.

The green and black outlines looked distorted through the night-seeing optic that gathered starlight and moonlight and amplified it in a luminescent monochrome green color. Silhouettes and glowing images confused his eyesight until his vision finally adjusted to the picture it saw.

"From the left I count seven long tubes on stationary guns, the 175-millimeter pieces," Reung said. "They cannot easily move those."

Then he shifted the scope to the right.

"I count seven more long tubes, but these extend from tracked vehicles. They move easily," Reung said. "Those guns on these mobile artillery pieces fire either 175-millimeter or 155-millimeter rounds. I cannot tell with this awful telescope. No matter, though. Whichever they shoot, I do not like them. They cause terrible damage. I also see many tanks, mostly the smaller M48 series, but they have a few of the larger M60 main battle tanks too. Those big ones are useless in these forests. The smaller ones can maneuver somewhat, but not very well."

"With all of this armor and artillery here, clearly they anticipate our attack from this point," the guerrilla said.

"Perhaps," Reung said, counting tanks under his breath. "Then perhaps they anticipate our attack from the north, along the coastline, and have these units standing in reserve so that they can maneuver reinforcements where they may need them."

"Our people and the regiment from the 320th Division have only B-40 rocket grenades and B-41 artillery. How can we attack such heavy armor as they have here?" the soldier asked his leader.

"We can take them in the trees," Reung said and smiled.

ON HIGHWAY 1 AT NHA TRANG

DAVID KENNERLY HAD arrived in Nha Trang at midday on Monday greeted by turmoil. The highway reminded him of the parking lot at the Super Bowl, except the shoulder-to-shoulder crowd extended for as far as the photographer could see. Then today, thunder had awakened him before dawn. He saw no clouds and quickly realized that the North Vietnamese had begun shelling the city. The pushing and jostling of the hundreds of thousands of refugees on the roadway and in the city square suddenly turned to a panic-driven stampede.

Two days earlier, the ARVN's Third Airborne Brigade had tried to make a stand where their units straddled Highway 21 below An Khe

Pass, serving as a blocking force for the ARVN garrison defending Nha Trang. For the last two weeks of March, the North Vietnamese had shown them no activity. Then the day that Da Nang fell, battalions from the 320th, 316th, and 10th NVA divisions came roaring down their throats.

Lieutenant Colonel Truong Quang Thi had led his light infantry battalion back to the top of An Khe Pass after its victory at Cheo Reo. While other battalions of the 320th NVA Division mopped up at Ban Me Thuot, Cheo Reo, Pleiku, and Kontum, his unit marched back to their post atop the highest point on Highway 21, ready to react should the remaining ARVN in the coastal regions attempt any counteroffensives.

When the day came to finally strike the ARVN Third Airborne Brigade, positioned down the slope from Truong's battalion, his soldiers led the charge.

With mortar volleys into the ARVN bunkers and followed by superficial probes by small units of his infantry, Truong Quang Thi succeeded in drawing several companies of the enemy forces into a counterattack up the pass where the bulk of his NVA battalion waited. His ambush worked perfectly, and his warriors decimated the pursuing units who had given his soldiers chase.

"When I was still a boy," Truong told his officers that evening as they quietly celebrated that first day's victory, "many of our fathers who fought beside Chairman Ho Chi Minh and General Vo Nguyen Giap achieved one of their greatest victories at this very place. They held this same ground where our battalion now stands and annihilated an entire division of French Union soldiers using the same ploy as we did today."

The Communist soldiers smiled proudly, hearing this history that several of them already knew from their school days in Hanoi.

"The French Union Army had several regiments also garrisoned at Kontum," the lieutenant colonel continued. "The embattled division called them for help, believing that they could attack our fathers from two sides. This narrow highway and steep terrain proved their undoing, and our Viet Minh army decimated those regiments too."

The following day, Truong Quang Thi mobilized his battalion before dawn and struck the heart of the Third Airborne Brigade with the full force of his battalion. Just as David smote Goliath with a stone, Truong's light infantry sent the much larger ARVN unit reeling.

When the Third Airborne Brigade's leaders saw that not only did they face a very determined NVA battalion, but behind it came nearly three enemy divisions, the ARVN folded their tents and ran toward the sea. Upon reaching Nha Trang, without word to anyone, the brigade's command group boarded helicopters and fled south. The remaining units, in disarray, splintered and fled on foot and by boat.

As David Hume Kennerly hurried to the airport that same Tuesday morning to also flee from Nha Trang, Lieutenant Colonel Truong Quang Thi and his battalion already stood on the hilltops outside the city. The NVA commander could see the airfield from where he sat and watched the busy aircraft traffic amidst the incoming shells of his division's artillery.

With a bag full of exposed film hanging off his shoulder and three cameras dangling from his neck, the White House photographer boarded his outbound Air America chopper flight to Saigon.

"I think this is it," he shouted to the pilot as he sat in the jump seat behind the Huey helicopter's center console.

"It what?" the pilot said, easing upward with the collective handle, turning the power full throttle, and easing the cyclic control forward for takeoff.

"The war," Kennerly said. "The handwriting's on the wall. The North Vietnamese will be in Saigon in a matter of weeks."

CAM NE HAMLET, SOUTH OF DA NANG

WITH HIS FORCE of 450 poorly armed Viet Marines hiding in the trees just beyond the checkerboard of rice paddies north of the Cam Ne hamlet complex, Lieutenant Colonel Tran Ngoc Toan slipped quietly to the darkened farmhouse. He heard a man try to muffle a cough inside, so he approached in the shadows and peered in the window.

Squatting by the doorway, an old friend sat with an American M14 rifle pointed into the night. He had heard the Marine approaching, but had not yet seen the intruder.

"Nguyen!" the colonel called in a loud whisper to the older man. "*Chu hoi! Chu hoi!* I surrender! Don't shoot."

The man with the rifle relaxed and smiled.

"Toan, I thought you died at Hue!" Nguyen said and immediately hugged his friend when he walked around the corner of the farmhouse.

The old farmer had once led Viet Marines when their corps first began, training under the caring and proud hands of the United States Marines based at Da Nang. He had risen to the rank of brigade sergeant major and then retired to what he had hoped would be a quiet life of growing rice in the shadow of Hill 55, southwest of Da Nang.

"I knew you would not run," the lieutenant colonel said to the sergeant major. "I am saddened that you did not, but I am glad for the sake of my 450 men who wait among the trees that you have held your ground."

"I am sure the dirty bastards will eventually seek me out and kill me, as they have murdered so many of our brothers around here," Nguyen said. "I intend to take as many with me as I have rounds for this rifle. Then I will detonate two cases of hand grenades that I have hidden under the floor. I will trip the wire once I get my house full of the scum. I will blow them all to hell with me."

"You should come with us," Toan told his friend. "We could use your grenades, and your leadership."

"Do you intend to start your own guerrilla war with these imbeciles?" the sergeant major said and laughed.

"I intend to lead these Marines to Saigon, if necessary, where we can regroup with our brigades and send these monsters back to Hanoi, wrapped in sheets," Toan said.

"As ignorant peasants, we fools who toil in the rice fields have great freedom to move about while our North Vietnamese lords ride along the roadways," Nguyen said. "My neighbors, who are also my trusted friends, tell me the latest news that the soldiers tell them as they invite them in their homes to dine. Sadly, my brother, we have no more Marine Corps. All but a few who fled to Saigon and joined what is left of the 468th Brigade there have either died fighting these curs, or have gone to Khe Sanh or right here to Hill 327 as prisoners."

"What of the great line of defense from Nha Trang, cordoning off Saigon?" Toan asked.

"I know nothing of any defense," the sergeant major said. "All that I hear told describes the panic that jams all highways southward."

"We will not surrender," the lieutenant colonel said, sighing in the darkness, sitting cross-legged on the floor by his old friend.

"Everyone speaks of the American evacuation," the sergeant major said. "They have many great cargo ships off the coastline, and thousands of people have gotten on boats to escape to the United States.

Perhaps you may pursue that option if you can manage to sneak more than three hundred miles on foot without being arrested or shot. That is how far I estimate you must travel to reach friendly lines, if they still exist when you get there. At any rate, I am staying here. I cannot walk three hundred miles, but I can damned sure fight!"

The lieutenant colonel took his friend by the shoulder and squeezed it with his hand. He knew the old man was right and would rather die fighting than to succumb to exhaustion while running away.

"We cannot sneak very far down Highway 1 wearing these tiger-stripe uniforms," Toan said.

"Have your men strip and bury those clothes and their helmets tonight," the sergeant major said, "and I will bring you as much peasant clothing as my trusted friends and I can gather from our closets or steal from our not so trustworthy neighbors. Most of them have abandoned their homes anyway, so they will never miss the articles. For now, I will go with you back to your hiding place with what clothes I have here. Perhaps those men who will wear them can then come with me to visit my friends and raid a few vacated houses."

By dawn, Tran Ngoc Toan and his 450 Marines had buried their uniforms and had dressed themselves as peasants, hiding their faces under wide-brimmed conical straw hats. They filled their pockets with grenades from the two cases hoarded by the old sergeant major, leaving him six for his planned self-destruction and final attack on the Vietnamese Communists. Marines who carried sidearms threw away their gun belts and holsters along with their helmets and other gear, filled their pockets with ammunition, and tucked the pistols in their trousers' waistbands. Those men who had carried rifles buried them and everything else they discarded.

Cautiously the Viet Marines slipped through the forest and across the rice paddies following their colonel and, in groups of two, three, and four, melded into the massive sea of peasants still streaming southward.

Chapter 16

RACE FROM NHA TRANG

"THE BOOGERMAN'S A coming," Staff Sergeant Roger Painter called into the room where two of his five American Consulate Marines had just rolled from their cots, suddenly awakened not only by their boss's shout, but by the rumbles of the distant artillery crunching in the hills northwest of Nha Trang. "It's no April Fools' joke, sports fans. This is the real deal. Hustle down to the conference room ASAP. The skipper wants us there five minutes ago."

When the corporal on watch had heard the first rounds impact, he had immediately notified Painter, the Nha Trang consulate security force's Marine NCO in charge. The staff sergeant, in turn, had called Consul General Moncrieff Spear.

After a telephone call to the American embassy in Saigon, Spear faced the reality of the moment. Nha Trang today stood in immediate peril. Based on the intensity and nearness of the gunfire, the North Vietnamese Army could move on the city by sunset.

The soft-spoken diplomat had stubbornly held faith in Major General Pham Van Phu's albeit badly decimated II Army Corps, which now amounted to hardly more than remnants of the defeated Twenty-second ARVN Division, who had fled to the sea at Qui Nhon, and the Third Airborne Brigade, now beaten on Highway 21 and themselves running. While the northern provinces and Central Highlands collapsed, Spear had gone out of his way to avoid raising sensitivities among Nha Trang's population by not sending a massive exodus of staff to Saigon. As provinces fell, he quietly allowed the workers from those outlying offices to proceed to Saigon. However, he did not send their corresponding workers at Nha Trang south as well. Thus, as more and more satellites closed, more and more of his consular staff found themselves searching for matters to keep themselves busy. He also had not bothered to have the emergency evacuation plan dusted off, or even updated.

Meanwhile, the small, cliquish American community in Nha Trang began to rumble with concern despite Spear's efforts to quell public discontent by preaching to them Ambassador Graham A. Martin's party line of reassuring rhetoric. Each day, more and more of the concerned citizens came knocking on the consulate door, begging for Air America seats to safer climes. Then with the sudden fall of Da Nang came the flood of demands for outbound seats. By then the opportunity to establish a sound or even reasonable evacuation process had literally overnight been overtaken by events.

In a matter of days the Nha Trang consulate swelled with transient CIA and USAID workers en route from Da Nang, who stopped there for a respite and had now gotten themselves stranded. Other similar recent arrivals used the consulate as a base of operations in their support functions at nearby Cam Ranh Bay, where the South Vietnamese government had established a refugee center.

When April dawned in Nha Trang, the consulate found itself in a pickle. With the NVA's artillery thundering in the nearby hills, the massive exodus from the beautiful seafront city became overwhelming. Air America, Bird Airways, and World Airways could not cram enough planes into the pattern fast enough to accommodate the rush.

Pham Van Phu and his staff had several days earlier laid their plan of giving up Nha Trang, but had kept it tightly under wraps. The diminutive general had told his subordinate commanders to hold the front only long enough for him and his staff to depart, and then he could not care less what happened, especially to the Americans.

When General Fred Weyand had visited Phu at his headquarters on the first stop of his fact-finding mission, the MR 2 and II ARVN Corps commander had assured the American army's chief of staff that Nha Trang would stand. With their backs to the sea, Phu said his army would hold off the NVA on a line north of the city. He had told the American a wonderful and most gracious straight-faced lie. The American then conveyed that lie to the public, saying to reporters who trailed him, "The South Vietnamese forces are not demoralized in any sense of the word."

When April 1 dawned in Nha Trang, the only ARVN forces anyone could see had deserted their posts when their leaders had boarded planes for Saigon. The desperate soldiers ran amok as their fellow ARVN had done in Da Nang. They held people at gunpoint, robbing them of any gold they carried, raped the women, and murdered the men. These former saviors of the South Vietnamese people commandeered any form of transport they saw and fled south or out to sea.

At the airport, roving bands of ARVN deserters soon began attacking the aircraft that landed and forced their passage aboard several flights. By midafternoon, as the NVA now landed artillery shells in the city itself, no safe place existed in Nha Trang.

Admiral Noel A. M. Gayler, United States Navy, commander in chief, Pacific, and operational commander of the United States Support Activities Group, read an intelligence report from Tom Polger, the CIA station chief in Saigon, issued with a message date-time group of 1 April 75, that said that with the NVA pressure now exerted against the ARVN defensive forces in MR 2, Nha Trang would fall in the next two to seven days. The admiral immediately sent a message to Rear Admiral Donald E. Whitmire, commander of Navy Task Force 76, directing him to send helicopter landing ships to lie one mile off Nha Trang's coast, should the Americans at the consulate there need evacuation.

No one at the American consulate in Nha Trang ever saw either message. Phil Cook, the consulate deputy, had by early afternoon put the Marines to work shredding and burning everything classified and destroying all encrypting equipment. They did, however, maintain their communications center radios and telephones.

As he did the first thing each day, Cook had gone to Major General Pham Van Phu's headquarters for his regular morning briefing. There he encountered not the swaggering peacock general, but a man on the brink of nervous breakdown. Phu stood before the American diplomat broken and disheveled. In the city, the mayor had already dismantled the police force and government, in his own mental collapse, and now on the telephone begged and sobbed for the general to send soldiers to save him. At the same time Phu's army had just lost its last skirmishes with the 10th and 320th NVA divisions, which now bore down upon Nha Trang like an avalanche. With Phil Cook now presenting a new thorn in his side, the general could not rid himself of the consulate deputy fast enough.

With the artillery closing fast, and the army headquarters already looking like a ghost town, no one had to tell Phil Cook what he needed to do next.

As the American drove away, Pham Van Phu exploded from his office in a rage. "Get out!" he shouted to the few loyal soldiers who had remained near him. "Get out now!"

Without even taking his hat, the mad general ran from his office and out of the headquarters building to where his helicopter sat.

"Get out!" he screamed again in the courtyard and then ran for the chopper.

Major General Phu would later claim that he had simply relocated his headquarters to Phan Thiet. One other passenger had managed to board the general's Huey just as it lifted off, an NCO academy instructor. If Phu had truly moved his headquarters as he claimed, then the single soldier represented the army that he now led.

By the time Phil Cook had reached the American consulate, his suspicions drove him straight to the telephone where he tried to reach the MR 2 commander. No one answered. Wanting to make certain of what his gut shouted to his mind, the consular deputy drove back to the ARVN II Corps headquarters and now found it deserted.

He immediately called Moncrieff Spear by radio and urged him to consider without delay breaking and burning, and getting the hell out of town. The ARVN had already fled, and no one now stood between the NVA and Nha Trang.

. With so much poor planning and little thought toward evacuation, the departure from the American consulate quickly degenerated to chaos.

Hardly any of the Vietnamese who had worked as valued field agents for the CIA had even received contact. All of these people would certainly meet with an executioner's bullet if they fell into the Communists' hands. While the intelligence agency's senior field supervisor grabbed his staff and choppered to the Nha Trang airfield, a handful of his younger, more conscience-prone subordinates backed off boarding their Saigon-bound plane and returned to the consulate, driven by strong feelings of collective guilt from seeing the agency now abandoning these people.

Riding a helicopter back to the consulate, the young CIA agents teamed with an agent from the DAO and through the day made repeated forays into the city, seeking out their endangered Vietnamese colleagues. One by one the American agents encountered these trusted friends and employees, often finding them waiting at designated rally points as instructed by their handlers' standing operating procedures and emergency contingency plans. Without the young, conscience-driven Americans seeking out and evacuating their Vietnamese partners, these people would have very likely suffered summary executions much like those currently happening to so many like them in Da Nang.

While the DAO and CIA agents made their humanitarian excursions back and forth into Nha Trang through a hole in the consulate fence, hidden by shrubs and overlooked for repairs, Staff Sergeant Painter and his five Marines found themselves almost overwhelmed trying to stem the flow of Vietnamese slipping through the consulate gates and over its high, chain-link fence. When the first helicopter had landed in the consulate parking lot, a surge of more than a hundred people blew through the front gate. Someone had forgotten to lock it.

It took all five Marines and several of the CIA and DAO staff to shove it shut again. Then, as one person turned his back from one breach to stop another, a new group of Vietnamese filtered through.

As the Air America helicopters ferried load after load of passengers from the consulate parking lot to the Nha Trang airport terminal, the number of Vietnamese passengers who remained for transport there seemed to grow rather than shrink. Phil Cook began to lose his patience and told the Marines to crack down and keep the people from slipping through or over the fence.

As Staff Sergeant Painter and his Marines turned from diplomatic nice guys to club-wielding aggressors, now accompanying stern orders with smashing billy club shots to shoulders, heads, and faces, the crowds outside the consulate, now numbering in the thousands, turned vicious. They began tearing angrily at the gates and fences.

Mild-mannered Consul General Moncrieff Spear had sat in his office, agitated at seeing the CIA and DAO staff repeatedly slipping back to the helicopter assembly area with new faces in tow each time. The

Marines also agitated him, seeing the sentries now slapping people back with blood-marred police batons and threatening them with shotguns.

Everything had fallen into disarray. With the sun lying low above the mountains, it seemed to him that the entire day had failed itself. It had begun badly and had gotten worse.

Then when the telephone rang, and George Jacobson, the Saigon embassy's field operations special assistant to Ambassador Martin, told him to get out now, he did just that. The tall, often soft-spoken diplomat slipped on a hogleg pistol nosed into a black leather shoulder holster and bounded down the stairs. Without a word to anyone, he left on the next helicopter bound to the Nha Trang air terminal, leaving all his woes and chaos behind in the unruly consulate parking lot.

A half hour later, Phil Cook came knocking on the consul general's door and found the boss gone. He called George Jacobson in Saigon, who then told him that Spear had followed orders and that he should too.

"Get your staff, and get those Marines, and get the hell out of there now," Jacobson growled. "That's an order."

By six o'clock, Phil Cook had loaded out the last passengers and began gathering his American cohorts who had helped him supervise the impromptu evacuation from the consulate parking lot while Roger Painter and his Marines held their fingers in the dike. The last flight out would be hairy since the men holding back the angry human tide would no longer stand in that breach. Thus every moment counted.

With bags in hand, Staff Sergeant Painter, Sergeant Michael A. McCormick, and Corporals Robert L. Anderson, John G. Moya, Levorn L. Brown, and Jimmie D. Sneed bounded up the back ramp of the Air America CH-47 Chinook helicopter, and bid farewell to the consulate.

"Go ahead and get your men on that plane," Phil Cook told Roger Painter when the helicopter ramp came down on the tarmac at Nha Trang airport. The Marine looked down the concrete apron where a silver with blue trim Air America Volpar Turbo Beech 18 executive twin aircraft sat with its left engine softly whistling at idle while it waited for passengers.

"Grab a seat anywhere," Painter shouted as he led the five men to the plane.

The aircraft's copilot climbed down the steps on the side hatch and waved to the Marines, each with a satchel of their clothing in one hand and a rifle or shotgun in the other. He stood by the fuselage beneath the aircraft's twin tail and shouted at the staff sergeant, "Drop your bags here by the cargo door, and get your men inside."

Staff Sergeant Painter looked back at his Marines and began running them aboard, and then stopped.

"Sergeant McCormick," he said. "I need you to jump back on that chopper before it leaves and get back to the consulate. We left our service record books and pay records on the front desk. We're screwed without those! Especially the pay records. We'll sit tight until you get back!"

McCormick dropped his valise by the others and glanced up at the plane's tail section where he took a mental picture of the white letters Air America painted on the fuselage above the aircraft's registry, N3674G. Then with his rifle in hand he ran for the helicopter that had now begun to rev its twin rotors for takeoff.

"Can you get one last trip to the consulate for me?" he shouted to the pilot.

"I can get you there, but I have no fuel to wait," the pilot said. "I am heading for Cam Ranh after that."

"Fine," McCormick said and climbed aboard.

In a matter of minutes, the big chopper set down on the consulate parking lot and lifted away just as the Marine's feet hit the ground. Already, in only a matter of ten minutes, Vietnamese had begun to tear down the fence, hoping to get aboard any other helicopters that might happen to land.

Grabbing the stack of manila folders on the security office's front desk, the Marine ducked out the consulate's side door, away from the people who had already managed to break through the fence. They ran into the vacated building and began trashing several stacks of files that had not made it to the burn barrel before the consulate staff's hasty departure.

Mike McCormick didn't look back, but found the hole in the fence, behind the shrubs, where the CIA and DAO agents had made their forays and ducked out into the darkening city. With six sets of Marine Corps service record books and pay records under his arm, the young sergeant began jogging a straight shot back to Nha Trang airport.

"Where's a cyclo when you need one?" he said to himself, looking for one of the normally hundreds of bicycle-driven carriages that had until this evening crowded Nha Trang's streets. He looked at his wristwatch as he jogged and saw that his few-minutes journey back to the consulate had already taken nearly half an hour.

"They had better wait," he told himself as he now began to sprint, clutching the records tight and pumping the rifle with his other hand as he ran.

NHA TRANG AIRPORT TERMINAL

MONCRIEFF SPEAR PACED the now blockaded Nha Trang terminal nervously, at one point tripping over the feet of the DAO officer who had made several of the forays after Vietnamese friends earlier that day. He snapped at the man, who then burst into laughter. The sight and now growling of the gangly, otherwise soft-spoken diplomat, with the loosely strung shoulder-holstered hogleg pistol slapping his ribs as he paced had sent the young defense attaché assistant over the edge. The tension simply broke.

"Just us left," Spear said, taking a quick appraisal of the terminal. "Good. Our helicopter should be here any second."

Outside, hordes of Vietnamese civilians with suitcases and boxes stacked beyond belief huddled all along the terminal boarding areas. Beyond them bands of armed ARVN soldiers, now desperate for escape, roamed the tarmac, ready to take on any challengers.

With immediate security falling quickly apart, the consul general had ordered that when the next aircraft landed, it should taxi discretely to the opposite end of the airfield, far from any roving bands. He had then ordered a helicopter to set down at the side of the terminal where he and the remaining handful of Americans could scramble aboard. The chopper would then ferry the last of his staff to the waiting Air America Volpar.

Just as the Air America Chinook's wheels touched the concrete outside the terminal, Spear, Phil Cook, and a handful of other Americans scrambled inside its open side hatch. It lifted off the ground just as a thousand Vietnamese rushed for a departing ride.

Marine Corporal Jimmie Sneed stood guard outside the door of the Air America plane and snapped to attention when he saw Consul General Spear and the others dash toward him. Appropriately, he crisply saluted his boss by presenting arms with the Remington 870 riot-model

12-gauge shotgun with which he stood his sentry watch while waiting on Sergeant McCormick to return.

Moncrieff Spear dashed aboard ahead of everyone else and strapped himself into the forward seat.

"Give us just a couple more minutes, sir," Staff Sergeant Painter said to Phil Cook as the last American climbed aboard. "I have a man inbound and should be here any minute. We cannot leave a Marine behind."

"Right," Cook said, saddling himself into one of the empty seats and finally relaxing after running nonstop for the past fourteen hours.

With the evening light fading quickly to darkness, Jimmie Sneed did not see the gaggle of desperate ARVN stragglers running at the plane until they had already reached him and their leader had put the cold, steel end of his rifle to the Marine's head. Not hesitating to think, the corporal shoved his shotgun's barrel straight up and caught the ARVN lieutenant under the chin with its muzzle.

"Back off," Sneed said to him. "That plane's full of armed United States Marines who will slaughter your men once I blow off your head."

The lieutenant suddenly smiled and raised his hands, holding his rifle above his head. He stepped back from the aircraft, and then he and his men ran back toward the terminal's floodlights.

"Gentlemen," Moncrieff Spear shouted from his seat, where he had sat by the window and had watched the frightening exchange. "We're leaving! Now!"

"Sir, Sergeant McCormick!" Staff Sergeant Painter shouted. "We cannot leave a Marine behind. We never."

"You will tonight, or you and your Marines can get off and find other accommodations," Spear snapped without looking back.

"Get in the plane, Corporal Sneed," the staff sergeant then said, leaning out the door. "First, make sure you clear your weapon outside."

The corporal smiled and began jacking the shotgun's pump action back, expecting to see a shower of aught-four buckshot cartridges spit out of it. His heart had nearly stopped when he looked into the wide eyes of his staff sergeant.

"Don't tell me that damned gun was empty!" Painter growled at the corporal.

"I guess I forgot to load it this morning," Sneed said with a sick smile as he handed the empty weapon to the staff sergeant and climbed inside the plane.

SWEAT STREAMED DOWN Mike McCormick's face as he ran down the airport apron, past the active runway and to the far taxiway and fence line where he had left his fellow Marines waiting. He still had all their pay records and SRBs tightly in his clutch.

He jogged across the spot three times, his head turning 360 degrees as he ran, and found nothing but bare concrete and asphalt. His bag was gone. The plane was gone.

"I knew it!" he cried out. "I damned well knew it. They left me here to die!"

He looked at the floodlights of the terminal and watched the crowd that had again settled in to wait. The sky had fallen silent, and the artillery had stopped. One silhouette of a man taller than the other people stood off the corner of the building, marking his position by the glow of the cigarette that he smoked. He didn't look Vietnamese.

"Leave me like this," McCormick said under his breath as he began to jog, heading toward the light and the tall man standing in the shadows a few yards from the side of the building. "If I die, they will go home poor. Without pay records, they're screwed."

The idea of even that low level of revenge at leaving him behind made the Marine feel better about his situation. Only very slightly better.

"Ah, another friendly," the man said, seeing McCormick jog toward him. "I thought that I had the honor of the last man out."

"Not much honor in that," the sergeant said, smiling through his sweat-dripping face. "I ran from the consulate, and they were supposed to wait for me."

"I saw the plane take off nearly half an hour ago," the stranger said. "I tried to catch it too. Luckily, I have my trusty little handheld and managed to raise Air America at Cam Ranh. They've diverted an inbound flight to drop in and swoop us out. I'm afraid you'll have to put in a little more PT before we sit down. We've got to get out to the far runway when we hear his engine. He won't wait."

"Let's go now," McCormick said anxiously.

"Give it a few minutes more," the stranger said calmly. "We don't want to draw a crowd, or gunfire, do we? I think we can run the distance between the time we hear his engine and he sets down out there."

The tall man had hardly finished his words when the distant beat of a Huey caught McCormick's attention. "Like now," he said.

Both Americans quietly walked into the darkness and then ran for all their worth. When the UH-1N twin-turbine utility helicopter flashed on its landing light, it caught the two men waving happily at it from the runway's center stripe.

Like diving out of a hot LZ, the two new friends bellied aboard the chopper as it tilted its nose and raced skyward. Beating the air as it climbed, the Huey streaked past a suddenly stirred crowd that charged after the aircraft.

"Damned near out of fuel, boys," a gray-haired crew chief shouted at the pair as the wind whipped through the open side doors. "We'll drop off at Cam Ranh for gas, then chop on to Saigon. Good to have you aboard."

Mike McCormick fell into the gray nylon stretcher-style seat at the back bulkhead. His sweat had soaked through the outside cover of top and bottom service and pay record folders. He tried to wipe away the stain, but then quit.

NVA FIELD HEADQUARTERS NEAR BAN ME THUOT

"ANOTHER CIGARETTE I see," Tran Van Tra said, smiling at the North Vietnamese Army's chief of staff, General Van Tien Dung.

"Tran, my friend," Dung said, "join me, and have a cup of tea and some of this delicious breakfast fruit."

An aide pulled a chair from the small table and offered it to the Viet Cong leader to sit.

"You see the map?" Dung said. "This is why I have indulged myself with another cigarette this morning. Hanoi has authorized us to proceed now directly to Saigon."

"What of Nha Trang," General Tran said. "The 10th, 316th, and 320th divisions can enter the city at any minute."

"No," Dung said, "I have sent orders for them to turn southward and proceed toward Saigon. The rats have abandoned the ship, and thus we no longer have any reason to pursue the city. It is ours if we want it, but the prize is Saigon. Nha Trang is now meaningless.

"The Tenth Division will divert forces to clear out what remains around Cam Ranh, but the 316th and 320th must maneuver their units straight away to Saigon."

"It will be good to go home again," Tran Van Tra said, sipping the tea that the aide had placed before him.

"General Le Trong Tan will also redeploy to the Saigon tactical area with the bulk of his forces, but leave behind a sufficient garrison in Da Nang to continue establishing public order," Dung said. "I have directed him to be in position east of Xuan Loc by April 11. He will direct that battle, which I regard as the key to our whole success in finally liberating Saigon. Whoever controls the crossroads at Xuan Loc virtually controls access to Saigon. That is why I have placed this most important battle in the hands of Le Trong Tan.

"Meanwhile we will redeploy the majority of our forces from here to surround Saigon, along with four newly activated reserve divisions leaving Hanoi today. Let me show you how I have formed our plan on the map."

The two men walked to a blowup of the Saigon region that showed a layout of a fifty-mile radius surrounding South Vietnam's capital. One clear plastic overlay identified all the ARVN defense positions and headquarters locations by unit designations and strengths, and the second overlay plotted the North Vietnamese Army's and their Viet Cong reinforcements' lines of attack.

"Here you see the enemy's forces and positions," Dung said, flipping down the first overlay, "at least what measure of an army that they have remaining in existence. Minuscule now compared to the twenty-one full divisions that we shall press upon them. Our best estimates say that Nguyen Van Thieu has no more than ninty thousand soldiers, including his own personal legions, to defend Saigon. Against those forces, we will deploy more than three hundred thousand highly motivated warriors from the field and have nearly a hundred thousand more coming from Hanoi."

"As Sun Tsu Woo wrote more than two thousand years ago," Tran said, agreeing with his colleague's ideal, "win your battles with decisive force! To do less wastes much."

Dung smiled as he dropped down the second overlay, showing the NVA forces' planned positions and projected axes of approach.

"We will surround Saigon from no less than five extensive battle-fronts," the senior general said, pointing on the map to the dashed lines arching across five sectors that ringed the city. "Our forces will attack along six primary axes and four secondary axes, moving from six different sectors."

Touching the overlay with a black ballpoint pen, General Dung pointed to a sector south of Saigon.

"You see the Eighth Division here, now deploying to coordinating positions on the Mekong River?" Dung said, tapping the pen on the map. "They have little resistance and will attack mainly to block any retreats on the river or to the sea. The Eighth Division will attack on an axis from the southwest along a parallel line to QL-4 and cover the right flank of the southwestern Long An front. One division can easily cover that responsibility."

"This left flank of the Long An front," General Tran Van Tra said, pointing to the sector southwest of Saigon, "presents more resistance than the forces shown on this overlay. I can tell you from my many bitter experiences there."

"I agree. You learned many valuable lessons from the attack that you planned and led on Saigon in 1968, and we now will profit from those experiences," Dung said. "Accordingly, I have put four full divisions and a reserve regiment there, under command of the 232nd Tactical Force to cover that left flank. That includes the Third, Fifth, Ninth, and Sixteenth divisions, and the 271B Regiment. They will attack on this axis toward Saigon, proceeding from the southwest out of their coordinating positions on the Mekong and moving on a line parallel to QL-4 on its north side.

"Here I have the Second Army Corps, comprised of the 304th, 324B, and 325th divisions, and the Third Gold Star Division. They will close on Saigon from the southeast along two attack axes. Their primary assault will follow an axis that follows Highway QL-15 to Long Thanh, parallel to the southeastern QL-15 front, and then once on the outskirts of Saigon, feint southwestward to the lower deepwater reaches of the Dong Nai River, crossing it at this bridge, seven kilometers east of Nhon Trach. From there they will enter Saigon from the point of the far left flank of our eastern Bien Hoa front. The Second NVA Corps will also execute this second attack axis that neutralizes Dat Do City and then proceeds southwest along QL-15 and blocks access to the seaport south of Phuoc Le. This second axis will cover the left flank of the southeastern QL-15 front.

"Up here," Dung said pointing to the sector east of Saigon, "our Fourth NVA Corps will attack the eastern Bien Hoa front on two axes, one north and one south of Highway 1. This is our key offensive. Controlling those crossroads is vital.

"Here at Xuan Loc, we have our wonderfully flamboyant Brigadier General Le Minh Dao and his Eighteenth ARVN Division standing the sentinel. He has one regiment forward and two in reserve. Behind him, at Bien Hoa, our fat friend General Nguyen Van Toan sits with a regiment in garrison. Just south of him we have the remains of their Marine commando 468th Brigade, no more than one regiment in strength. Next to them the ARVN have their Third Tank Brigade and the two reserve regiments of the Eighteenth Division. We have the 314th, 6th, and 7th divisions and some reinforcements from the Second Corps supporting our attacks on Saigon from the east.

"You see, the enemy has anticipated that our primary attacks will come from the north," Dung said, with a smile.

"Of course we will not disappoint them," Tran Van Tra said, smiling too.

"Of course not," the senior general said. "We will give them all that they can handle with our secondary attacks.

"I have divided the 320th Division among the First and Third corps, here in the north at Binh Dong and then here at the west by Cu Chi.

"First from the north, the First Corps will attack Saigon on a secondary axis that covers the left flank of the northern Binh Duong front, using detached regiments from the 320th Division. They will augment the 312th and 338th on their assault along the Dong Nai River, taking out the Fifth ARVN Division's right flank. Their intermediate objectives include the hamlets of Ben San and Co Mi and the junction where QL-13 meets Highway 1 at the Saigon River bridge, thus entering the city at that point.

"The Third Corps will cover both the right flank of the Binh Duong front, assaulting the left flank of the Fifth ARVN Division and the entire western Cu Chi front, dealing with not only the Twenty-fifth ARVN Division and their heavy artillery, but the Eighth and Ninth ARVN Rangers too. For this reason, I have provided the Third Corps with the majority of the 320th Division, as well as the 316th, 70th, and 968th divisions.

"Again, these are all secondary fronts, meant more to distract, waste, and block the enemy, while our primary attacks converge from the south and the east."

"A very comprehensive plan, General Dung," Tran Van Tra said as the two men returned to the small table and poured more tea.

"Now, my friend," Dung said, taking a slice of orange and sucking the pulp into his mouth, speaking as he chewed, "I hope that you have not grown too comfortable at your headquarters here."

"Comfort does not describe my accommodations, as you well know, my friend," Tran said with a smile.

"Good," Dung said. "You will immediately relocate your head-quarters to the eastern sector of the Saigon tactical area. Tomorrow, I will move the supreme command headquarters from here to Loc Ninh, only 110 kilometers north of Saigon and just forty-five kilometers from Song Be Airfield. Very convenient."

"Loc Ninh as command headquarters will sit well with Chairman Pham Hung," Tran Van Tra said. "Does he not reside near Loc Ninh?"

"Indeed," General Dung said, "I am due to pay him my respects upon arrival tomorrow, and you must as well too."

Pham Hung had quietly overseen all Communist operations in South Vietnam and stood not only as General Tran Van Tra's superior, but lofted politically above General Van Tien Dung as well. The squat, simple man lived in a humble home in a rural setting, yet carried the clout of the fourth highest ranking member of the politburo in Hanoi.

The regime in Hanoi had kept Pham Hung out of the public eye and applauded his humble existence. In this way he freely operated in South Vietnam, literally serving as the politburo's hands, eyes, and ears there, ultimately controlling and approving all major Communist force activities throughout the country.

Pham put on no pretenses, living in a bamboo hut with a thatched roof overlooking a checkerboard of rice paddies. A simple rice farmer nearing sixty years of age, gray haired, squat, and burly, appearing much as a peasant, the unassuming old man stood as one of the most powerful men in all of North or South Vietnam. His influence both here and in Hanoi literally controlled millions of lives.

UNITED STATES NAVY SEVENTH FLEET HEADQUARTERS

VICE ADMIRAL GEORGE P. Steele, commander of the United States Navy's Seventh Fleet, had to man his battle station and go to general quarters against a stone wall of hand-wringing bureaucrats in Washington, DC, who fretted by the minute about President Ford tromping on the edges of the War Powers Act. Steele needed some fast authorization to put

Marines on the merchant ships, and the gray serge suits on the Potomac kept stalling his efforts.

Murders and mayhem rocked through nearly every ship. One of them had even encountered an act of high-seas piracy by a gun-wielding band of refugee cowboys who took over the bridge of one vessel for a time. Rapes, killings, and violent disputes occurred below decks on an hourly basis. Messages begging for security help aboard these containers of human strife came from the shipmasters by the stackful each day. The Seventh Fleet commander felt compelled to immediately station Marines aboard those floating disaster areas. Each minute delayed potentially cost lives, yet the suits kept putting him off.

Finally, in desperation, Steele and his boss, the Commander in Chief, Pacific, Admiral Noel Gayler, bluntly laid the issue at the feet of the Chief of Naval Operations and the Joint Chiefs of Staff. Those officers, like the President, went against all the bureaucrats' wishes and issued the green light.

President Ford, now in disgust, broke his silence and went before television cameras at Palm Springs, venting his frustrations not only with Congress, but with Nguyen Van Thieu's faulty leadership and panic-stricken actions. He told reporters that South Vietnam's president should have kept his army in its defenses in the Central Highlands and northern provinces and that he saw the massive attempt at redeploying those forces a major blunder in the war. He said that now his staff had begun considering evacuation operations of the more than six thousand Americans presently in South Vietnam, should matters there continue down the current negative path.

The President then laid a bombshell on the media. He told the reporters that despite the vocal opposition of most Democrats on Capitol Hill, and a few Republicans too, he stood prepared to land military forces in South Vietnam. He said that while restricting the use of military power to go to war, the War Powers Act allowed the President the authority to land military forces in any combat theater where American citizens' lives hang in the balance. He said he would certainly not hesitate to send ashore Marine landing forces to evacuate the Americans from besieged and strangled Phnom Penh, Cambodia, or from South Vietnam.

The approval for Marines aboard the refugee ships, in light of President Ford's heated remarks and commitment to protecting American lives, now seemed pale in comparison to the other possible prospects that he raised.

Before the grunts of First Battalion, Fourth Marine Regiment broke into their security detachments and scattered themselves among the vast sea of ships that lay in the waters off Nha Trang and Cam Ranh, now overwhelmed with those cities' evacuees, Major Carl A. Shaver, the battalion's operations officer, hosted an operational skull session aboard the USS *Dubuque*, along with his commanding officer, Lieutenant Colonel Charles E. Hester, for the battalion landing team's officers and staff.

During the night the *Dubuque* had rendezvoused with the USS *Frederick* and the USS *Blue Ridge*. The armada of American ships now only awaited the arrival of the aircraft carrier, the USS *Hancock*, underway from Pearl Harbor along with its escort.

Mike boats from the various vessels rounded up the conference's concerned parties and delivered them to the LPD's side. A crowd of battle-ready Marines, chomping and stamping to get into the thick of a good fight, quickly filled the ship's quarterdeck.

Shaver covered the plan of action, deploying detachments of Marines to each of the refugee vessels and providing basic immediate action, deadly force, and policing guidelines. Companies Alpha, Bravo, Charlie, and Delta became Security Forces Alpha, Bravo, Charlie, and Delta, retaining the same captains in command and their subordinate structures, with only name change and cosmetics. Among the gathering he heard a few hums and haws and several groans. Then came the question that everyone wanted to ask.

"Obviously, this shipboard security is an intermediary mission," one voice piped from the back of the room. "When do we land the landing force?"

The response brought little more than a shrug and a sigh because no one up the chain of command, at least at this side of Planet Earth, knew an answer to the question. Yet the grumbles of frustration and two-hour-long exchange of commentary sent a distinct message to anyone who cared to listen.

Every Marine present ached to get into battle and badly wanted to push the North Vietnamese not only back to the DMZ, but through Hanoi and out the Chinese border, if they could. To a man, not one of the men gathered on the quarterdeck believed that the United States would ever stand by and do nothing and give up South Vietnam. None of the Marines could imagine how America, with all the money spent, equipment invested, and more than fifty-six thousand lives sacrificed in this cause, could ever turn its back. Such betrayal violated every principle of honor that American history ever preached.

On the ships, to a man, every one of the Marines who spread themselves among the refugee ships and assumed the roles as caretakers and policemen longed to see the moment when the order would come to land the landing force and finally save South Vietnam.

While the First Battalion, Fourth Marines set about their shipboard work, Brigadier General Richard E. Carey, the Ninth Marine Amphibious Brigade commander, Colonel Dan C. Alexander, 9th MAB's chief of staff and the commander of the Amphibious Evacuation RVN Support Group (the Thirty-third Marine Amphibious Unit's redesignated name because of its humanitarian mission), and Colonel Alfred M. Gray, the newly designated commander of Regimental Landing Team 4, examined options and scenarios for a host of possible contingencies. All of them seemed to involve the eventual evacuation of Saigon.

HIGHWAY 1 NEAR CHU LAI

DUST CHOKED TRAN Ngoc Toan, and he tried pulling his white muslin shirt over his nose and mouth to filter the air. It helped little. Ahead of him and behind him the 450 Viet Marines that remained of the 147th Brigade scattered themselves among the thousands of people who inched their way down Highway 1, pushing toward Saigon.

At night, they camped much in a group, making their fires near each other. Toan's battalion sergeant major, the highest ranking enlisted Marine who managed to escape the beach at Tan My, worked his way from group to group, counting heads, listening, and reassuring.

Pushing slowly past Chu Lai, the Viet Marine lieutenant colonel began to notice what seemed an endless caravan of southbound military trucks loaded with North Vietnamese soldiers. Scattered among these troop transports rolled long semi trailers with tarp-covered, cigar-shaped cargos. Other trucks accompanied these, and Toan clearly recognized them as mobile missile launchers.

"I fear for Saigon," he finally whispered to his sergeant major, who walked at his side. The two men kept their heads down as they plodded in the bar ditch along the highway. Their faces hidden under straw hats, the pair spoke softly without looking at each other.

"Tens of thousands of fresh troops in these trucks," the sergeant major said, agreeing with his commander's sentiments. "These do not come from battle, but come from Hanoi. They wear new uniforms. Look closely too, and you will see that they have conscripted ARVN prisoners as drivers."

"I noticed that," Toan said. "I also see that they have begun transporting SA-2 missiles on the long trailers, and their mobile launching systems accompany them. We never saw these big SAMs except near the DMZ, where they shot down countless numbers of the Americans' B-52 bombers. Now they bring them toward Saigon."

The sergeant major trudged onward and looked out the corner of his eye, watching more of the trucks roll past him.

"I too fear for our home."

ALGIERS, DEMOCRATIC AND POPULAR REPUBLIC OF ALGERIA

"LADIES AND GENTLEMEN of the international press, please listen," Madame Nguyen Thi Binh, spokeswoman and foreign minister for the Provisional Revolutionary Government, said in an Algiers hotel conference suite. "We understand that General Duong Van Minh has offered to negotiate peace on behalf of the Saigon regime. We are anxious to talk with him. He speaks a voice of reason within the corrupt government of Nguyen Van Thieu, who leads our people daily to more needless suffering. We hope very much that peace can be achieved with Big Minh representing Saigon."

Her news conference ended without questions. It cast another empty peace overture toward the West and set Capitol Hill strategists scrambling. Perhaps a negotiated settlement with North Vietnam had not lost all hope. They readily bought the ploy that Nguyen Van Thieu, from the Communists' perspective, presented the only stumbling block to finally saving Saigon.

Chapter 17

THE NOOSE CLOSES

SAIGON, RVN—FRIDAY, APRIL 4

"STORK TWO-ONE-eight, climb to and maintain flight level three-two-zero, report passing two-eight-zero, cleared to vector heading one-three-six, information India, squawk six-two-five-niner and ident, contact Clark center on guard frequency two-eight-niner-point-five," the Tan Son Nhut departure flight controller said in a rapid-fire litany of aviation shorthand, radioing the monotone drone of instructions in the outbound Air Force C-5A Galaxy flight deck crew's headsets as the gigantic cargo aircraft banked southeastward and ascended through twenty thousand feet at its best-rate-of-climb attitude and airspeed.

"Two-one-eight with the information, roger, and good day, sir," the aircraft's pilot in command, Captain Dennis "Bud" Traynor, responded as his copilot, Captain Tilford Harp, switched the aircraft's radios to the next flight center frequency.

Picking up its southeast heading of 136 degrees and climbing through twenty-three thousand feet, the strategic transport's four immense General Electric TF-39 turbo-fan engines, their eight-and-one-half-foot diameter intakes agape like the mouths of a quartet of bowhead whales, sucking air, compressing it, supercharging it with fuel, and combusting the volatile mix through each of their twenty-seven-foot-long bodies, exploded forty-three thousand pounds of constant thrust out the exhaust end of each jet and sent the three-quarters of a million pounds of aircraft loaded with 332,500 pounds of JP-5 kerosene, 328 passengers, their personal possessions, and a flight crew of sixteen, droning skyward at more than three hundred miles per hour, above a bed of growing cumulus clouds. The aircraft's wings stretched nearly 223 feet and easily lifted its 247-foot-long, 65-foot-high body as it pushed higher into the cold blue of a late afternoon sky.

Built by Lockheed-Georgia, and already having circled the planet for nearly six years as a proud representative of the Sixtieth Military Airlift Wing from its home station at Travis Air Force Base, California, the awesome craft, serial number 68-218, still turned heads. C-5 Galaxies, like great trains, ships, and skyscrapers, possess a titanic beauty unique in the world.

The big plane had shuddered slightly as it began pressurizing the crew stations, passenger cabin, and cargo bay, passing above eight thousand feet mean sea level, racing for its thirty-two-thousand-foot cruise altitude. As it climbed higher and higher above the Mekong Delta of South Vietnam, the flight engineer monitored the four sets of engine gauges and saw the cabin pressurization indicator moving slowly but holding a positive volume well in the green.

"Thelma, sweetheart, I need a favor," Twila Donelson called to her colleague Thelma Thompson just before takeoff. Twila was an American attached to the Defense Attaché's Office in Saigon, and Thelma Thompson was another DAO member who had drawn orphan escort duty for a one-way ride home. "Would you mind terribly if you moved upstairs into the rear passenger area, in the tail section? They have 145 children up there with just six attendants. You'll make it lucky number seven for them. As shorthanded as they are up there with those children, I think they would really appreciate some help."

Thelma smiled and nodded happily at Twila and left the lower cargo bay where the remaining 102 of the total 247 South Vietnamese orphans sat, along with forty-seven other passengers on this first flight of Operation Babylift. Because most of the children averaged no more than one year of age and suffered from malnutrition and other health problems, they required close attendance.

Satisfying two goals, helping the children and evacuating an important and deeply appreciated portion of his staff, Major General Homer Smith, the defense attaché in Saigon, had assigned as orphan escorts forty-four women from his American staff, many of whom were qualified nurses. Along with them he wrangled aboard the flight a handful of other evacuees like Helen Drye, an American DAO employee, and her young daughter Theresa; Laurie Stark, an American school teacher; and Sharon Wesley, who had worked for the American Red Cross and Army Special Services for several years in South Vietnam and had remained in Saigon after her job and the United States military had pulled out in 1973.

Tending to the crowd of crying babies in the main cargo bay, Clara Bayot, Barbara Stout, and Mary Ann Crouch busily changed diapers and tried their best to ease the infants' tears. Beyond them, Ruthanne Gasper, Dorothy Howard, and Joan Pray worked with groups of five children each. Juanita Creel, Elizabeth Fugino, Vera Hollibaugh, and Beverly Herbert did likewise with their charges of orphaned Vietnamese infants.

Most of the babies had wound up in the New Haven Nursery in Saigon after spending hungry months at poor foundling homes scattered across the country. Pronounced ribs, potbellies, and gaunt faces seemed the common denominator among the children, such as Bach Thi-Kim Cuong.

The newborn infant's family had abandoned her only days after her birth, sometime in late April at Soc Trang hamlet, and thus she came to live at the Khanh Hung Orphanage on May 6, 1974. No one knew the baby's identity, family, or birth date, so the nuns gave the little girl a name, Bach Thi-Kim Cuong, and decided that she could recognize the day that they found her lying on the orphanage doorstep as her birthday. What difference would that few days make over the years, anyway?

The Sisters of Providence, who operated the orphanage, had very little and baby Bach already had badly suffered starvation, so the nuns persuaded an American colleague, Sister Susan McDonald, a missionary nurse at the New Haven Nursery in Saigon, to take the severely underweight and malnourished infant.

Bach Thi-Kim Cuong learned to sit up and crawl at her new home, under Sister Susan's gentle hand, along with a hundred other children just like this baby girl from the Mekong rice lands. Her first memories of life formed there.

After she lived in the Saigon orphanage nearly a year, an English couple, Colin and Diane Felce, at long last finalized arrangements to adopt little Bach. They had finally overcome the mountains of paperwork and had passed all the grueling tests and screening. The arduous process seemed ironic in the face of the devastating conditions from which these children came and their current meager existence. Why should these children languish while bureaucrats slowly processed stacks of papers, spinning mountains of red tape, when families on the other end wanted them so badly?

With the war rapidly closing the noose around Saigon, and because baby Bach Thi-Kim Cuong had a place to go, she received priority to board this first flight of angels.

Unfortunately, the bustle of loading the children so quickly had not allowed time to process much paperwork to accompany the babies. So workers attached hospital bracelets to the children's tiny wrists containing only sketchy information, such as "Baby Cuong, destination London."

Besides the 247 orphans and their forty-four American babysitters, along with an additional United States Air Force medical crew of ten, brought aboard to look after the sick and very fragile among the children, a mix of twenty-seven other homebound Americans, mostly civilian government employees, also rode in the aircraft. The Thirteenth Air Force, based at Clark Air Base, Philippines, held operational authority over the airlift and had coordinated the flight of this C-5A Galaxy, along with a C-9 Nightingale, as the inaugural sorties of President Ford's Operation Babylift.

The C-5A's afternoon mission from Saigon to Clark Air Base had originated with the big cargo jet delivering one of the first loads of expedited military supplies summoned by General Fred Weyand during his telephone conference with President Ford. Once the ground crews had rolled off the war goods, they quickly prepared the main bay and upstairs passenger areas to receive the orphans and American evacuees.

At 4:03 p.m., the twenty-eight wheels on the Galaxy's landing gear quickly sucked inside the belly of the mammoth aircraft as it lifted from the runway at Tan Son Nhut. It passed over Saigon like a football stadium on wings, its engines humming their telltale drone, and climbed through the building afternoon clouds as it followed the Mekong River southward. Sparkling like mirrors in the sun, the thousands of rice paddies that spread throughout the broad river delta shrank smaller and smaller as the great aircraft lifted itself higher and higher aloft.

"Good afternoon, Clark center, stork two-one-eight with you passing flight level two-eight-zero for three-two-zero, heading one-three-six degrees," Captain Traynor radioed the en route air traffic control center.

"Roger, two-one-eight, squawk ident," the traffic center controller responded.

At 4:15 p.m., twelve minutes into the flight, Captain Harp pressed the ident button on the aircraft's radar transponder. This sent a momentarily strong signal of the aircraft's identifying code to the air traffic control radar, causing the numbers to show brightly on the flight center's cathodal sweep screen. Suddenly, a deafening boom shook the gigantic aircraft. The cockpit lurched up, then slammed down violently. As the transport plunged into a deadly dive, it immediately ran up three hundred knots on the injured plane's airspeed indicator.

"What was that?" Captain Traynor shouted as he immediately pulled down his oxygen mask and hauled back on the control column, trying to raise the big plane's nose. Instead of blue sky, he now saw the watery green Mekong Delta filling the Galaxy's front windows.

"Oh, dear God!" the aircraft's crew chief cried out as he looked through the window of the door that opened onto the lower deck and cargo bay. The 13.5-foot-high, 19-foot-wide, and 148-foot-long hold had filled with a massive tornado of fog, spinning aircraft debris, personal belongings, and human beings in its wind. At the aft end of the aircraft, where the twister generated its force, a huge, gaping hole shown.

"Sir," the crew chief shouted on the intercom to his commander, "the aft cargo doors and ramp have blown off the aircraft. It looks like a large part of the rear, lower airframe has torn off too."

"No pressurization, sir," the flight engineer followed.

"The explosion must have severed the control cables to the rudder and elevator," Captain Traynor said to his copilot. "I get no response out of the tail, and I've got reaction from only one set of wing spoilers and aileron."

"Mayday! Mayday! Mayday!" Captain Harp called on the radio and switched on the emergency locator radio beacon, broadcasting a Mayday signal on the international distress frequencies. The incessant sirenlike radio chirp of the emergency signal filled the cockpit.

"Two-one-eight declaring emergency, attempting return to Tan Son Nhut," the copilot continued.

"Two-one-eight, Tan Son Nhut tower," a voice responded on the radio, "cleared for emergency landing, runway two-five left. If able, come about to heading three-one-zero."

As the C-5A gained airspeed in its dive, the increased lift on the wings caused the aircraft to shallow its dive and its nose to rise. Soon the big plane slowed to a stall and rolled to the right, again diving hard. With the increase in airspeed on the wing surfaces, the lift again brought the plane's nose up.

"I have no pitch control and very little attitude with just one wing spoiler and aileron working," Traynor told his copilot. "By adding power in the dives, we shallow out sooner, and we roll to the right. Using the throttles to control pitch and letting it roll to the right, I think we can bring it back around to the northwest heading. Harp, you take care of the roll with that one wing control while I bring us about and try to control our descent by manipulating these power settings."

The sudden decompression of the aircraft dislodged everything and everyone inside the cargo area. The violent storm of debris and tornadic winds, with the sudden lack of oxygen, instantly killed many of the passengers in the lower bay. Several of those people seated toward the rear were sucked out the massive hole in the tail of the plane.

"Almost there, Harp," Captain Traynor told his copilot as both men watched their heading indicator slowing ticking its way to the final approach heading for runway 25L at Tan Son Nhut. Airspeed soared with each dive and fell as the nose came up, bringing the rate of descent from four thousand feet per minute to a little more than fifteen hundred feet per minute. The pronounced time lag from power adjustment to aircraft response taxed the full energy and fiber of both pilots to their outer limits.

They watched as the altimeter wound backwards, now showing less than six thousand feet. The parallel runways at Tan Son Nhut lay far in the distance.

On the last shallow turn to final, from their heading of 310 degrees, pushing left to 250 degrees, lining up with the runway, the plane suddenly dropped.

"Too slow!" Traynor said, pushing the throttles as the altitude rapidly disappeared, cursing the lag in response. "We can't make the runway now! We've got to belly into the marsh. Level the wings as best you can, Harp. I've got full power to keep the nose up as high as I can get it."

Its wheels still locked inside its vast underbelly, the great Galaxy splashed into the watery flats of the Mekong Delta, sending a spray of water and mud over its massive body. Moving at more than 250 knots, the gigantic plane began to plow a deep trench through the muck and then skidded into a patchwork of flooded rice fields.

Still traveling at high speed, the C-5A slammed through a paddy dike, and the impact sent the plane bounding back into the air. It rode airborne for nearly a half mile and then crashed back into the rice paddies, spraying more mud and water over its back as it now dug itself deeply into the ground. The impact as it struck the rice paddy dike fractured the wings and tail from the aircraft, causing the Galaxy to separate into four parts as it finally came to rest.

Thelma Thompson had sat in her tail section seat terrified from the first moment that the explosion from beneath the deck under her feet had put a spinning fog all around her. She had almost passed out from the horror and the sudden lack of air. Then as oxygen at last began to again fill her space, clearing out the fog and giving her the feeling that perhaps the worst had passed, suddenly she found herself seeing daylight through the roof as her chair ripped from the floor, and a cascade of mud and water enveloped her.

The careening and banging seemed to last an eternity during those few seconds of touchdown and crash landing. It stressed every part of her body. Then the final slamming, with the aircraft breaking apart and her seat crashing into debris that used to be part of the plane, had made her think she would surely die.

As suddenly as it had all begun, it ended.

Able-bodied and injured women and the few men aboard who had survived immediately grabbed children from the upper deck and rushed them out the massive holes in the aircraft's broken body, tromping through the knee-deep rice fields, carrying the babies to a paddy dike. Back and forth they hurried, hauling the mud-covered infants.

When Thelma Thompson managed to push herself out of the wreckage, her body throbbed with severe pain. As she stepped from the gash across the roof and side of the aircraft where she had ridden, she noticed that the ground was nearly even with the top of the plane. Recalling how the galaxy had sat on its trucks and wheels at the airport before takeoff, she realized that now this same ground-level spot on the aircraft had earlier towered sixty-five-feet above the tarmac.

Helicopters descended on the crash site almost immediately with emergency rescue and medical professionals racing to the great air-craft's remains. They climbed down into the hellish chamber that had once served as the Galaxy's cargo bay. It had filled with water, mud, and muck and reeked of kerosene from the aircraft's ruptured fuel cells.

As more and more rescue workers arrived, a stream of mud-covered babies began to fill the outbound medevac choppers. They piled the black-caked, limp children into the rapidly moving brigade of chop-pers, letting the medical workers at Third Field, the former army hos-pital at Tan Son Nhut, sort the living from the dead.

At the hospital, nurses and doctors began their triage by washing a shower spray of water over the babies, clearing away the thick mud so that they could determine if the child still lived.

At the end of the day, 141 of the 149 orphans and attendants who sat in the airplane's massive cargo bay had died. The violent churn of debris in that chamber, chopping through everything inside like blades in a great blender, had killed most of the victims during the first sec-onds of the disaster. Some of the people survived the mayhem but suc-cumbed from drowning after the crash. A handful died from having the massive vacuum pull them out of the plane at high altitude amidst a stream of whirling, knifelike debris very likely as well, killing them in-stantly.

While many in the upper passenger compartment suffered serious injuries, such as Thelma Thompson, whose later compensation barely covered her medical expenses, only three of the people seated there died in the crash. Five of the sixteen-person flight crew also perished, as did three members of the ten-person medical team and three other passen-gers not connected with the babylift operation.

Helen Drye and her daughter Theresa died in the crash. So did Thelma Thompson's friend Twila Donelson. Thelma credited her sur-vival to the last-minute move that she made from the cargo bay to the upper-level seating in the tail section.

Laurie Stark and Sharon Wesley also died in the crash, as did Clara Bayot, Barbara Stout, and Mary Ann Crouch. Ruthanne Gasper, Dorothy Howard, Joan Pray, Juanita Creel, Elizabeth Fugino, Vera Hollibaugh, and Beverly Herbert also died in the airplane that day.

Although bruised and badly frightened, one-year-old baby girl Bach Thi-Kim Cuong survived the disaster. She later flew to England and joined her new parents Colin and Diane Felce. While many occidental families gave their adopted Vietnamese orphan children Western names, the Felces preserved their new daughter's Indochinese heritage by giving her the name Safi Thi-Kim Felce.

In total, of the 328 passengers and 16-member crew, 175 passengers and eleven of the crew made it out alive, thanks to the brilliant and determined actions of pilot in command, Captain Dennis "Bud" Traynor, and copilot, Captain Tilford Harp.

For their decisive leadership and heroic airmanship, Captains Traynor and Harp each received the Air Force Cross for their valor during the horrifying final fifteen minutes of the last flight of C-5A Galaxy, serial number SN 68-218.

Because of the violent nature of the explosion that took out the Galaxy's rear fuselage and aft cargo ramp and doors, Air Force officials immediately feared that a saboteur had managed to put a bomb on the plane. Only days later did officials discover that faulty latches, or a failure to properly close the latches to the rear doors, had in most probability caused the explosion. Once the aircraft neared its cruise altitude, its internal atmospheric pressure apparently caused the latches to give way and snapped off the doors with explosive force, tearing away part of the fuselage and rear ramp as well as the hatches.

Some speculated that with so many infants aboard the flight and given that high altitude inflicts a greater level of discomfort on babies, the crew may have allowed cabin pressure to build higher than the typical atmospheric equivalent of eight thousand feet. Perhaps they may have pushed it down a bit to five thousand feet to make conditions more comfortable for the children. With possibly faulty latches, or with the latches failing to lock securely before takeoff, the higher than typical pressure may have exacerbated the problem to excess.

According to the flight crew, however, all systems had functioned normally during preflight inspections and at the time of launch.

Lawsuits later pursued by surviving family members of those killed in the crash pointed blame at Lockheed, citing faulty aircraft systems.

When the C-9 Nightingale carrying out the second flight of Operation Babylift launched that next morning, two fully armed United States Air Force security policemen rode shotgun. They had flown from their Third Security Police Group headquarters at Clark Air Base at two o'clock that morning to make the Nightingale flight at eight o'clock.

Every flight after that carried two of the 3rd SPG/CC armed security policemen aboard it. Striving to remain in compliance with the War Powers Act, none of the United States Air Force policemen remained in Saigon overnight, but commuted from the Philippines daily. However, as the North Vietnamese Army closed on Saigon and increased their assaults on defending ARVN units, the daily-enlarging detachment of Clark Air Base security policemen's commutes rapidly segued into an around-the-clock, ever-increasing air evacuation operation.

LOC NINH, NEWLY RELOCATED NVA FIELD HEADQUARTERS

GENERAL TRAN VAN Tra sat at a simple, clean table inside a plain-looking house in Loc Ninh, sipping tea and silently reading a copy of the April 5 edition of *Pacific Stars and Stripes* that Colonel Vo Dong Giang had an aide smuggle to Song Be Airfield the evening before and then take to him that morning at the supreme headquarters for the forward forces of the North Vietnamese Army. An aide had to read the general the newspaper, but he knew from the photographs and his limited understanding of English that the plane crash had tragic consequences. He understood the headline, "178 Die on Babylift Crash at Tan Son Nhut."

The incorrect number of deaths seemed consistent for the newspaper, missing the toll by twenty too many. Viet Cong undercover agents had already made a full report with more accurate numbers than the United States Information Agency publication could gather. Although he had a tedious time trying to speak or even read English, he understood a few words based on his fluent French abilities. So the general slowly studied the words and deciphered them quietly as he sipped his tea. An aide would read the whole thing to him soon enough.

Through his long career as a soldier of the people, first against the French, then against the Americans and their puppet regime in Saigon, he had held responsibility for the deaths of thousands of people. However, as a man and a father, to know of the death of so many innocent babies caused his heart to ache.

"Such a terrible thing," he said to General Van Tien Dung as he too came to the table and sat with a fresh cup of tea.

"Yes, and the Saigon regime immediately looks to blame us for killing these children," Dung said.

"So be it," Tran said philosophically. "Both our side and theirs carry the blood of thousands of children already. It is the nature and cruelty of war. The weakest and most vulnerable get caught under its coarse heel."

"Today, we conclude our planning discussions and move forward full force with the operation," Dung said happily. "I read a novel maybe fifteen years ago by an American writer, Jack Kerouac, who died five or six years ago. He was an innovative thinker and very much a socialist, I think, perhaps even a member of the Communist Party in Paris. His book that I read, *On the Road*, remains very popular among liberal young Americans and many liberal Europeans, especially in London and Paris. Now, our illustrious Comrade Le Duc Tho, the way he came here for our meeting, riding that motorcycle from Song Be Airfield with the leather satchel on his shoulder, tall and striking, like a college boy on his life's first adventure, he reminded me of Kerouac's main character, Sal Paradise, so seemingly carefree and so willing to flaunt himself at risk."

Tran Van Tra looked up and smiled, appreciating the comparison. He too had considered the risk when one of Vietnam's founders of the Communist Party and most revered leaders, Le Duc Tho, had ridden up on the sputtering motorcycle, wearing the stiff troopers' helmet, the breezy blue shirt and khaki trousers, and the black leather satchel looped over his shoulder. He considered how the great British chieftain from the desert war of the early 1900s, Colonel T. E. Lawrence, had died. To have survived capture by the Turks and to have ridden at the forefronts of the great campaigns across the Arabian wastelands leading the Bedouin armies, accomplishing what many thought impossible, only to die in a tumble while riding a motorcycle seemed to him tragically wasteful. As the inspirational leader of the Viet Cong, winner of the 1973 Nobel Peace Prize for his negotiations opposite Henry Kissinger in Paris, a member of the politburo in Hanoi, and a founder of the Vietnamese Communist Party, revered by many as second only to Ho Chi Minh, Le Duc Tho's adventurous personal risk seemed inconsiderate. His death or injury could have a devastating impact on the political power structure throughout North and South Vietnam.

After his flamboyant entrance to that meeting, Le Duc Tho announced that the politburo had named General Van Tien Dung as supreme commander of all forces for the onslaught of Saigon. Their host, the humble rice farmer Pham Hung, became chief political officer, holding an equal stature to General Dung. Tran Van Tra and General

Le Duc An assumed the posts as deputies to Dung and Hung, respectively. Le Truong Tan received the honor of holding operational command of the forces in the field and figuratively became General Dung's second in command. Tran Van Tra now felt like an automobile hood ornament, striking and lofty, but of little operational importance.

After the meeting he became sullen and spoke rarely, choosing only to say things that truly mattered. The general privately blamed his loss of command significance on the failure of his forces in 1968 when he had planned, organized, and led the Tet Offensive attacks on Saigon. Although still quite powerful in the Hanoi hierarchy, Tran Van Tra had crippled himself badly in that embarrassing loss. The American press had made it seem like a Communist victory, yet the defeat of his forces had badly hurt his credibility with Hanoi as a leader. Clearly, Van Tien Dung held the complete confidence of the politburo, Party First Secretary Le Duan, and even fellow South Vietnamese Communist Le Duc Tho.

The Communist leader had examined Dung's maps and planning for the upcoming siege of South Vietnam's capital. With only minor changes, Le Duc Tho and one of the plan's masterminds, First Secretary Le Duan, approved it and promised unanimous consent from the Communist Party in a matter of days, once Le Duan had presented it to the Central Committee.

Meanwhile, Tho sent General Dung and his armies into action, initiating the preliminary skirmishes in the Mekong Delta regions south of Saigon.

"My morose but dear friend, Tran Van Tra," General Dung said, finally breaking the long silence, watching the Viet Cong leader picking his way through the newspaper, "I must tell you a thing that I promise will bring a smile to your face while we wait for our comrades Pham Hung and Le Duc An."

Tran Van Tra looked at Dung, took off his glasses, and wiped the glow of sweat from his face with a handkerchief.

"Please do, then," Tran said. "My spirits do seem a bit down today, and a cause to smile would be nice."

"Our Tenth Division, as you know, has enjoyed great success in defeating the ARVN forces at Cam Ranh," Dung said.

Tran Van Tra nodded, agreeing.

"On their advance to Cam Ranh," Dung continued, "they confronted the city of Da Lat, which has an airfield and other strategic benefits, west of Cam Ranh. As they approached Da Lat, the citizens there invited our forces to come into the city before anyone had commenced a battle."

"Very gracious of the citizens," Tran said, "and quite wise of them."

"They invited the Tenth Division forces to the city not because they feared the artillery or gunfire, but to restore order!" Dung said and laughed hard. "These fatherless ARVN scum had invaded Da Lat and held the people there in complete terror, raping, murdering, and looting. The community's leaders came to our army for help, and peace. This truly represents the full meaning of the people's liberation and our purposes for unification."

Tran Van Tra smiled.

"MR. PRESIDENT, MR. Secretary of State, good morning, gentlemen," General Fred Weyand said, standing behind a briefing lectern set on the end of a conference table at a Palm Springs, California, resort with President Gerald Ford and Henry Kissinger seated at the opposite end with National Security Advisor Brent Scowcroft and a host of other high-level State Department, CIA, and NSA bureaucrats. Secretary of Defense James Schlesinger remained off the guest list and conspicuously absent, despite Weyand's position in the Pentagon.

"First of all," the general began, "I flew home on April 5 with my heart in my throat. This C-5 crash has simply devastated many of us, especially General Smith, who lost so many treasured friends who were also DAO employees. The deaths and injury of these children not only broke our hearts, but presented us with a serious political and operational dilemma.

"The decision to keep the planes flying is the only real choice we had. First of all, if we cancelled the operation as a result of the crash, we would take a political bath. International opinion and domestic reaction would remain focused on the loss. Continued evacuation in the face of disaster, saving many thousands of lives despite these 150 or so deaths, offsets the balance of the loss. Secondly, Communist forces have begun movement toward Saigon, so the evacuation process remains a prudent action."

"Of course, you have my support and concurrence," President Ford told the general. "I know Graham Martin has spoken quite frankly about this, again championing his cause of not pulling the pin and folding the tent so quickly, but I think it is best that we err on the side of caution. I hope that Ambassador Martin is correct in his estimation of the capabilities of Saigon's forces, but we must act in a practical manner too. We will keep these planes flying."

"Mr. President, that brings me to the crux of my briefing," General Weyand continued. "CIA Station Chief Tom Polger had his staff put together an assessment of enemy forces, and I know you have read it. Very dismal reading, indeed. Saigon looks to be outnumbered by at least two to one, and probably more than that. However, as we know, the army on the road has greatest vulnerability when compared to the army standing at its citadel with all of its defenses, stores, and equipment at hand.

"Given that the North Vietnamese now field more than three hundred thousand forces north of Saigon and possess all the abandoned arms and equipment from I Corps and II Corps, the ARVN must receive a massive infusion of equipment, munitions, and materiel in order to hold their defenses adequately."

"Fred," President Ford said, "what do we need? Bottom line?"

"Sir," the general then said, "in addition to the $700 million already authorized, and by the way, thank you for expediting the first loads of that authorized equipment, South Vietnam will require at the very minimum an additional $733 million in military supply."

"We need to go to Congress and ask for another $733 million in emergency aid, in addition to that already approved on the current budget authorization?" President Ford asked.

"At the very least, sir," Weyand responded. "More importantly, it is a matter that cannot wait. They need the additional materiel today."

That same morning, President Ford called leaders from the House of Representatives and the Senate, both Republicans and Democrats. They turned him down flat.

Through the increasingly difficult days of April, President Ford kept asking Congress to grant the aid, repeatedly. No one on Capitol Hill would stand up with him. Congress turned their backs on him, and they turned their backs on the people of South Vietnam.

Chapter 18

THE SIEGE BEGINS

SAIGON, RVN—TUESDAY, APRIL 8

TWO AMERICAN-MADE Northrop F-5A Skoshi Tiger fighter jets, rolling in staggered formation, each loaded with six MK-82, 500-pound "snake eye" bombs latched on their wing pylons and half a dozen MK-77, 250-pound napalm canisters clustered under their bellies, roared down the parallel runways at Saigon's Tan Son Nhut Air Base. As the sleek duo thundered toward the sky, their twin General Electric J85 engines running full thrust with afterburners afire, leaving wakes of black exhaust smoke swirling in their trails, South Vietnamese Air Force First Lieutenant Nguyen Thanh Trung nudged his Skoshi Tiger's dual throttle levers forward with his left hand while stepping hard on the left rudder pedal, turning the nosewheel, and brought his fighter jet onto the active runway.

The ground crew had traded off the weight of two of the Mark 82 bombs in exchange for additional nine-yard belts of 20-millimeter cannon ammunition for the plane's two big guns. Trung had the double duty of flying top gun on this three-plane sortie, covering the high side of the attack while his comrades focused on putting their loads of "snake and nape" down the enemy's stack. When they wrapped up their work, he would pile his four bombs into any positions his colleagues might have missed.

The youthful father of three adoring daughters and husband of a devoted and beautiful wife had spent nearly a year away from this family that he valued and cherished even more than his own life learning to fly the F-5 jet and master air combat maneuvering at Williams Air Force Base near Phoenix, Arizona. Trung had done well in his training and now often flew the top gun slot because of his superior dogfighting skills.

These days, however, the task of flying top gun had changed from a formerly mundane lookout duty to a highly stressful combat chore. The North Vietnamese had begun incorporating the multitude of A-37 Dragonfly light attack aircrafts and a handful of F-5As and Es that they captured intact in the northern provinces, with their previously small air force of formidable Soviet-built Mikoyan-Gurevich MiG-21 Fishbed jet fighters, with their wide array of air-to-air and air-to-surface rockets, bomb payloads, and twin 23-millimeter cannons.

As North Vietnam had begun flying more and more combat missions with their growing air force, they now seized the majority ownership of the skies across South Vietnam with the increasing numbers of SA-2 and SA-3 surface-to-air missiles that they deployed southward, as near to Saigon as Phuoc Long Province. The Communists also took full advantage of Phuoc Long's air facilities at Song Be Airfield as the primary base for their air and missile defense operations. The former AFRVN airfield's tarmacs now displayed rows of MiG-21s and A-37 Dragonflies with red stars painted on their wings and tails.

Beyond the station's perimeter, missile launch trailers loaded with ready-to-fire SA-3 SAMs stationed on the high ground, buttressed by quadbarreled 23-millimeter antiaircraft guns, guarded the skies. Farther out from the airfield and NVA supreme command headquarters, scattered in an arc looking southward at Saigon, larger, longer-range, and higher-reaching SA-2 SAM batteries lay in ambush for any AFRVN aircraft that happened to venture within range.

As Lieutenant Trung pushed the throttles forward and kicked in both afterburners, his right hand applying slight back pressure to the pistol-grip control stick, his thumb resting on the top-hat trim switch, his Skoshi Tiger with four 500-pound snake eyes under its wings put its nose toward the blue and climbed like a rocket. Rolling to the right and picking up the trails of his two companions, he switched his radio to its intercom frequency and called the pair to report he had launched.

In the distance he saw his flight partners turning from their northerly heading and climbing toward the west. They had obviously encountered the signatures of SAM batteries kicking in their high-power radar, trying to lock and fire. Trung knew that today's mission, like so many in the past few days, would doubtlessly end with the two planes ahead of him making another bomb run on the trees and river near Cambodia. They would not tempt their fate against any MiGs or SAMs.

Seeing his two comrades depart their planned route to go bomb an uninhabited jungle made Nguyen Thanh Trung feel better about what he now had to do. Again, today, they would hurt no one.

"I have a warning light," Trung called to his companions. "Looks like hydraulic failure. Returning to base."

The sound of two clicks of a microphone button told the lieutenant that his fellows had received his message and acknowledged. Gently he turned his wrist easing the stick to the right while adding power, dropping a wing but continuing to climb, and made a shallow bank toward Saigon.

This morning, when he had said good-bye to his wife and three daughters, he held the manila envelope that the civilian architect and Viet Cong spy at Tan Son Nhut Air Base, Dang Quang Phung, had given to him three months ago. He had tucked it behind the seat of his plane when he first saddled up, along with a few toiletries wrapped in a bath towel hidden in his helmet bag. Inside the sleeve of his flight suit, he had squirreled away several small photographs of his wife and their three little girls.

Kissing them farewell today had put his abilities to conceal his emotions to the ultimate test. While the mother and daughters had hugged his neck and wished him well and had said they would see him this afternoon when he finished at work, the lieutenant knew that he would not see them again until the war had ended. Even worse, he feared that the antiaircraft batteries surrounding Saigon, and the fighters that would surely come after him, might well shoot him down and kill him.

Standing in the front doorway, putting on a happy mask, he fought back his tears and overwhelming grief as he held his wife a bit longer than usual and kissed her for what he knew could be the last time.

When the control tower at Tan Son Nhut called him on his radio,

Trung did not respond. He pointed his plane at the Presidential Palace in the heart of Saigon, and sent the F-5 into a high speed dive toward the massive, monolithic structure that symbolized South Vietnam's leadership.

Marine Corporal David Norman had stood watch at the American embassy all night, so he stripped down to his white skivvy shorts and T-shirt and had now gone to enjoy the outdoor breeze while relaxing on a chaise longue set beneath the green-and-white awning on the rooftop patio of the Marine House. From his vantage point atop the nine-story, French-hotel-style building, he could see the Presidential Palace over the treetops on the next block.

He had just closed his eyes, imagining himself back home, when the coursing sound of Nguyen Thanh Trung's diving fighter sent him to his feet. With the increasing unrest in Saigon, the Marines had begun keeping loaded weapons with them at all times, even when relaxing in their skivvies on the Marine House rooftop. Dave Norman immediately grabbed his M14 rifle and charged its chamber with a fresh 7.62-millimeter round from the loaded magazine locked in its well.

With the rifle on his hip, he searched the sky and caught a glimpse of the plane just as the fighter stood on its tail, in a hard right turn back skyward, and sent a snake eye exploding on the palace lawn.

"You Commie motherfucker," Norman snarled, slamming the .30-caliber rifle into his shoulder and unloading his magazine at the climbing and turning aircraft.

Neil Davis happened to have his motion picture news camera on his shoulder as he walked from the Presidential Palace when the bomb exploded and the plane climbed away. He watched the F-5 climb skyward, turn, and start a second, more shallow run at its target.

The NBC News contract motion picture photojournalist brought the jet into focus in his camera lens and let the film roll. He followed Trung's plane as it made its second run and put another Mark 82 squarely on the Presidential Palace lawn. The Australian kept his camera humming as the aircraft made another steep turn and then climbed to the north and disappeared.

Dave Norman had grabbed a second loaded magazine, jammed it into the rifle, and managed a few distant shots at the fleeing airplane. He wondered if he had managed to even hit the fast-moving fighter.

After the second bomb had gone astray, like the first, Trung pointed his plane's nose to the ground and firewalled the throttles. He kept the aircraft just above the treetops, racing northward to Song Be Airfield. Not only did he want to make himself a difficult target for the AFRVN jet fighters that no doubt had now scrambled to pursue him, but he also did not want to risk getting shot from the sky by an overly zealous NVA rocketeer directing an SA-2 missile battery on the arch above Saigon who may not have gotten the word that Lieutenant Trung's F-5A Skoshi Tiger now flew friendly to their cause.

The few minutes that it took him to fly from Saigon to Song Be seemed to last forever. Already, the events of this morning's sortie, all of which had transpired in less than half an hour, seemed to have lasted a whole day. Nguyen Thanh Trung's heart pounded. His stomach hurt. He worried that he might even throw up the tea and toast that he had eaten for breakfast.

At least he would no longer have to live the lie of each day with cloak-and-dagger subterfuge, fearing that someone would discover his treason. That liberated honesty in his spirit felt good.

However, he had not dared to tell his wife about his turncoat decision six months ago, nor of his planned mission that he had executed today. She would learn his secret soon enough, when Saigon's television and radio news reports would break the story of his act of defiance against Nguyen Van Thieu's regime. The American media would call him a disgruntled South Vietnamese pilot acting in protest to the president because Thieu had lost such great credibility with his armed forces.

Although Trung had surely felt a loss of trust with President Thieu, it did not come from the recent failures in the northern provinces or Central Highlands. Nguyen Thanh Trung's bitter discontent emerged from the murder of his father and the wrongful imprisonment of his brother by the very government he had, until last fall, sworn to defend with his life.

Not an act of revenge, not an extraction of a tooth for a tooth— Nguyen did what he did to help end the fighting, to protest the violence. He wanted the killing to stop. He hoped that his act today would somehow motivate the warring sides to end the bloodshed. The lieutenant simply wanted peace.

Tears streamed from the young lieutenant's eyes as he skidded onto the runway at Song Be. Ahead of him crowds of cheering North Vietnamese soldiers ran across the tarmac to greet their comrade, today a hero of the people.

As Trung smiled and waved to the men, with tears on his cheeks, his sobs came not from joy, but from profound heartache. Paramount in his mind, as he clutched the sleeve of his flight suit, holding to the photographs of his beloved family tucked there in the zipped-shut pocket, he thought of what possible misfortunes now confronted his devoted wife and three darling daughters.

LIEUTENANT TRUNG'S HOME IN SAIGON

WHILE SMOKE STILL boiled from the grounds in front of the Presidential Palace, two jeeps with four military policemen wearing green-and-white-striped helmets slammed to a stop at Nguyen Thanh Trung's former home. Behind them a white van with two other policemen stopped.

They surrounded the house, as though they had cornered a bank robber, as the two policemen from the van kicked in the front door. The troops clapped handcuffs on Trung's terrified wife and dragged her screaming to the van. Behind the distraught mother, as a gathering crowd of neighbors watched in shock from the fringe, two other officers led and carried the three bewildered and frightened little girls.

Following a day of intense interrogation, Saigon police concluded that the wife had known nothing of her husband's treason. Nonetheless, they locked her and the three small children in jail.

As his wife and daughters endured humiliation and abuse in Saigon's prison, Nguyen Thanh Trung flew his absconded F-5A Skoshi Tiger to Da Nang. Now, as a captain in the Vietnamese Communist air force, he had a mission to oversee the preparations and planning for the air attack on Saigon, which he would lead.

AL FRANCIS SAT stroking the black beard that covered his face, intent on reading the gloomy CIA reports produced by Saigon Station Chief Tom Polger's staff. Then, as though to underscore the information that he studied, agreeing with the very logical conclusions that the intelligence analysts had reached, that without significant outside help Saigon was doomed, the first bomb struck the Presidential Palace, rattling Francis's small, obscure office's windows. When he saw the smoke rising above the treetops and heard the roaring jet delivering its second shot, he laughed at the absurdity of the politics that now surrounded him.

He had learned a valuable lesson in the difference between pragmatic reality and stubborn idealism at Da Nang. Holding to blind hope while not accepting resounding evidence to the contrary had cost him dearly. An awakening came to him in the chaos of that collapsing city, and now he recognized those same telltale signs in Saigon. Here, blind hope, driven by an unrelenting master, still prevailed.

When he had finally reached Saigon, and had gotten a nap, he joined his longtime friend and mentor, Graham Martin, in the ambassador's suite. He had considered Martin a confidant and teacher and had enjoyed the favor of standing in the senior diplomat's inner circle. So when he had collapsed on the couch in the boss's private office chambers and opened his soul to the man, the cool and condescending response that Martin gave him stung deeply.

"Da Nang is lost, and General Truong's army is no more," Francis had said with a sigh, expecting some consolation from his boss.

"No," Martin said with a superior whisper coming from deep in his throat, "MR 1 is not lost. I have information to the contrary."

The ambassador had earlier met with President Thieu and his generals and had listened, smiling, nodding, and fully endorsing the South Vietnamese leader's bizarre pipe dream plan to cordon off what little remained in South Vietnam's control, reconstitute the MR 1 and MR 2 forces that now straggled by increasing numbers into Saigon, and then retake Da Nang and the northern provinces. Tactical, logistical, and intelligence experts wondered what these two aristocratic politicians had been smoking. While the plan sounded grand, it had no substance. The army had no troops, the stragglers had no will to fight, and most significantly, they had no arms or supplies. The enemy now held those chips and bore down like the flail of God on what remained of Thieu's army.

The former Da Nang consul general immediately lost his composure and blurted out, "But sir! I have spent the past several days on shipboard with the remains of Truong's army. MR 1 has fallen, I tell you. If you don't believe me, take a helicopter and go there and look for yourself!"

"How's your health?" Martin purred, after a long silence, speaking again from deep within his throat in a soft, feigned caring, condescending voice. "With this thyroid problem you had so recently, you've got to be drained after all you endured at Da Nang. What about taking a little breather?"

"I'm fine, sir," Francis said, putting his feelings in check.

Graham Martin stood as the former consul spoke and put his hand across Al Francis's back as he led him sanctimoniously from the ambassador's office and ushered him out of his circle of favor. The young and aspiring diplomat had dared to contradict his lordship. For that sin, he would pay with his lot now cast into the embassy's backwash of lower, inconsequential offices and do-nothing chores.

As the fighter plane disappeared, Al Francis hurried into the hallway outside his lower-floor office and joined a gathering crowd of other embassy workers shocked by the attack. He still had the smile on his face.

COUNTRYSIDE NORTHWEST OF CU CHI BASE

IN LESS THAN a day, news of the heroic bombing of the Presidential Palace reached the camp where Le Van Reung and four guerrillas from his Viet Cong squad squatted by a fire, watching a pot of rice seasoned with chunks of smoked pork and bean sprouts boil. They had considered the aerial stunt a great joke and grand insult to the pompous leader of their enemy. Its symbolism motivated them as they prepared to eat their evening meal. After dark, with full stomachs and high spirits, they would commence their advance against the ARVN's Twenty-fifth Division and begin their run at Cu Chi.

Throughout the five arching battlefronts, Communist soldiers similarly prepared for the coordinated attacks that would launch the sieges toward Saigon with the war's final victory as their prize.

With Nha Trang and Cam Ranh now fallen behind the Communist tide, President Nguyen Van Thieu and his remaining council of generals, headed by the MR 3 commander, Lieutenant General Nguyen Van Toan, adjusted the plan that promised to save Saigon. Rather than anchoring the new DMZ at Nha Trang and extending that line to Tay Ninh, on the Cambodian border, they adjusted the new dividing zone southward to the coastal city of Phan Rang, pivoting the line at the critical crossroads of Xuan Loc and then extending it westward again to Tay Ninh.

The heavyset, flush-faced General Toan graciously accepted charge of Phan Rang and overall administration and operational control of the plan. Consistent with the general's crony politics, he activated one of his inner circle friends, Major General Nguyen Vinh Nghi, who had earlier lost his command of MR 4 because of his bald-faced, shameless corruption. Despite the man's questionable character, Toan placed Nghi in charge of the remaining regiments of the Airborne Division and sent him to operate from the new headquarters at Phan Rang.

Subordinate to both generals, Brigadier General Le Minh Dao busily drilled and prepared his Eighteenth ARVN Division soldiers for their defense of Xuan Loc. While General Toan sat securely at his Bien Hoa headquarters, and General Nghi's forces covered his southern flank, General Dao and his reinforced division, augmented by tanks, artillery, and a few helicopters, stood in the breach.

Xuan Loc stood at the crossroads to Saigon, and Dao knew that the Communists' main forces would have to come through his defenses in order to take South Vietnam's capital. Despite his soldiers' nearly overwhelming dread of what they knew must come, they feared the wrath of their commander even more. While many other ARVN divisions suffered mass desertions as the enemy approached, Dao's Eighteenth Division stood fast behind their guns.

FOREST NORTHWEST OF CU CHI BASE

"QUIETLY, QUIETLY," Le Van Reung whispered into the ear of his young comrade as he yanked him by the arm. The boy had volunteered to walk on point of their patrol within the Viet Cong battalion's advance toward the flank fighting positions of the Twenty-fifth ARVN Division. He stepped too heavily and walked too quickly and did not pay careful enough attention to his trek.

"You will kill yourself and me too," Reung scolded.

"Those ARVN have no patrols tonight," the boy retorted. "They crouch like cowards behind the walls of their bunkers."

"Why do you believe such nonsense!" Reung said. "The enemy fought well enough at Ban Me Thuot. These stories of our enemy fleeing at first sight of our forces have no value except to entertain the uninitiated, like you."

"Then do not stand so closely to me," the lad said, still walking at a fast pace along the trail that soon crossed the highway.

The tribe of guerrillas who walked behind their squad leader, widely spaced and disciplined combat veterans, increased the interval between themselves and the new point man. At only fourteen years of age, he had seen plenty of fighting, but had not participated as a soldier until he joined their group after they had conquered Ban Me Thuot.

Many new teenaged recruits had enthusiastically volunteered after that battle. This boy had appeared in their camp one night, carrying a bedroll and his father's old M1 rifle with one clip of very green, badly corroded ammunition for it.

"You step behind me," Reung finally said to the boy, yanking him by the shirt. "You will trip a mine walking the way you do."

"Mines?" the boy said.

"Booby traps and such," Reung answered, walking quickly, trying to build a properly wide interval between him and the lad. "Our own people have put many along trails like this, and they will kill us just as quickly as the ARVN might."

Just as the veteran of more than ten years of jungle fighting had finished his lecture and turned his eyes to the trail ahead of him, he felt the light tingle of monofilament fishing line press into the skin of his shin.

"Mine!" Reung screamed and dove as hard as he could backward, throwing his hands and arms over his head and trying to get face down on the ground before the blast.

The boy stood with his mouth and eyes still wide open when the hand grenade tied to the side of the sapling exploded. At just three paces behind Le Van Reung, the young soldier only saw the flash and never heard the bang. His body pulverized by shrapnel and blast concussion, he tumbled several more paces and landed flat on his back, looking up at the stars with empty eyes.

"Am I alive?" Le Van Reung said when he finally opened his eyes and saw several faces circled around him while two comrades knelt at his legs.

"Security out!" he suddenly ordered, now gaining more of his senses.

"We have security out," a soldier said softly to him and knelt by his head to keep him calm.

"Help me up," Reung said. His ears rang so badly that his voice sounded like an echo inside his head. When he tried to raise to his elbows, the soldier pushed him back to the ground and shook his head.

"Lay still, and be quiet," the guerrilla kneeling at his legs then growled at him. "You have bad wounds on your legs, so we must carry you when we leave. For now, help me by lying still."

Reung tried to look to see what went on, but in the darkness he saw only silhouettes and the gaps between the trees where the trail cut through them. He felt the painful pinch of a tourniquet crushing through the muscle of his lower thigh, just above his knee, and it took his breath.

"Your femoral artery has torn in two," the soldier said to him in a matter-of-fact voice. "I must stop this bleeding or you will die."

"Do what you must," Reung said. "I will deal with the pain."

The soldier tending Reung's wound ripped up his own shirt and tied a big knot in one of the strips and stuffed it onto the still-oozing artery. Against that knot he tied a second tourniquet and then twisted the strap tight with a stick.

Le Van Reung wanted to scream, but bit his index finger and knuckle instead.

"Give him some water," the soldier who had managed to stop the bleeding said to the guerrilla kneeling by the squad leader's head.

"I was a surgical and trauma nurse at Pleiku, in the ARVN," the soldier then said to Reung. "I think you will lose this leg. It seems badly broken, and you have extensive tissue and artery damage. By the time we get you to our field hospital, the lower leg will have even more damage because of the lack of blood to it. I had to shut off everything to stop the femoral artery's bleeding. The blast tore it to shreds. Do you have any questions?"

"What about my other leg?" Reung said.

"Ugly looking, but alive," the soldier then said and smiled. "Cuts mostly, lots of shrapnel in it. You will pick metal from it for years to come."

A guerrilla took the dead boy and put him across his shoulders and began trekking behind the point guard who now led the patrol toward the rear.

Le Van Reung put his arms around the necks of two of his VC comrades, and they raised him to his one foot. While they held him still, the soldier who tended his wound tied the mangled leg to the other one, taking several wraps so that it could not move.

"This will minimize the pain of that bad leg moving so much," the soldier said

They laid Reung on a makeshift stretcher that they fashioned from tying several of the soldiers' shirts onto parallel poles. With a man at each corner, they too moved out, following the guerrilla who carried the dead boy.

NORTHERN FLANK OF THE CU CHI FRONT

THE NIGHT SKY came alight with shell bursts from the Twenty-fifth ARVN Division's array of tanks and 175-millimeter artillery firing its final protective fire along the northern flank of the Cu Chi front. Nguyen Duc Qui sat by a bank of radios and clapped his hands as he heard the report flowing from the 320th NVA Division's first assault units as they pushed across the Saigon River and broke through the right flank of the South Vietnamese Army's line.

Behind his division's regiments, elements of the 316th, 70th, and 968th divisions forded the river and then deployed southward toward Cu Chi, north of Highway 1. With their first strike, they had put the ARVN forward units into a hasty retreat under a hail of artillery and tank fire.

Watching the flash signatures of the stationary units and comparing them with the reconnaissance reports that the Viet Cong guerrillas had gathered days earlier, the heavy artillery of the NVA's 68th Artillery Regiment plotted those enemy positions as targets and opened fire on them.

Cui's regiments had launched their attacks as a light infantry assault group with no more than rifles, automatic weapons, B-41 rockets, B-40 rocket-propelled grenades, and 82-millimeter mortars. First contact had raised some resistance from the ARVN defenders along the river. When the second wave then struck, the violence of the RPG, mortar, and rocket barrage with the heavy fire from the rifles and automatic weapons apparently shook the ARVN soldiers' confidence, and they began to retreat. As the South Vietnamese forces fled their bunkers guarding the river, they called in the final protective fire from their artillery and tanks.

Not only had the NVA taken control of a several-mile-long stretch of the Saigon River, opening their northern flank route to Highway 1 and Dong Zu Base at Cu Chi, but they now had a clear avenue to their remaining objectives Hoc Mon, Ba Diem, and finally Saigon. All that stood between the Third NVA Corps and South Vietnam's capital was the level of determination displayed by the Cu Chi front's defenders, the Twenty-fifth ARVN Division, and the Eighth and Ninth ARVN Rangers.

NVA FIELD HEADQUARTERS AT LOC NINH

"WHAT ARE YOUR thoughts on Xuan Loc?" General Van Tien Dung said to Tran Van Tra, who had just finished reading the morning situation report from General Le Truong Tan. "We take the ARVN off balance with our assault, capture a good measure of their positions, take control of the crossroads, and then send our forces back even farther behind our original line of departure, virtually losing ground to the enemy in his counterattack."

"Not surprising," Tran said, taking off his wire-frame glasses. "At some point I fully expected the ARVN to finally show some resistance. Not all of their leaders have issues with corruption and ineptness. I see a very strong and determined leader in Brigadier General Le Minh Dao, whose Eighteenth Division we have now engaged. These latest events suggest to me that perhaps we did not fully appreciate the determination of this force or its leader."

"Is this a touch of animosity speaking?" General Dung said.

"Of course, I would not be an honest soldier if I did not admit that I would rather have command of those forces than see General Tan doing it," Tran Van Tra admitted. "However, I would not be a good soldier either if I consciously allowed any personal issues to influence my assessment of the situation at Xuan Loc."

"So this is your honest candor?" Dung said.

Tran Van Tra nodded. "Honestly," he then said, "this setback may well do our armies good. Sometimes a small defeat enables a much greater victory."

"A positive thought in the face of such otherwise negative news," Dung said.

The supreme commander of North Vietnam's armed forces walked to the small, simple square table where Tran Van Tra sat and picked up the report that the Viet Cong commander in chief had just read. General Dung then pulled out a small chair and relaxed on its wooden seat. He looked at his old philosophical friend and then cracked a smile across his furrowed and formerly frowning face.

"At first I felt a good deal of anger about this," Dung admitted. "Like you, I suspected that the command had not fully appreciated the very strong likelihood of a massive counterattack. Until now, the enemy has cut and run. In some instances, they fled their defenses while we still consolidated our force and had yet to attack them. This totally confounded me. Certainly, I had not, nor had anyone else, expected such good fortune.

"News from the western front at Cu Chi reports that our Third Corps enjoyed great success against the enemy, pushing them well south and east of the Saigon River and encountering few instances of counterattacks. While I am grateful that the progress has come so easily purchased, I am not foolish enough to believe that those enemy units can fall back much farther without finally locking their heels and putting up a hard fight. When they retreat to Hoc Mon and Phu Cuong, I expect that we will encounter determination very much like that which General Tan has found at Xuan Loc.

"The short-lived victory that we celebrated at Xuan Loc, only to have it so forcefully wrestled from our clutch, certainly will remind General Tan to not count out the ARVN with their backs to Saigon. I suspect that our hero from Da Nang will also look to regain some respect too with the face that he lost in his retreat. I pity those soldiers with General Dao now."

"They have the prerogative to surrender," Tran Van Tra said.

"As they should have done yesterday, instead of counterattacking and retaking all they had lost," Dung said and laughed. "It is such a shame that we did not engage them more forcefully while we had them aboveground. Now with this snake, Dao, back in his den, bunkered well, and today reinforced with artillery and tanks, this fight may take a good bit of time and effort to finally win."

UNITED PRESS INTERNATIONAL, SAIGON BUREAU

"COFFEE, DIRCK?" Al Dawson said as Dirck Halstead squashed into a vinyl-covered sofa chair in the United Press International Saigon news headquarters where its bureau chief and lead reporter sat pecking a story on a teletype.

"No thanks," the *Time* magazine photojournalist said, not wanting to disturb his friend and knowing how wicked the UPI office brew could get after a few hours of simmering.

"There are some Cokes and other things in the refrigerator, if something else will do," Dawson said, not looking away from his work. "Just a minute and I will finish punching this tape and get it fed on the wire. I am on deadline for this story, so I can't stop right now."

"Don't let me interrupt you," Halstead said, wandering to the refrigerator and popping open the door. He found several cans of Orange Crush on the bottom shelf and took one.

"Big story?" Dirck said, pulling the tab on the can and tossing the tin strip into a trash can filled with yards of perforated, yellow paper tape next to the teletype machine where Dawson clacked at the keyboard.

"The Battle of Xuan Loc rages on the outskirts of Saigon," Dawson said.

"A little exaggerated maybe, Al," Dirck said, sipping the sweet orange drink. "Last time I drove to Xuan Loc, it took quite awhile to get there. Bien Hoa takes at least half an hour to drive."

"Relatively speaking," Dawson countered. "Xuan Loc is the gateway to Saigon."

"I thought that was Bien Hoa," the photographer said.

"Did you come here to piss me off, or what?" Dawson said. "Compared to Da Nang and Nha Trang, Xuan Loc sits on Saigon's doorstep."

"I'm just trying to rattle you a little," Halstead said and gulped down more of the Orange Crush.

"I don't rattle," Dawson said as he jumped from the swivel chair and gave it a kick back toward his desk, sending its seat spinning as it glided on its pedestal's six wheels.

"For a little guy, you talk awfully tough," the photographer said.

"That's because of my massive endowment and rugged looks," Dawson, a slight-built young man with long brown hair hanging over his collar and ears, boasted.

"Now that your breaking news story has hit the wire, what's the scoop?" Halstead said.

"First," Dawson said, taking a Coke from the refrigerator and pulling open its tab, "Xuan Loc is a great story, and if I can get a chopper ride in there, I will take you with me. We have that really flamboyant, tough talking general in charge there."

"Le Minh Dao" Dirck said, interrupting.

"Like a peacock with a megaphone," Dawson said. "By himself he makes good copy. However, they kicked serious ass yesterday and last night."

"No news," Dirck said. "They lost Xuan Loc and got it back. Story's cold."

"The NVA have pulled out all the stops and have committed their reserves and reinforcements to this fight, and General Dao still holds the crossroads and the city," Dawson said. "His Eighteenth ARVN Division has stopped the Communist push dead in its tracks."

MARINE CORPS PUBLIC AFFAIRS OFFICE, OKINAWA

"LET'S PLAY A game," Captain Jerry Shelton said to Staff Sergeant Joe Carr and newly promoted Sergeant Steve Tingley, who had pinned on his third chevron April 1.

"What the fuck are you talking about, Skipper?" Carr said in his typically swarthy tone, still tempering it with respect to the commissioned officer who had just spoken to him.

"The game's called 'Where in Hell Is Marshal Lon Nol Now?' " Shelton said and laughed.

"Nobody bought that goodwill tour bullshit the other day when he packed bags and headed out of Cambodia," Carr said.

"Khmer Rouge commenced fire before Nol's plane even landed in Bangkok," Tingley offered. "This about Phnom Penh, Skipper?"

"Lon Nol's in Indonesia, by the way, vacationing at the invitation of the president in Jakarta, in case you gave a shit about the game. At any rate, while he tours the world, his capital and government are on the verge of collapse. Today, President Ford ordered the immediate evacuation of the American embassy, all US citizens in Phnom Penh, and several thousand third-country nationals trapped there," Shelton said. "I just got word that Admiral Noel Gayler has passed orders from CINCPAC (Commander in Chief, Pacific) to III MAF to launch the 31st MAU ashore and commence Operation Eagle Pull."

"Skipper, can I go?" Tingley said, in a pleading whine.

"Shut the fuck up, beak face," Staff Sergeant Carr snapped.

"Bite me where your mama used to kiss me last," Tingley cracked, grabbing himself in the crotch and laughing.

"You stupid shit," Carr said. "Bite me where your mama kissed me last? I'll put my foot up your ass."

"I need you here," Shelton said and flashed a sideways look at the staff sergeant. "You've got the community relations job with Mr. Nakaoshi and Mr. Nishizato."

"Skipper, Herb Nakaoshi does everything, and I just watch," Tingley pled. "Nishizato takes care of everything else. I don't even speak Japanese. Tompkins can keep the books and budget reports. I've shown him how."

"Tingley," the captain said, trying to keep a friendly tone, but remaining firm, "I need a correspondent who can launch tonight and be on that ship by morning. I doubt you even have any 782 gear drawn. More importantly, I know how badly you write. You take great photos, but your writing sucks."

"Sir," Staff Sergeant Carr offered, "My man Killer Carl Ebert has the bubble. He's next in line for deployment. He can shoot good pictures and writes well enough."

"Better send him up the hill to get packed and then get him to Futima air station," Shelton said. "They have a C-130 to Cubi Point launching at 1800, and I want him on it. From there he can hitch a ride on the logistics helicopter out to the MAU, aboard the USS *Okinawa*. Make sure he knows where to go and who to see, so write this down and give it to him. Have Sergeant Ebert report directly to Colonel John F. Roche, Thirty-first Marine Amphibious Unit commander, and have him also see Lieutenant Colonel George P. Slade, the commanding officer of Battalion Landing Team Two-Four."

"Lance Corporal Carlson deployed from here with two-four. Where is he now?" Staff Sergeant Carr said.

"Not sure at this moment," Shelton said. "Last message from Gunny Thurman said that the amphibious task force had finally rendezvoused and now stood ready on station off the coast of South Vietnam, near Vung Tao. That's a port on the coast, somewhere southeast of Saigon. He's on the *Blue Ridge* with Brigadier General Richard E. Carey, Colonel Al Gray, and the 9th MAB command element. He said nothing about our gung ho lance corporal, and you know Carlson. He's unquestionably out there among the grunts somewhere, refusing to show his face for fear he might have to go sit in the headquarters. He could be with two-four, but he could just as likely have jumped ship and gone hunting with his old buddies at one-nine. Sergeant Ebert needs to get out to the *Okinawa* as best as he can and link up with Colonel Roche and Colonel Slade, tonight if possible. They'll marry him up with Carlson, if the lad is anywhere nearby."

"Either that," Carr growled, "or he's caught a chopper into Saigon and has set up shop at Mimi's Whorehouse down on Tu Do Street."

GULF OF THAILAND, 130 MILES SOUTHEAST OF PHNOM PENH

AT 6:00 A.M., APRIL 12, a dozen Marine Corps CH-53D Sea Stallion helicopters from Marine Heavy Helicopter Squadron 462, based aboard the USS *Okinawa*, carried the 360-man helicopter assault teams of Second Battalion, Fourth Marine Regiment from the decks of the *Okinawa* and the amphibious dock ship, USS *Vancouver* (LPD 2), 130 miles to the heart of besieged Phnom Penh, flying in groups of three and separated by ten-minute intervals. Once ashore, those forces immediately secured perimeters of the athletic fields where the helicopters had landed, designated as Landing Zone Hotel, and commenced Operation Eagle Pull, the evacuation of the Cambodian capital.

A half hour after the final three choppers from HMH-462 had headed inbound, twelve CH-53D Sea Stallion helicopters from sister squadron, Marine Heavy Helicopter Squadron 463, launched to ferry out the last of the American embassy passengers from Phnom Penh.

Once ashore, the inbound aircraft then entered a holding pattern at Point Oscar, an aerial position thirty miles from the city. From there the helicopters, moving three at a time under the guidance of Air Force air traffic controllers on the ground at the landing zone and stationed in the air aboard an HC-130 forward air controller (FAC) aircraft, flying high above Phnom Penh, moved to LZ Hotel. The choppers remained in the landing zone only long enough to board evacuees and then launch. During any delays, the birds waited airborne instead of sitting on the ground.

As the helicopters quickly dropped to the LZ, picked up a load, and departed to the ships, several thousand Cambodians crowded around the athletic fields. Most had simply come to see the show. While the heavily armed Marine security force stood almost shoulder to shoulder, keeping the citizenry well away from the evacuation, 107-millimeter rocket fire and 82-millimeter mortar rounds, shot by advancing Khmer Communist forces, began falling closer and closer to the landing zone.

Ambassador John Gunther Dean and the acting Cambodian president, Saukham Khoy, along with remaining members of the American staff, boarded the last evacuee helicopter from Phnom Penh. It flew President Khoy to the *Okinawa* and then delivered the ambassador to Ubon Air Base in Thailand.

Before noon, the 360 Marine security force members had retrieved the last of its riflemen and returned to the ships without firing a single round during the entire operation. As they departed Phnom Penh, however, the Khmer Rouge closed on the athletic fields and now moved their fire dangerously close to the launching helicopters.

Two air force HH-53 Jolly Green Giant helicopters, extracting the ground controller team, took several hits from ground rifle fire. The second Green Giant took a 12.7-millimeter heavy machine gun round in its tail rotor section. Despite vibrating heavily due to the tail rotor damage and suffering a few oil leaks, both helicopters and their air traffic controller teams returned safely to their home base at Udorn.

With the departure of the Americans and the last remnants of the former Khmer Republic government, the Khmer Communists, led by Pol Pott, assumed control of Cambodia. In the four-year rein of Pol Pott's ruthless government, the Khmer Rouge, under the direction of Pott's second in command, Ta Mok, nicknamed the Butcher, put more than 3,979,000 Cambodians to death.

It would be none other than General Tran Van Tra who would lead Vietnam's forces into Cambodia in 1979, finally liberating the Khmer people from the horror of Pol Pott's bloody regime.

HIGHWAY 1 NORTHEAST OF SAIGON

"I THOUGHT WE would get a helicopter to Xuan Loc," Dirck Halstead said, bouncing in the passenger seat of a dusty brown Mercedes sedan that Al Dawson had borrowed from a friend and now manuevered through heavy traffic past the American consulate at Bien Hoa, en route to Brigadier General Le Minh Dao's Eighteenth Division headquarters.

"Don't complain. We did good just getting this car for the day," Dawson said, turning the air conditioning fan switch to high speed.

"Would have been nice to fly," Halstead said. "In this car, we'll be lucky to get back by tonight."

"Just a quick in and out. Grab pictures, I do a short interview with the general, and we get out," Dawson said, laying on the horn and pushing through the crowds of refugees that packed both sides of Highway 1.

"He's supposed to take us to see the front line, right?" Halstead said, counting rolls of film in the side pouches of his camera bag.

"Right," Dawson said. "We talk at his headquarters, then board his chopper, and go straight to the front."

"Exciting," Dirck said, looking out the window at the sea of faces that lined the roadway.

"I want to ask you something, and I want an honest answer," Dawson said.

"Sure," the photographer said, now closing his eyes and lying back in his seat.

"Nguyen Cao Ky wants to overthrow Nguyen Van Thieu," Dawson said.

"Ever since Ky lost the election, what, now eight years ago?" Halstead said sarcastically.

"I mean a *coup d'etat*," Dawson said. "He mentioned it just the other day, maybe now a week or so ago. That's why Nguyen Van Thieu demanded that Prime Minister Tran Thien Khiem resign and why he fired half his cabinet and then had Assembly Speaker Nguyen Ba Can form a new government with Deputy Prime Minister Tran Van Don as the new PM in place of Khiem."

Dirck Halstead kept his eyes shut and said, "I heard that Nguyen Cao Ky had approached Khiem and a few others."

"Such as whom?" Dawson asked. "Trust me, I have a point to my interrogation."

"General Cao Van Vien, chairman of the Joint General Staff, for example," Dirck said, now sitting up and looking at the roadway.

"Le Minh Dao ever creep into the conversation?" Dawson said.

"Yeah," Dirck said. "My friends at the embassy say that Dao is the first person whom Nguyen Cao Ky approached."

"Check," Dawson said, "and the CIA too."

"I have not heard the CIA slant, but I did suspect as much," Halstead said.

"Spooks did not want to touch it with a ten-foot pole," Dawson said. "Kissinger apparently still buys the heavy line of bullshit that Graham Martin keeps preaching: how Saigon will prevail in the end and that negotiations will save the day. The CIA said that Ky is too extreme a character for the Communists to embrace and believe that General Duong Van Minh, good old Big Minh, is their man. The Communists keep bantering his name, so if anyone steps to the plate for South Vietnam in place of Thieu, whom the NVA hate, I think that person will be Big Minh."

"Alan," Dirck said, "they could have Mickey Mouse holding Ky and Thieu by the balls, and the NVA will not stop until they own Saigon. You know that, and I know that, and damn it, the CIA knows it too. People, just open your fucking eyes, for crying out loud!"

"To talk to anyone at the embassy, on the record, they express the utmost confidence in the Army of the Republic of Vietnam and have full faith that President Nguyen Van Thieu and his forces will finally prevail," Dawson said facetiously. "Talk to any midlevel or below, and it's like they know they live in Fantasy Land, but have to pretend they're all Goofy. Meanwhile, just check out how many of them have hooked up with General Smith's folks and have boogied on the around-the-clock outbound flights from Tan Son Nhut. Slowly but surely, they're abandoning ship while 'Ahab' Martin steers the *Pequod* after Moby Dick with his head up his ass."

"Guy in the air force at Tan Son Nhut told me that everyone there is based at Clark and just flies in and out for the day," Dirck said.

"What day?" Dawson said and laughed. "Check the flights. They don't stop. We have one C-141 Starlifter after another taking off all day long, and then at night, nothing but a steady stream of C-130 Herculeses going nonstop. I've seen the same air force ground security guys there for days now, and there must be at least fifty or more of them running around in their tiger stripe camouflage. Anyway, I think it's good that they are here, keeping these flights under control. Look what Da Nang turned into."

"The DAO folks have been shipping people out by the planeloads since the C-5 crash," Dirck said. "They're taking this mess pretty seriously and evacuating everyone that they can, regardless of what Ambassador Martin says. When I get ready to yank my ripcord, I am going to the DAO."

"So back to the matter at hand," Dawson said. "Do you ask General Dao about Nguyen Cao Ky's coup and the cabinet shakeup, or do I?"

"Why would I want to ask him about that?" Halstead said. "You're the one with the story. Anyway, he will deny it. You know that no one in his right mind would admit to something like that, not even when the NVA are breathing down your neck. I have ten dollars that says he tells you the story is merely a bad rumor."

"I have other sources," Dawson said. "Dao won't say a word. But I am going to ask him anyway, just for the record. I have good information that Ky's friend General Cao Van Vien ratted him out to President Thieu's cousin Hoang Duc Nha, in exchange for amnesty."

"The old Texas hedge," Dirck said and laughed. "Ky thinks Vien is backing him, and at the same time Vien has his backside covered with Thieu. No matter who comes out on top, Vien keeps all his poker chips."

"A contact at the embassy told me that General Dao had too much on his plate with Xuan Loc to get involved with Nguyen Cao Ky in the first place," Dawson said. "In the second place, I hear that besides bellowing and ranting and putting on a loud show, General Dao is a man of honor and conviction. I also hear he watched the movie *Patton* a dozen times and wanted to find out where George C. Scott got his uniforms made."

Both men laughed.

The dusty brown Mercedes bounced down the deeply rutted dirt road that led to General Le Minh Dao's forward headquarters, west of Xuan Loc. Even at this rear area location, incoming NVA 130-millimeter artillery fell within sight of the command post. ARVN soldiers scurried about like busy ants cleaning up after a storm.

"My friends!" Le Minh Dao shouted from the doorway of his command bunker. He strutted to the car where Dirck Halstead busily rigged two cameras and draped their straps around his neck. "What a beautiful day! We are now turning this battle around, you know?"

"No, I didn't know that, General," Al Dawson said, flipping open his notebook and jotting down the quote.

"We have stopped the enemy dead in his tracks now for a week, and he cannot move past us," Dao bragged. "ARVN forces have begun to fight inspired and driven because our division has shown them how to beat these Communist dogs and send them running home."

The general then laughed at his comment and slapped the side of his green combat utility uniform trousers leg with a two-foot-long rosewood swagger stick with a polished, copper-jacketed .30-caliber bullet fastened on the tapered end and the shiny brass shell casing from the same round mounted on the butt. Dao wore a glossy green helmet with a large silver star fastened to the center of the front.

Both journalists looked at the strutting general and thought of George C. Scott's portrayal of the great American warrior general, George S. Patton. Boisterous, coarse, loud talking, and full of himself, all General Dao lacked was an ivory handled, chrome .45-caliber revolver riding on his hip.

MACHINE GUN AND rifle bullets snapped through the air above the two journalists' and the general's heads as they leaped from the olive green UH-1E Huey utility helicopter as it touched the ground with its skids in the center of a debris-strewn roadway in Xuan Loc. Enemy dead littered the pummeled landscape. Some corpses, burned beyond recognition, still smouldered, filling the air with a wretched stench. Dirck Halstead began clicking his camera in nearly every direction, freezing the horror on film, while Alan Dawson ducked low, looking for something substantially impervious to gunfire and shrapnel to squat behind.

Le Minh Dao strutted down the middle of the roadway, seemingly oblivious to the hail of gunfire, artillery, and mortars that now struck close to the spot where the helicopter beat its wings for a hasty departure. Then, before the chopper could clear the landing area, several panic-stricken ARVN soldiers, covered in white, disheveled and ragged from enduring days of intense battle, dashed for the departing bird.

"Stop! Cowards!" General Dao screamed at the men and pulled his Colt M1911A1 .45-caliber semiautomatic pistol from a shoulder holster that he wore and opened fire on three of the men who now clung stubbornly to the helicopter's skids.

The chopper never slowed its progress and flew fast from the fighting with the trio of deserters holding onto its undercarriage for dear life.

"I think this may represent the most brutal fighting of the war," Dao said cooly as he shoved his pistol back in its holster and looked at the two journalists, who both now squatted behind a wrecked and burned truck.

Halstead framed the general in a wide-angle shot with smoking dead bodies from both sides scattered here and there and a Catholic church steeple rising from behind a high stucco wall with two great solid iron gates in the background. Bullet and shell holes pockmarked the wall and heavy gunfire still chewed at the bell tower, leaving wisps of smoke and dust drifting in the air as each new round struck it.

"General, we're under fire!" Dawson shouted incredulously at the man.

"Oh, this?' the general responded. "Nothing to fear. We are in defilade to their direct fire here. Everything, except their mortars and artillery, pass well over our heads. Come out, gentlemen, look around. Meet my men."

Dirck timidly walked to the corner of the truck and squatted again, snapping a different angle of the Eighteenth Division commander.

"I'm fine right here," Dawson called back from where he knelt behind the truck. General Dao laughed and slapped his trousers leg with his swagger stick.

"Show yourselves!" the commander then bellowed, still slapping his leg with the polished rosewood stick. His shiny green helmet with its single silver star gleamed in the bright midday sunlight as the egotistical commander stood amid several bodies of his fallen enemy on the dirty, debris-littered, artillery-riddled roadway.

"Come out!" the general shouted again. "I am standing in the middle of this street, and you men still cower in holes. What sort of warriors are you?"

One by one, faces began to appear from holes and behind walls, hundreds of faces, dirty, white with blast dust, haggard, and ragged.

"These are the finest, the bravest soldiers in all of our republic!" General Dao then said to Al Dawson, who now sat cross-legged, writing in a notepad balanced on his knee. Dirck Halstead took frame after frame as he began to scurry to one soldier after another, snapping close-ups and medium shots of the defenders of Xuan Loc.

"I have to agree with you, General," Dawson called back to him.

"Forget those three cowards you saw run," Dao said, waving his arm in the direction that the helicopter had departed. "I would not dirty this sacred ground with their blood, not among these valiant men, not among their dead, nor even the dead of our enemy that you see scattered here."

Dawson jotted notes while Halstead kept his camera working.

"We met the Communists nose to nose here on this street," Dao said in a coarse voice, slightly breaking from emotion. "We sent them running! They have brought tanks and every kind of artillery that they possess to bear on us here. We stand! We fight! We prevail!"

Dao walked up the street to a low bunkered machine gun nest and pointed his swagger stick at the men inside it.

"Each day and night they run straight at these brave lads behind these guns," Dao shouted to Dawson. "Each day and night, these men turn back those assaults."

Le Minh Dao then walked back to the wreck where Dirck had rejoined his colleague.

"This is why the Communists will not succeed in their quest to seize Saigon," Dao said in a now quiet voice. Then he turned and stormed to the center of the street.

"These lawless invaders of my homeland will not succeed!" Dao roared, again slapping his leg with the swagger stick to punctuate his words. "This division of heroic patriots who keep the wolves at bay, here at Xuan Loc, will inspire courage among all of the Republic of Vietnam's armed forces. The Eighteenth Division will then step to the forefront of that great legion and will lead the offensive that sends these Communist dogs cowering back to hell."

General Dao then turned his eyes toward the street corner behind the wreck where the two American journalists had taken shelter from the ongoing barrage and raised his swagger stick over his head, motioning it in a circle. A moment later the helicopter returned.

The whole time of their visit to the front, the shelling and gunfire had never relented. Dirck Halstead and Alan Dawson ran to the waiting chopper, still ducking the sounds of the bullets high over their heads. Fully erect, Le Minh Dao walked.

COASTLINE NORTH OF VUNG TAO

PASSING NHA TRANG and Cam Ranh, Lieutenant Colonel Tran Ngoc Toan and his 450 Viet Marines who had escaped the disaster at Tan My veered off the main track of Highway 1 and followed the coast. They made their way south, scattered among refugees looking for boats to take them to sea and to the several ships whose silhouettes lay on the horizon.

Although the sight looked tempting, the Viet Marines knew better than to attempt crossing that several-mile stretch of open sea. Even with adequate numbers of the small boats that fought the strong tidal currents among the treacherous rocks and reefs, overloaded with fleeing refugees, the odds of finally reaching the ships stood against them.

By land, they faced few encounters with enemy forces. So far, those had remained friendly. The Communists that passed them, mostly riding in the backs of trucks, merely waved to the crowds along the roadways. The NVA had no time to waste searching through the refugee masses for South Vietnamese soldiers. They presented them little threat and would only serve to distract the army from its primary objective: Saigon.

The 450 Viet Marines had now walked for more than two weeks, mingled among the endless flow of battle-fleeing peasants and deserters, since they left the old sergeant major's rice farm southwest of Da Nang. Finally, they reached a place where the sounds of gunfire and shelling echoed from several miles to their northwest.

"Beyond those hills and trees, somewhere over the horizon, lies Xuan Loc," Tran Ngoc Toan told his battalion sergeant major as the two men squatted by a small campfire in the rocks above the beach where the South China Sea washed rhythmically across the sand below them. Hundreds of other small fires twinkled in the darkness as refugees hunkered by them, some cooking rice and others wishing that they had rice to cook.

"The battle sounds fierce," the sergeant major said. "It also fires two directions, which I regard as good news."

"Yes," Toan said, "our forces have made a stand."

"Soon this coastline will turn westward, and we will find the Mekong River and Saigon River flowing into the sea," the sergeant major said. "We cannot go much beyond that point."

"I hope that the port at Vung Tao remains free," Toan said.

The sergeant major, squatting on his heels, using a piece of stiff, rusty wire to stir the driftwood coals that burned in their small fire and wishing that he had rice to boil over it, nodded to his commander.

"Once these people have gone to sleep for the night, I want our Marines to assemble on the beach among these rocks below us," the lieutenant colonel said. "Have a relay of men surreptitiously mingle among our camps and ensure that everyone has the word."

Shortly past midnight, the Marines walking alone, in pairs, and a few in small bunches casually made their way down the cliff to the beach and gathered among the rocks. No one spoke or uttered a sound. While the majority of them waited silently, representative leaders from each small bunch squatted in a circle around Lieutenant Colonel Toan.

"With the sounds of the fighting to our west, and now behind our position, I believe that we have begun to emerge beyond our enemy's front lines," Toan said in a low voice while the roar of the waves crashing across the beach and the wind covered the sounds that he made.

"Tonight we will at long last assemble again as a military unit in formation. We will deploy in a column, one platoon at a time, spread over typical patrol intervals. Have each squad spaced about five minutes apart," Toan said. "I want four scouts working ahead of the lead element at all times, with two scouts relaying information to the main body. If they encounter anyone, they should make no contact. The scout will move rearward from that location and inform a runner who will then intercept the head of our formation. I will come forward and deal with the encounter appropriately. Any questions?"

The lieutenant colonel looked at each face of the men sitting in the small circle.

"What if we make contact with the enemy from the rear?" one man finally asked.

"Excellent question," Toan said. "Minimize contact. We have few weapons, so any firefight will not bode well for the squad who engages. Our best defense remains our elusiveness and ability to hide. If we hear gunfire, all squads will disperse to cover well away from our track and hide. Hopefully, if the enemy encounters you and takes you prisoner, they will likely assume that your squad or what few men they actually see represent the full measure of the group.

"If there is no further enemy activity beyond the initial contact, we will wait one hour in position before movement. Then as one squad moves out, we will dispatch a runner to the trailing squad, informing them that we have moved, and relay that word backward, until we again have the column moving at safe intervals on our route."

Through most of the night the Viet Marines slowly trekked southward, following the coastline. Then as the sky began to show the first gray light of morning, a runner slipped through the trees and met Lieutenant Colonel Toan.

"Sir," the runner said quietly, his teeth showing brightly in a gaunt-faced smile, "we spotted a patrol, moving ahead of fixed positions, coming our way."

"What do you make of it?" Toan asked.

"They look like ARVN because their helmets are round, not flat," the scout then said, smiling even more.

The commander passed back word to hold the formation's position, and he slipped quietly through the trees for half a mile until he too saw the soldiers walking in the increasing light. They wore American-style helmets and carried American-made weapons.

"Take cover, in case they are Viet Cong wanting to look like our people," Toan said. Then he stepped forward another fifty yards, took cover behind a tree, and shouted to the lead man in the patrol.

"*Chu hoi*!" he cried out. "Do not shoot!"

Immediately the patrol jumped to the sides of their trail and dove for the ground, pointing their rifles toward the trees where Tran Ngoc Toan hid.

"Step to the open, and put your hands above your head!" the patrol leader shouted.

Toan swallowed the lump in his throat and moved from the cover of the trees into the open meadow and stood on a narrow trail where he held his hands up high.

"VC!" the leader shouted at him. "You are VC! On your face!"

"No!" the lieutenant colonel said and knelt to the ground, keeping his hands well above his head where the soldiers could clearly see them.

As they came closer, the darkness of their uniforms revealed the tiger-stripe pattern of fellow Marines. Toan smiled, and tears began to roll from his eyes.

"I am Lieutenant Colonel Tran Ngoc Toan, commanding officer of the 4th Battalion, 147th Brigade, Marine Corps of the Republic of Vietnam!" he cried to the men, still kneeling.

Then the skinny and ragged Marine raised his face toward the patrol leader and said, "I assume that you come from the 468th Brigade or a unit that escaped from Da Nang. I have 450 survivors from the massacre of the 147th Brigade on the beaches at Tan My, nearly one month ago. Please send for your commander and take me to General Bui!"

That morning, Major General Bui The Lan, commandant of the South Vietnamese Marine Corps, did not wait for the survivors of the lost brigade to come to him at his Vung Tao headquarters. He rode out to the trail and met the haggard tribe of warriors as they marched the final miles of their long escape.

During the more than two weeks that Tran Ngoc Toan and his 450

Viet Marines had struggled southward from Da Nang, remaining faithful to each other and to their country and corps, General Bui had spent each day gathering Marines as they too straggled to Vung Tao. After feeding the men and putting them back into uniforms, he sent them to join the growing brigade and prepare to again fight.

MAI THAO VILLA IN NORTHWEST SAIGON

"MY GOD!" Kieu Chinh cried as she banged on the front gate at Mai Thao's villa courtyard. "Please, Mai, open the gate!"

"What has happened?" Mai Thao said as he pushed the decorative iron and wood doors apart and allowed the sobbing actress to hurry inside. He immediately took her in his arms and held her close to him.

"I just came home from Singapore," Kieu said, her eyes flooding tears. "You know I have a diplomatic passport because of my relationships with India and the motion picture industry, so President Thieu gave me ambassador status."

"Yes, yes," the novelist said, trying to help his friend regain composure. "Of course, it's diplomatic. What about your passport?"

"When I got off the plane at Tan Son Nhut, they took it from me!" she cried. "The police there confiscated it."

"We can ask our friend Senator Tran Van Dong to get it back for you," Thao said confidently. "Why on earth did you come back here to begin with?"

"I was afraid," she said. "My husband and my in-law family, I worried for them. I came home because of my duty as his wife."

"Your husband, of course, is nowhere near, is he?" Thao said.

"No. When I got home, I found the house empty. My husband's family had all flown out of the country already, and he is with the army fighting," she said. "Thank God my three daughters are at school in Canada, or else I don't know what I would do."

"I think everything will be all right. Just settle down, and have a martini with me," Mai Thao said, escorting the actress into his house. "Tomorrow or the next day, Senator Dong will obtain your passport for you, and you will simply buy a ticket to Canada."

"How can I buy a ticket to anyplace?" Kieu again sobbed. "I have no money!"

Mai Thao raised his dark eyebrows and frowned. And then he sighed.

"I had quite forgotten," he said. "Our illustrious President Thieu and his corrupt cabinet have declared a state of national emergency and closed all the banks and frozen all assets. Mine too!"

"What shall we do?" Kieu said.

"I shall have a martini," Mai Thao said and smiled confidently. "Relax, and we will resolve the problems. Your three daughters sit safely in Canada, your mother-in-law has flown to the Philippines, your husband remains with his unit, so you really have to worry about no one but yourself."

"Thank you, dear friend," Kieu said, sitting on the jade green couch and taking a martini. The warmth of its spirits trickling down her throat helped her to relax.

"You know," she said, "I have not seen my father since 1956. My sister in Paris can communicate with him and tells me that he has spent five years in prison and now has poor health. He is so terribly poor in Hanoi. I love him so very much, and I have missed him each day since I last saw him. I was only fifteen years old.

"He sent me to stay with his friends here in Saigon, and I married their son. I have done my best to be a dutiful wife, and they have treated me so very well. My mother-in-law has allowed me to be a movie star because she trusts me.

"When I made that first movie, *The Quiet American*, and Burt Reynolds kissed me, so that everyone saw it on the film, I was so frightened. My husband and his family accepted that as just part of my work.

"Now I am torn. I could stay here, and when the Communists come, I could once again see my father. Then, on the other hand, I have my three daughters in Canada. What shall I do?"

"Your duty, my dear," Mai Thao said. "You love your father, but he is old. Poor health will take him, and then where will you be? The Communists will most certainly jail you, if they do not first shoot you. Kieu, my precious flower, your duty remains with your daughters, just as your husband's duty remains at the front with his soldiers."

"You make it sound so simple when it seems so complicated and difficult for me," she said, wiping her eyes with a napkin.

"We can often decide upon solutions to many problems with great ease," Thao said. "Living with the decisions that we make regarding them can often come quite hard."

PRESIDENTIAL PALACE, SAIGON

"PETER, PETER, HURRY!" Ky Wahn shouted to his friend and fellow Associated Press colleague Peter Arnett. "They will start before we can get there."

Hurrying up the walkway to the steps of the Presidential Palace, the AP correspondent and his photographer joined a crowd that included every member of the Western press.

Vice President Tran Van Huong stepped to a lectern covered with microphones and in his broken English told the world, "Nguyen Van Thieu has resigned as President of the Republic of Vietnam, effective today, April 21, 1975. By constitutional authority I humbly accept the office of president and will now pursue a path toward a negotiated peace with the North Vietnamese."

Immediately, when the small man disappeared back up the steps among a crowd of soldiers and cabinet officers, the journalists ran out the gates toward the American embassy, hoping to find Ambassador Graham Martin willing to now speak about the issue of Saigon falling to the Communists.

Already, the bureaucrats in Washington, DC, admitted to an ongoing evacuation of American citizens from Saigon since early April and offered the press an estimate of slightly more than thirteen hundred United States citizens still remaining in South Vietnam, including diplomats, military officials, and civilian press corps. They announced that shuttle flights for members of the press and other Americans wishing to leave the distressed capital would commence immediately.

Graham Martin met the announcement with yet another dialogue of double-talk. He revised upward the number of Americans in Saigon from thirteen hundred to fifteen hundred and then finally to eighteen hundred. He said that the evacuation flights would be for American citizens only and those Vietnamese citizens whose relationships with the United States might jeopardize their safety. He added that under no circumstances would the United States allow any military-service-age male clearance to depart the country. The United States would not be party to any draft dodging or desertions.

He then told the media that while President Huong held the leadership office for the interim, the United States would fully support him and would further support the person who finally sat as President.

Behind closed doors, while Nguyen Van Thieu stormed about his now nearly empty villa, vowing that he would remain in Saigon and face the Communists, the CIA, and American embassy politicians jockeyed to place General Duong Van "Big" Minh in power.

In 1963, weeks before President John F. Kennedy's death, in the coup that overthrew and assassinated President Ngo Dinh Diem and his brother Ngo Dinh Ngu, a young General Duong Van Minh, along with a young Tran Van Don, now deputy prime minister and defense minister, and a young Tran Thien Khiem, now reluctant to step down as prime minister, had sat at the center of the murderous plot and helped put Nguyen Van Thieu in power.

Now, with Thieu ranting in open defiance, the new incoming President Big Minh told the Americans that they must eliminate the former South Vietnamese president from their political arena and at least get him out of the country. Thieu's continued presence and visibility now only distracted the Communists from any negotiations.

Not to be outdone, PRG spokesman Vo Dong Giang, the press's beloved Colonel Ba, followed the breaking news of Thieu's resignation and eminent departure with new demands by the Communists. He stood proudly and told the journalists that all remaining American military advisors, now disguised as civilian contractors, along with all visible American military people must leave Saigon posthaste. He capped the demands with a headline: Ambassador Graham Martin and his henchmen must also depart immediately.

Giang told the reporters that Martin had not acted in the spirit of diplomacy, but had orchestrated and directed South Vietnam's military operations from his diplomatic office and had stood as a pillar under the corrupt Saigon regime remaining in power.

On April 25, wearing an expensive gray suit and escorting more than twenty thousand pounds of baggage, former President Nguyen Van Thieu boarded a plane to Taiwan, where he would remain for the interim with his wife and his eighty-nine-year-old mother at the villa of Nguyen Van Kieu, Saigon's ambassador there. Heavily guarded in addition to President Thieu's ten tons of baggage rode more than three and a half tons of gold from South Vietnam's national treasury, thus accounting for the closing of the banks and seizure of all assets from depositors. Thieu had shipped two and a half tons of the gold by sea while he carried a full ton of it by air with him.

Weeks later, when finally responding to the increasing barrage of questions about the absconded riches, he claimed that he took the three and a half tons of gold ingots to purchase weapons and build an army to retake South Vietnam from the Communists.

When news of the deposed President's planned departure had surfaced, one day before Thieu left Saigon, former Premier and Vice President Nguyen Cao Ky sought an audience of reporters by holding a self-ingratiating rally where he challenged the sitting government and dared them to place him at the helm against the Communists.

"Anyone who flees our beloved country while the enemy advances upon us is a coward!" a colorfully bemedaled and festooned Air Marshal Nguyen Cao Ky, decked in his finest dress uniform, shouted over the loudspeakers. He clearly spoke the words for Nguyen Van Thieu to hear on his final night in Saigon.

As Ky bellowed his patriotic rhetoric and beat his breast bravely, thousands of Vietnam's most wealthy and influential citizens flocked to Tan Son Nhut Airport. Using hoarded black market American greenbacks, they bought and bribed passage aboard the dwindling numbers of commercial flights out of Saigon. Calamity now began to overwhelm the streets of the city as chaos overtook order.

As Vice President Huong announced President Thieu's resignation and his own ascension to the crumbling throne, Brigadier General Le Minh Dao and his valiant soldiers of the Eighteenth ARVN Division, now reinforced by elements of the First Airborne Brigade, prepared for the North Vietnamese Army's final thrust on Xuan Loc. They would not last another day.

Already, several advancing Communist divisions maneuvered around the northern flank of General Dao's stubborn Xuan Loc battlefront and laid in their artillery positions to attack Bien Hoa.

Refusing to surrender, the Eighteenth Division fought until the NVA finally overwhelmed the Fifty-second Regiment, which stood the long sentinel over the critical crossroads of Highway 1 and Highway 20 in Xuan Loc, and overran the division's flanks, wiping out the Forty-eighth Regiment, which had guarded the city's western edge. The fierce Communist drive killed many hundreds of the embattled ARVN soldiers and took a great number of the valiant warriors prisoner, including the Eighteenth Division's commander, Brigadier General Le Minh Dao, who stood fast to the end at the crossroads with his Fifty-second Regiment.

What remained of the Eighteenth ARVN Division and the Airborne Brigade finally managed to retreat southward toward the hamlet of Ba

Ria, along Interprovincial Highway 2, out of the central thrust line of the NVA's Bien Hoa front attack axis.

Finally tucking Xuan Loc behind them and holding full control over the vital crossroads there, all twenty-one divisions of the NVA forces now sat poised along their five battlefronts surrounding South Vietnam's capital and at last stood ready to make the final run to claim their prize, Saigon.

Chapter 19
RING OF FIRE

SAIGON, RVN—SUNDAY, APRIL 27

"HOW DOES LIFE treat you at Ben Cat?" General Van Tien Dung said to General Tran Van Tra, who busily made notes on a tactical map spread across a long table at his new forward command post, only forty miles from the city limits of Saigon. "Putting you and General Tan in concert with each other has proved to make a most impressive symphony."

"I am very pleased today, sir," Tran Van Tra said, showing his old friend a rare and genuine smile.

"Tran, you flatter me with your humble subordination," Dung said and walked to the table to examine the adjustments and maneuvers that Tran Van Tra plotted. "I would have thought you would greet me with a haughty celebration after such a decisive annihilation of Bien Hoa. General Tan has his forces occupying the city and now positioned to begin shelling Saigon."

Tran Van Tra smiled again and said, "The Americans departed Bien Hoa in such a hurry, they left their flag flying atop their consulate. It still flutters there now."

General Dung laughed. "General Tan told me that pig Nguyen Van

Toan not only left his flag but most of his staff at his headquarters in Bien Hoa. He fled to Vung Tao instead of Saigon and clambered aboard the first boat that would take him to the American ships."

"We will occupy Saigon no later than Wednesday," Tran Van Tra said. "I am confident that we could overwhelm the city today, if we chose to do it."

"It serves our political objectives much better to wait and allow all the Americans and other Westerners to leave safely," Dung said. "We begin shelling the city tomorrow, but only the outskirts. This will prompt the ones still lingering, hoping for this negotiated peace to materialize, to realize that all we really seek is a Saigon government that will finally surrender to us."

"This idiot that assumed the presidency after that crook Nguyen Van Thieu has communicated the most ridiculous proposals for a negotiated settlement," Tran Van Tra said. "Reports from Colonel Vo Dong Giang read like a comedy. First Tran Van Huong offered to send an emissary to Hanoi to negotiate a settlement that would leave Saigon intact. Now he has returned to Colonel Giang's front door offering to free all the political prisoners now behind bars in their jails and will make a special presentation of the eighteen journalists that they imprisoned more than two months ago and have yet to adjudicate. I wanted to advise Colonel Giang to tell Huong that we will free our people ourselves on Wednesday. However, I told the good colonel to simply make no reply to this or any further offers."

"I hope that you kept his notes," Dung said, chuckling. "Our infamous Paris peace negotiator Le Duc Tho and our senior political officer Pham Hung will find them most amusing when they arrive here tonight."

"Elsewhere in Saigon's political turmoil," Tran said, "Colonel Giang reports that Nguyen Cao Ky continues to gain a following with his ranting. Last night more than six thousand people attended another of his political rallies. The fascist peacock has vowed that he will remain in Saigon and fight to the end. He said that the current regime has run from the battle, giving away the nation, and now negotiates to save themselves while betraying Saigon."

"His voice will fall silent on Wednesday, if he does not flee with the Americans," Dung said. "Tomorrow night we fly an air attack on Tan Son Nhut, shutting their airport down, and then begin our artillery barrage before dawn. It will send a clear enough message for the Americans to leave Saigon."

"The Associated Press today has reported that now the Americans have forty-four of their warships, more than three hundred aircrafts, and six thousand Marines waiting off the coast of Vung Tao," Tran Van Tra said.

"So many?" Dung said, in a voice undisturbed by any real concern with the news. "I had seen reports of their aircraft carriers *Coral Sea* and *Hancock* sailing off our shores, but I had not realized that they had involved so many vessels. Well, they will need all that room for everyone that they can carry out before we assume command of Saigon. They have the next two days to get it done."

Then the senior general walked to a sofa chair and sat down, stretching out his legs.

"For now we wait," Dung said, closing his eyes. "President Huong will resign this afternoon, and Big Minh will assume the title as their president tomorrow. Pham Van Ba, in his illustrious role as chief delegate in Paris, has conveyed to the Americans that we will most willingly negotiate with the new regime. In two days, possibly three, we will convene those negotiations and most graciously accept the new government's unconditional surrender."

AIR VIETNAM FLIGHT FROM SAIGON TO SINGAPORE

KIEU CHINH FELT a great relief fill her heart as the Air Vietnam Boeing 727 left the runway at Tan Son Nhut Airport, bound for Singapore. Her friend Tran Van Dong, still holding the status as a senator in South Vietnam's National Assembly, had managed to obtain her passport from the foreign minister, even though his department had now voided it as a diplomatic voucher. It provided Kieu little more than identity and helped a vice president of Air Vietnam brush her past the American air force and South Vietnamese police inspectors at the terminal gate.

The thirty-four-year-old motion picture star sat on the plane with a one-way ride to Singapore. She had no money nor any sort of renewed visa. She hoped that the one which allowed her to be in Singapore for much of the year might still allow her entrance.

Early that morning she had kissed her dear friend Mai Thao good-bye. The prior evening, they had eaten dinner together at his villa with Tran Da Tu and his wife Nha Ca, celebrating Kieu's success in regaining her passport, obtaining a plane ticket from Air Vietnam, and the next day departing to Singapore. As the plane now descended on its final approach to landing, she thought of her friends once again.

Nha Ca especially feared the Communists because of her condemning books citing the atrocities that the North Vietnamese had committed at Hue in 1968. Tran Da Tu also worried for her, but Mai Thao philosophically suggested drinks all around to sooth those concerns.

"What is this?" Kieu Chinh cried out as two uniformed Singapore policemen met her as she stepped off the Jetway.

"Your passport," one officer said as he opened her purse while the other clasped her hands in steel cuffs behind her back. Finding the black leather-bound document, the officer flipped it open and compared the photograph inside with her face.

"Very beautiful, Miss Chinh," he said. "Unfortunately, this document no longer has validity. Your government has cancelled your status to travel. As an undocumented alien, we must take you to jail."

NVA FIELD HEADQUARTERS AT LOC NINH

THE FORMER SOUTH Vietnamese pilot, now a captain in the North Vietnamese Air Force, Nguyen Thanh Trung had found a small roll of cellophane tape and used it to fasten the photograph of his wife and three daughters on the instrument panel of his A-37 attack jet when he launched from Da Nang Air Base on April 26.

Shortly after his arrival at Song Be Airfield near Phuoc Long City, a staff car carried him to NVA supreme command headquarters at Loc Ninh. There he went over his bombing plan with the deputy commander of the North Vietnamese Air Force, who had flown from Hanoi to congratulate Trung on his mission and to receive final coordinating instructions from Supreme Commander General Van Tien Dung.

"You have only one day to make your mark," General Dung explained to the two airmen. "April 28 is your only opportunity because the following morning we commence our full assault on Saigon. The artillery will prohibit any aerial maneuvering, except to allow the American helicopters to fly out a very narrow corridor to the southeast."

While Nguyen Thanh Trung led his flight of five A-37 Dragonfly attack fighters off the runway at Song Be Airfield in the fading late Monday afternoon sun on April 28, General Duong Van Minh held up his right hand and swore his allegiance to the Republic of Vietnam as he officially took the seat as South Vietnam's president.

At 4:30 on Sunday afternoon, President Tran Van Huong, who held the office for only six days, resigned under direct pressure by United States Ambassador Graham Martin. That night, the South Vietnamese National Assembly voted 134 to 2 to appoint Duong Van "Big" Minh the new president.

In his inaugural speech beneath the crystal chandeliers of the Presidential Palace, Minh said to the Vietnamese Communists, listening by way of their spies and through the news media in attendance, "We sincerely want reconciliation. You clearly know that. Reconciliation demands that each element of the nation respect the other's right to live. I propose to you an immediate cease-fire as a manifestation of our goodwill and to quickly end the soldiers' and people's sufferings."

Almost simultaneously, Radio Hanoi, broadcasting on a wide range of international channels, announced to the world that all "third force" citizens in South Vietnam should rise up against the regime and join the revolution. Contrary to several weeks of diplomatic jockeying by North Vietnamese diplomats in Paris to place Minh in office and oust Nguyen Van Thieu and his regime, Hanoi also blatantly rejected any chance of negotiations with the new Big Minh government.

Newsmen clambered to Colonel Vo Dong Giang's door, pleading for a comment. He only said, "Our troops continue to advance," and closed the door.

In Washington, DC, Director of the CIA William Colby sent top secret messages to the president, secretary of state, and forces at the battlefront that stated: "We now believe that Hanoi has been deliberately holding back militarily in order to allow time for the evacuation process and for a government of surrender to be established in Saigon."

Kissinger reacted by taking the helm of all further communications with Hanoi, via the North Vietnamese and PRG emissaries in Paris. He cautioned Graham Martin and his staff to cut all further communications with the PRG at Tan Son Nhut. He and Graham Martin still stubbornly clung to their convictions of a negotiated cease-fire with the

Communists and salvation of Saigon, despite the clearly unambiguous declarations immediately made by Hanoi following Big Minh's assumption of power in Saigon.

General Le Truong Tan's Fourth NVA Corps launched several 122-millimeter *Katusha* rocket strikes from the eastern suburbs into the center of Saigon as Big Minh and his colleagues celebrated his new office amid the gold brocaded walls and lushly carpeted great hall of the Presidential Palace. To the south, General Le Duc An's 232nd Tactical Force opened their artillery barrage, closing Highway 15, Saigon's last remaining overland escape route to the sea.

Dropping from the increasingly overcast sky, aglow with broad streaks of orange from a breathtaking sunset, Nguyen Thanh Trung hurled his light attack jet at Tan Son Nhut Air Base, releasing the plane's entire load of a dozen MK-81 250-pound bombs into the flight line of AFRVN F-5A Skoshi Tigers and F-4J Phantom IIs.

As he flew his popup and looked down toward the earth through the top of his aircraft's canopy as the bombs struck in a line, demolishing several of the exposed aircraft, the second plane of his flight of five A-37s released its bomb load.

One after another, the captured South Vietnamese jets delivered a very loud message, its thunder heard at Big Minh's presidential reception: the end for Saigon had now come. The clock ticked, and soon North Vietnam's tanks would roll into the city.

AMERICAN EMBASSY, SAIGON

"GUNNY, I AM not authorizing anyone leaving the embassy on some wild adventure like you have in mind," Consul General Richard B. Peters said to Marine Gunnery Sergeant Robert W. "Bobby" Schlager, his former staff noncommissioned officer in charge of the Marine Security Guard detachment at the United States Consulate at Bien Hoa. "Getting all the equipment shipped out and everything shredded and burned had greater importance than anything else. Also, pulling down the flag when we left would have also incited a panic, and we might not have been able to drive away from the consulate. The flag provided cover for us. So leaving it flying on the rooftop mast has to fall out as one of those matters that we cannot now correct."

"Sir," the balding, blond-headed Marine pled, "if I devise a plan that will work, won't you at least give me the green light to try? Major Jim Kean, our Marine Security Guard company commander, said he had no problem with me going if I found a good way to do it."

"Bobby," Peters said, "the crowds have become so unyielding outside the gates that your fellow Marines had to pull you over the wall just to get you inside the embassy when you got here from Bien Hoa. How on earth do you propose to try to penetrate through that turmoil, which is now much worse, and even make it across town, much less to Bien Hoa. The Communists now own Bien Hoa. It is simply too late."

"If I come up with a way of getting the flag, will you at least allow me the chance?" Schlager again pled.

"See the deputy if you have a viable plan," Peters said, exasperated with the argument, and left the marine.

Deputy Consul General Charles Lahiguera stood in a small circle of other midlevel managers, and Gunnery Sergeant Schlager gave him a polite nudge.

"I got a green light, of sorts, from Mr. Peters. He said to see you," Schlager said. "Come on, our ride is waiting on the roof."

"Wait a minute, Gunny," Lahiguera said, climbing the concrete stairs in an outside ladder well hidden behind the embassy's exterior blast wall. The embassy staff had the lacework of concrete bricks installed across the face of the building after the rocket attacks of the 1968 Tet Offensive. "This adventure sounds a little too simple, and my gut tells me to stop and consider the risks."

"I've got an Air America pilot sitting on the roof in his Huey right now, and he says he can get us in and out of Bien Hoa, no sweat," Schlager said, still jogging up the steps. "This time of the day, the NVA will have a hard time seeing us with the sun setting and all. We zip right to the roof, I cut the lanyards, grab the flag, and we zip right off. No sweat."

"You cannot go without me," the consulate deputy said, jogging up the steps. "Someone has to take responsibility. If I stayed here, then I would be alive to suffer the consequences if you get killed. So if I go, and you get killed, I at least die with you."

"That's the way to think about it, sir!" the gunny shouted and banged open the steel door that exited to the helicopter landing pad on the embassy roof.

Inside the gray UH-1N, twin-turbine Huey utility helicopter, a pilot wearing a blue denim shirt, khaki trousers, and David Clark radio headset over a blue baseball cap with "USS Coral Sea CVA 43" embroidered on its front waved at Bobby Schlager and Charlie Lahiguera.

"Sir," Gunny Schlager said to the consulate deputy, "just climb up front in the right seat. You get a real good view there. I'm riding back here where I can jump out and in quick if I have to."

"What about the rest of the crew?" Lahiguera said.

"You're looking at him, coach," the pilot said, tapping his chest with his thumb and then pulling up on the collective control handle, turning the throttle, and tilting the cyclic control forward as the young diplomat slipped on a headset with boom mike and fumbled with the shoulder harnesses on the helicopter's right front seat.

"Just push those couplings together, and pull the little metal tabs down," the pilot said on the intercom, trying to explain how the harness's Koch fittings snapped together. "You gotta get out, just flip up the tabs, and they pop right off."

The diplomat sat still, taking special care to touch nothing. Through the green Plexiglas beneath his feet, the tops of buildings and street lamps raced past the speeding helicopter. Ahead, artillery and rocket bursts lit the sky as the sun sank behind the western horizon.

"Sir," Gunny Schlager said, plugging his headset into the overhead intercom terminal, "our pilot's a Marine. Well, former Marine anyway. Flew Hueys with Third Wing and delivered cargo to the Rockpile up on the DMZ by balancing on the skids in a hover while the ground crew grabbed the gear off his chopper's deck. You ever see the Rockpile?"

"Pictures of it, Gunny," the deputy said.

"Really narrow mountain of rocks, isn't it?" the gunny then added. "Comes right up to a razorback ridge about two feet wide along the top."

"Yes, it looked that way in the photographs," Lahiguera said. "It did not look like it had enough room for a helicopter landing zone on top."

"It doesn't," the pilot interjected. "That's the gunny's point. To deliver goods to the Rockpile, we had to kind of balance the helicopter by a skid, or with our CH-46s, let down the tail ramp and balance on that. We set the bird in a hover and anchored with the tailgate. Marines came on, got off, unloaded cargo, pretty cool."

"Amazing," the midlevel diplomat said.

"We're going to do a variation of that drill when we go to get the flag," Gunny Schlager said.

"We can't land anyplace below?" Lahiguera said.

"Surrounded with VC and NVA," the pilot said. "I took a dash past the consulate when the gunny asked me to make the trip. Lots of bad guys on the streets. Tanks, troops, lots of stuff. We'd never make it up again."

"Won't they shoot us down hovering over the little rooftop capo where the flagpole is?" the deputy said.

"I think we got about half a minute to zip on, cut the lanyard, and zip off," the pilot said. "It'll take them that long for the thought to register to start shooting. By then, we'll be saying *sayonara*."

"Oh, you guys have this all figured out, timed down to the second," the consulate deputy said, sarcastically. "You know we're going to die!"

"Some day, coach," the pilot said. "It happens to the best of us."

"Nothing like going down in a blaze," the gunny said and laughed.

"Okay, Gunny," the pilot said, "you got that gunner's belt on?"

"Roger, skipper," Schlager said, sitting on the deck with his feet out the helicopter's sliding side door.

"Coming on your side," the pilot said. "Be quick about it!"

Just as the helicopter dipped over some high trees, it came face-to-face with the small, square capo that stood on the top of the Bien Hoa consulate headquarters building. Atop the little building, on the short flag mast, the United States flag fluttered, showing the recent tears of many bullets shot through it while it flew.

Bobby Schlager stepped onto the Huey's skid and then knelt, pulling his full weight against one of the helicopter's floor deck rings anchoring the long safety strap of the gunner's waist belt that he wore. Balancing his knees against the skid and bracing himself against the tension of the safety strap that held him, he took both hands and clasped the flag as it violently fluttered and popped in the wash of the chopper's main rotor.

Holding the flag tight with his left hand, the Marine reached down with his Ka-Bar utility knife and sliced through the thick nylon rope behind each of the brass snaps holding the American colors to the pole.

Just as Bobby Schlager stood up on the rail with the flag in one hand and the Ka-Bar knife in his other, several dozen North Vietnamese soldiers on the ground among a string of their Soviet-built T-55 tanks, momentarily stunned by the surprise of the Air America helicopter stopping at the rooftop just above them, opened fire on the aircraft. A sudden spray of .30-caliber rounds shot from their AK-47 and SKS rifles popped through the skin and Plexiglas windows of the helicopter.

At the same time that the Marine had stood on the rail and the Communist soldiers opened fire on them, the pilot dropped the bird's nose and gave the chopper a full-throttle departure.

With the consulate's national colors clutched tightly in his left hand, fluttering in the wind, and the Ka-Bar knife now clamped between his teeth, Bobby Schlager extended to the angry, still-firing Communist soldiers a lasting farewell gesture, shoving his right hand's middle finger skyward for them to see and appreciate.

TU DO STREET, THE HEART OF SAIGON'S BAR DISTRICT

"GET IN, GIRLS, you go stateside, *di di mao*," Sergeant Gregory E. Hargis called from the pedestal-mounted driver's seat of the walk-in style delivery van that he and the other embassy Marines had nicknamed the bread truck. Normally used for performing maintenance around the American compound because of the ease with which a person could simply walk in and out of the vehicle with its passenger door slid open, Hargis had now converted it to a downtown bar-girl evacuation bus.

"Oh, it's you, Greg," sang out a leggy prostitute with long black hair, dressed in tight-fitting denim jeans and a braless, red, slinky silk knit top with the name Amy written in blue sequins across her jiggling breasts. She wore big, round, red Elton John–style sunglasses rimmed with imitation sapphires that covered half her face, and she rocked along Tu Do Street on thick, high-stepping, four-inch-heeled platform pumps. Next to her, two similarly clad playmates of the Saigon bars waved happily at the Marine.

"Where we go?" they chimed together.

"You go stateside," Hargis called back. "You go big PX (post exchange), beaucoup GIs. Lots of boom-boom. Buy you Honda."

"Greg! You so crazy!" the three girls cackled.

"Girls, VC come. NVA come," the Marine then said in a serious voice. "I'll take you to Tan Son Nhut and put you on a C-141 heading out to Clark Air Base this afternoon. Then you'll go stateside. You get in now. The VC will definitely kill you if you stay here."

By the time the Marine had idled the length of the boulevard, lined by such illustrious nightspots as Mimi's, Moulin Rouge, Club Tiger,

Venus, and Mona Lisa and had stopped on the corner beneath the gigantic, lightbulb-covered Rex Hotel sign to count noses, he had the bread truck packed with fifty Tu Do Street hostesses.

Hargis's staff noncommissioned officer in charge, Master Sergeant Juan "John" Valdez, had himself made several trips to the Saigon strip rescuing the girlfriends of many of his young Marines who stood embassy watch. He quietly slipped them aboard outbound air force C-141s and C-130s, one or two girls at a time.

Not one to devote a lot of effort to such covert tactics as hiding one or two Tu Do hookers among a group of school teachers, Greg Hargis believed in going for maximum impact. So taking a break from an afternoon of shredding and burning chores, he absconded with the embassy bread truck and went to the city's center, prowling the streets for working girls who wanted to leave Saigon.

He had already convinced the United States Air Force ground security crew at Tan Son Nhut that what he proposed had a noble purpose, and personally vouching for each girl, he easily won the guards' cooperation. However, the platoon of bubbly young women needed some sort of documentation to account for the fifty boat spaces that they occupied on the aircraft.

"Look, sir," Hargis said to a chief master sergeant processing paperwork for the boarding passengers, "these young women certainly are not missionaries, but they're good girls, very resourceful, and get by really well on their own in a tough place like Saigon. So move them somewhere like Oceanside or Laguna Beach, and they will do great."

The senior air force sergeant just looked up at Hargis and said, "Put down their names here, real names. None of this Amy, Suzi, Kim, and Lolita bullshit."

Then the sergeant pointed across the sheet of information blocks and said to the Marine, "You put your name in this box. That means you accept responsibility for them. That clear?"

"Yes, sir," Sergeant Hargis said. "Where do I sign?"

Almost immediately following the crash of the Operation Babylift C-5A Galaxy, the Thirteenth Air Force began daily shuttle flights, striving to evacuate all American citizens living in and around Saigon to Clark Air Base in the Philippines, where they could catch flights to places like Australia, New Zealand, Thailand, and the United States.

By April 21, the shuttle flights operated around the clock, one after another, averaging a launch from Tan Son Nhut every twenty minutes.

While air force C-141 Starlifters transported qualified refugees and Americans by day, C-130 Herculeses carried similar loads throughout the night, never falling below the three-planes-per-hour pace. The Third Security Police Group from Clark Air Base now had thirty-six military policemen based at Tan Son Nhut on temporary duty for the duration of the emergency.

In the eight days of around-the-clock evacuations, the Air Force C-141 and C-130 flights successfully transported out of Saigon's Tan Son Nhut Airport more than forty thousand Americans and South Vietnamese refugees.

Simultaneously, as the Air Force evacuation flights increased in frequency, the civilian carriers who had serviced Saigon began to disappear. Pan American, Bird Airways, and World Airways jets no longer arrived. By Monday afternoon, even Air Vietnam launched its final voyages from Saigon.

Meanwhile, United States Air Force transports jammed the taxiways and flew nonstop, shuttling out the few remaining Americans and thousands of South Vietnamese citizens identified by the defense attaché and the American embassy as persons important to the government of the United States. These people included CIA operatives whose names had now fallen into the hands of the Communists by way of volumes of highly classified documents left behind unburned at consulate offices across the country. Other South Vietnamese refugees included public service professionals, government workers, loyal employees of the American facilities, friends, families of friends, friends of news media, and a scattering of sweet-smelling hookers from Tu Do street.

THE WHITE HOUSE, WASHINGTON, DC

"SIR, DR. KISSINGER is holding for you," White House Chief of Staff Donald H. Rumsfeld said to President Gerald Ford after Deputy Assistant Chief of Staff Dick Cheney had passed him a note, interrupting the President's late afternoon meeting. Ford sat in the Oval Office discussing economic and energy strategy with several of his key policy advisors: Ken Rush, William Seidman, Elliot Richardson, Rogers Morton, and Frank Zarb.

"Henry," President Ford said, "what's the news?"

The secretary of state had just received a telephone call from Gra-

ham A. Martin, who conveyed the tragic news that at two minutes before 4:00 a.m., Saigon time, the North Vietnamese had attacked Tan
Son Nhut Airport with more than one hundred fifty 122-millimeter
rockets and 130-millimeter artillery shells. Some of the rockets struck
outside the Defense Attaché's Office compound, killing two United
States Marines standing guard there.

When the attack began, an Air Force C-130 had taxied onto the active runway and took a direct hit, setting it ablaze. The aircraft's five-
man crew and two Air Force security police riding shotgun on the plane
managed to clear all the passengers from the aircraft and led them to
shelter under concrete abutments nearby. The aircrew and two security
policemen then ran to a second C-130 preparing to depart and managed to get aboard and flew on to Clark Air Base.

"We have approximately four hundred passengers stranded under
the concrete abutment with a dozen or so Air Force security police providing them protection," the secretary of state told the President. "General Smith immediately suspended further flight operations for the time
being."

"We have the names of the Marines?" Ford said.

"Corporal Charles McMahon, Jr., of Woburn, Massachusetts, and
Lance Corporal Darwin D. Judge of Marshalltown, Iowa," Kissinger
said.

"Can you be here by seven o'clock?" the President said.

"Yes, sir," Kissinger replied.

"I will see you then," Ford said and put the telephone receiver back
in its cradle.

The President took a blank note sheet from a small wooden tray
and jotted a message on it. Folding it in half, he waved at Dick Cheney
to come forward and handed him the paper.

"Get this to General Scowcroft," the President said.

Cheney immediately had the note hand carried to Lieutenant General Brent Scowcroft, deputy director of the National Security Council.
Folded inside the small sheet with *The White House* embossed in dark
blue block letters at the top, President Ford had written, "We'd better
have an NSC meeting at 7."

UNITED STATES CONSULATE, CAN THO

WHILE FIFTEEN OF Clark Air Base's Third Security Police Group sentries spent Tuesday morning squatted behind the concrete barriers along the runways at Tan Son Nhut, protecting the four hundred stranded evacuation passengers, exchanging automatic weapons fire with either Viet Cong guerrillas or renegade ARVN soldiers now rapidly deserting the front lines en masse, Consul General Francis "Terry" McNamara faced a similarly stressing dilemma at Can Tho, the last remaining United States consulate in South Vietnam.

"But sir!" Terry McNamara pled with Ambassador Graham Martin. "Saigon is completely surrounded. We have no other means of getting to the embassy except by air. We're cut off too. We need those four helicopters to evacuate people here at Can Tho."

"I'm in no mood for this," Martin snapped back. "Send the four helicopters now, with no passengers aboard any of them. Besides, you have other options for evacuation. What about the four LCM landing crafts and the rice barge that you bought from the Alaska Barge and Transport Company? You might even be able to get Air Force planes into your airfield too."

"Fixed-wing operation would draw every VC and NVA for miles," McNamara said. "We already explored that idea and realized that the first plane would never make it off the ground. So our only option is that we drive the landing vessels down the river to the coast."

"I will ensure that a ship is sitting right there to pick you up," Martin said firmly. "Trust me. You will get out of there in fine shape."

In less than an hour, McNamara, a former navy officer, walked down to the docks and found Staff Sergeant Boyette S. Hasty swearing and chewing out two Filipino clerks that worked for the CIA section and an American CIA logistics man.

"Sir!" Hasty snapped, wheeling on his toes, still showing his hackles bristling. "Our loyal and faithful CIA staff has already launched a bug-out operation of their own. You recall the four helicopters that were supposed to go to Saigon? Two may have actually flown north, as ordered. However, two have definitely flown south, loaded with the bulk of the CIA pukes and their tribe. They also had their people load all their South Vietnamese operatives in our two best LCMs, the ones I had outfitted with machine guns, and they ripped them off too."

"That leaves us with two LCMs and the rice barge?" McNamara said.

"Correct, sir," Hasty said. "Two LCMs with no machine guns and one leaky old rice barge. The son of a bitches abandoned us here and even ran out on three of their own people."

"Nothing we can do about it now," the consul general said and took a seat on a bench in the shade of a wooden awning built onto the pier. "Do you have a total head count of whom we have to take with us downriver?"

"My five Marines, you, your remaining staff of thirteen, and numbnuts here from the CIA makes the American count an even twenty head," Hasty said. "Then, according to my paperwork, we have 298 other folks that have to go with us."

"Divide the number down the middle and spread us among the two LCMs," McNamara said. "If we try to deploy that old barge, it will just slow us down. We'll be a bit crowded, but it's only sixty miles down the Bassac River to the sea. If we get the people down here now, we can make it to the ocean before dark."

"Sir," Hasty said, "have you considered exactly where that sixty miles of river takes us?"

"Smack through the heart of some of the nastiest VC and North Vietnamese haunts in MR 4," McNamara said. "That's why we will all dress like Vietnamese, including the rice straw hats."

"Two really bad stretches," Hasty said. "Just a few miles past that first bend we have one area guaranteed to rouse a few VC attacks. Then, where the river narrows, and they can hit us with rocks from the shore."

"We'll take all that we can carry from the armory and hope that's enough," McNamara said. "Oh, and what about your new bride and her family?"

"Got them all packed and ready to go when you give the word," Hasty said. The Marine staff sergeant had married a South Vietnamese woman only days earlier and had instructed his wife, her mother, and her brothers to stand by for immediate departure.

"You need to get your wife and her family right now," McNamara said. "Get back here as fast as you can because we need to shove off. Saigon is already under artillery attack."

An hour later, Consul General Francis "Terry" McNamara sat at the coxswain station of the lead LCM studying the controls. When the CIA had departed without notice, commandeering the two helicopters and two landing crafts, they had also taken with them the seamen capable of operating the flat-bottom boats.

From prior navy experience, McNamara and one other member of the consulate staff were the only two people remotely skilled enough to operate the two diesel-powered vessels. For nearly twenty minutes the two former navy men studied the controls, helm, and gauges.

Finally, McNamara looked up and said with a shrug, "I can do this." Then he turned a switch, pushed a handle forward, and fired the engine.

Black smoke boiled out of the water aft of the boat, and the people standing inside the boat clapped and cheered. Then the consul general climbed out of the first LCM and walked back to the second and instructed his colleague on the start-up procedure.

In a moment, the two landing crafts with more than 318 passengers divided between them cruised into the center of the broad-reaching waters of the Bassac River.

"Here's a little something that me and the boys fixed up for you," Staff Sergeant Hasty said with a smile and handed Terry McNamara a gray steel Navy combat helmet. Neatly painted in half-inch tall black letters laid in an arch above a white star read the word *Commodore*. Then in a straight line beneath the star the Marines had painted, *Can Tho Yacht Club*.

McNamara laughed with Hasty, admiring the artwork and creative thought. He tossed to the deck the conical straw hat that he had worn and plopped the helmet atop his head.

SINGAPORE AIRPORT TERMINAL

TEARS STREAMED FROM Kieu Chinh's eyes as she hugged and kissed the four men in her motion picture crew in Singapore who had come to her rescue. When the police had taken her to jail, she called her producer, who then took a collection from everyone connected with her last project.

Not only did they obtain her release from the Singapore prison, with the proviso that she would depart the nation immediately, but they had bought her an around-the-world airline ticket.

"This will take you anywhere you want to go," the producer said as his three colleagues huddled by him at the gate for the Singapore Boeing 747 jetliner. Two police officers stood nearby to ensure that the actress departed the country.

"Maybe they will let you stay in Paris with your sister," another of the producers said.

"I hope," Kieu said, her voice choked with tears.

Her first leg of the journey took her to Hong Kong. There, police stood outside the customs gates, so she stayed on the neutral side and looked for a flight to Europe. The next plane departed for Rome, and because that was close to Paris, she boarded the flight.

TAN SON NHUT AIRPORT, SAIGON

THUNDERSTORM CLOUDS BEGAN to build across the southern horizon, and breezes from them cooled the concrete taxiway where the fifteen Air Force security policemen and the four hundred stranded passengers from the rocketed C-130 sat with their backs locked against the concrete abutment that separated them from their attackers.

The shelling had let up, but automatic rifle fire still grazed across the tarmac, keeping the passengers and SPs pinned behind the cement wall. They had no water, and despite the sky filling with clouds, the high temperature and humidity had taken their toll. Several of the people now moaned from heat sickness and dehydration cramps.

Once the sun had risen, and the shelling had seemed to subside, a sudden flurry of activity swept over Tan Son Nhut Air Base. South Vietnamese soldiers and airmen swarmed the flight lines and started every aircraft that would fly. Dozens of helicopters, jammed with deserting soldiers, launched directly from the aprons in front of their hangars. Fighter jets, attack aircraft, observation planes, light private airplanes, and several South Vietnamese Air Force transports took off from every direction, on the runways and taxiways and even diagonally across the flight lines.

Some of the aircraft headed south and west, but most headed toward the sea where the American armada of warships and merchant vessels lay, now picking up refugees by the boatloads.

As the chaotic launch of every aircraft in any sort of flying condition took place, the pilots let external fuel tanks, loads of bombs, and rocket pods just tumble to the runway behind them as they rotated into the air, littering dangerous debris across most of the taxiways and runways, especially near the terminal and hangar areas.

While the planes made their mass getaway, NVA and Viet Cong

gunners targeted the fleeing aircraft, sending another barrage of 130-millimeter artillery and 122-millimeter rockets into the airfield. One AFRVN C-130, just beginning its takeoff roll, took a rocket through the wing, setting the aircraft ablaze. As its passengers and crew ran from the burning plane, a column of black smoke signaled General Homer Smith, who had watched the spectacle from the DAO compound next door, that any further flights at Tan Son Nhut would only involve rescuing the American airmen on the ground with the stranded passengers.

"Look, a C-130 coming in hot," a sergeant said, seeing the silhouette of the aircraft banking low from a truncated base line in the pattern to a very short final approach.

"Get everybody on their toes, ready to run when he stops," a master sergeant called down the line. "When the plane comes parallel to us, send the people running to the ramp fifty at a time. We'll cram as many aboard as they'll let us."

"Maybe we can get half on this one," an airman suggested to the master sergeant.

"I'll cram all four hundred, plus myself, if they'll let us," a staff sergeant down the line said anxiously.

"We may have to," the master sergeant said and pointed across the airfield where hundreds of Vietnamese deserters came running toward them.

Just as the C-130's tires skidded on the runway, the pilot used every breaking maneuver in the book, making a near record-setting short-field landing and then gunned the plane's four big engines, turning directly across taxiways, weeds, and gravel, going directly to the stranded passengers.

He had not yet stopped when the back ramp came down, and the loadmaster stood in the opening, pumping his arm up and down, encouraging the people to run to him. The exhausted passengers crammed themselves inside the plane, leaving only a handful still waiting outside, along with the master sergeant and seven of his security policemen, who had set up a base of covering fire for the aircraft.

Taking shelter again behind the concrete, the remaining few dozen passengers and eight Air Force SPs watched the C-130 race across the gravel to the main runway and then hurl itself skyward with the sudden ignition of eight jet-assist takeoff bottles mounted inside the fuselage above the wheel wells, roaring an impressive array of white and blue flames that scorched the runway.

"Tallyho, another plane and a Jolly Green Giant," an airman said, pointing to the horizon as a second C-130 made a similar combat approach and short-field landing. Behind it raced a CH-53D helicopter from the USAF Fifty-sixth Special Operations Unit from Nhakon Phanom Royal Thai Air Force Base, flying low and hot along the airport perimeter, heading straight for the remaining SPs and evacuees.

"Put those people on that plane while we provide cover fire," the master sergeant told his crew. "Once they're aboard, we'll fly home on the chopper."

As the air force C-130 carried the last passengers to Clark Air Base, the Jolly Green Giant delivered the remaining Air Force security policemen to the deck of the aircraft carrier USS *Midway* (CVB 41), which had now joined the growing armada of United States Navy vessels. Now, four aircraft carriers, the *Midway*, the USS *Coral Sea* (CVA 43), the USS *Hancock* (CVA 19), and the nuclear-powered attack carrier USS *Enterprise* (CVAN 65), along with the helicopter carrier and amphibious assault ship USS *Okinawa* (LPH 3), provided the aviation operating platform for the final chapter of the evacuation of Saigon, phase four of Operation Frequent Wind.

THE WHITE HOUSE, WASHINGTON, DC

EVEN BEFORE HIS 7 p.m. National Security Council meeting had convened, President Ford did not have to wait for much more input. With the deaths of two United States Marines and NVA rocket and artillery attacks closing Tan Son Nhut Airport, the President knew the end loomed only hours away. While still talking energy and economic strategy a few hours earlier, he made the decision to finally pull the plug on Ambassador Graham A. Martin and Secretary of State Henry Kissinger's last-ditch efforts to negotiate a settlement with North Vietnam, saving Saigon from the Communists.

They had hoped the USSR would make the difference, but that proved a pipe dream. Soviet President Leonid Ilyich Brezhnev had pattered and stalled, continually renewing American diplomats' false hopes that somehow the Russians would pressure Hanoi into backing off. Waltzing a narrow line with Henry Kissinger's detente initiatives, but still kowtowing to the ironfisted hardliners in the Kremlin, Brezhnev took the politically expedient course of action, doing nothing while smiling at both sides.

However, despite the diplomats' zeal, President Ford faced the grim reality that with each passing minute, while Graham Martin puffed smoke and flashed mirrors, the lives of thousands of people lay wagered like chips in a dangerous poker bluff. America had no hole card. No aces or kings. No flushes or straights. Not even a pair. Just a handful of nothing.

A good poker player has to know when the bluff has backfired and his wager is spent. He has to know when to fold his hand and save the chips he still owns.

When the men sat down for the seven o'clock meeting, President Ford simply said, "Tell Ambassador Martin that the evacuation has now transferred to military operational control. We have no choice but to send in the helicopters, get our Americans out, and try to save as many friends as we can."

"Should I send the signal to the Seventh Fleet to initiate phase four of the operation?" Lieutenant General Brent Scowcroft said.

"Yes, General Scowcroft, notify the command center to send the flash message to launch," President Ford said.

"Anything else, sir?"

"That's it, Brent. Just get them out as quickly and as safely as we can. We cannot afford any more American lives lost at this late date."

Chapter 20
FREQUENT WIND

SAIGON, RVN—TUESDAY, APRIL 29

"PUT YOUR BACKS into it, Marines!" Sergeant Duane R. Gevers jokingly shouted to Sergeant Steven T. Schuller and Corporal David E. Norman, who busily hacked at the base of a large pepper tree growing in an island in the embassy's front parking lot.

"Kiss my sister's black cat's ass," Schuller said, resting his ax against his leg and wiping sweat from his face with the back of his arm. Dave Norman kept swinging his blade, slowly chipping away at the hardwood heart of the tree.

"You about done with that?" Gevers said, seeing the depths of the cuts made by the two men in each side of the tree. "I'm heading out back to get the water truck. I bet I can pull it down the rest of the way. We'll just slap the tow chain on the trunk and snap it off."

"Yeah, Gevers, give it a try," Schuller said. "I'm whipped on this Paul Bunyan shit."

Norman kept hacking at the trunk and spoke between strokes. "Good thing we started chopping on this awhile back."

"Yeah, every time I got a chance I'd sneak out here and give it a few licks, hoping that Ambassador Martin didn't see me," Schuller said, now chopping again on the side opposite of the cut Norman had made.

"The old man would have put our butts in a sling," Norman said. "He didn't want to see anything going on that made it look like we would bug out anytime soon. That's the shits, having to come out here at night and work on cutting this tree down. No way the helicopters could ever land on this parking lot with this tree standing."

As the two Marines hacked at the hardwood trunk, the deafening roar and whistle of the duce-and-a-half tactical water truck's diesel engine came from around the corner of the embassy's main structure as Duane Gevers tromped the throttle and jammed through several gears on the big, tandem, all-wheel-drive military vehicle. Blowing the air horn at his two friends, he backed the truck close to the tree.

Dragging a thirty-foot-long, heavy steel tow chain from the cab of the vehicle, the sergeant fastened one end of it to the truck's rear towing rings pinned to its heavy steel frame. Norman and Schuller made several wraps around the tree trunk and then hooked the chain back into itself.

Back in the cab, Gevers gunned the engine, honked the air horns once more, and popped the clutch on the big truck. It lurched in the air as it jumped forward, spun all eight back tires as it hit the tension on the chain, and then yanked the tree off its trunk. With the wide-spreading tree now in tow, Sergeant Gevers never slowed down, but kept the truck running and headed it to the rear of the embassy with its heavy, leafy load rolling and bucking like a roped wild steer.

Steve Schuller and Dave Norman picked up their shirts and two axes and happened to glance at the embassy doorway where Graham Martin stood with his small dog clutched under his arm.

"Don't let on like you see him," Schuller said, turning his eyes toward the ground. "He'll have us digging that hole through the fence for him next."

"Hole through the fence?" Norman said, now walking with the sergeant toward the rear of the building.

"Oh yeah, that's the latest of his hairbrain schemes to save Saigon," Schuller said, taking one last glance to see the ambassador still standing on the steps. "He's decided that he needs a tunnel dug through the wall to the French embassy so he can boogie next door at his own whim and keep negotiations with the Commies alive."

"I wonder if he's actually mentioned this idea to the French?" Norman said.

"I don't think so," Schuller said. "If they had given him any sort of notion that they might play ball, we'd be digging a tunnel right now."

ROOFTOP OF THE AMERICAN EMBASSY, SAIGON

"WE'VE GOT A problem, Major Kean," Master Sergeant Juan "John" Valdez said to Jim Kean, the commanding officer of Company C, Marine Security Guard Battalion. Kean had arrived in Saigon from his Hong Kong headquarters shortly after Da Nang had fallen. Given the catastrophic situations that he assessed, based on his own common sense values as a Marine officer, he concluded early on, despite the confident rhetoric espoused by the embassy leadership, that South Vietnam would fall in a matter of weeks. He thought it best that he stick around.

"I see it," Kean said, seeing the high voltage electrical wires running through the radio tower on the embassy roof. "Any way we can tell if the wires are live?"

"Lick your finger and touch one," Valdez said sarcastically.

"You can tell when I clip them with these bolt cutters," Sergeant Greg Hargis said, starting up the thirty-foot-high antenna derrick.

"Hold on," Kean said, worried that even if the young sergeant only got a hard jolt from the electricity, it would knock him back to the roof. The three-story fall alone might kill him.

"Sir, we have no choice," Valdez said. "We've got helicopters inbound right now. We can put two, maybe three CH-53s on the parking lot and a couple of CH-46s at a time up here. But we can't get anything on this deck until we cut all these guy wires and electrical lines and drop this antenna tower."

"Let's at least stand under him," Kean said, moving under the tower, beneath where Sergeant Hargis climbed.

"I don't know, sir," Valdez said. "I think it would be best if we just let Hargis hit the deck."

"Nobody's going to fall, Top," Hargis called back, and with his leg hooked over a crosspiece on the tower, he reached for the first electrical line with the long-handled bolt cutters. "Hey, Major, look at it this way. It's a fifty-fifty shot that it's off."

Just as the wire snapped in two, the heavy steel door on the embassy roof entrance slammed. It startled the major and the master sergeant so badly that they stumbled backwards. Sergeant Hargis laughed at the sight and cut the remaining electrical wires.

"What's going on?" Gunnery Sergeant Bobby Schlager shouted as he and Corporal Stephen Q. Bauer walked onto the roof, intentionally slamming the steel door shut just as Hargis cut the wire.

"Clearing out an LZ, Gunny," Kean said. "You slammed that door on purpose, didn't you?"

Schlager grinned, "Oh no, sir. Just a strong coincidence. Sorry if I startled you."

"You guys look like shit," Valdez said, noticing the black tinge to both men's fair skin. "All that soot on you come from working in the burn room? Take a look in the mirror. You both have grown Hitler moustaches too."

Schlager pulled a handkerchief from his back pocket and wiped his nose. Then he offered the black-stained cloth to Bauer. The corporal looked at the stained handkerchief, then at the gunny, and casually pulled up his shirttail and wiped the two thick black streaks from under his nose.

"Had to take a breather," Schlager said, lighting a cigarette. "Just from my estimate, we have burned more than $2.5 million in small bills. I think we still have close to a million dollars left to burn."

"Not taking any samples are you, Gunny?" Kean said, jokingly.

"I wish," Schlager said. "Everything is brand-new currency, wrapped in numerical sequences, so they have the serial numbers on all this cash. Treasury will just print more bills to replace them, so it's basically just paper and green ink we're really burning."

"Timber!" Sergeant Hargis shouted like a lumberjack, cutting the last of the heavy cables that guyed the antenna tower to the roof. As the thick steel rope snapped, the derrick crashed across the black asphalt-covered flat deck covering the embassy. Working with wrenches and hammers, the Marines soon had the mast taken loose from its mounting and heaved it over the back side of the building, letting it drop on top of the pepper tree that Duane Gevers had dumped.

"They're already getting people lined up out front," Kean said, looking down at the parking lot. "Choppers must be getting close. We'd better let them know that we have this pad clear and they can use it too."

SOUTH CHINA SEA, SOUTH OF SAIGON

BRIGADIER GENERAL RICHARD Carey, commander of the Ninth Marine Amphibious Brigade, stood on the bridge of the USS *Hancock*, watching the swarm of aircraft, both fixed-wing and helicopters, filling the air from the runway decks of the five flattop ships. While phase four of Operation Frequent Wind had begun at just a few minutes before 11:00 a.m., the helicopter-borne evacuations did not get into full production until afternoon.

Although the choppers now roared toward Saigon as the fast movers flew high cover for them, this final phase of the last act of a long war had actually begun nearly two weeks earlier as Marine Corps logisticians and operations planners began nighttime sorties into Saigon, visiting the Defense Attaché's Office compound and the American embassy, secretly putting the pieces in place for the evacuation.

Commanding officer of Regimental Landing Team 4, Colonel Al Gray, had even sent clandestine ground security forces ashore as early as April 25.

While the ambassador had dragged his feet, General Homer Smith had seen the tea leaves in the bottom of the cup. Almost around the clock he had processed out evacuation loads every twenty minutes, filling many of the air force planes that flew out of Tan Son Nhut nonstop. Each night, as the South Vietnamese National Police sounded a curfew, thus stopping the transit of passengers from the DAO, now nicknamed Dodge City, to Tan Son Nhut. As a result of the curfew, anywhere from two hundred to six hundred South Vietnamese evacuees wandered the halls and grounds of Dodge City until morning.

As the days moved to the weekend and throngs of South Vietnamese people frantically crowded around the DAO compound, as well as around the United States Embassy, trying to obtain tickets out of Saigon on the evacuation flights, Colonel Gray met with General Smith and agreed that at least a platoon of Marines at Dodge City to help maintain security might prevent any potential disasters. Clearly, as the obvious end of the current Saigon drew nearer, panic began to overtake the heretofore well-behaved crowds, and now they began to push hard in desperation.

On Friday afternoon, helicopters delivered Third Platoon, Company C, First Battalion, Ninth Marine Regiment to Dodge City. Under the leadership of platoon commander, First Lieutenant Bruce P.

Thompson-Bowers, the Marines dressed in civilian clothes so that they would not draw attention to themselves as a military force or incite protests from the PRG that America now violated the Paris Accords.

A favorite response by many of the Marines whenever anyone might raise the question of the Paris Accords was, "What are they going to do? Shave our heads and send us to Vietnam?" The diplomats' deep concern of possibly violating the agreement that had clearly meant little more than toilet paper to the Communists often raised the ire of the Marines. To these soldiers of the sea, any feared consequences of violations of the Paris Accords seemed ridiculous. The leathernecks would rather have had their helicopters headed into Hanoi to assault the heart of the Communist leadership than to execute a plan that in their majority opinion constituted little more than quitting and running. They took the pill bitterly.

As the weekend passed and Saigon stood surrounded, Al Gray consulted with embassy officials and dispatched a similar platoon of Marines to assist with security at that site too. When the first flight of helicopters landed on the roof and the parking lot, armed and uniformed Marines took up their positions within the compound on what remained of American soil in South Vietnam.

ROOFTOP OF THE AMERICAN EMBASSY, SAIGON

"DAMN IT, GET down!" David Norman shouted to Corporal Stephen Bauer, who had emerged from the open ladder well door followed by several of the regimental landing team Marines. They immediately hit the deck and scrambled to stacks of sandbags where the embassy Marines had built firing positions to cover the helicopters during landing, loading, and launching.

"What's going on?" Bauer called back to him.

"Cowboys!" Norman said just as a spray of automatic fire danced across the rooftop. "I think I have him spotted, but every time I raise up for a shot, he hoses down the area."

"Can we open fire on these guys?" one of the regimental Marines shouted.

"If you don't have a trigger lock on your rifle, I suggest you use it," Norman answered. "I think this cowboy's got some friends working with him too. The last forty-six that landed here drew a bunch of rifle fire, and one guy couldn't pump out that many rounds."

Just as Corporal Norman had made his comments, the beating wings of another inbound CH-46 echoed across the compound. The aircraft raced over the treetops and then pulled to a hover over the embassy roof and began a descent.

Suddenly bullets began pinging across the helicopter platform and dinged through the chopper's skin. Norman, who had lain at the end of the rooftop, looked up and saw the pilot's eyes opened wide and his mouth moving fast, as though he had yelled over his flight helmet's boom microphone at someone.

Seeing the pilot's alarmed expression, Norman raised himself above the sandbags and began shooting his rifle rapid fire at the building inside which he had concluded the cowboy hid. As the corporal opened fire, the other Marines joined him, focusing their fire onto the same upper-floor target area.

An embassy staff officer crouched in the doorway of the stairwell, leading a string of outbound passengers for the waiting helicopter. They had come to the embassy via the armed shuttle buses, driven by the RLT-4 Marines, on a set of routes that they called trails, interconnecting pickup points in the heart of Saigon for the departing American citizens. Earlier in the afternoon, Ambassador Martin had announced that all American citizens must now leave South Vietnam, by order of President Ford.

The fleet Marines had devised the network of trails that extended across Saigon and connected the embassy with the DAO compound. The routes had names like Santa Fe, Oregon, and Texas trails. In classic Western fashion, the armed Marines rode the trails, picking up Americans as they made their runs from Dodge City to the embassy and back, dodging through sporadic small-arms ambushes laid by Saigon's bushwhacking cowboys.

By sunset, the city had turned to a seething pit of entrapped and panic-stricken citizens. Tens of thousands of deserting ARVN soldiers now rampaged the streets, shooting, looting, raping, and killing. They knew they faced their end, and with no way out, they struck at the very heart of what they had for many years protected with their lives.

Hundreds of thousands of people jammed every avenue surrounding the American embassy and the Defense Attaché's Office compound.

Finally, the turmoil reached such an impossible level that the armed shuttles had to cease their operations.

At sea, hundreds of airplanes and helicopters swarmed to the armada of American ships. Beneath them, thousands of small crafts and barges pushed their way to the United States vessels. While they felt deep resentment and now even hatred for the Americans in the end turning their backs on their long-fought and costly war, the desperate South Vietnamese still flocked to their old protectors for final salvation.

As the South Vietnamese helicopters landed on the decks of the navy ships, crews immediately pushed the aircrafts over the sides, making room for other choppers to land. Now and then a light airplane would dip low over the water and people would leap out, some to their deaths. Then the pilotless aircraft would crash into the sea in the midst of the countless small boats that dotted the water.

No one could even estimate how many of South Vietnam's people died at sea that day and night. No doubt thousands.

Through the midst of the turmoil, as tens of thousands of South Vietnam's population fled toward the waiting American ships, the man who had said that anyone who ran from Saigon was a coward, former Premier Nguyen Cao Ky, landed a helicopter that he commandeered and personally piloted to the deck of the USS *Blue Ridge*. Dressed in a clean flight suit, with a silk scarf around his neck, he quickly ducked below decks to the senior officers' staterooms. Meanwhile, navy deck crews pushed the Huey that he had flown into the churning South China Sea.

BASSAC RIVER SOUTH OF CAN THO

THICK CLOUDS LOOMED over the swampy jungles along the Bassac River as Marine Staff Sergeant Boyette Hasty stood watch at a gunner's station on the LCM piloted by Consul General Terry McNamara. He had just begun to relax and believe that they might actually slip past any Viet Cong or NVA patrols watching the river when a sudden stream of machine-gun fire chopped through the water and cut across the raised front ramp of the landing craft.

"Everybody down!" he screamed and immediately opened fire with his rifle at the shoreline where he now saw twenty or more Communist guerrillas jumping into boats. He waved at Sergeant Terry D. Pate and

Corporal Lee J. Johnson to also open fire and help try to suppress the Viet Cong from closing in on them.

In the LCM that trailed the craft piloted by McNamara, Sergeant John S. Moore, Hasty's assistant NCO in charge, along with Sergeant John W. Kirchner and Corporal Lawrence B. Killens also opened fire on the Viet Cong that now entered the river from both sides.

Terry McNamara pushed the throttle levers full forward and kept hitting them, trying to encourage more thrust from the diesel engine that pushed the heavy landing craft through the water at hardly more than a dozen knots. Meanwhile the Viet Cong rode in the long wooden canoelike sampans, powered by small gasoline engines. The shallow-drafting boats skimmed quickly through the water, easily closing on the bulky LCMs.

Slamming magazine after magazine into his rifle, Boyette Hasty kept thinking of the nonchalance that Ambassador Martin had shown when he took the four helicopters from Can Tho and left these 318 people to fend for themselves. Pouring round after round into the prows of the Viet Cong boats, the Marine sergeant thought of the callous disregard for life and utter disloyalty that the American CIA contingent at Can Tho, along with their local operatives, had shown them. To him, their betrayal had now risen to a capital crime. They commandeered two of their helicopters, stole the consulate's two best landing crafts, with their machine guns and food and water provisions too, and left the remaining Americans, including one of their own people, twisting in the wind.

At this point, had he seen any of that bunch of CIA wastes of skin, he would have opened fire on them too.

"They're gaining on us!" McNamara shouted, crouching low and steering the flat-bottom boat in the center of the river, trying to maximize the distance between the pursuing Viet Cong and his two LCMs.

"We're getting low on ammo too," Hasty called back.

"That fog up there?" McNamara said, pointing to what looked like a gray curtain stretched across the river and surrounding jungle swamps.

"Rain, sir," Hasty said. "I think it's rain!"

In a moment, a hard downpour shrouded the two landing crafts as Terry McNamara steered onward, glad that he had a steel helmet covering his head.

Within seconds, as the rain pounded the two hard-driving landing crafts, the density of the downpour cloaked both shores from view, and the Viet Cong suddenly quit firing at them, losing the two vessels in the rain.

The heavy deluge kept both boats covered as they cruised past the dangerous narrows they had dreaded before they had launched on their Can Tho Yacht Club expedition down the Bassac.

As though God had kept an eye on their travel, the clouds parted and the rain stopped as the two vessels left the river and entered the South China Sea.

"Where is the ship!" Terry McNamara shouted at himself when he scanned the horizon in every direction and saw nothing but horizon. Graham Martin had promised him that a ship would be waiting at this very spot, waiting to pick them up. The bitterness of a day of betrayal wore deeply into his emotions, and he clamped his jaws tight in order to refrain from bringing distress on his passengers.

"Staff Sergeant Hasty," McNamara shouted. "Get these passengers prepared for some rough going. We're heading into the open water. These flat-bottom boats have a miserable ride, so try to make everyone as comfortable as you can. We need to get far away from shore, however. Those VC will come hunting us."

EARLIER IN THE afternoon, First Lieutenant Johnny Johnson and his detachment of security Marines aboard the Military Sealift Command vessel *Pioneer Contender* had lain off the mouth of the Bassac River, exactly where American embassy coordinators had instructed them to rendezvous with the evacuating contingent from Can Tho. In the afternoon sun, his sentries spotted two LCMs emerge from the river, into the open water, and make way for the freighter.

Two helicopters had landed on the amphibious dock ship USS *Vancouver* (LPD 2) earlier that afternoon and had discharged the bulk of the CIA employees from Can Tho. Therefore, the master of the *Pioneer Contender* concluded that between the people aboard the two LCMs and the two helicopters, the evacuation of the Can Tho consulate had succeeded perfectly. He turned his ship to the east and proceeded to rejoin the fleet.

AS TERRY MCNAMARA and his charge of twenty Americans and 298 South Vietnamese refugees pressed their two landing crafts beyond sight of shore, he knew that as long as he remained on his easterly course, he would eventually find friendly ships. After a sixty-mile harrowing ride down the river, a firefight with Viet Cong, and now an empty sea, the commodore of the Can Tho Yacht Club reassured himself that the situation could not get much worse. At least with nighttime they could more easily pick up the position lights of seagoing vessels and steer toward them.

AMERICAN EMBASSY, SAIGON

WITH DARKNESS CAME bitterness and open hostility among the endless sea of people that pressed themselves against the locked gates of the American embassy. Regimental landing team Marines stood picket duty around the compound walls and used their rifle butts to smash the fingers of South Vietnamese who attempted to climb the fence and get inside. The people had quickly realized that the ticket to evacuation rested on their cunning or their sheer brute strength to slip through the gate as the Marines opened it for the last of the shuttle buses to enter, or to climb over the barbed wire–topped barrier that surrounded the compound.

"One more bus!" Sergeant Terry Bennington shouted to Sergeants Bobby Frain and Steve Schuller, now manning the front gates with him. Behind the trio of embassy Marines, a dozen RLT leathernecks stood in groups of six on each side. As Bennington and his two fellow MSG sentries unbarred the gate and let it fly open, allowing the bus inside, the regimental Marines joined them in pushing the entrance shut against the unyielding tide of people pushing the other direction.

As the bus slid past and several dozen South Vietnamese rushed inside, Bennington radioed Major Kean on the roof to let him know the shuttle had arrived.

"I think we just let in another four Viet Cong corporals," he said on the radio. "They'll sure feel funny waking up in Guam."

Steve Schuller had just turned and laughed at Bennington's comment when in the corner of his eye he saw the crazed ARVN soldier lunging at him with his rifle, a bayonet fixed at its muzzle. He jumped to dodge the thrust but felt the blade sink into his side. Then from his other side he saw Terry Bennington swing his M14 rifle straight up, catching the angry attacker on the chin with a vertical butt stroke. It sent the mad soldier tumbling backwards, and the regimental Marines pushed the gates shut.

"Man down," Bennington shouted on his handheld radio.

"How bad?" responded Major Kean.

"Sergeant Schuller took a bayonet through his side," Bennington said. "I had him go take a break and plug the hole. I'm sending him topside to be radioman for you. He's no good down here now."

In the courtyard on the opposite side of the embassy compound, Colonel John Madison and his staff from the United States Joint Casualty Resolution Team worked feverishly, processing refugees by the hundreds. On the forms he filled out the names and gave them copies of the papers that provided them a presidential parole for entry into the United States. The parole stated that the person named faced great risk if he or she remained in Vietnam and therefore would receive refuge in America.

Ousted Cambodian President Lon Nol had received just such a parole and now applied for a driver's license in his new hometown of Honolulu. Nguyen Cao Ky received his days ago, while still grandstanding among his faithful. Ky's wife had already flown to San Francisco ahead of him, along with thirteen other women and children, also waving the parole papers at the customs guards they rushed past. As VIPs, they did not have to wait in lines or endure any searches. Ky's wife went to stay with relatives in the San Francisco Bay area, where she would await the arrival of her husband.

As the Joint Casualty Resolution staff filled out the papers, verifying mostly that the refugee put a correct name in the blank on the form, Colonel Madison then sent the processed Vietnamese passengers in groups of twenty to the rooftop and to the parking lot to board the outbound transport choppers. As the night grew later and later, he noticed that many of the people had begun to get jumpy, worried that not enough time remained to get them out.

It seemed that every time he sent a new bunch to the landing zones, twice as many new faces appeared.

"Look, all of you will get out," the colonel told the people. "Just relax. We're not leaving anyone behind."

THE WHITE HOUSE, WASHINGTON, DC

A FEW CHERRY blossoms still lingered on the late-blooming trees that grew along the Potomac near the Jefferson Memorial. President Gerald Ford stood by one of the tall windows behind his desk in the Oval Office, looking toward the river and the now leaf-covered cherry trees that, although they blossomed beautifully, never bore fruit.

A gift from Japan, the *sakura*, the nonbearing fruit tree, raised an ironic parallel in the President's mind. How much like them was Vietnam now? For ten years America had cultivated the small nation, spilled its sons' and daughters' blood urging it to bloom. Today, just as the trees that lined the Potomac by the Jefferson Memorial had done in the recent weeks, the blooms dropped to the ground. Vietnam would never bear its costly fruit.

"Sir," a voice came from the curved door that disappeared into the Oval Office wall.

"Don, come on in," the President said to Chief of Staff Don Rumsfeld.

"Update on the situation in Saigon," Rumsfeld said, handing the President the two-page flash message.

"It says that the South Vietnamese are trying to storm the gates at the embassy and at the DAO compound," President Ford said. "I'm afraid that this will only lead to big trouble. Order the Marines and remaining embassy staff to evacuate now. No more South Vietnamese evacuees. I want only Americans on these helicopters now."

"One other thing, sir," Rumsfeld said. "Kissinger wants to see you about Ambassador Martin. Apparently, the secretary of state has gotten wind of a plan the ambassador is trying to hatch that gets him to the French embassy, where he can continue negotiations with the North Vietnamese."

"Tell Henry," President Ford began to say, "no, I will talk to Henry. Have him come on over."

"He has that State Department black tie dinner tonight," Rumsfeld said.

"I think that can wait until we get this done," President Ford said. "History will appreciate the reasons for his tardiness at that dinner."

"Yes, sir," the chief of staff said and walked toward the door.

"Don," President Ford said, "when you send my evacuation order to Saigon, be sure that you specifically address Ambassador Martin. I want him out of the embassy on the next helicopter. Is that clear?"

AMERICAN EMBASSY, SAIGON

"SIR, GENERAL CAREY on the horn," Steve Schuller called to Jim Kean.

The major took the handset and put it to his ear. "Yes, sir, Major Kean here," he said.

"Major," the 9th MAB commander said, "we just got a flash message from the President. The President directs that no more Vietnamese evacuees fly out on your helicopters, only Americans. The Dodge City and the Alamo at the DAO compound are clearing as we speak. I want you people to start doing the same.

"Now, very important! The President specifically directed that Ambassador Martin depart the embassy on the next helicopter out."

Jim Kean immediately jogged down the stairs and found Ambassador Martin seated behind his desk. His aide-de-camp, Brunson McKinley, stood by the desk when the Marine stepped inside the ambassador's suite.

"Sir, I just received orders from President Ford, via General Carey, that all further evacuations of South Vietnamese cease and that all the remaining Americans now evacuate," Kean said.

"I'm awaiting a response from the French ambassador," Martin said in a tired voice. "We still might have a chance if I can get over there and go to work."

"Sir," Kean said. "President Ford specifically ordered you out on the next helicopter."

The gray man, whose face now looked drawn and haggard, stood and looked around his office.

"Well, I guess that's it then," Martin said in a calm and low voice.

Major Kean had already taken down the United States flag and had carried it in his hand, folded in a triangle, when he came to Ambassador Martin's office. As the beaten diplomat stepped out of his spacious grand suite for the last time, Kean handed him the embassy's national colors.

As Graham Martin waited for his helicopter to set down on the roof and his signal to board, Brunson McKinley, jogged down to the courtyard to get an update of the situation down there for the ambassador before he departed.

"Colonel Madison, how goes it? Making any headway?" McKinley asked.

"This is a mess. Everyone is very concerned about being left behind. It's past 2:00 a.m., and I see no end to it," Madison said.

"We've got six more helicopters inbound, so all these people will be fine on them," the aide-de-camp reassured the colonel. "However, my bird looks to be landing, so I need to run."

Marine Major Gerry Berry sat in the left front seat of his CH-46 Sea Knight helicopter, idling his aircraft's twin rotors as he awaited Ambassador Graham A. Martin to step aboard. He had already loaded more than thirty of the remaining staff and now only waited for Martin.

"So long, Major," Martin said as Jim Kean assisted him up the short climb of stairs into the side door of the helicopter. Then the major looked at pilot Gerry Berry and gave him a thumbs up.

Kean took a few steps back and knelt to the ground as the twin-rotor helicopter cycled up and then raced into the darkness, headed to the American armada seventeen miles off the point of Vung Tao in the South China Sea.

"Tiger, tiger, tiger," Berry called on his radio to the command vessel, USS *Blue Ridge.* "Tiger, tiger, tiger."

"Go ahead, Tiger," responded the voice on Berry's radio.

"Tiger's out of his cage," Berry said, signaling that he had the ambassador aboard.

A few moments later, Jim Kean walked into the courtyard and called Master Sergeant John Valdez to his side.

"Top, it's time for us to start packing up and getting on the roof," Kean said. "Start rounding up our Marines, and we will fall back and barricade ourselves inside the main building. It's got to be coordinated because as soon as you pull the guys off the wall, the people will flood through."

"Aye, aye, sir," Top Valdez said and caught the attention of Terry Bennington and Steven Bauer.

Major Kean walked to Colonel Madison and took him aside from the crowd of several hundred South Vietnamese still waiting for the helicopters.

"What do you mean!" Madison exploded. "The ambassador has just assured me that all these people will be taken on the next six helicopters."

"Sir," Kean said, "the ambassador has just left."

"What do you mean?" Madison said.

"Last bird off the roof had him on it," Kean said. "You need to get your people back inside the building, and then I'm pulling my Marines off the wall."

"No, you don't, mister!" Madison stormed. "We've got a responsibility for all these people!"

"Colonel, the President of the United States has ordered you and me to get out of here. No more South Vietnamese evacuees," Kean said and walked away.

DAO COMPOUND, SAIGON

A CIRCLE OF automobile, bus, and truck headlights ringed the six landing zones at the Defense Attaché's Office compound, nicknamed Dodge City, and its annex, nicknamed the Alamo. Gunnery Sergeant Russ Thurman and Lance Corporal Eric Carlson busily snapped pictures as the Marines who had stood the security around the compound's perimeter fell back and boarded the waiting helicopters.

Among the crowd, a few American news reporters and photographers lingered. Each of them wanted to outwait the other to be the last man aboard the last helicopter out.

Dirck Halstead had developed masterful skills at lingering and now had managed to outwait everyone. As Marines gathered other reporters and photographers and pushed them on departing birds through the long night that now had lasted into the early hours of morning, Dirck had slipped from one cluster of activity to another.

Finally, he had no place to run when Gunny Thurman cornered him.

"Look, if you're waiting on the last chopper out, this is it," Thurman said. Having served multiple combat tours in I Corps and having cut his public affairs teeth on escorting journalists much like Dirck Halstead, he knew exactly the photographer's motives.

"So we better head out then," Dirck said, walking with the Marine, both men shooting photographs of the activities in the headlights.

As they sauntered toward the waiting CH-53D Sea Stallion, Halstead saw two Marines run toward the main buildings.

"What's going on there?" he asked.

Russ Thurman saw the two running Marines and recognized them both. Captain Raymond J. McManus and Master Sergeant William East. They had led their team of explosive ordnance technicians through the entire DAO compound, wiring and setting thermite charges throughout the complex of structures. Now with the last helicopter preparing to depart, the two senior Marines from their team went to their control point to detonate the incendiary explosives.

"They're going to burn the building," Thurman said and jogged to the helicopter.

Dirck Halstead started to wander over to the place where the two Marines knelt, but heard the helicopter turning up the speed of its main rotor and instead ran up the rear ramp.

He watched out the rear of the helicopter as the two Marines stood and then ran for their waiting ride.

As the helicopter lifted, most of the Marines and the few civilians inside looked out the open rear door as the headlights of the cars, buses, and trucks shown in the now empty circle that had since noon the prior day served as the landing site for hundreds of Marine helicopters and a number of air force Jolly Green Giants.

With the headlamps now a distant ring of light, every building at Dodge City and the Alamo suddenly came aglow with white and red light. Although built of concrete blocks and steel, the structures literally melted to the ground, destroying everything within their walls.

In the night sky, Dirck Halstead looked overhead and was amazed at the hundreds of lights from aircraft of all shapes and sizes. Several flew forward air control missions, keeping the thousands of sorties from any midair mishaps. Others, such as a team of Marine Corps EA-6B Prowlers, spent a day and a night jamming North Vietnamese antiaircraft fire control radar and communications signals, keeping a vast array of Communist SAM SA-7 antiaircraft missiles grounded.

Dozens of fighters from the *Midway, Coral Sea, Enterprise*, and *Hancock* flew high cover, along with the air force tactical jets based in Thailand and the Philippines that joined them. Seeing the immense array of ships as his helicopter finally landed on the deck of the USS *Okinawa*, Dirck Halstead suddenly realized just how massive this evacuation had been.

The *Time* photographer, finally feeling safe and relaxed, took out a cigarette and lit it, his first in a dozen hours. He had almost forgotten that he smoked them. As he took the first long, satisfying pull of the tobacco, he wondered if Al Dawson, Peter Arnett, Neil Davis, Hugh

Van Es, or any of his other friends that he had left on the streets of Saigon, busy covering their stories, had managed to catch one of the buses to the embassy or the DAO compound.

Dirck stood on the deck in the darkness, his cameras put away, and felt sad for the nation he had left behind. He had stood on Red Beach in Da Nang in March of 1965 and had photographed the first Marine Corps ground combat units as they came ashore. Tonight, he rode with some of the last Marine Corps combat units to set foot in South Vietnam.

SOUTH CHINA SEA, SOUTH OF CAN THO

"LIGHTS!" TERRY MCNAMARA shouted. "Send up the flares!"

Boyette Hasty had been lying back on the deck with his wife, his mother-in-law, and his brothers-in-law, exhausted, when the consul general yelled.

They had first spotted what looked like ship lights an hour or two after dark. Then the lights disappeared for a time. They had shot flares skyward every twenty minutes, trying to get the ship's attention, but had thus far failed.

Since early evening, they had also taken turns calling "Mayday" on the PRC-25 radio that Hasty had managed to leave in the cockpit of the boat. He was thankful that the CIA had not seen it because they had absconded with everything else. As it was, the radio had proved only worth occupying a man's time. No one ever answered any of their distress signals. Then they saw the lights.

Throughout the night they chased the distant white and yellow glows. Sometimes the sea reflects lights from distant cities, making them look like ships on the water. He wondered if all they really chased was a ghost, teasing them for half a dozen hours. Hasty had nearly given up and had lain back to relax when Terry McNamara stirred him again.

"Sergeant Hasty," McNamara said, his voice filled with joy, "I can see the ship. They have stopped!"

Marine Captain David A. Garcia and his security detachment of Marines aboard the *Pioneer Contender* had seen the flares hours earlier and had watched them curiously. They supposed that the fire in the sky came from NVA or Viet Cong because they had already picked up their passengers from Can Tho. At least the CIA field staff from Can Tho had allowed them to believe that lie. Then Captain Garcia realized that the flares signaled distress, and he requested that the shipmaster stop the vessel.

Now, only a few hours before dawn, April 30, Terry McNamara and his civilian staff, and Sergeant Hasty and his Marines, along with the 283 civilian refugees that they had evacuated, happily climbed aboard the MSC ship. The consul general still wore his United States Navy gray helmet with the single white star and *Commodore, Can Tho Yacht Club* painted on its front.

Although the consul general exchanged words with the chief of the Can Tho CIA field unit, he never divulged to anyone what words he said to him. Sergeant Hasty and his fellow Marines had their own opinions about the conduct of the CIA at Can Tho and freely expressed them.

AMERICAN EMBASSY, SAIGON

"PULL THEM INSIDE, Top," Jim Kean shouted from the embassy doorway.

John Valdez, Bobby Schlager, Terry Bennington, and Stephen Bauer had stood ready with a base of fire while all the other sixty-eight Marines from Regimental Landing Team 4 scrambled inside the building. Now several hundred suddenly panic-stricken South Vietnamese who had waited in the courtyard for their flight, which would never come, rushed at them.

"Get inside!" Kean shouted as Bennington, Schlager, and Valdez ran for the doorway.

Stephen Bauer reached the door first, but before he could get inside, he suddenly found himself and his fellow Marines surrounded by Vietnamese screaming and clawing at them. The Marine quickly grabbed the four-inch by six-inch, eight-foot-long beam used for barring the door, put it over his shoulders, and ran at the crowd, spinning the beam at them, knocking several of the frantic people to the ground. While he stood there spinning the heavy length of wood like a helicopter rotor, his comrades ducked inside the embassy.

Yelling a few profane words at the people, he too jumped inside and slid the beam in the cradles across the door, barring the screaming people outside.

"Colonel Madison and his people have gone," Jim Kean told the seventy-nine Marines and four navy Seabees that now huddled together on the roof. "We're the last guys out. Now we just sit tight and wait."

ABOARD USS *BLUE RIDGE* IN THE SOUTH CHINA SEA

WHILE THE SECURITY team and embassy Marines waited on the embassy roof, another war raged on the Task Force 76 flagship and at Fleet Marine Force Pacific Headquarters in Hawaii.

As happens with most messages from higher headquarters, information copies abound and scatter to the four winds in the Pentagon. When President Ford's order to end the evacuation reached certain bureaucrats at Department of the Navy headquarters, typical of the office drones, they began nitpicking.

They had in hand a Presidential order that directed an end to the evacuation. Someone also realized that the helicopters had flown non-stop for more than twelve hours now, well beyond the *Naval Aviation Tactical Operations Procedures* book. As diligent bureaucrats, they issued a directive from the Secretary of the Navy ordering all flight operations party to Task Force 76 and Operation Frequent Wind to immediately cease.

When 9th MAB commander Richard Carey saw the order, he went ballistic.

"Get me Lieutenant General Wilson," he snarled. He merely had to inform his boss in Hawaii of the facts. He did not have to ask for help.

Louis H. Wilson, as a Marine captain in World War II, had earned the Medal of Honor heroically leading his infantry company against the Japanese on Guam. Nothing scared him. As commanding general of Fleet Marine Force, Pacific, his word stood above all others west of Kansas City. Nothing to Lou Wilson had greater value than the lives and safety of his Marines. Knowing that a detachment of them still sat on the United States Embassy in Saigon while the city surrounded them in chaos, and navy bureaucrats had now ordered that flight operations halt, leaving his Marines on that roof, sent him through the ceiling.

"General Carey," Wilson growled in his Mississippi southern gentleman's drawl, "I want you to inform the entire chain of command there of one important fact. I will personally court-martial anyone, no matter service or rank, who halts these flights until all our Marines in this evacuation are aboard those ships. Are you clear on that?"

"Sir, yes, sir," Carey said happily.

ROOFTOP OF THE AMERICAN EMBASSY, SAIGON

"CHOPPER COMING, MAJOR," Sergeant Schuller called to Jim Kean.

"Okay," the last officer in command of forces ashore in Vietnam said as the CH-46 landed on the rooftop landing platform, "next stick stand up and prepare to embark the chopper."

"Sir," John Valdez said, "we gotta get one more bird after this. When we board these guys, we still have a spillover of eleven bodies."

"We can't squeeze everyone aboard?" Kean questioned, not wanting to sit for another hour for the helicopter to make the round-trip.

"No way," Valdez said. "I got them in each other's laps as it is."

Kean walked to the window by the pilot and recognized Major Gerry Berry. Both men exchanged familiar smiles.

"I hate meeting like this," Kean said jokingly, raising a laugh from Berry. "We still have eleven of us on the deck here, all my embassy Marines. The last of Colonel Gray's men and the majority of my guys are loaded on your bird now."

Berry gave Kean a thumbs up and turned his eyes to the control panel. Then Jim Kean grabbed the pilot's sleeve in the open window.

"Make sure you come back for us," Kean said as firmly as he knew how. "Don't leave us here."

Chapter 21

GOOD MORNING HO CHI MINH CITY

IT WAS THE last thing Jim Kean wanted creeping in his head right now. He knew if he thought it, so might the ten other Marines who depended on him for leadership. He certainly could not let doubt paint itself on his face. He was their rock in a hurricane-whipped sea.

"Major Jim Kean, US Marine Corps," he said to himself, mocking his new rank, although not yet officially promoted to it. "Solid man. Cool head. Last commander of American forces in Vietnam. Got all the answers. Field-grade material. No sweat, not a drop."

But in his heart, hidden there, worming a rotten little hole, uncertainty nudged at him. Had they been left behind?

From the roof of the United States Embassy—four stories and a helicopter platform above Saigon—Kean could see for several miles. And at this moment, his world looked a mess with wrecked cars, trashed streets, and broken windows. Just beyond the courtyard fence, the embassy's once-beautiful Olympic swimming pool now floated with suitcases, clothing, guns, and chairs. During the night, with no facilities, the Vietnamese waiting to escape had even used the pool as a toilet.

By daylight, many of them had given up. No more choppers, they knew it. When the Americans barricaded themselves on the roof, the future was obvious. They had now gone home, or wherever, to wait for the Communists.

Still, scores of others faithfully sat, clustered in the courtyard below, waiting by their sacked-up belongings. Jim Kean could hear their distant mumbles and coughs. Babies cried. Always babies, everywhere in this country. He knew what they told each other, reassuring their faith. America would not forsake them, most certainly not. The helicopters would come again today, and they could leave too. They believed this and continued to wait, and hope.

The Marine blew a thick wad of spit off the roof, disgusted. He didn't want these people's useless vigil creeping around his brain either. The rest of his life would be time enough to wrestle with it, but not now. Nothing he could do, just feel bad for them.

And what about himself? His little covey of Marines? Were they just as stupid as those poor souls?

Kean scanned the empty sky. He strained his ears for the sound of a helicopter beating its blades against the morning air. But he heard nothing, saw nothing, for the dozenth time in the past twenty minutes. Nothing. Just a ball of orange sun about a fingernail's width above the horizon.

"Chopper will come. Give it a chance," he told himself. Then he looked at the people below who also waited, believing in the faithfulness of President Ford, America, and the United States Marines.

"Sure," his frustration answered in a sarcastic growl. Then he let fly with his pistol. Pumped a full magazine of .45-caliber lead into the embassy's satellite antenna, shooting it to hell.

Kean looked at the smoking barrel and shoved the piece back in the shoulder holster he wore. Then he looked at his Marines who sat silently, dazed, not really caring that their boss had just cranked off the last shots fired in anger by an American in Vietnam, killing an antenna.

"Now that was certainly a field grade thing to do," he said, looking at Master Sergeant John Valdez, who sat with his back against the two-foot tall parapet that surrounded the roof.

"Skipper, you're a major now, so I guess it was," Valdez said, pulling a long, Monte Cristo Havana from his shirt. "Have a cigar."

Kean took the panatela and twisted off its cellophane. He let the wrapper go and watched it drift off the roof. He thought about his wife, Rosanne, at home in Hong Kong. They had hardly had time to celebrate the news of his selection for promotion. And now, less than twenty-three hours ago, she had gotten word to him that she was going to have a baby, their fourth.

He was still a captain despite what his men called him, although in Saigon no one really knew what rank he actually carried. Dressed in a polo shirt, slacks, and a shoulder holster that held his own Colt Gold Cup pistol with fine walnut grips and engraved receiver, he could be anything.

The square-faced Marine commanded Charlie Company, Marine Security Guard Battalion, an odd outfit compared to most other of the corps's organizations. He had several hundred Marines scattered across the Asian part of Earth. He mainly oversaw their training and administrative needs. Outside that, his men worked for the ambassadors and came under the operational authority of the security officers of the respective embassies where they stood interior watch and bodyguard duty.

His largest crop of Marine security guards worked in Vietnam, sixty-two of them in Saigon alone. That's why he had come here in the first place. When the security boss for the Far East, Jim Ellis, had suddenly left Hong Kong for emergency discussions in Beijing, Kean knew he had better go to Saigon.

When he arrived on April 17, Kean recognized all the signs. Vietnam's northern provinces had fallen more than two weeks earlier. Hue, Da Nang, Chu Lai, and all of I Corps, his old hunting grounds from his previous tours, were gone. Marine First Lieutenant Sandy Kempner came to mind when he thought of those places now held by the Communists. Sandy had died up there. Now it was lost. And it would not be long before the whole country followed.

The public's nervousness was much like what he had seen in Cambodia two weeks earlier. Now Pol Pott and his Khmer Rouge had begun murdering those people by the millions. Kean had gone in and out of that disaster and then to Vientiane, Laos. There he watched the Laotian capital fall under joint occupation by the government and the Pathet Lao forces. Interestingly to Kean, the Pathet Lao men in uniform seemed to have taken on a more disciplined aspect. In fact, to him they looked more like North Vietnamese troops.

After he had arrived in Saigon, one day, and he couldn't put his finger on exactly which, Top Valdez and the others decided he was not a captain any longer. No ceremony, but they began to call him major. So did General Carey when he talked to him nearly four hours ago.

For that conversation, Kean had used a headset aboard one of the helicopters while it embarked passengers at the embassy. At that late hour, it was his only means of communication with the ships.

Nothing else worked now. Just a little backpack radio, a PRC-25, not much better than a walkie-talkie. Choppers, close in, were about all it could raise. With weak batteries, now, maybe not even those, it was as useful as a brick. But it kept a couple of Marines busy, twisting knobs and talking on the handset. Charlie and Nguyen Victor were probably laughing in the weeds, listening to the boys.

Undoubtedly, Kean thought, his superiors on the ships were looking for his debrief by now, certainly the general. Even if they assumed they had everyone aboard those last three birds, surely by now they realized they came out eleven short. They would at least be looking for the commander, the boot major.

"Nobody's forgotten us," he told himself. But that didn't help as he looked toward the sunrise, hoping to see the silhouette of a helicopter and saw only horizon.

They were done in, Kean and these marines. They just wanted to go home. Logically, they reassured each other, it was only a delay. Chopper had to get gas, probably, or had a flat. Some reason. There had to be a good one why the bird had not yet shown.

"They know we're here," Staff Sergeant Mike Sullivan said.

"But then that dead radio," the inside of his head retorted. "No answer. Sorry little backpack Prick-25 doesn't get that far anyway."

He looked at Bobby Schlager who lay next to him, listening to the staff sergeant call on the handset to an unresponsive world. Schlager heard Sullivan pretending to talk to some unreal chopper.

"Don't bullshit, man," Schlager whispered. "There's nobody there."

"Say, what are the ships, fifty or sixty miles out?" Sullivan spoke in return.

Schlager looked back at Sullivan and tiredly nodded his head, yes. It sounded right. Who cared?

"No way a Prick can call that far, anyway. Chopper will come. *Semper fi*, do or die. They'll come," someone behind the two said. Then they looked at the sun and silently prayed.

Take another drink of Jack Daniels Black, or was it the Johnnie

Walker? Black Label, you know. Best there is, at least in these parts. A half-gallon bottle of each was floating around, robbed from Ambassador Graham Martin's liquor box. What the hell. Now that everything's done but this waiting for the last bird out.

Somewhere, though, the ugly thoughts kept blurting out.

"Think they left us?"

"Shut up, asshole."

Steve Schuller, who had been lying against the wall, hurting, looked up. He heard the question. He had asked it too—in his head. But he didn't like his feelings about the answer.

The bayonet wound in his side throbbed. So he dug in his finger and pulled out the knot of T-shirt he had stuffed inside the hole, revealing black, dripping, syrupy blood. He sent the disgusting mess skidding a red streak across the embassy's roof.

The lanky sergeant took another drink from a canteen of piss-warm water. Then he doused a strip of fresh T-shirt he had ripped from what was left of the one he wore, nearly losing his breath when he shoved the wad inside. Then Schuller felt another rush of chill and sweat hit him, so he closed his eyes and sucked hard on his cigarette.

"Just gear down and cool it," he told himself. But the voices from somewhere over there, beyond his closed eyes, pulled at his ears and made him think it too.

"No man, really. They might believe they got us on that last bird."

Schuller opened his eyes to see who was talking, but didn't feel like turning his head.

"Think so? No way, man. The major, he told them. Got the crew chief, remember? Don't forget us, I heard him yell."

"They'll be here," a different voice interrupted.

It was Bennington, Terry Sergeant fucking Bennington. Schuller looked to him and gave him a wink. Skinny fart, but tough as shit.

He thought about the incident out at the gate the day before. The crowd, nonstop faces, going from the embassy wall to forever. Everybody wanted inside the gates and on the choppers. Bennington had stood next to Schuller on that watch.

They used M14 rifles, not because they shot a bigger round, but they presented a heavier club. They didn't want to kill the people, just hold them back. More stopping power with a 14's long stock and barrel.

Schuller remembered seeing the soldier. South Vietnamese, crazy, maybe drunk. Maybe both. He locked eyes with him and suddenly the guy lowered his rifle and charged.

The side step hadn't worked. Schuller felt the blade of the long bayonet fixed on the man's rifle pop through his shirt and his skin and bury in his gut. It felt as if it headed out the other side when Bennington stopped it.

He had seen the crazy soldier too, met him in the jaw with the steel tailpiece of his M14. Vertical butt stroke, they called it in boot camp. Terry was always the studious type, learned that hand-to-hand well. And Steve Schuller thanked God he did.

Terry Bennington stopped the assault dead in its tracks and took the soldier off his feet with the force of the rifle stock, sending the cuckoo man skidding on his back through a gap of parted people, all dodging the drama like when Moses parted the Red Sea.

Two sets of hands pulled Schuller backward inside the embassy compound, and two other Marines filled his slot at the gate.

He had known he was bleeding, but they had no hospital corpsman, not even a first aid kit. So the Marine took a break, lay against the building, sucked down some water, and stuffed T-shirt material into his wound. After a smoke, and a little more water, he went back to work.

Bennington sent Schuller to the embassy roof where he hailed chopper traffic with the PRC-25 radio that Staff Sergeant Sullivan now played with while they waited for rescue.

"Remember, before the others left? We sat for two hours with those guys," Schuller reminded his buddies. "No birds, just us and the world."

"Sure, that was sixty-eight marines, four Seabees, and an hour ago," David Norman suggested. "Maybe they think they got the whole herd."

"No way, Jack. They know we're here," Schuller said.

"So do the NVA," Bennington reminded the bunch. "How about all these pissed-off people down in the streets? Hope that bird gets here before we gotta deal with that."

Steve Schuller looked at the others, "I won't throw my hands in the air. No way! No POWs. They come up here, man, and it's the Alamo."

Jim Kean heard the talk and walked to the place beneath the platform where his men rested.

"Nobody forgot us," he told them in his most confident tone. "But like Bennington said, things could break at any time. So what should we do?"

John Valdez never said much, but the major's comment brought him to his feet. He looked at the others and then out to the streets of Saigon.

Poor, crumbling, frightened Saigon. He had gone over the wall a dozen times, rescuing special people, doing it as much for his Marines as for the people who needed out. Prostitutes mostly, girlfriends his Marines called them, but others too. Shine boys, bar keepers, corner hucksters, kids. People he had come to know out in the ville. Some of them seemed like the people back on his home streets in San Antonio. And that got to him.

"NVA will kill these broads," he had told the major. They weren't the Top's girls, but he cared about their lives.

Kean agreed. Who really gives a damn, or will know the difference? After it was done, scuttlebutt on the roof told of a C-130 full of whores that left Tan Son Nhut early yesterday. Top Valdez probably arranged that too, several Marines speculated, or at least had a hand in it.

"Can we vote on it?" Valdez said to the major and looked at the men who now gathered close.

Kean thought for a moment and agreed. It was their lives, if the chopper did not get here in time. He didn't want to think about that possibility. But if it came to it—with nothing to hold, no mission—they ought to have the choice.

The Marines voted. No discussion, no questions: No surrender. They would fight to the end, if the helicopter did not come, if it got to that.

With the vote taken, eleven to nothing, Jim Kean felt better. No doubts now, they would all go down together, if it came to it. But he didn't need the vote to know it. These guys would have fought anyway, and he knew he couldn't stop them. And he wouldn't have tried.

Stephen Bauer ambled back to the fire door where he stood guard with a mace can, squirting people's eyes anytime one brave enough, or desperate enough, tried to come through the broken glass in the little window. But no one had done that for several hours now.

Bennington and Dave Norman walked with Schuller and squatted again by the wall while Sullivan and Schlager flopped by the dead radio.

"Relax."

"Bird's coming."

"Give another hit off that Jack."

"Just zeed out, man. Too many hours and no sleep. Got the bugs crawling in your brain. Chill out."

Jim Kean walked to the ladder that led up to the helicopter pad and leaned his hip and elbow into the rungs.

It had been a tough three days, and the last twenty-four hours impossible to reckon. They had hauled out 140,000 Vietnamese, and who knows how many Americans. Nonstop crazy with two landing zones at the embassy and six at the Defense Attaché's Office compound, scattered across Dodge City and the Alamo, cycling helicopters in right behind those departing. No lull. Just pack them on and wave them off.

Most crews had taken the seats out of their choppers, buckled straps across the floors and told the people to hang on. They had packed in two and three times the numbers of bodies the birds' manufacturers said they could haul.

One HH-53D Jolly Green Giant driver, an Air Force captain named Joe Gilmartin, claimed carrying 150 souls in his chopper, which Boeing had rated as a 35-passenger aircraft.

People didn't care. They wanted to live. They wanted freedom, all so badly that they would risk death for it.

"Pile in some more," the crew chief would shout to Kean.

Throughout the day, he had worked the landing zone in the embassy parking lot. The pilot would haul back on his controls, lift the bird, set it down, and wave to load more people. They repeated this until the helicopter struggled so hard that the pilot knew it could not fly with another soul aboard. Then the big old green grasshopper-looking whirlybird rumbled and shuddered as it climbed in the air and disappeared over the treetops, ship bound with a fresh haul of despair and grief riding inside its belly.

With every load out, an equal number of infiltrators came over, under, or through the embassy wall. The population of the crowd waiting in the courtyard never really changed. And the marines didn't have time to check lists or papers. Just shove some more on another chopper and go.

Bennington had even started telling Kean on the walkie-talkie, "Major, I think we sent four more NVA corporals to Guam." It became the running joke.

Jim Kean smiled, thinking about what four North Vietnamese Army corporals would do in Guam. Then he bit the end off the cigar and sucked on it. The tobacco's sweetness tasted sharp and stung the tip of his tongue. He sniffed its aroma, a good one. Leave it to Top.

No matches, though. "Who's got a light?" he said. No one heard him. Kean looked around, but then decided to just settle and think. The cigar tasted good cold.

MAI THAO VILLA, NORTHWEST SAIGON

"MY DEAR, THE sun has risen. Dawn brings us a new day. It will be better than our last," Mai Thao said, rising from the sofa chair where he had fallen asleep. He looked for his martini pitcher and then remembered draining the last when he sat down and dozed while a ring of fire burned around Saigon.

Tran Da Tu and his wife, Nha Ca, had cuddled together on the fancy jade green couch with the beautiful gold brocade, hand-sewn thread work of Japanese cranes with their wings widespread decorating the heavy, silk-based fabric. Mai Thao swore that the birds looked more like the vile smelling African marabou, a type of stork that he had once seen close-up while visiting the London Zoo and caught a whiff of their dead, rancid odor. Ugly, black, long-legged creatures with bare necks and heads and a ring of white feathers at the tops of their shoulders where their ugly, thin, naked, red necks stretched half a meter to carry their lunking bald heads and monstrous yellow beaks. Feed on rotten carrion, they do, dead, decaying flesh. Wretched, foul birds.

Those marabou would feast today in Saigon, Mai Thao thought as he gazed at his two sleeping friends.

Moving quietly, the novelist walked to the kitchen and rummaged through the mess of several days, looking for a clean glass. His houseboy had disappeared on Friday, he supposed to escape the down-falling nation, just like most of his family and friends. They all had run when the getaway was still good.

The author had rested on his laurels and had depended on his highly placed friends to fetch him when the time to leave had come. Highly placed friends, indeed. Even Marshal Ky had finally taken down his valiant flag, while boasting his valor, and slipped out with the last big crowd to rush the exit. His kind talk a good fight, Mai Thao thought.

"Here I am, still standing in Saigon," he said to himself as he climbed the stairs to a balcony that overlooked the city. "Who is the coward, and who is the valiant one now?"

Then he laughed to himself, "And who is the fool?"

He looked at the glass of water that he had poured from a bottle he had found half full in the refrigerator. In it he noticed minute flakes of debris swirling in the liquid, soaked loose from the sides of the cleanest looking dirty glass that he found on the counter. He took a sip and dashed the rest over the rail, splashing into his well-kept flower garden on the edge of the patio below him.

Beyond the treetops, he saw black smoke filling the sky. It rose from every direction. The noise of battle, stubborn ARVN soldiers and Viet Marines fighting to save their country, had now grown strangely silent, except for a sporadic rifle shot or a pistol close by. Once in awhile an explosion crunched from a far distant place. People still died. Some still fought. Most had now, however, quit.

While shelling Saigon's outskirts and shutting down Tan Son Nhut, the Communists had virtually left his beloved city untouched, the novelist suddenly realized. He looked from the balcony as the newly dawning day cast its orange light across the rooftops of his home. The tall cathedral tower stood unblemished. Dense leaves still covered the trees surrounding it and other buildings, rustling in the morning breeze. Houses, hotels, the opera house, all remained undamaged. Except for the smoke that encircled the city, Saigon still looked much its old self.

However, the silence seemed odd, out of place. Mai Thao could not recall hearing such quietness. In the center of the city, he could hear a small helicopter still beating its wings, Air America still trying to salvage a few lives. Yet no horns honked. No bicycle bells chimed the morning as they had always done until now. No trucks. No cars. No people.

"My friends, you have awakened," Mai Thao said, seeing Tran Da Tu and Nha Ca step through the downstairs sliding door and walk onto the patio in the fresh day's light.

"There you are," Nha Ca said and smiled.

"We're going back to our house and wait for our fate there," Tran Da Tu said.

"Hold on, please," Mai Thao called back and hurried downstairs.

Reaching his two friends at the front door, Thao said, "Do not return to your house. I implore you, if you value your lives. Le, my houseboy, told me this one night, when I shared a glass or two of cognac with him, the Viet Cong have a list. You both are on it, and so am I. Kieu Chinh, and many others. Do you recall how the Chinese purged the intellectuals and artists from their society? The VC want the same thing. They want to rid themselves of us and our strange ways."

"Where else can we go?" Tran Da Tu said. "We have only our home."

"Then stay on the streets," Mai Thao said.

THE WHITE HOUSE, WASHINGTON, DC

"HENRY, WHAT'S THE problem?" President Gerald Ford said to the secretary of state.

"Apparently, we have left about a dozen Marines on the roof of the embassy," Kissinger said, dressed in a tuxedo.

"My God!" President Ford exclaimed. "How on earth did that happen? I thought they had reported everyone out."

"Initial reports indicated that all had been extracted, and the operation ceased," Kissinger explained. "Apparently, when the helicopter carrying out Ambassador Martin, Lady Ace Zero-Nine, made its radio report that they had the 'Code Two' aboard and 'Tiger is out,' meaning the ambassador," he said, reading from a message sheet, "the outbound flight of helicopters sent to pick up the remaining Marines apparently turned around. They misunderstood 'Tiger is out' to mean that they had all the remaining Marines aboard and were inbound with them. Lady Ace Nine and his wingman meanwhile returned to the embassy roof and picked up all they could carry, but had to leave behind eleven of the Marines. They naturally assumed that the other flight of helicopters would pick up the remaining men."

"The other flight had actually shut down," the President added.

"Precisely," Kissinger said. "I am expected at the State Department dinner tonight, but I cannot leave here until I know those Marines are safely aboard ship. So, if you don't mind, I will wait this out with you."

"Thank you," President Ford said and took a seat at the dining table where Henry Kissinger stood, dressed in his black tie, gripping the back of one of the side chairs, waiting for the telephone to ring.

"Those two Marines killed yesterday, Henry," President Ford said, "their bodies are still in Saigon."

"I also heard that bit of news when I got the call about the Marines left on the embassy roof," Kissinger said. "I understand that someone had called the hospital to retrieve the bodies, but were told that they had already been flown out. We have begun working through the French to obtain the two Marines, but it does not look promising. Not for the near future."

"We've also lost two Marine pilots at sea this morning," President Ford said. "Two enlisted crewmen escaped and were picked up, but the pilot and copilot, a Captain William C. Nystul and First Lieutenant Michael J. Shea, did not make it out of the aircraft. With the depth of the water and the conditions there, we are not hopeful of recovering their bodies either."

"I had not yet heard that news," Kissinger said, still standing behind the chair, gripping its back. "In contrast, however, we already estimate that our forces succeeded in evacuating more than 150,000 people. The Marines, Navy, and Air Force pilots flying those missions did a remarkable thing. They surpassed even our highest hopes for success. While we mourn the loss of those four Marines, we also need to appreciate what our servicemen accomplished today."

"Very true, Henry," the President said, "and I deeply appreciate their sacrifice. However, it still remains very difficult for me to sit here as President of the United States and watch South Vietnam collapse," President Ford confessed. "It looks like we just quit and ran. Yet I did all that I could for them."

ABOARD THE USS *OKINAWA* IN THE SOUTH CHINA SEA

"WHO DO WE still have airborne?" Ninth Marine Amphibious Brigade commander, Brigadier General Richard E. Carey, asked, now on the captain's bridge of the amphibious assault and helicopter landing ship USS *Okinawa*.

"One bird over Vung Tao, Swift Two-Two, inbound now," Major Dick Young, the brigade operations officer said.

"Anyone on deck fueled?" Carey asked.

"Lady Ace Zero-Nine might get going in fifteen or twenty minutes," the major said, "but the pilot, Gerry Berry, has already logged more than eighteen hours in the past twenty and has thirty-four sorties to his credit. He would do it, if you asked him, but I think he's already well outside the envelope. Purely a matter of safety."

"What's the current fuel status on Swift Two-Two?" Carey said, looking at the horizon through binoculars, trying to catch sight of the lone CH-46 Sea Knight as it headed toward the fleet of ships.

"Getting more critical by the minute," the operations boss said. "Ships have begun to track outbound, so that's a big factor. Right now, we're a good forty-minute flight each leg. He'll be riding on fumes when he lands. If you send him."

"Tell Swift Two-Two that, if able, they should turn toward shore, proceed to the embassy, and extract those Marines," Carey said. "Given the conditions in Saigon right now, with broad daylight, every second counts. Our guys sitting on that rooftop many not have fifteen minutes left to wait while we refuel another bird."

WESTERN OUTSKIRTS OF SAIGON

"WHAT IS THIS?" Nguyen Sinh Tuan said, raising his Leica M3 camera and focusing on Nguyen Duc Cui as he sat on the ground, massaging the leather of the brown oxford shoes that he had carried in his pack since the day he had made the blood-bound promise to his dying friend.

"I thought you had no film," Cui said, smiling as Tuan released the shutter.

"I had no more film for photographs of darkness," the photographer said. "They wanted pictures of that battle, and all that my lens could see was blackness and streaks of light. I had no film for that. However, I do have this roll of film to photograph today, Liberation Day!"

"It has not yet ended," Cui said. "We still have ARVN entrenched here at Hoc Mon."

"In a few hours," Tuan said and snapped another photograph, "their President Minh will formally surrender. He has already ordered his forces to lay down their arms."

"Those gunshots in that village tell me that these ARVN did not hear their president's orders," Cui said, still rubbing the leather.

"Then why do you soften your shoes so that you can wear them when we march into Saigon today?" Tuan said, smiling.

"I also heard about the trucks taking us into the city, once our troops have quieted these guns here," Cui said and smiled back at his friend.

COURTYARD OF THE AMERICAN EMBASSY, SAIGON

"NEIL!" A VOICE from outside the opened American embassy gates shouted.

"Here, over here," Neil Davis said, raising his hand above the back of the couch where he lay, watching the embassy roof.

"What are you doing lying on that couch in the embassy parking lot when we have ARVN soldiers running in the streets, shedding their uniforms, shooting, looting, burning? Hugh Van Es shot an outstanding still of an Air America Huey on the Pan American building, and a ladder of people climbing up to it. He'll get the Pulitzer Prize, and you're out here sleeping," Al Dawson said, stepping around the leather sofa that the South Vietnamese had dragged from the building after the Marines had locked themselves on the roof.

"We still have Marines on the roof, and I am waiting to see what happens. They'll no doubt send a helicopter for them, and I will have film of the last bird to leave Saigon," Davis said, lying back with his camera poised to shoot upward, should anything break.

Dawson sat on the arm of the couch and began watching the roof too.

"How do you know there are Marines up there?" the UPI bureau chief said.

"I had lain here to take a snooze about sunrise," Davis began. "Then I heard five or six shots. Pow, pow, pow, pow, pow from up there. So I start looking to see who did it. Once in awhile I get a peek of a head or upper body. They're not oriental, so they must be Americans, still on their own embassy. You know that the diplomats and brass all left first, so these guys must be Marines. Very simple deductive reasoning, my friend."

"What the heck are they still doing up there?" Dawson said, now captivated.

"You're the reporter," Davis said. "Go find the answer to that question. I'll wait here and film it."

ROOFTOP OF THE AMERICAN EMBASSY, SAIGON

"QUICK, COME HERE, Top," Jim Kean called, kneeling behind a stack of sandbags and looking at the street beyond the embassy compound fence.

"Big Minh!" Master Sergeant Valdez said. "Headed to the office to close up, I guess."

"What is this, six sedans and an armed escort?" Kean said. "They must be headed to the Presidential Palace to wait for the North Vietnamese to come knocking."

"I hope I don't see that," Steven Schuller said, now limping as he walked, suffering increasing pain from the wound in his side.

All the Marines crowded by the boss and watched as President Duong Van Minh and Premier Vu Van Mao drove to the Presidential Palace, where the Republic of Vietnam's leaders of two days would receive politburo boss Le Duc Tho and formally surrender South Vietnam to the Communists.

"What time you got, Top?" Sergeant Terry Bennington said, cupping his hands above his eyes, searching the distant horizon, as the other ten Marines kept their focus on the motorcade procession below.

"Why?" Valdez said, hopefully. "What do you see?"

"It's a helicopter!" Sergeant Bennington said, dropping his hands and beaming.

"Yeah, and the people on the ground hear it coming too. Look at them run!" Sergeant Duane Gevers said, now rushing to the steel door with Gunnery Sergeant Bobby Schlager and Corporal Stephen Bauer.

"Get deployed for his landing," Kean said. "Be ready for any ground fire too."

Screams and shouts echoed from the concrete stairwell behind the steel door that the Marines had now reinforced to keep shut.

"Go ahead and pop that big canister of riot gas," Kean said.

"This won't be pretty," Bauer said as he pulled the pins on two small CS grenades and dropped them inside the broken window in the center of the door.

Duane Gevers set off the big can of CS riot control agent on the roof, releasing a great white cloud of the irritating fog.

Swift Two-Two came in hot, dropping just over the deck and squatting on its wheels as the eleven Marines ran toward the open rear ramp. Tear gas spiraled and swirled over the roof and drifted toward the ground.

Despite its irritating properties, causing a person's eyes, nose, and sinuses to flood, the gas did not phase the screaming, anxious South Vietnamese who had waited all night for the helicopter and now saw it come. They rushed up the stairs and poured onto the roof just as Swift Two-Two parted from the deck.

"You getting this?" Al Dawson said to Neil Davis.

"I waited all night for this," the Australian responded.

NGUYEN GIAP TY RESIDENCE IN SAIGON

THE SUN BURNED Nguyen Giap Ty's eyes as he looked through the sheer lace curtains that hung over his living-room windows. Outside he saw a group of his neighbors walking toward his door and pointing. Although he could not hear their words clearly, the Viet Cong soldiers that his so-called friends led seemed intense and agitated as they tromped across his courtyard and garden.

The ARVN officer, recipient of America's Bronze Star Medal, answered the door when the Viet Cong slammed their fists against it, rattling the windows.

"Quiet, children," Ninh Thi Tran whispered, watching her husband unlatch the entrance to their home.

"May I help you?" Ty tried to say.

"Stand aside!" the first soldier who seemed to have authority over the troop said and pushed Ty away as he led his soldiers into the house.

Nguyen Giap Ty looked at the angry faces of his neighbors who crowded outside his front door.

"Why?" Ty said. "What have I ever done to hurt you? I thought you were my friends."

"He was an officer!" one of the neighbors shouted to the Viet Cong. "A criminal who lives on the sweat of our people!"

"Please simply take me, and do not harm my family," Nguyen Giap Ty pled.

"Yes," the senior Viet Cong said, "you will come with us now. Also, this woman, Ninh Thi Tran!"

"Why, sir?" Ty said, clasping his hands together in a prayerlike fashion, showing respect and subordination. "She has done nothing but secretarial work all of her life and has raised our five children. Please, sir, she has done nothing!"

"Quiet!" the senior soldier snarled and then turned to two of his soldiers who now held Ty. "Take him out of here now. You men take her."

Two other Viet Cong held Ninh Thi Tran by her shoulders and led her out the door behind her husband through the growing crowd of jeering neighbors. While the people watched, the soldiers tied both Ty's and Ninh's hands behind their backs.

Then the Viet Cong leader looked at Ty's oldest son, Nam, and growled, "You have two minutes to gather what you want of your personal belongings and leave this house. Don't come back."

Living as homeless orphans on the streets of Saigon for more than a year, Nam and his sister Bich-Van Nguyen took care of their three siblings. Tuong-Van Nguyen, the eldest daughter of Ty and Ninh, suffered most because of her Down syndrome disabilities. Vanny, the youngest daughter, and Son, the younger son, helped Nam and Bich with Tuong-Van, and together the four of them scavenged for food and shelter.

Eight years of hard labor, so-called re-education, took their toll on Nguyen Giap Ty and his wife, Ninh. Abandonment took its toll on their children.

Somehow, though, a resilient spirit among the Nguyen family kept them going through it all. Their children grew up and finally managed to escape from Vietnam aboard the clandestine boatlifts. They came to America and Australia. So did Nguyen Giap Ty and his wife and their disabled daughter, Tuong-Van, finally.

PRESIDENTIAL PALACE, SAIGON

AT 10:24 A.M., President Duong Van Minh issued a statement, broadcast to the North Vietnamese, offering the surrender of the Republic of Vietnam.

The announcement seemed to represent the latch on the gate because in a matter of minutes parades of victorious Viet Cong and North Vietnamese soldiers, walking, riding in trucks, and sitting on tanks and armored personnel carriers came streaming into Saigon from every direction.

Seeing President Minh's motorcade driving to the Presidential Palace, Neil Davis and Al Dawson ran to the capitol building after they had witnessed the last American forces leave Saigon. While Dawson found a good perch to watch from a distance, the Australian motion picture news photographer set up his camera on the front steps of Big Minh's headquarters.

He had his camera rolling when the Soviet-built T-55 tank, with soldiers waving the PRG flag, crashed down the palace gates and rumbled up the wide walkway to the great building's front steps. The Australian photojournalist stood, waved at the Communists, and kept his camera rolling.

Safely aboard the USS *Okinawa*, Major Jim Kean accompanied Brigadier General Richard Carey to the captain's bridge. As the last commander of American forces on the ground in South Vietnam, Kean signed the log beneath the signature of Graham A. Martin, America's last ambassador to Vietnam.

INTERNATIONAL AIRPORT, MONTREAL, CANADA

"HELLO!" KIEU CHINH cried on the telephone. Someone had finally answered.

"Who is this?" the voice responded.

"Kieu Chinh. I met you in Hollywood. Glenn Ford introduced us," the Vietnamese actress said.

"Oh, you're the girl from Saigon!" Tippi Hedren said, now recognizing her. "Where are you? In town?"

"No, oh no," Kieu said and again broke into tears. She had used her last Canadian dime to dial the telephone in Montreal's airport, where, with the fall of Saigon, a country friendly to America finally let her past the customs gate, despite her lack of documentation.

Leaving Hong Kong, Kieu Chinh spent the next twenty-four hours flying to Rome. She could not pass through customs there, but she did manage to call her sister in Paris. Flying to the French capital, the Vietnamese actress soon discovered that her sister's adopted homeland would not allow her entrance either. Her sister had met her at the De Gaulle International Airport, but could only wave at Kieu through the glass.

That night Kieu Chinh had flown to London and found a similar greeting, so she caught the next flight to Montreal.

This morning she began calling familiar names in her address book. Each call used another handful of change. William Holden had gone to play golf. Glenn Ford said that he could not recall who she was, and Burt Reynolds, the man she kissed for the first time on screen, did not answer.

She had one name left in her book, a woman she had met only once at a party in Hollywood. They had had a nice conversation, and Tippi Hedren had given Kieu her number in case she wanted to get together when she came back to town.

Kieu Chinh had come back to town all right, homeless and penniless, except for the last Canadian dime that she had dropped in the coin slot of the telephone to place the collect call.

"Poor girl," Tippi sobbed too. Both women had flooded with tears.

"I have no place," Kieu said. "I have no job, no prospects of work. I have no passport. I have no money. I only have a suitcase with a few of my clothes."

"What do I need to do to get you here?" the Alfred Hitchcock–film actress said.

"I still have my around-the-world ticket," Kieu responded. "The Canadian customs officers said that Saigon has now surrendered, so I have refugee status. They told me that I can board the plane to America if I have a sponsor and a place to go. That is what I desperately need."

"Kieu, now stop crying," Hedren said, still sobbing too. "Tell those people that you are coming here to live. We'll get you back on your feet in no time. Don't you worry anymore."

NVA HOSPITAL, CU CHI BASE

"HERE, LET ME help you up," a young boy said to Le Van Reung, who lay on a hospital cot at Cu Chi Base. "I have the radio on, and they are broadcasting our victory!"

The wounded Viet Cong soldier leaned on his elbow and looked at the stump where doctors had amputated his leg just above his knee. Until now all the wounds he had suffered had only made holes that soon scarred over. He managed to stay in the field with most of them. Now, he could not walk. He hated that thought.

Growing up, he had seen the men who had fought the French, their legs missing. They begged on street corners and could do little else. He could barely read. He only knew farming rice and fighting war.

He listened to the broadcast as the Hanoi correspondent spoke of the great liberation victory. Saigon existed no more, but Ho Chi Minh City had been born that morning at eleven o'clock when Le Duc Tho accepted Big Minh's unconditional surrender and immediately had the former ARVN general arrested, along with his prime minister.

The leaders joined members of the National Assembly, who had hoped to avoid prison by now kowtowing to the victors.

Colonel Vo Dong Giang laughed as he told the reporter how several members of the National Assembly had come knocking on his door with the artillery and rockets first bombarded Tan Son Nhut. They wanted shelter in his basement in exchange for cooperation with the Communists. He laughed long and hard as he told the reporter how he sent them away, cowering.

April 30, 1975, stood as a great day of jubilation for the new re-united Democratic Republic of Vietnam. Le Van Reung felt joy for his country, but lay on his cot at Cu Chi wishing that he had his leg back.

Nguyen Duc Cui, wearing the shoes of his fallen best friend, marched down the streets of Ho Chi Minh City that day, tears streaming from his eyes. Huong's spirit marched with him.

While the tricolor flags of the PRG flew with the red flags of North Vietnam, decorating every tall building in Ho Chi Minh City, more than 150,000 South Vietnamese refugees crowded into tent cities on Guam, Wake Island, Clark Air Base in the Philippines, and at Utapao Air Base in Thailand. Soon, United States Air Force transports would carry them to America, to improved, hardback tent cities at the Marine Corps's Camp Pendleton in California, at the army's Fort Chaffee in Arkansas, and at the air force's Eglin base in Florida.

Slowly but surely these broken souls would find resurrection. They would pursue the American dream. They would encounter American prejudice and poverty too. Many would fail, but most, despite the obstacles, would overcome.

In twenty years' time their grandchildren would emerge with no knowledge of life in a war-torn state. They, like most of the other Americans around them, would take their liberty for granted.

On the day Saigon fell, Nguyen Thanh Trung flew his captured American-made A-37 Dragonfly to Ho Chi Minh City and landed it despite the debris-covered and badly pocked runway at Tan Son Nhut. When he parked the small attack jet, he pulled the photograph of his wife and three daughters from the instrument panel and went looking for them.

While his comrades celebrated, while the Viet Cong constabulary established order and discipline on the chaotic streets, while they hunted down spies and arrested traitors, Trung searched for his family.

When he found no one at his home, and the few belongings that remained inside it trashed, he walked to the center of Ho Chi Minh City and the central police jail. There outside, sitting on a bench by the street, his beautiful wife and three daughters waited for him to claim them.

At first life came hard for the nation, and Trung lived as poor as he could ever remember in his whole life. Then after twenty years, the struggling country of starving people began to emerge and reach out toward the West.

Air Vietnam again began to fly passenger jets. First with old Soviet Aeroflot planes, flying junk iron and bricks, with no thrust and little lift. Then came the French Airbus, and finally the American Boeing and McDonnell Douglas jumbo jets.

Trung remained a pilot and helped Vietnam build its airline as their chief pilot. His three angelic daughters, who sat at the center of his life with his devoted wife, all became leading flight attendants for the airline.

His old F-5A Skoshi Tiger moved from the Da Nang Air Base to Ho Chi Minh City and the military museum. It sits there today, a symbol of his country's liberation.

MAI THAO VILLA, NORTHWEST SAIGON

MAI THAO SLIPPED through the small gate at the back of his garden and out into the narrow backstreet. He saw the men coming to his front door, led by Le, his former houseboy, who had warned him to leave Saigon. That night they had split a bottle of cognac, Le had nearly spilled the beans that like so many who served the wealthy, he moonlighted as a Viet Cong agent. Loyal to his cause, he duly reported every visitor and most of what Mai Thao said. Now they came to arrest him. He topped their list.

Nha Ca and Tran Da Tu also topped that list, a roster of artists and writers, dangerous to the new Democratic Republic of Vietnam. They needed re-education into the proper way to live life and treat their brethren.

While Mai Thao slipped out the gate and, through miracles and sly maneuvering, evaded the VC's capturing him for nine months, finally slipping free of Vung Tao in a sampan and catching a lift on an Indian freighter bound for Long Beach, California, his friends Nha Ca and Tran Da Tu did not manage quite as well.

A dozen years of hard labor, learning the error of their ways, greeted the two artists. Nha Ca spent most of those years sitting in a four-foot-wide cell. She ate once a day and saw little daylight. She paid for her sins with solitary. Her husband toiled digging roadbeds. When the enlightened government finally released them in 1988, they could hardly recognize each other.

Like their friend Mai Thao, they finally escaped Communist Vietnam too and made their homes near him in southern California.

DIRCK HALSTEAD WENT home to Washington, DC, and resumed his work as *TIME* magazine's senior White House photographer. He took assignments during the months that he did not cover the President and became one of the world's foremost photojournalists. He led the pioneer movement into digital photography and filmmaking and opened the horizons for photojournalism on the Internet.

David Hume Kennerly also succeeded in his world of photography, contracting for national and international publications.

Neil B. Davis, born in Tasmania on St. Valentine's Day, 1934, died in Bangkok on September 9, 1985. As a contract motion picture news photographer for major news networks, such as his service for NBC in Vietnam, he covered war on three continents, had seen it all, and won a Pulitzer Prize for his film coverage of the surrender of Saigon.

Like his friends Al Dawson, Derek Williams, and Hubert "Hugh" Van Es, Davis found that life in Bangkok pleased him best, and he settled there. Doing what he loved best, standing behind his lens, filming the drama of war, Neil Davis died.

In the summer of 1985, a segment of the Royal Thai armed forces splintered and attempted a *coup d'etat*. Just as he had done on the steps of the Presidential Palace, Neil Davis filmed the rebel Thai tank rolling at him. He waved at them, to show he presented no harm. They cut him down with a machine gun.

Neil remained in Ho Chi Minh City with friends, such as Peter Arnett, Dawson, Williams, and Van Es, for many weeks until one by one the Vietnamese Communist regime expelled them for insulting their host.

Arnett departed first. He found it easy to insult the new government.

Then came Van Es and Williams.

Van Es won the Pulitzer Prize for his picture of the helicopter on the roof with the ladder filled with people trying to scramble to it.

Days before the fall, Derek Williams married his longtime girlfriend in Saigon. He managed to get tickets out of Saigon for her and all of his in-laws. They flew to Thailand and settled in Bangkok. When the Viet Cong kicked him out of Ho Chi Minh City, he simply went home to her.

On the day that Saigon welcomed its new name, Ho Chi Minh City, the streets still remained dangerous. The American journalists banded together, trying to still cover the chaos but stay alive too.

That day Ha Thuc Can and Ky Wahn showed their Viet Cong credentials to the Americans, not on purpose but by necessity.

Angry VC, recognizing the round eyes and light skin of the men, put their guns on them. They wanted to kill some of them, sassy talking, back talking Westerners, like Peter Arnett and Hubert Van Es.

Always diplomatic and quick to think on his feet, and use them when opportunity offered, Al Dawson tried to explain to the soldiers that the members of his group were journalists, certainly not CIA.

The gun-wielding VC did not hear it, but only wanted to march the reporters to the nearest wall and shoot them, or at best case cart them to jail.

Ky Wahn then introduced himself to these brethren of the red, blue, and yellow cloth.

"These are my friends," he said.

The VC shrugged and let the men go.

Al Dawson stayed longest. More than three months he rattled cages in Ho Chi Minh City. Finally, Hanoi had enough of him and showed him the door too.

The Marines went home. America tried to forget her war. After a ten-year letting of blood, the forgetting took effort. Even after thirty years since the last day of that war, tempers still run at the high end of anybody's thermostat. Tops still blow easily when a young know-it-all buff on that bad war tells an old vet that he lost that war. It was an illegal bad war. He deserved to lose it.

Even with wrinkles, gray hair, and a mellowed-out attitude, guys like Master Sergeant Joe Carr, a crusty old retired jarhead, will still throw furniture. Insult the man and his service, insult the sacrifice that he and his brothers and sisters paid for that ten-year cultivation of fruitless cherry blossoms, Old Joe Carr will throw a chair, bust a nose too, and curse like hell when he does it. The man did set a high standard at cursing.

Half of those last four dead Americans never did come home. Captain William C. Nystul and First Lieutenant Michael J. Shea at last word still lay in the deep of the South China Sea off the coast of Vung Tao. They rest amid the wreckage of hundreds of helicopters and planes and sunken boats and rafts. They rest among many thousands of those that they tried to help, people they died for, people who also died that same day.

One year after Corporal Charles McMahon, Jr., and Lance Corporal Darwin D. Judge fell under that rocket blast outside the gates at Dodge City and the Alamo, they finally got to come home.

McMahon, a good Irish lad from Massachusetts, had a lot of passion in his family. They would not let their senator, Edward Kennedy, rest until he got the boy home to Woburn. Kennedy stayed on the job, and he brought both Marines home. God bless him.

Brigadier General Le Minh Dao went to the Communist prison. Re-education, they called it. Poor student, that one. They never let him out.

Chapter 22

REFLECTIONS

GOODNIGHT SAIGON IS the fourth book that I have written about the Vietnam War. It is without a doubt the most difficult of any I have ever written, and I suspect it will remain the most difficult book that I will ever write. This, primarily because I am too close to the subject. I know too many details. I know too many of the faces.

I was a sergeant in the United States Marine Corps, stationed in the Southeast Asian theater when these events took place. Therefore, a bit of my soul lies scattered among these pages, along with pieces of many others' souls.

Included among these are those of our enemy at the time, as well as those of our allies and brothers in arms.

I spent much of the fall season of 1994 in Vietnam, researching this book, interviewing South Vietnamese veterans and civilians caught up in the demise of their nation, many who spent years in prison. I also interviewed many veterans from the other side: Viet Cong soldiers, North Vietnamese Army troops, and their leaders.

Then, through all of 1995 and part of 1996 I traveled across the United States, interviewing American leaders, such as President Gerald R. Ford, as well as our own generals, line commanders, grunt veterans, news photographers and reporters, and many South Vietnamese civilians and soldiers, and leaders too, who managed to get away.

Of all these people, three stand out most in my mind: Nguyen Giap Ty, a retired South Vietnamese Army lieutenant colonel who held the position of master of the Port of Saigon when the city fell; Nguyen Manh Tuan, a South Vietnamese Army lieutenant colonel whom North Vietnamese forces captured in the massacre at Cheo Reo; and Nguyen Duc Cui, a North Vietnamese communications officer for the 320th Division who marched through Saigon wearing the shoes of his best friend, who had fallen in combat more than five years earlier.

Nguyen Giap Ty stands out because even at the time I interviewed him at his small apartment in Philadelphia, the winter of 1995, nearly twenty years after the war's end, he and his family had not yet found a lasting sanctuary. They had not stopped their struggle. As a United States Marine Corps veteran, it broke my heart to see it.

Ty's wife, Ninh, worked at the Defense Attaché's Office compound in Saigon while Ty managed the port of Saigon. Ty and Ninh both could have escaped days before the country fell, yet they remained at their posts helping others to flee. They remained at their stations, serving a greater good.

Once they reached the end of their work, they tried to make their flights. Unknowing and perhaps uncaring people, then in a bitter irony, ignored them. These gatekeepers refused to look at the Nguyen family's documents that authorized them to board the departing aircraft. Understandably, for the people who turned them away, Ty, Ninh, and their children were simply one more family of faces among a sea of others, all desperately struggling to leave the falling city, all waving papers, or even money.

Ty and Ninh spent several years in prison, enduring Communist Vietnam's infamous re-education camps. During those years, all but one of their children managed to sneak out of the country as "boat people."

When the Communists finally let Ty out of prison, he and his wife and their mentally disabled daughter, Tuong-Van, also joined the boat people exodus and got out of Vietnam under the cover of darkness. On those ships, they faced utter starvation, pennilessness, and the loss of all personal possessions. Tuong-Van nearly died from the heat, dehydration, and malnutrition.

Ty, Ninh, and Tuong-Van managed to survive the ordeal at sea and finally landed in the Philippines, but they could not remain since they had no documentation nor any money to bribe any officials. From there they went to Australia, where their daughter, Vanny, had married a citizen of that country. However, she was not financially able to support her parents and her sister, much less able to sponsor them as refugees.

Once they had regained some health, Ty, Ninh, and Tuong-Van departed Australia for the United States, where their two sons, Nam and Son, and remaining daughter, Bich, now lived in Philadelphia.

In the city that bore America's independence, the family spent several months struggling to get on their feet. Ty worked in a local produce market owned by another Vietnamese expatriate, shipping out fruits and vegetables. They finally managed to rent a small apartment for themselves and had begun to rebuild their lives when the United States Immigration and Naturalization Service entered their world with astonishing news for them.

Since the Nguyen family did not come to the United States first, the INS bureaucrats refused to classify Ty, Ninh, and Tuong-Van as refugees. As a result, the family had to obtain tourist visas to remain in America. Furthermore, they had to join the increasingly long line of immigrants waiting for citizenship quotas, and the delay would easily stretch far beyond the expiration dates of even the longest running visas they might hope to receive.

Then the bureaucratic nightmare began to worsen. The INS refused to extend their visas when the first ones expired. Ty and his family now faced being deported by the very country that they so deeply loved and had loyally served for more than ten years. Furthermore, the deportation would send them back to Vietnam, where they had suffered so greatly and fought so hard to escape.

Because they had left their native home without documentation or authorization, Ty, Ninh, and Tuong-Van faced certain imprisonment upon their return. The INS just shrugged it off as not their problem. Furthermore, the Clinton administration busily worked to establish trade and diplomatic relations with Vietnam and did not want to offend the Hanoi government by granting Ty, Ninh, and their daughter refugee status.

Shortly after my last conversation with him, in 1996, I lost contact with Nguyen Giap Ty and his entire family. It was well past the INS deadline too.

I do not know if Ty and his family succeeded in staying in America or went back to Vietnam. I suspect that they may have fled Philadelphia for some other place in America where they could blend in and disappear.

The United States Army awarded Ty the Bronze Star with combat V for valor, for rescuing a squad of American soldiers out of a minefield near Chu Lai. Despite his heroism and sacrifice for America, the INS still wanted to deport the man, his wife, and their child back to Vietnam and to certain imprisonment.

I think of Nguyen Giap Ty, Ninh, and their family quite often, and I include them in my prayers.

Like Ty and his wife, Nguyen Manh Tuan also spent many years in the Vietnamese Communist re-education camps. Tuan lost his entire family, and all of his dreams seemed doomed after his capture by North Vietnamese at Cheo Reo. However, his story has a bright ending, if not inspirational.

Tuan commanded an artillery regiment with the ARVN II Army Corps in Pleiku and Kontum, in the Central Highlands. He spoke eloquent English after the years that he spent in the United States, graduating command and staff college and training at the United States Army's artillery school at Fort Sill, Oklahoma.

When the Communists released Tuan from prison, he had no place to live and no money, and the government would not allow him to hold any sort of regular job. Dressed in prison rags, he was literally left to panhandle on the streets of Ho Chi Minh City, the former Saigon.

Tuan, however, refused to beg. He considered himself a better man than to sit on the streets and ask for handouts. Battling for survival, he noticed people with broken bicycles and offered to fix them in exchange for a few dong (the currency of the Socialist Republic of Vietnam).

So on a busy street corner each day, he set up his shop on a flap of cardboard, which also served as his bed at night, and repaired bicycles. He felt lucky if his customers had tool kits with their bikes. Otherwise he had to use his fingers or tools that he improvised from scraps of wood or metal.

Eventually, Tuan located his wife and children. However, they had disowned him. So for the next year, he lived on the streets of Saigon, shunned by his family, repairing bicycles often with little more than his fingers and earning only pennies.

One day, an old friend happened past Tuan and recognized him. While this man had served in the South Vietnamese Army with Tuan, he had also joined the Viet Cong too and at war's end had landed himself a decent job as manager of a foundry. The friend went to local Communist Party leaders and tried to persuade them to allow Tuan to work, if only as a custodian sweeping the factory floor. However, they remained steadfast that as long as people loyal to them during the war needed jobs, they would not give one to a former enemy, especially a lieutenant colonel.

Despite the denial, Tuan's friend still allowed him to take up residence in the foundry, where he could secretly sweep the floors at night when no one watched.

Living in the factory, Tuan also learned metallurgy and spent his free time between bike repairs developing skills in metal crafts, electroplating, grinding, and manufacturing tools.

Finally, Tuan decided to try making hand tools on his own and thought that he could perhaps sell a few of them on Saigon's growing black market. However, a man with no money and no way of legally obtaining financial backing, much less the means of purchasing even the most meager materials and equipment, faced a significant challenge.

Tuan had told himself many times since the day the Communists captured him that he had only two choices, to live or to die. If he chose life, then he must persevere against whatever obstacles he faced.

Undaunted and determined to live, he went to the local dump and began salvaging wires, metal containers, whatever materials he could use to fabricate the equipment that he needed to craft his tools. He even swept up the Carborundum dust from the factory floor at night and glued the abrasive grit to strips of fabric that he attached around cylinders of his own creation, thus making grinding wheels from scratch.

In a rickety shed that he built from scraps, and illegally tying his electrical power input to that of the factory, Tuan began to cut, grind and chrome plate scissors and shears of his own design. He made them from discarded scrap metal and gleaned his needed chemicals and other such products from the waste fluids dumped by the factory.

Tuan began selling his scissors on the streets of Saigon. Eventually, people who use fine shears in their work, such as barbers and tailors, sought out Tuan and placed orders with him. His business began to grow to the point that he had to employ and train people to help him. So he hired others like himself: people homeless and persecuted because they were South Vietnamese veterans or family members of these men. They all worked illegally in Tuan's black market, built-from-scraps scissors factory.

At this same time, the Communist government in Vietnam was undergoing an internal struggle and began some dramatic changes. The people were tired of starving and living without even their most basic needs fulfilled under the hard-line regime. The unrest reached into the higher levels of government as younger, more liberal-thinking people began to replace the aging old guard. Eventually, in the late 1980s, the government of Vietnam began to liberalize and allow private enterprise, private ownership of farms and factories, privately owned homes, and free-market trade that opened its doors to the world. Hanoi even extended its hand toward the United States and sought to establish treaties and diplomatic relations.

With this liberalized government, Tuan's friends who had clout with local Communist officials convinced those leaders to allow Tuan to operate and expand his factory in the open. The government expressed no objections, but also offered no help.

In a matter of three years, Tuan built his factory and began filling international orders for his high-quality, handcrafted scissors and shears. He formally named his business the Nguyen Dinh Scissors Factory and gave his products the brand name of Kevi.

By 1990, Tuan employed 320 workers at his Saigon factory and manufactured 245,000 pairs of scissors and shears annually. While his Kevi scissors and shears sold widely throughout eastern Europe, they also moved with increasing popularity in free-world markets too, such as Australia, New Zealand, and Hong Kong.

In 1992, Nguyen Dinh Scissors Factory won a contract with Corporation Franco Asiatique, a French firm, to produce two million pairs of scissors for $1.8 million in United States currency. This contract gave Tuan and his family of workers a bright future and solidly established them as a major industry in Vietnam.

After I had spent most of a day interviewing Tuan and touring his factory, as I prepared to depart, he handed me a farewell gift—a pair of his Kevi brand barber shears. To this day, I use those scissors regularly, and they remain sharp and tight and cut hair cleanly with a crisp snap. In my mind, they are the finest quality barber shears I have ever seen.

To me, Nguyen Manh Tuan embodies the resilient spirit of the Vietnamese people and exemplifies what it means to never quit. He is wealthy today by anyone's standards, yet what makes him rich in my eyes comes not from the thickness of his wallet, but from what lives in his heart.

His face and that of Nguyen Giap Ty symbolize the South Vietnamese and the fall of South Vietnam to me. Deep sadness, great frustration with heartless bureaucratic governments, on both sides, yet not utter failure, but hope.

Then there comes the perspective of the enemy, the North Vietnamese Communists and the Viet Cong. Until I knew these men as humans, I only saw them as angry faces beneath turtle-shell hats, aiming down Russian-made rifles. Like many of my fellow Marines, I believed these people heartless, uncaring, cold to human life. In a word, evil. As quick to crank a bullet in my back as look at me.

Near Cu Chi, in a national cemetery for Communist soldiers killed in action, I met Le Van Reung, a Viet Cong guerrilla who lost his right leg to a "friendly" booby trap on his way into Saigon, the day before the city fell. He had fought my brother Marines in Da Nang years earlier. He led the assault on Ban Me Thuot from within the South Vietnamese defensive circle, a virtual suicide mission. Yet he survived all of that only to lose his leg, and nearly lose his life, while casually walking toward Saigon.

As his reward for a lifetime of service to the Viet Cong cause, the Hanoi government made him caretaker of the Vietnam National Cemetery at Cu Chi, and official overseer of the shrine and mass grave of 2,473 unknown Communist soldiers buried there beneath a gray granite tower erected on a wide, flat marble footing. For his caretaker work and national service, his government gave the one-legged Viet Cong veteran a retirement of about eighty dollars per month.

Talking to him seemed haunting in one respect, but very familiar in another. After all, we both were veterans of the same war. We had common feelings, common ground that made us more alike than different.

In Saigon, when I interviewed General Tran Van Tra, commander in chief of the Viet Cong, on the second or third occasion, we talked about these apparent common links among warriors, even people from opposing sides.

I told the old general, "Had I seen you in my sights twenty years ago, I would have killed you."

He told me, "Had I the chance then, I would have killed you too."

Then he added, "But isn't it nice that we can now be friends."

The aged warrior had gained my consideration. He wasn't such a bad guy. Or was he? Like a pendulum, my emotions swung wide each way with every contrasting event.

That night, in Saigon at the hotel where I stayed, my friendly bartender whispered to me in confidence, between straight shots of Scotch, that he had some important information that I needed to know. Something terribly secret, but terribly important for him to tell me about a man whose name I had mentioned the previous night: Brigadier General Le Minh Dao, commander of the ARVN's Eighteenth Division.

We had talked about General Dao's valiant stand at Xuan Loc, a town only a couple of hours' drive north of Saigon on Highway 1. We talked about how he fiercely led his division and had held the overwhelming power of the North Vietnamese Army at bay for many days while thousands of people managed to evacuate from Saigon. The general had sacrificed himself and his division for the people of his country.

The bartender whispered, "General Dao is alive!"

"Where?" I asked. "I want to see him!"

The bartender shushed me, told me to speak lower, and then said, "I was released from re-education only last month. I was with General Dao when I was a captain in the Eighteenth Division at Xuan Loc. I was with him in prison too."

I whispered to the bartender that the Vietnam government press service and foreign ministry in Hanoi had told me that General Dao had been released and had left the country. "They say he is somewhere in America." I said.

"No!" the bartender whispered emphatically. "He is in prison, north from here. I was with him. They will never allow him to leave. He will die in chains. They hate him, and he will not bend their way."

Checks with both the State Department and the Immigration and Naturalization Service turned up empty. They had no record of Le Minh Dao's ever coming to America, despite the Hanoi government's insisting that he had.

During the autumn of 1994, I zigzagged my way throughout Vietnam, border to coast, from Saigon to Hanoi. I met Montagnards in the western mountains, next to Laos and Cambodia, who had not seen a Westerner in more than twenty-five years. For their children, I was the first one they had ever seen. With rifles on their shoulders, deep in the wild country where they live, these natives of the woodlands frightened away my Communist escorts but surrounded me with warmth and jubilation. America was back! It was hard to leave.

Later, in Da Nang, I talked with a woman, Huynh Thit, who had served as a cost accountant for the commanding general of the First Marine Air Wing, based there and at Phu Bai and Chu Lai. Since the Americans only gave Huynh passage for herself and not her family too, she chose to remain in Vietnam when the city the French called Tourane, succumbed. Defiantly loyal to America and her South Vietnamese cause, Huynh Thit continues to be persecuted by the Communists still today. She cannot hold a job, not even after so many years, and so she illegally teaches English to earn money to buy her food. The woman still wanted badly to come to America, but only with her family in tow.

A cyclo driver who had served as one of the South Vietnamese Marines who defended Da Nang to the bitter end introduced her to me after I talked to him in the place where he lived, squatted in the burned-out hulk of what used to be the United States Consulate. When I left Da Nang to fly to Hanoi, she was at the airport to say farewell to me. The Marine cyclo driver had carried her there, I am sure, for free. Huynh Thit hugged my neck long and hard. She still loved her Marines.

I passed her name and address to retired Marine Corps Commandant General Al Gray, hoping that he or some of his well-placed friends might find a way to help her.

A few days later, I met Nguyen Duc Cui in Hanoi, on what turned into an emotionally challenging afternoon.

My interview with him came after a surreptitious, high-speed, and very unauthorized tour of the brig where the North Vietnamese had, for so many years, incarcerated and tortured, some to death, American prisoners of war. My trusty guide, Hoang Huy Chung, followed the little side-trip adventure with a serene visit to a neighborhood where the tail section of an American B-52 jutted out of a lotus pond.

In a twisted way, the aircraft wreckage symbolizes for the Communists their victory. I assume, however, that since they did not want me to see the infamous "Hanoi Hilton," it likely reflects a perspective of their shame.

While we kept the driver turning left at each corner, taking us around and around the old prison with its high, barbed wire–topped, pinkish brown stucco walls and matching buildings, Hoang must have seen the deep sadness that filled my heart and expressed itself on my face. He offered honest words of consolation, trying to ease my feelings. War truly is an ugly experience for anyone. He added that today the facility no longer houses prisoners, but serves the Vietnam government with an important internal mission, too sensitive, however, for him to reveal to me.

Nonetheless, it still looked like a jail, harsh and ugly, badly in need of a salvo of napalm.

After making several passes, trying to see the place where my brothers in arms had year upon year languished so horribly, many of them succumbing there in slow, torturous deaths, and without seeming to look at it or stop, since the government had strictly forbidden my even noticing the "Hanoi Hilton," my nervous-wreck escort finally succeeded in prying me away and directed our driver to the park where the bomber had crashed. As we proceeded to the park, where all of us could stretch our legs, I felt smugly proud of myself. Hoang would have died of heart failure had he known that while we circled the famous military keep I had secretly pointed my camera out the car window and snapped half a roll of color slides of the jail that helped to endear Jane Fonda in the hearts of so many millions of America's Vietnam War era veterans.

At the park, several dozen elementary schoolchildren surrounded me and cheered me because I was American. Their teachers explained that the preteen students had learned of America in school, and they were excited and very happy to actually see a citizen of my country in theirs.

As the giggling youngsters departed, I then noticed a man scowling at me. When I made eye contact with him, he approached and spoke angrily at me. He too recognized me as an American and gave me a taste of his bitterness.

Thus, sitting in the front room of Nguyen Duc Cui's home that afternoon, sipping hot tea, talking about the battles and the end of the war with him and his old friend, Nguyen Sinh Tuan, a documentary photographer with Cui's unit, the 320th NVA Division, I struggled with my mixed emotions.

Tuan showed me his camera and took my photograph, while Cui smiled quietly. Apparently, Tuan, just like photographers I had known in the Marine Corps, was an outgoing and friendly fellow. Cui, on the other hand, seemed sullen, almost too quiet.

He explained that when the people at Hanoi's foreign press office had told him that I had served as a United States Marine, it troubled him. He did not know how he could handle meeting in a social presence his former enemy face-to-face, much less tell this person of the part he had played in the war and the final campaign that led to North Vietnam's victory.

I told Cui about the angry man I met in the park, how he had spit at my feet and stormed away. My escort, Hoang, said something in Vietnamese, trying to soften the moment, but Cui cut him off. Then he fought back tears.

The war had been very difficult for him. He told me that he did not like Americans very much, even now. He understood how the man in the park felt, but disagreed with his actions toward me.

"We were only soldiers, then, after all," Cui said.

We talked about sacred honor, duty, and obligations as warriors, and we agreed on every point. Over time, Cui relaxed.

Then, after an hour of talking, he told me how much alike he now realized that we were, and how sad this made him feel. We both had lost dear friends in the war. We both stood loyally with our countries when our duty called us.

I told him that I had also discovered those same feelings when I had talked to some of his comrades in the south a week or two earlier.

Cui told me of his best friend, Huong Chinh, who died in the war far west of Da Nang under the bombs dropped by American B-52s. He told me how his friend had bought a pair of shoes after their last class in college in Hanoi and had carried those shoes with him for two years as they fought in South Vietnam.

He told me how he promised as his friend lay dying that he would take the shoes and carry them in his pack until he could put them on his feet and march with them in Saigon in the victory parade.

Tears streamed from Cui's eyes as he told me the story, and my heart ached too. I could see his friend. I could understand such a promise. I know I would have done the same thing. So would most any good soldier, any good Marine, for his buddy.

At the end of war's mess, only battered soldiers stand, bleeding and heartbroken, weary of it all. Our enemy really is not the man in the trench with the rifle, but the man in the white tower, safely insulated from the fight a thousand miles, or a world, away. As warriors we are but instruments of our nations, loyal and serving. We are all pretty much the same.

I hold little use for politicians. The older I grow, the less respect I have for them. On most occasions, I avoid meeting nearly any of these swindling baby kissers who talk out of both corners of their mouths. Once, at a dinner gala in Georgia, I even refused to shake a certain senator's hand because I simply knew too much about him. For personal gain, political power, money, or simply a change in the spin of the news that day, men like him put men like Cui and me on the battlefront, facing each other, killing each other, while in a different place, in a different time, we might have been friends.

For me, Nguyen Duc Cui offers assurance that God's will eventually does prevail, and everything finally does even out, no matter how we silly humans try to bend it. Meeting Cui in Hanoi, identifying with him as a fellow warrior, but under different flags, getting to know each other's honor, our shared decency as men, helped put the war to rest, for both of us.

Goodnight Saigon first formed in my mind as a chronicle of how and why South Vietnam, and America, lost the war. After meeting and getting to intimately know many of the people who appear in these pages, my objective changed.

While *Goodnight Saigon* must tell its perspective of this history, it has a greater obligation to reveal the humanity of it. The participants, from all sides, were people. Simple human beings, like most any of us, with fears, hopes, joys, and tears.

In the Baptist church where I attended Sunday school as a child and let Christ in my heart, I learned the song, "Jesus Loves the Little Children." In its verses the song says He loves "all the children of the world. Red and yellow, black and white, they are precious in His sight . . ."

When I consider the insight that I gained in Vietnam, researching this book, discovering that my former enemy is more like me than different from me, how he too cries at the loss of his brothers and sisters, and how he too abhors war, but how he will always unflinchingly stand willing to fight for his people, the words of that old Sunday school song ring out in my mind. We should try harder to love each other, all the children of the world.

—*Charles W. Henderson, Chief Warrant Officer,*
United States Marine Corps (Retired)

Appendix

CHRONOLOGY OF SIGNIFICANT EVENTS 1973–1975

(Revised and reprinted from *U. S. Marines in Vietnam: The Bitter End*, *1973–1975*, with permission from History and Museums Division, Headquarters, United States Marine Corps)

1973

27 JANUARY—The United States, Republic of Vietnam (South Vietnam), Democratic Republic of Vietnam (North Vietnam), and the Provisional Revolutionary Government of South Vietnam (Viet Cong) sign a peace agreement in Paris, France. The Paris Accords provide for three commissions to oversee the implementation of the agreements and resolve any differences. The commissions are the four-party Joint Military Commission (JMC) representing each of the belligerents, a two-party JMC representing North and South Vietnam and an International Commission of Control and Supervision (ICCS) consisting of representatives from Canada, Poland, Hungary, and Indonesia.

27 MARCH—The Marine Advisory Unit of the Naval Advisory Group in Vietnam is disestablished and replaced by the United States–Vietnamese Marine Corps Logistics Support Branch. This is the last day of the sixty-day cease-fire period during which the North Vietnamese release American prisoners of war and in turn the United States turns over to the South Vietnamese its military bases and withdraws its last military forces from the RVN.

29 MARCH—The United States Military Assistance Command, Vietnam (USMACV), officially ceases to exist, replaced at 1900 Saigon time by the United States Defense Attaché's Office (DAO).

13 JUNE—The United States, South Vietnam, North Vietnam, and the Viet Cong sign the implementation agreement to the Paris Accords.

30 JUNE—Less than 250 United States military personnel, which includes the 50 at the DAO, remain in South Vietnam, the maximum allowed by the Paris Peace Accords.

1 JULY—New fiscal year begins with a reduction from $2.2 billion to $1.1 billion dollars in United States assistance to South Vietnam.

15 DECEMBER—Communist troops ambush a JMC-sanctioned MIA recovery mission, killing a United States Army officer and wounding four American and several South Vietnamese soldiers.

1974

JUNE—Lieutenant Colonel Anthony Lukeman replaces Lieutenant Colonel George E. Strickland as chief, United States–Vietnamese Marine Corps Logistics Support Branch, Navy Division, DAO.

1 JULY—Fiscal year 1975 begins with funding for South Vietnamese military forces set at $700 million, down from $1.1 billion.

DECEMBER—The North Vietnamese Army (NVA) 968th Division (later the 968th Corps, which merged the 10th, 316th, and 320th NVA divisions under command of Lieutenant General Hoang Minh Thoa) moves into South Vietnam's Central Highlands from Laos, the first overt deployment of a North Vietnamese division into the south since the cease-fire agreement.

31 DECEMBER—NVA units encircle Phuoc Long City (Song Be), capital of Phuoc Long Province, near the Cambodian border in Military Region 3 (MR 3).

1975

7 JANUARY—The NVA captures Phuoc Long Province.

27 JANUARY—The last allied Mekong River convoy from South Vietnam enters Phnom Penh. The Cambodian Communist Khmer Rouge have successfully halted resupply to the embattled Cambodian capital, threatening the downfall of the non-Communist Cambodian government.

10 MARCH—The NVA attacks Ban Me Thuot in the Central Highlands, marking the start of its Spring Offensive of 1975.

19 MARCH—The South Vietnamese abandon Quang Tri City and Province.

24 MARCH—Quang Ngai City and Tam Ky in I Corps fall to the advancing NVA.

25 MARCH—Hue falls to the Communists.

26 MARCH—The NVA captures the former United States Marine Corps base at Chu Lai.

30 MARCH—The NVA enters the major port city of Da Nang and captures Da Nang Air Base.

12 APRIL—Marines of the Ninth Marine Amphibious Brigade execute Operation Eagle Pull, the evacuation of American and other foreign nationals from Phnom Penh, Cambodia, just before the city falls to the Khmer Rouge.

21 APRIL—Nguyen Van Thieu resigns as president of the Republic of Vietnam (South Vietnam) and departs Saigon four days later for Taiwan, leaving the control of the government in the hands of his vice president, Tran Van Huong.

28 APRIL—General Duong Van "Big" Minh becomes the new president of the Republic of Vietnam.

29 APRIL—Marines of the Ninth Marine Amphibious Brigade execute Operation Frequent Wind, the evacuation of Americans, foreign nationals, and various Vietnamese officials and citizens associated with Americans from Saigon to ships of the Seventh Fleet.

30 APRIL—The North Vietnamese Army enters Saigon and places General Minh and his cabinet under arrest. Organized South Vietnamese resistance to the NVA has collapsed.

12 MAY—A gunboat of the new Cambodian Khmer Rouge regime seizes an American ship, the SS *Mayaguez,* in the Gulf of Thailand.

14 MAY—Marines of Battalion Landing Team 2/9 (Second Battalion, Ninth Marine Regiment), in United States Air Force helicopters, make a helicopter assault on Koh Tang Island, off the Cambodian mainland where the crew of the *Mayaguez* is believed to be held. At the same time, Marines from Company D, First Battalion, Fourth Marine Regiment board the *Mayaguez* only to find it deserted. The Cambodians in the meantime release the crew of the *Mayaguez,* who later are recovered at sea by the United States destroyer *Wilson.*

15 MAY—With the recovery of both the *Mayaguez* and its crew, the Marines withdraw from Koh Tang Island. The American forces sustained total casualties of fifteen killed, three missing in action (later declared dead), forty-nine wounded, and twenty-three other personnel killed in a related helicopter crash. United States forces inflict an unknown number of enemy casualties.

INTERVIEW NOTES AND BIBLIOGRAPHY

PERSONAL INTERVIEWS

Arnett, Peter—Correspondent, Associated Press, Saigon Bureau. Arnett remained in Saigon after the Americans left and witnessed the ensuing chaos of Saigon during and after the evacuation and during the Communist takeover of the city. His photographer was Ky Wahn, who turned out to be a Viet Cong. (Also CBS cameraman, Ha Thue Can, who worked with Morley Safer, turned out to be Viet Cong.) When confronted by NVA and Viet Cong, Ky Wahn saved Arnett by telling the Communists that the Western journalists with him were his friends. Multiple interviews in person—Los Angeles, California; Bangkok, Thailand; and various locations in Ho Chi Minh City (Saigon) and surrounding areas, Socialist Republic of Vietnam, October 1994.

Babel, Philip A.—Sergeant, United States Marine Corps. Babel was one of the last eleven Marines on the roof of the American embassy in Saigon. Interview in person, Hotel Saigon, Ho Chi Minh City (Saigon), Socialist Republic of Vietnam, October 1994.

Bauer, Stephen Q.—Corporal, United States Marine Corps. Bauer was one of the last eleven Marines on the roof of the American embassy in Saigon. Interview in person, Hotel Saigon, Ho Chi Minh City (Saigon), Socialist Republic of Vietnam, October 1994.

Bennington, Terry J.—Sergeant Major, United States Marine Corps. As a sergeant, he was one of the last eleven Marines on the roof of the American embassy in Saigon. During evacuation he told Captain Kean, in reaction to their inability to identify evacuees from infiltrators, "I think we just sent four NVA corporals to Guam." Interview in person, Hotel Saigon, Ho Chi Minh City (Saigon), Socialist Republic of Vietnam, October 1994.

Berry, Gerald L. "Gerry"—Major, United States Marine Corps. Berry piloted the CH-46 Sea Knight helicopter that flew Ambassador Graham Martin from Saigon and made the call via radio that the ambassador was successfully aboard the helicopter and outbound to the ship. Call sign for Martin was "Tiger." Berry radioed, "Tiger, tiger, tiger. The tiger is out of his cage." As Berry departed, he could see the last eleven Marines on the embassy roof. He advised General Carey that eleven Americans still remained behind. Berry recalled, "You could see the end coming. We made the next to the last pass and left the last eleven. There was no doubt in my mind that the Marines would be left. If I was one of those Marines, I would have had all the anxiety in the world, not knowing how much time remained before the North Vietnamese overran me." Interview in person, Hotel Saigon, Ho Chi Minh City (Saigon), Socialist Republic of Vietnam, October 1994.

Carey, Richard E.—Lieutenant General, United States Marine Corps. In 1975, while a brigadier general, Carey served as commanding general of the Ninth Marine Amphibious Brigade and operational commander of the evacuation of South Vietnam, dubbed Operation Frequent Wind. Carey spent much of his time during the war's final hours fighting with Navy, Defense Department, and State Department officials who wanted to call an end to the evacuation flights. Navy officials claimed the pilots had flown too many hours and this presented too great a risk for the Americans who remained to be evacuated. State Department and Defense Department officials echoed these feelings, asking for a halt until daylight.

Carey and his boss—Fleet Marine Force, Pacific, commander, then-Lieutenant General Louis H. Wilson (later Commandant of the Marine Corps)—went to quarters. Wilson, a recipient of the Medal of Honor, told General Carey that he would personally write charges against any officer who halted those flights before "his" Marines were evacuated, and that they would continue until that time or until the president ordered them halted. Interview by telephone, Dallas, Texas, August 1994.

Chinh, Kieu—Vietnamese actress, the most popular motion picture star of that time in South Vietnam. In America in the 1990s, she won acclaim in the motion picture, *The Joy Luck Club*. Chinh was closely associated with South Vietnam leaders such as Nguyen Cao Ky, Nguyen Van Thieu, and General Duong Van "Big" Minh. Her escape from Saigon required clandestine maneuvering and cloak-and-dagger tactics simply for her to get out of the country. Then once out, she had no place to go, and no country would accept her since she had no money or passport (confiscated by the crumbling South Vietnamese regime along with all her bank holdings). Kieu Chinh's odyssey took her literally around the world.

In mid-April, she was in Singapore making a motion picture. When she heard that it would be a matter of days before her country fell, she hurried home to Saigon. Upon her arrival, police took her passport. She then discovered that the government had frozen her assets and had taken all her money. Stranded in Saigon with no money, except for the few Vietnam piasters in her purse, she sought out friends to help her. One, a vice president of Air Vietnam, put her on a plane to Singapore—no money, no passport. Police there arrested her and held her in jail, giving her an option of either leaving the country or returning to Vietnam. Friends from her film company, still on location in Singapore, bought her an around-the-world plane ticket. She flew to Hong Kong, Tokyo, and then to Paris, where she saw her sister through a glass wall, but could not make contact with her. No country would allow her entrance.

Finally, she landed in Montreal, Canada, the day Saigon fell and was then allowed entrance as a refugee. She called every American film star she knew, and they turned their backs on her. She left messages for Burt Reynolds, but got no response from him. Glenn Ford said he did not remember her. Robert Weiss was never available and would not return her calls. William Holden had gone to play golf. Finally, she dialed Tippi Hedren's number, a woman she had met only once, but who represented her final resort, and used the last of her money to pay for the call. Ms. Hedren, instead of sending Kieu away, said, "Stop crying. Of course I will help you." Hedren sent Kieu money and a plane ticket to Los Angeles, sponsored the Vietnamese actress for citizenship, and shared her Hollywood home with her, putting Kieu on her feet. Multiple interviews, telephone interviews by the author, and an in-person interview on videotape conducted for the author by photojournalist Dirck Halstead, Chinh home in Studio City, California, January 1995.

Cui, Nguyen Duc—Communications Officer, 320th NVA Division. Cui joined the NVA in 1968 with a school classmate, and both were immediately sent to the Da Nang area. The two young men began their military service as line soldiers in the infantry. In 1968, his classmate was killed by a B-52 strike. He describes in vivid detail the experience of the attack. Cui's friend had bought a pair of new shoes in Hanoi when the two of them had joined the army. He kept them in his pack so that he could wear them as they marched victoriously through the streets of Saigon at the war's end. As he died, he made Cui promise to take the shoes from his pack and keep them until he reached Saigon, and there to put them on his feet and wear them in the victory parade.

In December 1974, Cui's unit at that time, the 559th Division, moved from Da Nang westward into Cambodia and linked up with the 320th Division. After the probe on Phuoc Long, they quietly awaited orders in bivouac. In February, they positioned themselves for the March 10 attack on Ban Me Thuot. With Ban Me Thuot secure, his units then marched from Ban Me Thuot, crossed the Saigon River, and overtook Cu Chi Base. His units faced South Vietnamese tanks while on the attack of Saigon, armed with rifles and artillery such as RPGs and B-51s. He had to keep communications open in the face of South Vietnamese constantly cutting his lines.

He explained that most of the attacks his forces used involved three prongs, one to set up a base of fire and the other prongs to attack on the flanks. His unit's mission was to take over Cu Chi and use the road to Saigon to advance the division into the South Vietnamese capital.

Before daylight on the morning of April 30, 1975, Nguyen Duc Cui stopped and washed his feet in an irrigation canal, then took out the shoes from his pack, wrapped in an oil cloth for seven years, and reverently put them on his feet. He then wore the shoes into Saigon, marching with them to the gates of the South Vietnamese Presidential Palace. There his longtime friend, documentary photographer Nguyen Sinh Tuan photographed Cui. Interview in person, Cui home, Hanoi, Socialist Republic of Vietnam, October 1994.

Dang, Tra Bach—Communist Party Leader, Saigon. He participated in planning the final offensive launched against Saigon. He commented that the Paris Accord represented an impediment to their ultimate goal of total unification of Vietnam under Communist authority. He said that since the Saigon government violated the agreement first, that opened their opportunity to strike. Violations he cited are highly disputed by both the South Vietnamese and the American leaders. He observed much of the collapse from his villa in Saigon where he held secret meetings with Communist military leaders and other political leaders. He had a reputation as a very nasty and cold-blooded man. Interview in person, Dang villa, Ho Chi Minh City (Saigon), Socialist Republic of Vietnam, October 1994.

Dawson, Alan—Bureau Chief, United Press International, for both Vietnam and Cambodia. Remaining in Saigon after the evacuation ended, he wrote a book of his observations and experiences during the fall of Vietnam, *55 Days: The Fall of South Vietnam* (published by Prentice Hall, 1977, Englewood Cliffs, NJ: 366 p. DS552D3). He made many firsthand observations of President Nguyen Van Thieu, noting that the president was a chronic micromanager. After witnessing the fall of Da Nang, he made his way by hook and crook back to Saigon, hitchhiking, grabbing chopper rides, and walking.

Dawson accompanied *Time* magazine photojournalist Dirck Halstead to Xuan Loc, where he recognized Xuan Loc as an effective last stand, and the valiantness of the South Vietnamese soldiers who stood their ground there. He observed that once Xuan Loc fell, it spelled rapid doom for Saigon, and that the importance of the stand made at Xuan Loc, buying time for Saigon, could not be overstated. Dawson lost his car at the embassy on the last night, so he mingled with the crowds. He fully expected anti-American sentiment, but was surprised at how little it existed. He noted that always in Vietnam there was noise, but the last night in Saigon, there was no noise, only haunting quiet.

From the roof of the Caravel Hotel, he and other journalists could see the rim of the city in flames. However, for the first time in his eight years of covering Vietnam, Saigon was quiet. On the morning of April 30, he was on the roof when he watched the last helicopter lift from the embassy with the last Marines. He recalled he was astonished because the city was full of NVA by then, tanks even rolling down the street in front of the embassy.

Dawson had an excellent Vietnamese interpreter and covered the formal surrender of South Vietnam for UPI. He remained in Saigon four months after the Communist takeover and was the last Western journalist expelled from Vietnam after the war. Unlike Peter Arnett, Dawson did not want to remain in Vietnam after the Communist victory. An evacuation bus that was supposed to have picked him up, along with several other western journalists, as well as thirty-seven Japanese correspondents, but the bus never arrived at their rendezvous point. Once he had adjusted to operating under the Communist regime in Vietnam, he dickered with the NVA to let him stay. Interview in person, Intercontinental Hotel, Bangkok, Thailand, November 1994.

Ford, Gerald R.—President of the United States. President Ford oversaw and directed all American activities relative to Vietnam in 1975. In that respect, he sought from Congress last-minute aid to South Vietnam in an effort to reassure Nguyen Van Thieu and prevent panic. Congress turned him down flatly. President Ford said that he agreed with military leaders' contingency planning and preparation of American military forces, should they be required to land in Vietnam.

Ford personally monitored the entire evacuation with Secretary of State Henry Kissinger at his side during much of that time. President Ford said, "It was a very difficult thing to be President of the United States and watch South Vietnam fall." When aides advised him that infiltrators were getting inside the embassy walls and mixing with legitimate evacuees, that numbers were not going down appreciably, he cut off flights and ordered Ambassador Graham Martin out. He said, "I want the ambassador on the next flight." Doctor Kissinger passed down this order, saying, "That's it, no more flights."

The orders confounded Navy and Defense Department officials who interpreted that President Ford meant all flights; thus they stopped all traffic once the helicopter carrying the ambassador had launched. This accounts for the more than two-hour delay between the flights bringing out Ambassador Martin and his staff and the final flights that retrieved the remaining Americans. At that time, seventy-nine Marines and four Navy Seabees remained on the embassy roof. Three helicopters were finally dispatched, contrary to President Ford's orders. When the third helicopter radioed eleven Marines still on the roof, Brigadier General Richard Carey ordered Swift Two-Two on the mission, the final helicopter. It is at least a forty-minute flight from the USS Hancock (the ship from which Swift Two-Two launched) to the embassy, accounting for the final delay for the last eleven men. Swift Two-Two had just completed a run from Vung Tao, and had no time to refuel, so they made the last flight dangerously low on fuel.

President Ford said of David Hume Kennerly, his photographer, that he had "a tendency to embellish his stories for dramatic effect," such as his going to Vietnam with General Frederick Weyand's fact-finding mission in late March/early April 1975. Ford said that Kennerly asked if he could go with the assessment team, and the President approved it, but he did not specifically send Kennerly other than for Kennerly's purposes. Interview in person, Waldorf Towers, New York, New York, December 1994.

Gevers, Duane R.—Sergeant, United States Marine Corps. Gevers was one of the last eleven Marines on the roof of the American embassy in Saigon. Interview in person, Hotel Saigon, Ho Chi Minh City (Saigon), Socialist Republic of Vietnam, October 1994.

Giang, Vo Dong (Colonel Ba)—Colonel, Army of the Provisional Revolutionary Government and National Liberation Front (Viet Cong), and Colonel, North Vietnamese Army; Deputy Foreign Minister, Democratic Republic of Vietnam (North Vietnam). He was a regimental commander near Da Nang in the mid-1960s and mentioned in the book, *Silent Warrior*, relative to his experiences while commanding forces in the field there. Giang sat with General Tran Van Tra as the North Vietnamese representatives to the Joint Military Commission and International Oversight Committee, formed by the Paris Accords in June of 1974. Giang provided a perspective of the Communist view in Saigon during the final campaign, especially during the final days and hours of the war. Interview in person, Giang home, Ho Chi Minh City (Saigon), Socialist Republic of Vietnam, October 1994.

Gray, Alfred M.—General, United States Marine Corps, and Commandant of the Marine Corps. As a colonel in 1975, he was an integral planner of the final evacuation operation. Colonel Gray commanded the Fourth Marine Regiment and Regimental Landing Team 4, reinforced, which served as ground forces in the evacuation of Saigon. His Marines provided security around the Defense Attaché's Office compound and provided a hundred Marines assigned to Captain Jim Kean's personal supervision at the embassy. Gray's Marines also provided assistance and security aboard the many civilian maritime service refugee ships. Interview in person, General Gray's private office in Crystal City, Alexandria, Virginia, November 1994.

Halstead, Dirck—Photographer for *Time* magazine and *Life* magazine. Colleague of the author, working jointly with him in all interviews for *Goodnight Saigon*, videotaping the majority of interviews for the production of a video documentary of the same subject. In April 1975, while accompanying United Press International's Southeast Asia bureau chief, Alan Dawson, he observed the valiant stand at Xuan Loc by the Tenth ARVN Division, commanded by the flamboyant Brigadier General Le Minh Dao. Halstead photographed action at the embassy and Defense Attaché's Office compound during the evacuation and later photographed activities aboard the ships. He departed Saigon on the last evacuation helicopter from the Defense Attaché's Office compound. Multiple interviews in person—Halstead home in Washington, DC; Los Angeles; Bangkok, Thailand; and in cities throughout the Socialist Republic of Vietnam, September, October, November, and December 1994, and January and February 1995.

Kean, James H.—Captain (Major Selectee), United States Marine Corps; Commanding Officer, Company C, Marine Security Guard Battalion. Headquartered in Hong Kong, he came to Saigon on April 17 because of the impending collapse of the South Vietnamese government and was a key military officer on the ground in the evacuation operation at the United States Embassy in Saigon, 1975. He was the senior Marine among the last Americans to leave from the roof of the embassy and is technically the last United States military ground commander to serve in South Vietnam. Multiple interviews, telephone and in person at various locations—Los Angeles, California; Bangkok, Thailand; and Ho Chi Minh City (Saigon), Socialist Republic of Vietnam, October 1994.

Kennerly, David Hume—Official White House Photographer for President Gerald R. Ford. Kennerly witnessed and photographed many of the events in the White House as President Ford and Secretary of State Kissinger watched South Vietnam fall. Kennerly traveled to South Vietnam with General Frederick Weyand's fact-finding mission during March and April 1975. Kennerly witnessed the chaos and concluded that the remainder of South Vietnam, including Saigon, would soon fall. Upon return to Washington, DC, he imparted these observations to President Ford. Among Kennerly's more memorable photographs of that time is the picture of Dr. Kissinger, dressed in a tuxedo, standing behind a chair, gripping its back, a solemn expression on his face as he awaited news of the extraction of the last Americans, the eleven United States Marines stranded on the rooftop of the United States Embassy in Saigon. He was supposed to be at a state dinner, but remained in his office until he was notified that the Marines were safe aboard ship. Multiple interviews, telephone and in person, Los Angeles, California, September 1994.

Ky, Nguyen Cao—Former Premier and Vice President, Republic of Vietnam. He held the rank of air vice marshal, commander of the South Vietnamese Air Force, and had flamboyantly played to be named president of South Vietnam when President Nguyen Van Thieu resigned. At one time, the CIA feared that Premier Ky was leading a coup to take over what remained of the South Vietnamese government when Tran Van Huong was named president on April 21, 1975, in accord with the South Vietnamese constitution, to succeed President Nguyen Van Thieu. When former President Thieu departed South Vietnam, Ky labeled him a coward and said that anyone who would flee in the face of the enemy was also a coward. Ky remained in Saigon until late afternoon on April 29, when he flew his personal helicopter to the deck of the USS *Blue Ridge*. His observations and actions provided valuable insight into the political death throes of South Vietnam during the final days. Multiple interviews by telephone, Hong Kong, China, July and August 1994.

Ky, Nguyen Xuan—Saigon Regional Viet Cong Commander. Throughout the war, Ky was a close ally of Tra Bach Dang. Among his guerrilla forces were spies, assassins, and terrorists who for years carried out most of the actions committed in and around Saigon. He was also a member of Vietnam's Communist Party's Central Committee and headed the Communist Party in Bien Tra Province. Interview in person, Dang villa, Ho Chi Minh City (Saigon), Socialist Republic of Vietnam, October 1994.

Lam, Tony—Councilman Westminster, California. First Vietnamese-born refugee elected to public office in America following the war, Lam was elected to the city council, Westminster, Orange County, California. In 1975, Lam owned and directed the South Vietnamese company, Lam Brothers Corporation, in Saigon. His company dehydrated grain and made fish meal, providing much of the dehydrated grain and meal to feed the South Vietnamese Army. In his life he has been a refugee three times: first as a boy in 1946 at the French camp at Hai Phong, then in 1952 when the country was divided and he fled south, and lastly in 1975 as he successfully evacuated from Saigon and settled in southern California. He could not believe that Saigon could or would fall, even in the face of the chaos. His perceptions reflected those of many powerful people in Saigon. He was a wealthy man in Saigon, but after the fall he had little. However, he and his wife and six children, three boys and three girls, evacuated on a flight from Tan Son Nhut Airport and considered themselves blessed because they were escaping with their lives. Interview videotaped by Dirck Halstead at Tony Lam's city council office, Westminster, Orange County, California, February 1995.

Luong, Nguyen Thien—Viet Cong Commander. Luong led forces attached to North Vietnamese Army 320th Division. Luong's guerrillas were part of the forces that initiated the attack on Ban Me Thuot. He redeployed his forces to Cheo Reo when word of the massive evacuation by the ARVN II Corps reached NVA headquarters. His forces played a key role in blocking the evacuation route at Cheo Reo and annihilating the ARVN II Corps and attached ranger battalions. Multiple interviews in person, the Veterans Association complex in Ban Me Thuot, Veterans Association Headquarters in Pleiku, and battle sites at Cheo Reo, Socialist Republic of Vietnam, October 1994.

Norman, David E.—Corporal, United States Marine Corps. He was one of the last eleven Marines on the roof of the American embassy in Saigon. While at his quarters at the Marine House, which is today the Saigon Star Hotel, Norman saw the renegade South Vietnamese Air Force F-5 jet dropping its bombs on the Presidential Palace. Norman grabbed his M14 rifle and opened fire on the aircraft from the rooftop of the Marine House. Interview in person, Hotel Saigon, Ho Chi Minh City (Saigon), Socialist Republic of Vietnam, October 1994.

Phung, Dang Quang—Civilian Architect at Tan Son Nhut Air Base and Viet Cong Spy. Phung is a native son of Pleiku and came to Saigon after studying architecture in France. Hired as a young man by the South Vietnamese government, Phung served for many years as a member of the team that designed and laid out many of the structures at Tan Son Nhut Air Base. He used the opportunities afforded him there to provide the Communist forces with detailed internal information, structure-specific information, and exact measurements of the air base. Prior to the attack on Saigon, Phung provided Viet Cong and NVA contacts with updated layouts of Tan Son Nhut and its defenses. Many of these blueprints were passed to the South Vietnamese pilot who defected to the Viet Cong with his F-5 jet. After the war Phung retired to the countryside where he lives on a farm a few kilometers east of Cu Chi. Interview in person, Vietnam National Cemetery near Cu Chi, Socialist Republic of Vietnam, October 1994.

Reung, Le Van—Viet Cong Guerrilla. Reung fought for more than ten years in the Central Highlands, in the southern reaches of I Corps, and in the areas of Da Nang and Chu Lai. In November 1974, he was among the forces probing Da Nang defenses. Following the successful assessment attack of Phuoc Long, in January 1975, his unit moved southward to infiltrate Ban Me Thuot, where his guerrilla forces attacked from within the stronghold's defenses. Once Ban Me Thuot had fallen, Reung moved with his unit toward Saigon by way of Cu Chi. During their battle to regain control of the Cu Chi Base, Reung tripped a Viet Cong booby trap and lost his leg. Following the war and his recovery from his wounds, he was placed in charge of the care of the Communist veterans' cemetery near Cu Chi. Among the thousands of NVA and VC graves at the cemetery is a giant monument that overlooks a mass grave containing the remains of 2,473 unknown Communist soldiers. Interview in person, Vietnam National Cemetery near Cu Chi, Socialist Republic of Vietnam, October 1994.

Schlager, Robert W.—Gunnery Sergeant, United States Marine Corps. Schlager was one of last eleven Marines on the embassy roof. He served as noncommissioned officer in charge of the Marine security forces at the Bien Hoa consulate. When Bien Hoa fell, Schlager evacuated to the Saigon embassy by car. When he came within a few blocks of the embassy, he could see the chaos of the masses of people outside the embassy. He abandoned the car and made his way through the angry crowd. Since the embassy Marines could not open the gates to allow him inside, they had to pull him over the wall, a scene shot on film by CBS News cameraman, the late Neil Davis, and widely broadcast by the network. After getting securely inside the embassy, Schlager realized that the United States flag had not been taken down at the Bien Hoa consulate. He convinced an Air America helicopter pilot to fly him back to Bien Hoa to get the flag. The helicopter hovered over the rooftop while Schlager climbed on the aircraft's skids and cut the flag free from the lanyards that held it to its flagpole. All the time he was retrieving the flag from the Bien Hoa consulate rooftop, NVA and Viet Cong had the building surrounded and had opened fire on the helicopter. Miraculously, the pilot and Schlager escaped and flew the helicopter back to the embassy with the rescued flag. Interview in person, Hotel Saigon, Ho Chi Minh City (Saigon), Socialist Republic of Vietnam, October 1994.

Schuller, Steven T.—Corporal, United States Marine Corps. Schuller was one of the last eleven Marines on the roof of the American embassy in Saigon. While standing guard, he was stabbed with a bayonet by a South Vietnamese trying to bridge the gate at the embassy. Interview in person, Hotel Saigon, Ho Chi Minh City (Saigon), Socialist Republic of Vietnam, October 1994.

Sparks, Walter W.—Staff Sergeant, United States Marine Corps. As the staff noncommissioned officer in charge of the Marine Corps security forces assigned from Third Marine Division (based at Camp SD Butler, Okinawa, Japan) to the United States Consulate in Da Nang, in 1975, Sparks was one of the people that Consul General Albert Francis called the Black Box, the key staff who oversaw the Da Nang evacuation. Sparks had responsibility over the security and processing of the people boarding departing vehicles during the evacuation, mostly on barges docked across the street from the consulate. He and his remaining Marines eventually took the last barge out of Da Nang under heavy fire from the NVA and Viet Cong, who had by then flooded the city. After Da Nang fell, he worked with military efforts in Saigon and was finally evacuated to the Philippines with his Da Nang security force, who had only the clothes that they were wearing. Multiple interviews, telephone and in person, Sparks home, Jackson, Mississippi, January 1995.

Sullivan, Michael K.—Staff Sergeant, United States Marine Corps. Sullivan served as the staff noncommissioned officer in charge of Marine Security Guard Detachment, Company C, Marine Security Guard Battalion, United States Embassy, Saigon, until the arrival of Master Sergeant Valdez. Sullivan came to Saigon from Tehran, Iran. When Saigon fell, he was serving as assistant NCO in charge and was one of the eleven Marines marooned on the embassy roof. Interview in person, Hotel Saigon, Ho Chi Minh City (Saigon), Socialist Republic of Vietnam, October 1994.

Than, Le Cong—Vice Commissioner of the Forty-fourth Line Front, Viet Cong. Than led his units in the initial assaults outside Hue and Da Nang simultaneously as the assault on Ban Me Thuot took place and eventually converged his units on Da Nang as the city fell. His units occupied Da Nang. Than observed that as his forces entered Da Nang, the people were jubilant to see his soldiers and offered the men food and water. Interview in person, The Army Hotel, Da Nang, Socialist Republic of Vietnam, October 1994.

Thao, Mai—Most renowned of Vietnam's novelists. Thao published six different newspapers, was editor in chief of several more, and authored fifty books in forty years of writing. Chased by Communist secret service for twenty years and comparable to Ernest Hemingway in his lifestyle and bravado, he remained in Vietnam and witnessed the fall of Saigon with Tran Da Tu and Nha Ca. Following the war's end, the Communists put out a Black List containing the names of artists and writers, including Nha Ca, Tran Da Tu, and Mai Thao. While Nha Ca and her husband, Tran Da Tu, were imprisoned, Mai Thao managed to elude capture for nearly two years. (The writers' imprisonment aroused anger among the world art community, who for many years demanded their release.) In December 1977, Mai Thao managed to escape Vietnam by boat to Malaysia, where he lived for five months until relatives and volunteer organizations were able to sponsor his emigration to New York. An aggressive, hard-drinking man, his color and style flew in the face of the Communists, yet they dared not kill him. He never bent to their pressure. Interview conducted for the author and videotaped by Dirck Halstead at the Thao home, Westminster, Orange County, California, February 1995.

The, Hoang Duc—Colonel, North Vietnamese Army. Commanded the Thirty-eighth Regiment, Second NVA Division, operating in the Fifth Region, the northern provinces of South Vietnam, including Da Nang and Hue. His forces captured hundreds of thousands of tons of weapons, ammunition, and equipment abandoned by the fleeing ARVN. The's unit operated primarily at night; however, on March 29, they attacked in daylight, setting the ARVN north of Da Nang into flight, literally running from the Hai Van Pass into the city of Da Nang. Interview in person, The Army Hotel, Da Nang, Socialist Republic of Vietnam, October 1994.

Thi, Truong Quang—North Vietnamese Army Regimental Commander with the 320th NVA Division. Truong participated in the Cheo Reo massacre, his forces confronting the ARVN rangers on the flanks and rear. He explained that the North Vietnamese Army and the Viet Cong combined into three divisions, the 10th, 320th, and 316th NVA divisions plus the cadre of regional Viet Cong guerrillas, which formed the 968th NVA Corps. The 968th Corps had the mission of taking control of the Central Highlands. Multiple interviews in person, The Army Hotel in Ban Me Thuot, Army Headquarters in Pleiku, and battle sites at Cheo Reo, Socialist Republic of Vietnam, October 1994.

Thurman, Russell R.—Gunnery Sergeant, United States Marine Corps. Thurman served as a Marine Combat correspondent, photojournalist, and was the public affairs representative for the 9th MAB. He made observations throughout the evacuation, both aboard the ships and ashore. Thurman vividly recalled the chaos at the DAO compound and flew on the last flight out of that site. He explained that to make a landing zone at night, the Marines took all available cars and parked them in a circle. When they departed, they left the cars running and their lights on. Multiple informal interviews, telephone and in person, San Diego, California, August 1994.

Tra, Tran Van—General, Commander in Chief, Army of the Provisional Revolutionary Government of Vietnam, National Liberation Front (Viet Cong), and General, North Vietnamese Army. Tran was one of the master planners, along with General Van Tien Dung and Party First Secretary Le Duan, of Campaign 2/75, The Blooming Lotus, North Vietnam's final campaign that led to ultimate victory over South Vietnam. He shared with General Dung and Lieutenant General Hoang Minh Thoa overall command of Communist forces in the field during the final campaign. He provided vivid details of the whole operation from the Communist perspective. Multiple in-person interviews, Tran Van Tra's private office at army headquarters, Ho Chi Minh City (Saigon), Socialist Republic of Vietnam, October 1994.

Trung, Nguyen Thanh—First Lieutenant, Air Force of the Republic of Vietnam. Trung is the infamous South Vietnamese Air Force pilot who defected to the Viet Cong on April 8, 1975, flying his F-5 jet fighter to Song Be Airfield at Phuoc Long after dropping the plane's load of bombs on South Vietnam's Presidential Palace. On April 28, he led the aerial raid of five A-37 jets on Tan Son Nhut Air Base. Trung was regarded as a hero of Vietnam by the Communists, his F-5 jet set on a stone pedestal in front of the Army Museum in Saigon, and he became chief pilot of Vietnam Airlines. Interview in person, Trung home, Ho Chi Minh City (Saigon), Socialist Republic of Vietnam, October 1994.

Tu, Tran Da, and wife, Nha Ca—Husband and wife, he is a novelist and she is a poet. Nha Ca was imprisoned for eight years, much of that time spent in a four-foot-by-four-foot cell, while her husband, Tu, spent twelve years in a forced labor camp. Nha Ca began writing poetry at age thirteen and has published forty books. Her poetry incited the Communists' anger by denouncing the executions that they committed when they captured Hue in the 1968 Tet Offensive. Her novels and poetry were harshly critical of the Communists and warranted her placement high on their Black List following the war's end.

Tran Da Tu also authored more than forty novels, many critical of the Communists. During his twelve years of imprisonment, moved from labor camp to labor camp, he witnessed the deaths of many writers and artists and feared that his wife, Nha Ca, had also died. The couple had six children, with the youngest being only seven months old in 1975. When Tu and his wife were imprisoned, handcuffed, and chained, their children were chased into the streets. Their home, their publishing business and equipment were all taken by the Communists, and their children left to fend for themselves until relatives could find them and care for them. Nha Ca and Tran Da Tu provided firsthand witness accounts of the fall of Saigon and the horrible aftermath for those who opposed the Communists. Interview conducted for the author and videotaped by Dirck Halstead at the couple's publishing office, the *Viet Bao Kinhte Newspaper*, Westminster, Orange County, California, February 1995.

Tuan, Nguyen Manh—Lieutenant Colonel, Army of the Republic of Vietnam. An artillery battalion commander in South Vietnam's II Army Corps, he received his artillery training at Fort Sill, Oklahoma, and on March 21, 1975, he was captured by North Vietnamese and Viet Cong forces at Cheo Reo while leading a group of civilians and children in an effort to evade capture. He provided a colorful firsthand account of the massacre at Cheo Reo. Interview in person, at Nguyen Dinh (Kevi brand scissors factory), Ho Chi Minh City (Saigon), Socialist Republic of Vietnam, October 1994.

Tuan, Nguyen Sinh—North Vietnamese Army Enlisted Soldier and Documentary Photographer, 320th NVA Division. Tuan participated in the final campaign's early battles around Da Nang and in the

NVA victories at Ban Me Thuot, Cheo Reo, and Saigon. Interview in person, home of Nguyen Duc Qui, Hanoi, Socialist Republic of Vietnam, October 1994.

Ty, Nguyen Giap—Terminal Manager, Port of Saigon, 1975. Ty retired from the South Vietnamese Army as a lieutenant colonel in 1974 and was awarded the Bronze Star Medal by the United States for heroism, saving the lives of a platoon of American soldiers trapped in a minefield. He and his wife were both heavily involved in evacuating their fellow countrymen and believed they would surely be evacuated at the end. However, due to the chaos and collapse of what refugee evacuation process had existed, the Nguyen family fell in the backwash. Ty was arrested and sent to a re-education camp for the next six years. When Ty was released in 1981, the family spent the next ten years enduring Communist harassment and finally escaped the country without permission as boat people in 1990. Multiple interviews, telephone and in person, Nguyen home in Philadelphia, Pennsylvania, January 1995.

Valdez, John J. "Top"—Master Sergeant, United States Marine Corps. Valdez served as the staff noncommissioned officer in charge of Marine Security Guard Detachment, Company C, Marine Security Guard Battalion, United States Embassy, Saigon. He was the senior enlisted Marine among the last to leave from the American embassy roof. Interview in person, Hotel Saigon, Ho Chi Minh City (Saigon), Socialist Republic of Vietnam, October 1994.

Van Es, Hubert "Hugh"—Dutch photographer. During the chaos of the final day, he was trapped in the crowds of Saigon and could never reach any evacuation points in time; thus he involuntarily remained in Vietnam after the fall. He took the now-famous photograph of the Air America Huey helicopter hovering over the rooftop with people climbing aboard. Getting the photograph was purely luck, Van Es told the author in an interview in Bangkok in 1994. He said, "The right place at the right time. Someone said, 'Christ there is a chopper on the roof.' So I put on my longest lens, a 300 mm, got off six frames, and she was gone." He attended a conference held by Colonel Vo Dong Giang (Colonel Ba), in which the Viet Cong representative told the journalists that if they should get left behind, NVA and VC troops had been told to expect to see foreigners, and they should treat them with respect. Colonel Ba, however, advised them that they should remain in the city because he was not sure what could happen to them outside it. Van Es observed South Vietnamese soldiers stripping off uniforms, running to the river, and throwing their guns away. He told of a pile of rifles and pistols lying in the street, and kids playing with them. People were very scared, burning their papers, and making Viet Cong flags. Interview in person, Intercontinental Hotel, Bangkok, Thailand, November 1994.

Vinh, Trong—General, North Vietnamese Army, and North Vietnamese diplomat. Serving as a member of the North Vietnamese delegation to the Paris Peace Talks, 1972 through 1974, he described his impression of Henry Kissinger as that of a strong man, intelligent, but a man who negotiated by force, and this did not work for the Vietnamese. While seated at the Paris Peace Talks, he left his family in Hanoi to endure the bombing. Finally his family was evacuated from Hanoi, which helped him focus better on the talks. He held that the position of the Vietnamese Communists was that their negotiations must reflect their "victory on the battlefield," so the negotiations must come to the conclusion that supported the Communists. When the peace accord was finally adopted, he was able to return home. However, he was immediately dispatched to Saigon to participate in the Joint Military Commission and International Oversight Committee. His delegation was held on their aircraft in Saigon for twenty-four hours, in heat with no food or water, and not allowed to participate in the delegation. Because of the maltreatment by the South Vietnamese, the Communist delegation concluded that South Vietnam was not interested in implementing the accords. Multiple interviews in person, Vinh home and Hotel Metropole, Hanoi, Socialist Republic of Vietnam, October 1994.

Williams, Derek—CBS News sound-recording technician. Williams began working in the Far East in Cambodia and eventually wound up in Saigon. He had a Vietnamese girlfriend and had the same idea as a lot of people: marry her and get her on the registry so she could get out. He got the registry office to open on Sunday with money he had won in a poker game and got married. His wife's family, who remained in Saigon, eventually got out as boat people, launching on a Russian freighter from Vung Tao. Williams was in Phnom Penh,

Cambodia, when he heard the news of Ban Me Thuot and hurried back to Vietnam because of concerns about his wife. He noted that the American embassy got the story backwards with the outcome of Vietnam and Cambodia. They said the Khmer Rouge would hold a lovefest in Cambodia while the VC would create a bloodbath in Vietnam. The Khmer Rouge were the animals. CBS did not sanction anyone staying behind, but many had planned to stay. Then they saw a South Vietnamese soldier insanely pumping rounds from his pistol into a parked car, and a photographer taking pictures of him. The soldier, seeing the photographer, turned the pistol toward him and pulled the trigger, but it was out of bullets. Seeing that changed a number of people's minds. Seeing Ban Me Thuot fall, several Australian journalists predicted to Williams the fall of South Vietnam, nearly to the day. Interview in person, Intercontinental Hotel, Bangkok, Thailand, November 1994.

Wood, Christopher—Sergeant, United States Marine Corps. Wood served as the crew chief of the last helicopter from Saigon, Swift Two-Two, which flew with dangerously low fuel and rescued the eleven Marines left on the roof of the United States Embassy. When the crew of Swift Two-Two received orders to pick up the last Marines, the sun was already up. The three earlier choppers that picked up the bulk of rear guard Marines had departed the embassy still in darkness. When Swift Two-Two lifted from the embassy rooftop, tear gas swirled inside the cockpit so badly that the pilot had to set the aircraft down so that he could clear his eyes and then launch. As the aircraft launched with the final eleven Marines aboard, the low-fuel warning lights were flashing on the instrument panel. Interview in person, Hotel Saigon, Ho Chi Minh City (Saigon), Socialist Republic of Vietnam, October 1994.

BIBLIOGRAPHY

55 Days: The Fall of South Vietnam by Alan Dawson (published by Prentice Hall, 1977, Englewood Cliffs, NJ: 366 p.)

Air Force Magazine: A Galaxy of Heroes by John L. Frisbee, Contributing Editor, August 1991, Volume 74, Number 8 (published by the Air Force Association, Arlington, VA)

C-5 Galaxy Crash—Operation Babylift by Adopted Vietnamese International (published by AVI on their Internet site, www.adoptedvietnamese.org, 2004)

C-5 Galaxy Crash—Vietnam Babylift Personal Stories by Brock Townsend (found on the Internet at www.vietnambabylift.org, 2004)

Decent Interval: An Insider's Account of Saigon's Indecent End Told by the CIA's Chief Strategy Analyst in Vietnam by Frank Snepp (published by Vintage Books, a Division of Random House, 1977, New York, NY: 591 p.)

Dumb Bombs: Aircraft Weapons Loads fact sheet (published by Federation of American Scientists, Military Analysis Network, August 1994)

Mikoyan-Gurevich MiG-21 Fishbed fact sheet (published by Combat Aircraft, available on the Internet at www.combataircraft.com/aircraft/fmig21.asp, 2004)

Northrop F-5 "Freedom Fighter" aka Skoshi Tiger fact sheet (published by the United States Air Force Museum archives, Washington, DC)

Operation Babylift fact sheet (from United States Air Force Security Force Heritage and History, Lackland Air Force Base Museum.)

Operation Babylift—American Women Who Died in Vietnam by Vietnam Women's Memorial Project (A Circle of Sisters/A Circle of Friends, Washington, DC, 2004)

Operation New Life by Global Security (compiled from *Operation Babylift and New Life* by Lea Arakaki, Fifteenth Air Base Wing historian, USAF, and *The Command's Humanitarian Efforts* by Anne M. Bazzell, Pacific Air Force, Office of History, USAF)

Safi Thi-Kim Felce—An Adopted Vietnamese Story by Safi Thi-Kim Felce (published by AVI Adopted Vietnamese International, found at www.adoptedvietnamese.org, 2004)

The Victor: What Next in Asia? a special edition of *TIME* magazine containing the following news articles and commentary: *A Letter from the Publisher, The Last Grim Good-bye, The End of a Thirty*

Years' War, Last Chopper Out of Saigon, 'This Is It! Everybody Out!,' The Privileged Exiles, Now On to 'Camp Fortuitous,' Saigon: Memories of a Fallen City, 'You Are Always With Us, Uncle Ho,' Henry Makes the Best of It, After the Fall: Reactions and Rationales, The Final Comment: People, Rocky's Turn to the Right, Ending a Personal War, After Vietnam: What Next in Asia?, The Press: They Stayed (published by Time Inc., May 12, 1975, New York, NY: 22 p.)

U. S. Air Force Fact Sheet: C-5 Galaxy by Air Mobility Command (published by the Office of Public Affairs, Scott Air Force Base, IL)

U. S. Marines in Vietnam: The Bitter End 1973-1975 by Major George R. Dunham, United States Marine Corps, and Colonel David A. Quinlan, United States Marine Corps (published by History and Museums Division, Headquarters, United States Marine Corps, 1990, Washington, DC: 315 p.)

Vietnam: A History by Stanley Kornow (published by Viking Press, 1983, New York, NY: 750 p.)

Where We Were in Vietnam: A Comprehensive Guide to the Firebases, Military Installations and Naval Vessels of the Vietnam War 1945-75 by Michael P. Kelley (published by Hellgate Press, an imprint of PSI Research, 2002, Central Point, OR: 840 p.)

World Airways History: Ed Daly and the Beginning. . . by unnamed author (published by Yakety at www.yakety.com/worldstory.html, 1999)

INDEX

CHARLES HENDERSON is a veteran of more than twenty-three years in the United States Marine Corps, with a distinguished career spanning from Vietnam to the Gulf War, after which he retired as a chief warrant officer. In addition to writing his own books and for various publications, he also runs his family's cattle enterprise in Peyton, Colorado. He is the author of the critically acclaimed military classics *Marine Sniper* and *Silent Warrior,* which first chronicled the exploits of U.S.M.C. sniper Carlos Hathcock. He is also the author of *Marshalling the Faithful.*